Institutional Shareholders and Corporate Governance

Institutional Shareholders and Corporate Governance

G. P. STAPLEDON

B.Ec., LL.B. (Hons.) (Adel.); D.Phil. (Oxon.)
Centre for Corporate Law and Securities Regulation,
Faculty of Law, The University of Melbourne

CLARENDON PRESS · OXFORD
1996

Oxford University Press, Walton Street, Oxford OX2 6DP

Oxford New York
Athens Auckland Bangkok Bombay
Calcutta Cape Town Dar es Salaam Delhi
Florence Hong Kong Istanbul Karachi
Kuala Lumpur Madras Madrid Melbourne
Mexico City Nairobi Paris Singapore
Taipei Tokyo Toronto
and associated companies in
Berlin Ibadan

Oxford is a trade mark of Oxford University Press

Published in the United States
by Oxford University Press Inc., New York

British Library Cataloguing in Publication Data
Data available

Library of Congress Cataloging in Publication Data
Stapledon, G. P. (Geof P.)
Institutional shareholders and corporate governance/G. P.
Stapledon.
p. cm.
1. Corporate governance. 2. Institutional investments.
3. Corporations—Investor relations. 4. Corporate governance—Great
Britain. 5. Institutional investments—Great Britain.
6. Corporations—Investor relations—Great Britain. 7. Corporate
governance—Australia. 8. Institutional investments—Australia.
9. Corporations—Investor relations—Australia. I. Title.
HD2741.S762 1996 96–424
658.4—dc20
ISBN 0–19–826088–1

1 3 5 7 9 10 8 6 4 2

Typeset by Cambrian Typesetters, Frimley, Surrey
Printed in Great Britain on acid-free paper by
Biddles Ltd., Guildford and King's Lynn

Preface

This book grew out of a doctoral thesis written at Lincoln College, Oxford. I thank my D.Phil. my supervisor, Paul Davies, for encouraging me to research the role of institutional shareholders in corporate governance. I thank Paul also for his invaluable advice, support, guidance, and friendship both during the writing of my thesis and during the preparation of this book. My studies at Oxford were made possible by the funding of the Keith Murray Senior Scholarship. I am grateful to the trustees of the Keith Murray Trust for the interest that they showed in my research.

Persons who kindly assisted me in various ways with the research for the book are listed in Appendices A, C, F, and H, and in footnotes in the body of the book. Particular mention should be made of Stuart Bell of Pensions & Investment Research Consultants Ltd.; Peter Brierley of the Bank of England; Paul Cahill of the Department of Trade and Industry; Jonathan Charkham, formerly of the Bank of England; Sandy Easterbrook of ISS Australia; Matthew Gaved; Jenny Hill of the Faculty of Law, University of Sydney; Julian Le Fanu of the Institutional Fund Managers' Association; Chris Mallin of Nottingham Business School; Ian Matheson of the Australian Investment Managers' Association; Colin Mayer of the School of Management Studies, University of Oxford; Dean Paatsch of the Australian Institute of Superannuation Trustees Inc.; Julian Potter of the Institutional Shareholders' Committee; Dan Prentice of the Faculty of Law, University of Oxford; Ian Ramsay of the Centre for Corporate Law and Securities Regulation, Faculty of Law, University of Melbourne; James Rath of the Association of Investment Trust Companies; Richard Regan of the Association of British Insurers; John Rogers of the National Association of Pension Funds Ltd.; Melissa Wheeler of the Australian Investment Managers' Association; and the participants in the UK and Australian interview projects. Special thanks go also to Margaret Shade and Richard Hart of Oxford University Press.

Some of the material in Chapters 5, 8, and 10 has appeared, in an earlier state, in: P. L. Davies and G. P. Stapledon, 'Corporate Governance in the United Kingdom' in M. Isaksson and R. Skog (eds.), *Aspects of Corporate Governance* (1994) 55; G. P. Stapledon, 'Exercise of Voting Rights by Institutional Shareholders in the UK' (1995) 3 *Corp. Gov.: Inter. Rev.* 144; G. P. Stapledon, 'The Structure of Share Ownership and Control: The Potential for Institutional Investor Activism' (1995) 18 *UNSWLJ* 250; and G. P. Stapledon, 'Disincentives to Activism by Institutional Investors in Listed Australian Companies' (1996) 18 *Syd. L Rev.*

In closing, I dedicate this book to Lisa, in partial thanks for her boundless support, patience, understanding, and love durings its writing.

Melbourne   GEOF STAPLEDON
January 1996

Contents

PART 1
INTRODUCTION

Chapter 1
The Corporate Governance Systems in the UK and Australia

Chapter 2
The Growth of Institutional Share Ownership

PART II
INSTITUTIONAL INVOLVEMENT IN CORPORATE GOVERNANCE IN THE UK:
HISTORY AND CURRENT LEVEL

Chapter 3
The Participants in the UK

PART IV

INSTITUTIONAL INVOLVEMENT IN CORPORATE GOVERNANCE: THE POTENTIAL

Chapter 9

Chapter 10

PART V
APPENDICES

List of Tables and Figures

TABLES

FIGURES

List of Abbreviations

ABI	Association of British Insurers
ABS	Australian Bureau of Statistics
ACT	Association of Corporate Treasurers
AICD	Australian Institute of Company Directors
AIMA	Australian Investment Managers' Association
AIMA Corporate Governance Guidelines	Australian Investment Managers' Association, *Corporate Governance: A Guide for Investment Managers and a Statement of Recommended Corporate Practice (Australian Investment Managers' Association, Sydney, 1995)*
AIMG	Australian Investment Managers' Group
AIST	Australian Institute of Superannuation Trustees Inc.
AIT	Association of Investment Trusts
AITC	Association of Investment Trust Companies
ASB	Accounting Standards Board
ASC	Australian Securities Commission
ASFA	Association of Superannuation Funds of Australia Ltd.
ASX	Australian Stock Exchange Ltd.
ASX Listing Rules	Australian Stock Exchange Ltd., *Official Listing Rules (Australian Stock Exchange, Sydney)*
AUTIF	Association of Unit Trusts and Investment Funds
AUTM	Association of Unit Trust Managers
BCA	Business Council of Australia
BIA	British Insurance Association
BMBA	British Merchant Banking and Securities Houses Association
CA 1985	*Companies Act 1985 (UK)*
Cadbury Code	Committee on the Financial Aspects of Corporate Governance, *Code of Best Practice (Gee & Co., London, 1992)*
Cadbury Committee	Committee on the Financial Aspects of Corporate Governance
Cadbury Report	Committee on the Financial Aspects of Corporate Governance, *Report (Gee & Co., London, 1992)*

CBI	*Confederation of British Industry*
CL	*Corporations Law (see Corporations Act 1989 (Cth.), s. 82)*
CSO	*Central Statistical Office*
Cth.	*Commonwealth*
DTI	*Department of Trade and Industry*
EU	*European Union*
GDP	*Gross Domestic Product*
Greenbury Code	*Study Group on Directors' Remuneration, Code of Best Practice (Gee Publishing, London, 1995).*
Greenbury Committee	*Study Group on Directors' Remuneration*
Greenbury Report	*Study Group on Directors' Remuneration, Report (Gee Publishing, London, 1995)*
HMSO	*Her Majesty's Stationery Office*
IC	*Investment Committee*
IFMA	*Institutional Fund Managers' Association*
IMRO	*Investment Managers Regulatory Organisation*
IOD	*Institute of Directors*
IPC	*Investment Protection Committee*
ISC	*Institutional Shareholders' Committee*
LIBA	*London Investment Banking Association*
LIFA	*Life Insurance Federation of Australia Inc.*
Listing Rules	*London Stock Exchange, The Listing Rules (The International Stock Exchange of the United Kingdom and the Republic of Ireland Ltd., London, 1993)*
MBO	*management buy-out*
NAPF	*National Association of Pension Funds Ltd.*
NCSC	*National Companies and Securities Commission*
OECD	*Organisation for Economic Co-operation and Development*
PIRC	*Pensions & Investment Research Consultants Ltd.*
R&D	*research and development*
SGC	*superannuation guarantee charge*
SIB	*Securities and Investments Board*
Statement on Directors	*Institutional Shareholders' Committee, The Role and Duties of Directors—A Statement of Best Practice (Institutional Shareholders' Committee, London, 1991)*
Table A	*Companies (Tables A to F) Regulations 1985 (SI 1985/805), Table A*

Table A (Aust.)	*Corporations Law, Schedule 1, Table A*
UK	*United Kingdom*
US	*United States of America*
UTA	*Unit Trust Association*

Abbreviations of the names of fund-management firms are contained in Appendices E and G

Table of Cases

Table of Statutes

United Kingdom

STATUTORY INSTRUMENTS

Commonwealth of Australia

United States

Germany

PART I
Introduction

1

The Corporate Governance Systems in the UK and Australia

A. INTRODUCTION

This book contrasts the role of institutional shareholders in corporate governance in the United Kingdom and Australia. Corporate governance is the system by which companies are directed and controlled.[1] The companies of present concern are quoted public companies. The comparative aspect of the book is novel: the UK system of corporate governance has (along with that of the US) been contrasted commonly with the systems of continental European countries (especially Germany) and Japan,[2] but not with that of Australia. The UK and US corporate sectors are characterized by a relatively large number of quoted companies, a liquid capital market where ownership and control rights are traded frequently, and few inter-corporate equity holdings.[3] The corporate sectors of Germany and Japan are, in contrast, characterized by a relatively small number of quoted companies, an illiquid capital market where ownership and control rights are traded infrequently, and many inter-corporate shareholdings.[4] As a result, the UK and US corporate sectors have 'outsider' systems of corporate governance, whilst the German and Japanese systems of corporate governance are 'insider' systems.[5] The Australian corporate sector has traditionally been considered to possess the same basic characteristics as those of the UK and the US, and the Australian system of corporate governance is regarded as an outsider

---

[1] Committee on the Financial Aspects of Corporate Governance ('Cadbury Committee'), *Report* (1992) para. 2.5. The Cadbury Committee's *Report* and accompanying *Code of Best Practice* are referred to throughout this book as the *Cadbury Report* and *Cadbury Code*. For the context of the work of the Cadbury Committee, see V. Finch, 'Board Performance and Cadbury on Corporate Governance' [1992] *JBL* 581. Two other terms which are used throughout the book are (a) 'monitoring': this refers to any form of involvement, direct or indirect, at firm level or industry-wide, by institutions in corporate governance; and (b) 'portfolio company': a company in which an institution has a shareholding (and which thus forms part of the institution's investment portfolio).

[2] See e.g. J. R. Franks and C. P. Mayer, 'Corporate Control: A Synthesis of the International Evidence' in J. C. Coffee, R. J. Gilson, and L. Lowenstein (eds.), *Relational Investing* (1996). See further Ch. 10, Sec. B1.i.

[3] Franks and Mayer, ibid.   [4] Ibid.   [5] Ibid.

system, very similar to that of Britain. The supposedly strong similarity between the corporate sectors and systems of corporate governance of the UK and Australia explains the lack of a detailed comparison of the British and Australian systems of corporate governance.

In the context of its examination of the role of institutional shareholders, this dissertation seeks to demonstrate that the characteristics of the Australian corporate sector are, in fact, a hybrid of those of the corporate sectors of, on the one hand, the UK and US, and, on the other hand, Germany and Japan. The *quoted* corporate sector is not as significant a part of the economy in Australia as it is in Britain. Unquoted companies—in particular, wholly owned subsidiaries of overseas-based multinationals—have a comparatively larger presence in the Australian economy than in the UK economy.[6] Further, inter-corporate shareholdings and 'founding-family' shareholdings of 30% or more of the issued capital (which are in effect controlling shareholdings) are prevalent in the Australian quoted corporate sector but not in the UK equivalent. Thus, in relation to a large proportion of the Australian quoted corporate sector, as well as the Australian unquoted corporate sector, there is almost no market for corporate control. It is submitted that there are two systems of corporate governance existing side by side in Australia: an 'outsider' system in relation to widely held quoted companies, and a mixture of an 'outsider' and an 'insider' system in relation to large unquoted companies and those many quoted companies which have a controlling *non-institutional* share-holder. The regulatory framework affecting Australian public companies is, however, very much like that within which UK public companies operate.

The significance of the subject-matter of this book lies in the fact that (a) institutional investors collectively hold a very large proportion of the equity capital of the UK quoted corporate sector, and a sizeable proportion of the equity capital of the Australian equivalent; and (b) domestic quoted companies, in turn, occupy an extremely significant position in the UK economy, and a significant one in the Australian economy.

In regard to (a), the proportion of the listed UK equity market owned by institutional shareholders grew enormously between the early 1960s and the early 1990s. Whereas in 1963 individuals owned some 54% of listed UK

---

[6] The 500 largest non-financial companies (measured by sales revenue) operating in Australia at mid-1993 comprised 170 listed Australian companies, 2 listed New Zealand companies, 147 unlisted Australian companies, 122 unlisted foreign companies, and 59 government-owned companies: author's calculations from information contained in 'ABM Top 500 Companies', *ABM*, Dec. 1993, p. 64. Many of the listed Australian companies would have had an overseas shareholder with a controlling stake.

equities, and institutions owned 29%, by 1994 the positions had more than reversed: individuals owned only 20%, and institutions accounted for 60%.[7] Institutional share ownership has grown substantially in Australia as well, although not to the extent seen in the UK. In 1991 institutions owned 36% of listed Australian equities, whilst individuals owned 28%, and overseas entities (mostly UK and US quoted companies) owned 29%.[8]

Regarding (b), there were 11,100 public companies registered in Britain at 31 March 1990 (compared to about a million private companies), and about 2,400 of those UK public companies were quoted: either listed on the London Stock Exchange or trading on the Unlisted Securities Market.[9] The market capitalization of those quoted UK companies was equal to 77% of Britain's GDP in 1990.[10] The 100 largest listed UK companies accounted for 67.3% of total domestic market capitalization in 1990,[11] which means that the market capitalization of those 100 listed companies alone was equivalent to 52% of Britain's GDP in 1990. Domestic quoted companies were not in as dominant a position in the Australian economy in 1990. There were about 10,800 public companies registered in Australia at 30 June 1990 (compared to over 800,000 proprietary (private) companies), and just under 1,100 of those Australian public companies were listed on the Australian Stock Exchange ('ASX') at 31 December 1990.[12] The market capitalization of quoted Australian companies at the end of 1990 was equal to 42.6% of Australia's 1990 GDP.[13] The 50 largest listed Australian companies accounted for 70% of total domestic market capitalization on average during 1990,[14] and therefore the market capitalization of those 50 listed companies was equal to 29.8% of Australia's GDP in 1990.

The concern, in Part I (i.e. Chapters 1 and 2) of the book, is to provide a framework for and to put into context the matters to be discussed in Parts II, III, and IV. The remainder of the current chapter outlines the systems of corporate governance in the UK and Australia. This highlights the fact that institutional monitoring is just one element in a complex system of monitoring forces. Chapter 2 describes the growth of institutional share

---

[7] Central Statistical Office, *Share Ownership* (1995) 8.

[8] Industry Commission, *Availability of Capital* (1991) 140.

[9] Department of Trade and Industry, *Companies in 1989–90* (1990) Table A2; International Stock Exchange of the United Kingdom and the Republic of Ireland, *Quality of Markets Quarterly Review* (Spring 1990) 31.

[10] T. Jenkinson, 'Regulating Hostile Takeovers in the EC' [1992] (Spring) *Stock Ex. Q* 13, at 14.

[11] A. Peacock and G. Bannock, *Corporate Takeovers and the Public Interest* (1991) 25.

[12] National Companies and Securities Commission, *Eleventh Annual Report and Financial Statements* (1990) 23; ASX, *Fact Book 1995* (1995) 43.

[13] ASX, ibid., at 44.

[14] ASX, *All Ordinaries Index Companies Handbook* (1990) 19.

ownership in each country. The chapters constituting Parts II, III, and IV then provide the substantive, analytical body of the book. The chapters in Part II (i.e. Chapters 3, 4, and 5) deal with the history and current level of involvement of institutional shareholders in corporate governance in the UK. These chapters contain the results of a number of empirical studies undertaken by the author in the UK during 1991–3. Chapter 3 describes the different types of institutional investor in the UK, and emphasizes the importance of fund-management firms. It contains statistics on the proportion of the UK equity market which is controlled by the largest fund managers. Chapter 3 also introduces the trade associations which represent UK institutions. Chapter 4 details the various issues with which institutional shareholders have been concerned in the UK. Chapter 5 then describes the actual manner in which the institutions have involved themselves in the matters listed in Chapter 4. Chapter 5 is the major chapter in Part II. Part III deals with the history and current level of involvement of institutional shareholders in corporate governance in Australia. The three chapters in Part III (namely Chapters 6, 7, and 8) deal with the same subject matter as Chapters 3, 4, and 5, respectively, but from an Australian perspective. They also contain the results of a number of empirical studies undertaken by the author in Australia during 1993–4. Part IV (which comprises Chapters 9, 10, and 11) looks to the future—examining the possibilities for increased involvement by the institutions. Chapter 9 investigates the desirability of a greater level of institutional monitoring. The issue with which Chapter 10 is concerned is whether a significantly higher level of institutional monitoring can be expected in the future. The chapter points to a number of factors which operate as disincentives to detailed institutional monitoring. Chapter 11 provides a conclusion and lists some recommended reforms.

B. THE POWER STRUCTURE IN LARGE COMPANIES

The companies statutes of the UK and Australia contain a model of corporate management and control involving two main organs: the board of directors and the general meeting of members. However, the standard articles of association allow for the board to appoint and confer any of their powers upon one or more executive (or 'managing') directors, which in effect allows the creation of a third organ—executive management—if it is required.[15] Under the companies legislation, and standard articles of association (as interpreted by courts in the twentieth century), the board

---

[15] Companies (Tables A to F) Regulations 1985 (SI 1985/805), Table A (hereafter 'Table A'), arts. 72, 84; Corporations Law (hereafter 'CL'), Sch. 1, Table A (hereafter 'Table A (Aust.)'), arts. 79–81.

of directors is the most important day-to-day organ in the company. The board is given the power to manage the business of the company,[16] and the general meeting is not permitted to interfere with its exercise.[17] The general meeting does, however, retain ultimate power in that it has the right by simple majority to remove the directors without cause,[18] and by three-quarters majority to change the articles.[19]

The board of directors of a quoted public company usually consists of non-executive (i.e. part-time) directors as well as executive directors (who are employed as full-time officers of the company). The board, as an organ, would very rarely manage the business of such a company. In practice, the board of the average quoted company delegates to the chief executive (or 'managing director') and other executive directors the responsibility for day-to-day management of the company's business. It is the executive directors and other executive officers (who are not also members of the board), collectively called the executive management, who manage the company's business. The company's strategy is developed by the executive management, although it is normally necessary for the approval of the board to be obtained for major transactions or changes in strategy,[20] and sometimes necessary for shareholder approval to be obtained as well.[21] The board usually meets monthly, and performs (or is supposed to perform) the functions of reviewing strategy and monitoring the performance of the executive management.[22] This division of functions

---

[16] Table A, art. 70; Table A (Aust.), art. 66(1).

[17] *Automatic Self-Cleansing Filter Syndicate Co. Ltd.* v. *Cunninghame* [1906] 2 Ch. 34; *John Shaw & Sons (Salford) Ltd.* v. *Shaw* [1935] 2 KB 113, at 134; *Winthrop Investments Ltd.* v. *Winns Ltd.* [1975] 2 NSWLR 666, at 682–4. Note that during the nineteenth century it was assumed that the board of directors was an agent of the general meeting of shareholders, subject to its directions by ordinary resolution. This view was based largely upon the terms of deeds of settlement (see L. S. Sealy, 'The Director as Trustee' [1967] *CLJ* 83, at 89–90), the wording of the Companies Clauses Consolidation Act 1845, s. 90 (see *Isle of Wight Railway Co.* v. *Tahourdin* (1883) 25 Ch. D 320, at 330–2, 335), and the terms of private Acts of incorporation (see *Foss* v. *Harbottle* (1843) 2 Hare 461, at 492).

[18] Companies Act 1985 (UK) (hereafter 'CA 1985'), s. 303; CL, s. 227. Shareholders may cast their votes as rights of property—to advance their own interests: *North-West Transportation Co. Ltd.* v. *Beatty* (1887) 12 App. Cas. 589, at 593; *Ngurli Ltd.* v. *McCann* (1953) 90 CLR 425, at 447.

[19] CA 1985, s. 9; CL, s. 176.

[20] The Cadbury Committee recommended that boards should have a formal schedule of matters specifically reserved to them for their collective decision, and envisaged that such a schedule would include at least: (a) acquisition and disposal of assets of the company or its subsidiaries which are material to the company; and (b) investments, capital projects, authority levels, treasury policies, and risk-management policies: *Cadbury Report*, paras. 4.23, 4.24; *Cadbury Code*, para. 1.4.

[21] See Ch. 5, Sec. B.1.i; Ch. 8, Sec. B.1.i.

[22] See *AWA Ltd.* v. *Daniels* (1992) 7 ACSR 759, at 832–3, 864–8 *per* Rogers CJ (Comm. Div.); on appeal (*sub nom. Daniels* v. *Anderson*) (1995) 16 ACSR 607, at 664 *per* Clarke and Sheller JJA.

between the shareholders, the board, and the executive management is an inevitable consequence of the large size and scale of operation of most quoted companies.[23]

Under UK and Australian company law, directors and senior executives[24] owe their fiduciary and other duties to the company as a legal entity separate from its shareholders and creditors.[25] However, under the general law the 'interests of the company' means, whilst the company is solvent, the interests of the shareholders, present and future, as a group.[26] Although most industrialists,[27] and many commentators,[28] consider that the interests of large companies are an amalgam of the interests of a number of stakeholders such as shareholders, creditors, employees, customers, suppliers, management, and indeed the community, the general law still considers the company's interests to be those of the collective body of shareholders.[29] Legislation has altered the position slightly in

[23] It should be noted that quoted companies almost invariably have many subsidiaries. In some cases the main operational subsidiaries have a good deal of autonomy from the board of the quoted holding company: see A. D. Chandler, *Strategy and Structure: Chapters in the History of the Industrial Enterprise* (1962); O. E. Williamson, 'The Modern Corporation: Origins, Evolution, Attributes' (1981) 19 *J Econ. Lit.* 1537 (contrasting 'M-form' and 'U-form' firms). However, the present concern is with the executive management and board of directors of the quoted entity, because this is the apex of the organization and the point at which institutional involvement takes place.

[24] Directors' duties under the general law apply also to senior executive officers who are authorized to act on behalf of the company: L. C. B. Gower, *Gower's Principles of Modern Company Law* (5th edn., 1992) 553 (cited with approval in *Canadian Aero Service Ltd.* v. *O'Malley* (1973) 40 DLR (3d) 371, at 381). There are statutory duties in Australia which overlap with the general-law duties, and the statutory duties apply to 'officers' (which is defined to include executive officers as well as directors): CL, s. 232(1).

[25] *Percival* v. *Wright* [1902] 2 Ch. 421; *Esplanade Developments Ltd.* v. *Dinive Holdings Pty. Ltd.* (1980) 4 ACLR 826.

[26] *Greenhalgh* v. *Arderne Cinemas Ltd.* [1951] Ch. 286, at 291; *Peters' American Delicacy Co. Ltd.* v. *Heath* (1939) 61 CLR 457, at 512; Inspector's report on the Savoy Hotel investigation: described in L. C. B. Gower, 'Corporate Control: The Battle for the Berkeley' (1955) 68 *Harv. L Rev.* 1176.

[27] See e.g. Sir Hector Laing, 'The Balance of Responsibilities' in National Association of Pension Funds, *Creative Tension?* (1990) 59, at 60–1.

[28] The literature (much of which is American) is vast. For one of the earliest submissions, see E. M. Dodd, 'For Whom Are Corporate Managers Trustees?' (1932) 45 *Harv. L Rev.* 1145. From a UK perspective, see Lord Wedderburn, 'The Legal Development of Corporate Responsibility' in K. J. Hopt and G. Teubner (eds.), *Corporate Governance and Directors' Liabilities* (1985) 3; M. Stokes, 'Company Law and Legal Theory' in W. L. Twining (ed.), *Legal Theory and Common Law* (1986) 155, at 176–81; J. E. Parkinson, *Corporate Power and Responsibility* (1993) chs. 9–12. Note that in the US, towards the end of the 1980s takeover boom, many states adopted anti-takeover 'constituency' statutes, which empower directors to consider the interests of employees, creditors, the local community, etc. as well as those of shareholders: see L. Herzel and R. W. Shepro, *Bidders and Targets* (1990) 62–4.

[29] Many commentators also favour this position: see e.g. A. A. Berle, 'For Whom Corporate Managers *Are* Trustees: A Note' (1932) 45 *Harv. L Rev.* 1365; M. Friedman, *Capitalism and Freedom* (1962) 133; D. R. Fischel, 'The Corporate Governance Movement' (1982) 35 *Vand. L Rev.* 1259, at 1273: 'Do investors, as long as corporations lawfully may be

the UK: directors of UK companies have, since 1980, been required when performing their functions to have regard also to the interests of the company's employees.[30] In a book dealing with the role in corporate governance of a particular type of equity shareholder (namely, the institutional shareholder), it is inevitable that the issue of the position of shareholders *vis-à-vis* other stakeholders should be addressed. This is done in a later chapter.[31]

C. AGENCY COSTS INHERENT IN THE CORPORATE FORM OF FIRM ORGANIZATION[32]

It has been mentioned that the size and scale of operation of most quoted companies results in there being a division between the shareholders, the board, and the professional management. Although the groups usually overlap to some extent, it is important to appreciate the division and why it exists:

> The corporate form of firm organization has obvious advantages for shareholders (suppliers of capital) and managers. Shareholders can participate in the gains from entrepreneurial ventures even though they lack management skills; managers can pursue profitable business opportunities even though they lack large personal wealth. Both parties benefit from this division of labor.[33]

As well as benefits from specialization of function, there are also, however, certain costs inherent in the corporate form of firm organization. The most

formed for profit, have any duty to sacrifice profitable opportunities to benefit some other parties? And do managers . . . have any right or duty to sacrifice profitable opportunities to benefit some other party? Both questions have the same answer—managers should act to maximize the wealth of investors . . .' For some important factors affecting the debate in the UK, see D. D. Prentice, 'Directors, Creditors, and Shareholders' in E. McKendrick (ed.), *Commercial Aspects of Trusts and Fiduciary Obligations* (1992) 73, at 76–8.

[30] CA 1985, s. 309. See also, in the context of takeovers, Panel on Takeovers and Mergers, *The City Code on Takeovers and Mergers*, General Principle 9: 'It is the shareholders' interests taken as a whole, together with those of employees and creditors, which should be considered when the directors are giving advice to shareholders.' Note also that many of the privatized UK companies (especially the former public utilities) are subject to regulatory regimes which, mainly through pricing controls, effectively compel their boards to take into account the interests of consumers as well as the shareholders.

[31] See Ch. 9, Secs. B.2, B.8.

[32] Terminology taken from Fischel (n. 29 above), at 1262. In relation to why much economic activity takes place within and between firms rather than between individuals contracting in the market, see R. H. Coase, 'The Nature of the Firm' (1937) 4 *Economica* 386; A. A. Alchian and H. Demsetz, 'Production, Information Costs, and Economic Organization' (1972) 62 *Am. Econ. Rev.* 777; Williamson (n. 23 above) (use of firms involves a reduction in transaction costs).

[33] Fischel, ibid.; see also E. F. Fama and M. C. Jensen, 'Agency Problems and Residual Claims' (1983) 26 *J Law & Econ.* 327, at 333.

significant of these are 'agency costs'[34] (so called because the shareholders and directors/managers are, loosely speaking, in a principal:agent relationship). Agency costs arise because of a divergence between the interests of shareholders and managers:

> As residual claimants on the firm's income stream, shareholders want their agents—the firm's managers—to maximize wealth. Because managers cannot capture all of the gains if they are successful, and will not suffer all of the losses should the venture flop, they have less incentive to maximize wealth than if they themselves were the principals. Rather, managers have an incentive to consume excess leisure, perquisites and in general be less dedicated to the goal of wealth maximization than they would be if they were not simply agents.[35]

Agency costs comprise the costs incurred by the shareholders in monitoring the managers in order to minimize the divergence between their interests (see Section D below), 'bonding' costs incurred by the managers,[36] and the 'residual loss' resulting from the remaining divergence in shareholders' and managers' interests.[37]

The well-known thesis of Berle and Means was formulated in the US in the late 1920s when a mass of diffuse small holdings characterized the shareholding structure of those numerous quoted public companies which lacked a significant 'founding family' or corporate shareholding, and in which senior management and their associates had a negligible stake.[38] Berle and Means warned: 'Where ownership is sufficiently subdivided, the management can . . . become a self-perpetuating body even though its share in the ownership is negligible.'[39] They were concerned that the divergence between the interests of shareholders and managers was unchecked because of the lack of incentive for holders of insignificant shareholdings to monitor management. It is part of the aim of this book to show that the highly diffuse ownership structure described by Berle and Means did not exist in the vast majority of quoted UK and Australian companies in the early 1990s. Divergence between the interests of shareholders and managers is, nevertheless, still an issue. Since the study

---

[34] M. C. Jensen and W. H. Meckling, 'Theory of the Firm: Managerial Behavior, Agency Costs and Ownership Structure' (1976) 3 *J Fin. Econ.* 305, at 308–9.

[35] Fischel (n. 29 above), at 1262–3. This problem was pointed out by Adam Smith in the eighteenth century: A. Smith, *The Wealth of Nations* (1937) 700. Note that '[i]t is clearly an error to suppose that a firm managed by its only owner comes closest to the profit-maximizing firm postulated in the model firm of economic theory. The owner-manager of such a firm may or may not be motivated only by the search for profit. He may habitually consume on the job.': H. Demsetz, 'The Structure of Ownership and the Theory of the Firm' (1983) *J Law & Econ.* 375, at 382–3 (citing the example of the decline of the Ford Motor Company in the latter years of Henry Ford's life; suggesting that the company would have performed better if widely owned). [36] See n. 42 below, and accompanying text.

[37] Jensen and Meckling (n. 34 above), at 308.

[38] A. A. Berle and G. C. Means, *The Modern Corporation and Private Property* (rev. edn., 1968). [39] Ibid., at 82.

of Berle and Means, however, it has become clear that there are numerous devices, rules, and market forces which serve to reduce the divergence between the interests of shareholders and managers.

D. THE MONITORING ENVIRONMENT

A brief outline is given below of the range of devices and market forces which operate to converge partially the interests of shareholders and managers. This 'monitoring environment' is not treated in any detail because the purpose of the exercise is simply to put into context the discussion in the remainder of the book. The aim of this section is, then, to show how the monitoring role of institutional shareholders fits into the broader tapestry of monitoring devices and forces.

Market forces. There are several market forces which serve to align the interests of managers and shareholders. First, there is the market for corporate control—takeovers. Economic theory suggests that takeovers serve to redistribute resources from poor to good management teams. In addition, however, the *threat* of a takeover bid is said to motivate management to run the company so as to maximize the return to shareholders.[40] There is further discussion of the market for corporate control in Section E, below. Secondly, the capital market provides a discipline in that inefficiently managed firms may find it difficult to raise equity capital, and may have to pay a higher interest rate on debt finance. Thirdly, there is the product market: a poorly run firm may lose market share to efficiently run rivals, and may eventually become insolvent. Finally, there is the market for managerial talent, which is two-pronged: (a) managers have an incentive to run a successful firm because that will enhance their prospects for advancement, both within and outside the firm; and (b) because managers work as members of a team, there is an incentive for each manager to monitor other members of the team to ensure that his or her services are not undervalued by poor performance on the part of other managers.[41]

Corporate financial policy. There are theories which suggest that a

---

[40] There is an enormous literature in this area, which began with H. G. Manne, 'Mergers and the Market for Corporate Control' (1965) 73 *J Pol. Econ.* 110; see D. Scharfstein, 'The Disciplinary Role of Takeovers' (1988) 55 *Rev. Econ. Stud.* 85.

[41] See E. F. Fama, 'Agency Problems and the Theory of the Firm' (1980) 88 *J Pol. Econ.* 288; A. A. Cannella, D. R. Fraser, and D. S. Lee, 'Firm Failure and Managerial Labor Markets: Evidence from Texas Banking' (1995) 38 *J Fin. Econ.* 185; R. G. Hubbard and D. Palia, 'Executive Pay and Performance: Evidence from the US Banking Industry' (1995) 39 *J Fin. Econ.* 105.

company's management will choose the company's financial policy (debt-equity ratio and dividend policy) so as to minimize total agency costs, and hence maximize the market value of the company, and thereby (a) maximize their remuneration from incentive schemes linked to the market value of the firm; and (b) reduce the risk that a successful takeover bid will be made for the company.[42] This is an example of the 'bonding' devices to which reference was made earlier.[43]

Executive incentive remuneration. If a sizeable portion of managers' remuneration is linked to changes in shareholder wealth, the divergence between the interests of managers and shareholders will be decreased. One of the most common forms of incentive remuneration is the executive share scheme, and institutional shareholders in both the UK and Australia have been involved in attempts to ensure that executive share schemes provide a real incentive for managers to maximize shareholder value.[44]

Mandatory disclosure of information. One response of the law to the divergence between the interests of shareholders and managers has been to require management to disclose (through the board) to shareholders a steadily growing amount of financial and non-financial information,[45] to help the shareholders in assessing management's stewardship of the company's assets.

Audit. The primary purpose of the statutory audit[46] is to assist the collective body of shareholders, when examining the information to which reference has just been made, in making an *informed* appraisal of the stewardship of the management and the board.[47]

Non-executive directors. It has been accepted widely for several years that a major role of non-executive directors should be to monitor the performance of the executive management.[48] This topic is dealt with in detail in later chapters.[49]

Powers of the general meeting, and shareholder monitoring. The shareholders of all UK companies, and of Australian public companies,

---

[42] See S. J. Grossman and O. D. Hart, 'Corporate Financial Structure and Managerial Incentives' in J. J. McCall (ed.), *The Economics of Information and Uncertainty* (1982) 107; Jensen and Meckling (n. 34 above); F. H. Easterbrook, 'Two Agency-Cost Explanations of Dividends' (1984) 74 *Am. Econ. Rev.* 650; J. S. S. Edwards, 'Recent Developments in the Theory of Corporate Finance' (1987) 3 (4) *Ox. Rev. Econ. Pol.* 1, at 6–11; P. Aghion and P. Bolton, 'The Financial Structure of the Firm and the Problem of Control' (1989) 33 *Euro. Econ. Rev.* 286.   [43] See nn. 36–7 above, and accompanying text.

[44] See Ch. 4, Sec. A.1.xvii; Ch. 7, Sec. A.1.v.

[45] See CA 1985, Pt. VII; CL, Pt. 3.6. Listed companies are subject to further disclosure requirements imposed by the London Stock Exchange and the ASX.

[46] See CA 1985, s. 235; CL, s. 332.

[47] *Caparo Industries plc* v. *Dickman* [1990] 2 AC 605, at 626, 630–1, 661–2.

[48] See e.g. *Cadbury Code*, para. 1.1; Working Group of the Business Council of Australia, et al. ('Bosch Committee'), *Corporate Practices and Conduct* (2nd edn., 1993) 15.

[49] See Ch. 5, Sec. D.2; Ch. 8, Sec. D.2.

have the right by ordinary resolution to remove directors without cause.[50] For this reason the shareholders have ultimate power in the company. There are numerous other matters for which approval of the general meeting is required, either by the companies legislation, the articles of association, or the listing requirements of the London Stock Exchange and the ASX. Then there are various informal monitoring actions which are performed by shareholders—in particular institutional shareholders—of quoted UK and Australian companies. The formal and informal monitoring actions taken by institutions are, of course, the subject matter of this book.

Directors' and officers' duties. Directors and senior executives[51] of UK and Australian companies owe to their companies fiduciary duties of honesty and loyalty, and a duty of care and skill.[52] The Australian companies legislation also lays down statutory duties which largely cover the same ground as the general-law duties.[53] As far as executive directors and other senior executives are concerned, these legal duties serve as a deterrent to wrongdoing and extreme negligence, but one of their shortcomings is that they, 'unlike the market and market-linked devices, [cannot] create a more positive motivational environment. They lay down minimum standards, and do not as such provide an incentive . . . to achieve top-quality performance.'[54] In the case of non-executive directors, however, recent developments in the duty of care and skill in both the UK and Australia indicate that these duties now require non-executive directors to undertake the monitoring role which proponents of good corporate governance have cast upon them.[55] In the *AWA* case, the majority judgment in the New South Wales Court of Appeal said that 'the responsibilities of directors require that they take reasonable steps to place themselves in a position to guide and monitor the management of the company'.[56] It is to be doubted, though, whether the courts' changing perception of the duty of care and skill has served or will serve as an incentive for non-executive directors of quoted companies to play a

---

[50] CA 1985, s. 303; CL, s. 227. These sections do not, however, take away any rights of compensation for breach of contract of employment: CA 1985, s. 303(5); CL, s. 227(11); see further Ch. 4, Sec. A.1.xvii.   [51] See n. 24 above.

[52] See generally Gower (n. 24 above), ch. 21. Although these duties are owed to 'the company', under the general law the 'interests of the company' means, whilst the company is solvent, the interests of the shareholders, present and future, as a group: see nn. 24–30 above, and accompanying text.

[53] See CL, s. 232.   [54] Parkinson (n. 28 above), at 134.

[55] This point is developed in detail in G. P. Stapledon, 'The AWA Case: Non-Executive Directors, Auditors, and Corporate Governance Issues in Court' in D. D. Prentice and P. R. J. Holland (eds.), *Contemporary Issues in Corporate Governance* (1993) 187, at 204–14.

[56] *Daniels* v. *Anderson* (n. 22 above), at 664; see also *Commonwealth Bank of Australia* v. *Friedrich* (1991) 5 ACSR 115, at 184.

considerably greater monitoring role. This pessimistic view is based upon the fact that actions to enforce the duties of directors of quoted companies have been almost non-existent in the UK, and extremely rare in Australia. The reasons for this are set out in a later chapter.[57]

Regulatory investigation and inspection. In both the UK and Australia, there are statutory powers for regulators to investigate the affairs of companies, and take actions such as applying for the disqualification of directors.[58] The government's involvement in the UK has been *ad hoc*, with an extremely small amount of resources being devoted to this area.[59] Since the formation of the Australian Securities Commission in 1990, government has played a relatively larger role in the regulation of the Australian corporate sector, but from a very low base. It still does not approach a systematic monitoring device.

E. ADEQUACY OF PRESENT CORPORATE GOVERNANCE SYSTEMS

Many of those who argue for changes in corporate governance seem simply to assume that there is a need for change. It is important to recognize that there is an economic argument that efforts to enhance one or more of the elements in the monitoring environment just described may be more costly than beneficial. This argument finds favour especially with supporters of the nexus-of-contracts model of the company: 'contractarians'. Contractarians believe that a separation of ownership and control in large quoted companies is not merely inevitable but also economically efficient.[60] Put simply, they argue that the divergence between the interests of managers and shareholders is minimized largely by market forces, and that positive action (for example, bolstering the legal duties of directors) to reduce the remaining divergence is unjustifiable because this would lead to greater costs (from, for instance, a stifling of managers' enterprise) than benefits.

It is submitted that contractarians place excessive reliance upon market forces—especially the market for corporate control—as a means of monitoring corporate management. The following are some shortcomings

---

[57] See Ch. 5, Sec. B.3.viii.

[58] CA 1985, Pt. XIV; Company Directors Disqualification Act 1986 (UK); Australian Securities Commission Act 1989 (Cth.), Pt. 3; CL, s. 230.

[59] See V. Finch, 'Company Directors: Who Cares About Skill and Care?' (1992) 55 *MLR* 179, at 195–7.

[60] See e.g. Demsetz (n. 35 above); E. F. Fama and M. C. Jensen, 'Separation of Ownership and Control' (1983) 26 *J Law & Econ.* 301; for criticisms, see V. Brudney, 'Corporate Governance, Agency Costs, and the Rhetoric of Contract' (1985) 85 *Colum. L Rev.* 1403; M. A. Eisenberg, 'The Structure of Corporation Law' (1989) 89 *Colum. L Rev.* 1461.

with the market for corporate control, but it should be recognized that there are also shortcomings with the product market, the capital market, and the market for managerial talent.[61]

As far as the UK is concerned, the major shortcoming with the market for corporate control as a device for disciplining inefficient management is that empirical evidence suggests that there is in fact no link between poor performance and hostile takeovers. From a sample of contested and friendly bids in the UK in 1985–6, Franks and Mayer found no statistical difference in either the share-price performance or the dividend performance of targets of hostile bids compared to targets of friendly bids over the two years prior to the bid.[62] In addition, it was found that only 12% of targets of successful hostile bids had reduced or omitted their dividends in the two years prior to the bid, compared to a figure of 41% for a random sample of poorly performing firms (companies from the bottom 20% of the market measured by share-price performance). Franks and Mayer did find, however, that there was a significantly higher level of corporate restructuring—asset disposals and executive dismissals—associated with successful hostile bids compared to friendly bids.[63] An interpretation of these results is that the market for corporate control is a market in contending prospective strategies for firms rather than a mechanism for correcting past poor performance of firms.[64] That is, hostile bids occur where there is *ex ante* managerial failure (i.e. the prospect of improved performance in the future by an alternative management, even without poor performance by the incumbent management) rather than *ex post* managerial failure (i.e. poor past performance by the incumbent management).[65]

A second difficulty with the market for corporate control is that takeovers in the UK and Australia have historically occurred in 'waves'.[66]

---

[61] See Parkinson (n. 28 above), at 114–19, for a good summary.

[62] J. R. Franks and C. P. Mayer, 'Hostile Takeovers in the UK and the Correction of Managerial Failure' (1996) 40 *J Fin. Econ.* (forthcoming). See also M. L. Lawriwsky, 'Some Tests of the Influence of Control Type on the Market for Corporate Control in Australia' (1984) 32 *J Indust. Econ.* 277. [63] Ibid.

[64] Franks and Mayer (n. 2 above). Note, however, that Franks and Mayer (n. 62 above) also found that *un*successful hostile bids in the UK in 1985–6 were followed by a high level of executive dismissals. This is explicable in terms of 'a sequential interaction between the board [of the target company] and the [would-be] acquiror [whereby] the board infers from the takeover bid that the bidder possesses adverse information about the [senior management of the target]': D. Hirshleifer and A. V. Thakor, 'Managerial Performance, Boards of Directors and Takeover Bidding' (1994) 1 *J Corp. Fin.* 63, at 65–6.

[65] See J. R. Franks and C. P. Mayer, 'Capital Markets and Corporate Control: A Study of France, Germany and the UK' (1990) 10 *Econ. Pol.* 189, at 211–12. See also T. Jenkinson and C. P. Mayer, *Takeover Defence Strategies* (1991) 33 (finding a relationship between hostile bids and the corporate strategy of the bidder).

[66] In relation to the UK, see M. King, 'Take-over Activity in the United Kingdom' in J. A. Fairburn and J. A. Kay (eds.), *Mergers and Merger Policy* (1989) 99, at 100.

This raises a theoretical problem because '[t]here is every a priori reason for believing that [managerial] incompetence is not cyclical'.[67] Thirdly, takeovers are very expensive—there are direct costs in the form of payments to advisers and underwriters, and indirect costs in the form of consumption of managerial time and effort (with both types of costs being borne by both the bidder and the target).[68] Especially in the case of unsuccessful bids, these costs may be simply dead-weight costs which do not generate any offsetting benefits.[69] Fourthly, hostile bids require a very high bid premium.[70] If a potential bidder can see nothing other than an inefficient incumbent management in a potential target (and not also, for example, the possibility of strategic gains from a merger), then a bid is unlikely to be forthcoming unless it is a case of 'gross managerial failure'.[71] Lastly, and following on from the previous point, the market for corporate control serves to keep a management on its toes only where there is a real possibility of a bid emerging. In some sectors of the UK and Australian markets (for example, the banking sector in the UK, and the media sectors in both countries) there are, however, substantial regulatory barriers to takeovers. There are two further fetters to takeovers of Australian companies, generally: (a) takeovers of Australian companies by foreign companies require government approval;[72] and (b) takeovers of Australian companies are regulated by a statutory system, which means that tactical litigation—and hence increased transaction costs—are features of the Australian scene.[73]

---

[67] D. D. Prentice, 'Regulation of Takeover Bids in the United Kingdom' in K. Kreuzer (ed.), *Öffentliche Übernahmeangebote* (1992) 133, at 134.

[68] T. Jenkinson and C. P. Mayer, 'The Assessment: Corporate Governance and Corporate Control' (1992) 8 (3) *Ox. Rev. Econ. Pol.* 1, at 3; J. R. Franks and R. Harris, 'Shareholder Wealth Effects of UK Take-overs: Implications for Merger Policy' in Fairburn and Kay (n. 66 above), at 169–70.

[69] D. D. Prentice, 'Some Aspects of the Corporate Governance Debate' in Prentice and Holland (n. 55 above), at 37.

[70] See Franks and Mayer (n. 62 above) (premiums in hostile bids approximately one-and-a-half times the level in friendly bids). See also Prentice, ibid., at 38; M. Burkart, *Overbidding in Takeover Contests* (1994).

[71] J. C. Coffee, 'Regulating the Market for Corporate Control: A Critical Assessment of the Tender Offer's Role in Corporate Governance' (1984) 84 *Colum. L Rev.* 1145, at 1200.

[72] Foreign Acquisitions and Takeovers Act 1975 (Cth.). Of course, each country also has competition legislation: see Fair Trading Act 1973 (UK), Pt. V; Trade Practices Act 1974 (Cth.), Pt. IV.

[73] The UK's self-regulatory system, with the Takeover Panel, has ensured that tactical litigation is not a barrier to takeovers in the UK: see Jenkinson and Mayer (n. 65 above). This has been a factor behind the UK's opposition to the proposed Thirteenth EC Directive on harmonization of company law (1990 OJ (C 240) 7): see Jenkinson (n. 10 above), at 16. The market for corporate control has drawbacks other than those which affect its efficacy as a discipline on poor managerial performance. The most significant seems to be that takeovers break implicit contracts or, more likely, ensure that beneficial implicit contracts between shareholders, managers, employees, suppliers, and customers, simply do not arise in the

There are also shortcomings with the other monitoring devices mentioned earlier. As regards corporate financial policy, there is not yet a complete theory nor strong empirical evidence showing how agency costs determine an optimal debt-equity ratio and dividend policy for the firm.[74] In regard to incentive share schemes, one problem is that there is both UK and Australian empirical evidence showing little or no link between the remuneration of executive directors of quoted companies and the performance of those companies.[75] A second problem is that, whilst reducing (theoretically, at least) the incentive for managers to shirk, an executive share scheme actually compounds a different problem. There is an asymmetry between the attitudes to risk of managers and diversified shareholders (like institutions). A manager is inherently financially over-invested in his or her firm, and will therefore be more risk-averse than the firm's institutional shareholders, which have diversified portfolios of investments. The use of shares and share options as incentive remuneration serves to further decrease the diversification of the manager's income stream.[76] Compulsory disclosure and audit also suffer from defects. In regard to the audit, concerns have been expressed about whether in practice auditors 'work with' management rather than 'working for' the shareholder body.[77] There are also problems with non-executive directors as monitors of management performance—these are detailed in later chapters.[78] Finally, for reasons given already, neither the body of legal duties owed by directors and senior executives, nor the governments' regulatory regimes affecting companies, plays a significant role in motivating executive management to maximize shareholder return.

To recapitulate, monitoring by institutional shareholders fits within a broad tapestry of devices and market forces which operate to reduce the divergence between the interests of managers and shareholders. There are

---

outsider systems of the UK and the US: see Jenkinson and Mayer (n. 68 above), at 8; C. R. Knoeber, 'Golden Parachutes, Shark Repellents, and Hostile Tender Offers' (1986) 76 *Am. Econ. Rev.* 155, at 159–61; A. Schleifer and L. H. Summers, 'Breach of Trust in Hostile Takeovers' in A. J. Auerbach (ed.), *Corporate Takeovers: Causes and Consequences* (1988) 33; Franks and Mayer (n. 65 above), at 212–14. See further Ch. 9, at nn. 91–142, and accompanying text.

[74] See Edwards (n. 42 above); see also the criticisms in J. C. Coffee, 'Shareholders Versus Managers: The Strain in the Corporate Web' (1986) 85 *Mich. L Rev.* 1, at 27–8.

[75] See M. J. Conyon, P. Gregg, and S. Machin, 'Taking Care of Business: Executive Compensation in the UK' (1995) 105 *Econ. J* 704; A. Defina, T. C. Harris, and I. M. Ramsay, 'What is Reasonable Remuneration for Corporate Officers? An Empirical Investigation into the Relationship Between Pay and Performance in the Largest Australian Companies' (1994) 12 *C&SLJ* 341.   [76] See Coffee (n. 74 above), at 17–19.

[77] See D. Hatherly, 'The Future of Audit: The Case for the Shareholder Panel' (1994); Auditing Practices Board, *The Future Development of Auditing* (1992) 10–12; *Dairy Containers Ltd.* v. *NZI Bank Ltd.* (1995) 7 NZCLC 260,783 at 260,804. In relation to disclosure, see L. S. Sealy, 'The "Disclosure" Philosophy and Company Law Reform' (1981) 2 *Co. Law.* 51.   [78] See Ch. 5, Sec. D.2.ii.(b); Ch. 8, Sec. D.2.ii.

weaknesses in each element of that monitoring environment. In particular, the market for corporate control, which lies at the heart of the arguments of the contractarians, has serious shortcomings as a monitoring force. It is shown in later chapters that institutional monitoring is already a significant element of the monitoring environment in the UK quoted corporate sector, and a growing but less significant part of the Australian scene. Are there any reforms which would aid the operation of this monitoring device, but without unduly reducing managerial enterprise?[79] A leading financial economist wrote recently:

> For those with a normative bent, making the internal control systems of corporations work is the major challenge facing economists and management scholars in the 1990s. For those who choose to take a purely positive approach, the major challenge is understanding how these systems work, and how they interact with the other control forces (in particular the product and factor markets, legal, political, and regulatory systems, and the capital markets) impinging on the corporation. I believe the reason we have an interest in developing positive theories of the world is so that we can understand how to make things work more efficiently. Without accurate positive theories of cause and effect relationships, normative propositions and decisions based on them will be wrong. Therefore, the two objectives are completely consistent.[80]

This book adopts partly a positive approach, in that it aims to increase the state of knowledge about the extent and mechanics of institutional monitoring in the UK and Australia, and about how institutional monitoring interacts with other elements of the monitoring environment. It also has a normative aspect, in that it seeks to identify ways in which one part of the internal control system—monitoring by institutional shareholders—could be improved.[81]

---

[79] Note that there is some evidence that monitoring devices are substitutes for one another: see Ch. 5, at nn. 213–14, and accompanying text. If this is correct, an increased level of institutional monitoring would not necessarily entail greater total monitoring costs: see Ch. 9, Sec. A.1.

[80] M. C. Jensen, 'The Modern Industrial Revolution, Exit, and the Failure of Internal Control Systems' (1993) 48 *J Fin.* 831, at 873.

[81] In order to avoid confusion from the terminology, institutional monitoring is a part of the *internal* control system because it involves shareholders utilizing, or threatening to use, their powers under the corporate constitution. On the other hand, institutional monitoring forms part of an *outsider* system of corporate governance (see nn. 3–5 above, and accompanying text), because each of an institution's shareholdings is ultimately part of a widely diversified portfolio of investments, and institutions do not normally have other links with portfolio companies such as the creditor and boardroom links associated with German banks, for instance.

2
The Growth of Institutional Share Ownership

This chapter is divided into two sections, which deal with the UK and Australia respectively. Each section first presents a statistical picture of the growth of institutional share ownership in the post-World War II period. There is then a brief description of the main types of institution in each country, and finally an outline of the reasons behind the absolute and relative growth of institutional share ownership. The chapter is brief because an understanding of the background, size, and growth of the institutions' beneficial shareholdings is less important, for present purposes, than an appreciation of the position of the fund managers which manage the equity investments of the institutions. The latter topic is covered in Chapters 3 and 6.

A. UNITED KINGDOM

Table 2.1 shows the distribution of beneficial ownership of the listed ordinary shares of quoted UK companies over 1963–94. Institutional ownership of the listed UK equity market was 29% in 1963, 34.2% in 1969, 47.3% in 1975, 57.6% in 1981, 60.6% in 1992, and 59.8% in 1994.[1] Investment trusts and insurance companies were the major categories of institutional shareholder in the 1960s, but pension funds have been the largest category since 1975. The market share of pension funds in 1992 was more than five times larger than in 1963. The institutions' increased ownership of UK equities has come mainly at the expense of the direct holdings of individuals. The government's policy of 'wider share ownership' failed to reverse the trend during the 1980s.

---

[1] These figures are for pension funds, insurance companies, unit trusts, and investment trusts, collectively. Holdings of banks are not included. Many UK banks have fund-management arms which manage UK equities on behalf of pension funds and other beneficial owners, but the shares owned beneficially by banks are mostly either corporate holdings or the result of debt-for-equity swaps; they are not portfolio investments.

Table 2.1 Ownership of UK equities, 1963–94

Sector of beneficial owner	Beneficial ownership of listed UK equities (%)						
	1963	*1969*	*1975*	*1981*	*1991*	*1992*	*1994*
Individuals	54.0	47.4	37.5	28.2	19.9	20.4	20.3
Other personal sector (mainly charities)	2.1	2.1	2.3	2.2	2.4	1.8	1.3
Public sector	1.5	2.6	3.6	3.0	1.3	1.8	0.8
Industrial and commercial companies	5.1	5.4	3.0	5.1	3.3	1.8	1.1
Overseas	7.0	6.6	5.6	3.6	12.8	13.1	16.3
Banks	1.3	1.7	0.7	0.3	0.2	0.5	0.4
Insurance companies	10.0	12.2	15.9	20.5	20.8	19.5	21.9
Pension funds	6.4	9.0	16.8	26.7	31.3	32.4	27.8
Unit trusts	1.3	2.9	4.1	3.6	5.7	6.2	6.8
Other financial institutions (mainly investment trusts)*	11.3	10.1	10.5	6.8	2.3	2.5	3.3
Total	100.0	100.0	100.0	100.0	100.0	100.0	100.0

* From 1989 onwards, holdings in SEPON (the Stock Exchange account into which shares are placed while in transit between seller and buyer) are allocated one-quarter to 'other financial institutions' with the remainder being allocated proportionately across all beneficial sectors. Prior to 1989, SEPON is included entirely in 'other financial institutions'. SEPON accounted for only 0.6% of shares in 1991, 0.7% of shares in 1992, and 1.0% of shares in 1994: Central Statistical Office, *Share Ownership* (1995) 7; Central Statistical Office, *Economic Trends* (No. 480, 1993) 124, at 128.

Source: Central Statistical Office, *Share Ownership* (1995) 8.

The four main types of institution in the UK are insurance companies, pension funds, unit trusts, and investment trusts. Major *insurance companies* operating in the UK fall into three groups: companies limited by shares and listed on the London Stock Exchange; subsidiaries of other companies (including overseas-based insurance groups; UK banks; and a listed conglomerate); and mutually owned companies (i.e. companies whose members are the policyholders). Most of the equity investments of insurance companies are in their life funds, as opposed to their general (i.e.

household, vehicle, health, etc.) funds.[2] Whilst life policies originally provided cover only upon the death of the insured, 'endowment' policies—which mature at an age below the actuarial expectation of the life of the policyholder—have for many years made up the bulk of UK life policies. Endowment policies are a long-term savings medium as well as insurance in case of early death. Importantly, the two main types of endowment policy ('with profits' and 'unit-linked') tie the amount ultimately payable under the policy to the performance of the insurer's investments, either overall or in a particular fund. The long-term liabilities of life insurers mean that equities—which offer the prospect of both income and capital gain over the long term—are ideally suited as an investment for life funds.

In regard to *pension funds*, only those which are funded in advance are of present relevance.[3] State pension schemes are usually unfunded. They operate on a pay-as-you-go principle, with pensions being paid out of general revenue, and therefore have no equity or other investments. Nearly all funded occupational pension schemes are constituted as trusts, separate from their sponsoring entities.[4] They are either defined-benefit (or 'final-salary') schemes—where the investment risk is upon the sponsor (employer), because it undertakes to pay a pension equal to a fixed percentage of pre-retirement salary; or defined-contribution (or 'money-purchase') schemes—where the investment risk is upon the members, because contributions are fixed and benefits depend upon investment returns. Defined-benefit schemes are the more common in the UK. In both cases, but more so in the case of defined-benefit schemes, long-term assets such as equities are suitable investments for schemes which have a reasonable ratio of contributors and deferred pensioners to pensioners, and which thus have some long-term liabilities.

There are three ways in which the assets of funded schemes may be invested. First, small pension schemes often just take out insurance policies. These are called 'insured schemes'. They normally involve either a with-profits endowment policy or a deposit-administration contract

---

[2] The following draws on E. V. Morgan and A. D. Morgan, *Investment Managers and Takeovers: Information and Attitudes* (1990) 3–5; and E. P. Davis, *International Diversification of Institutional Investors* (1991) 2–4.

[3] On the history of pension provision in Britain, see L. Hannah, *Inventing Retirement* (1986).

[4] They may have individual trustees, but most large schemes have a corporate trustee (which is usually a wholly owned subsidiary of the sponsoring employer, the directors of which are usually senior executives of the sponsor and possibly also member representatives). A custodian trustee is another possibility: see N. Inglis-Jones, *The Law of Occupational Pension Schemes* (1989) 429–32. Local-authority schemes are not formally constituted as trusts. They are constituted under the Superannuation Act 1972, and regulated under the Local Government Superannuation Regulations 1986 (SI 1986/24). The local authority ('administering authority') is nevertheless in a position analogous to that of a trustee: see J. J. Quarrell, *The Law of Pension Fund Investment* (1990) ch. 4.

(which operates similarly to a bank account).[5] The policy(ies) of an insured pension scheme is treated like most other insurance policies: the premiums are pooled together with those of other policies into a large fund which is invested in the name of the insurance company. The insurance company is the beneficial owner of the underlying assets (equities, gilts, etc.); the scheme trustees own the insurance policy(ies).

The second way in which the assets of a pension scheme may be invested is in one or more 'pooled funds'. A pooled pension fund is one in which the assets of a number of different pension schemes are aggregated and invested, as one fund, by an external fund manager. Most pooled funds are either unit-linked insurance funds (known as life company 'managed funds') or authorized unit trusts.[6] Unit trusts are discussed separately, below. Regarding managed funds, a unit-linked insurance fund is not a separate legal entity: the life company merely keeps 'separate accounts recording the assets representing the fund, the current value of such assets and transfers of cash into and out of the fund'.[7] The fund forms part of the insurer's life fund, and is notionally divided into units. Trustees of pension schemes effectively buy 'units' in the fund, which are then liquidated as necessary to meet the schemes' obligations as they fall due.[8] In reality, however, the assets which comprise a managed fund are owned beneficially by the insurance company. The investing pension-scheme trustees own just their insurance policies.[9]

Thirdly, most large schemes are directly invested. Here, the scheme trustees invest directly in assets such as equities, bonds, real property, etc.[10] This task may be performed by the trustees themselves, or by in-house fund managers paid by the sponsor or the trustees, or it may be contracted out to external fund managers. The important point is that, in contrast to the position with insured schemes and managed funds, the

---

[5] Pension Law Review Committee ('Goode Committee'), *Report* (1993) paras. 2.4.23–2.4.26.

[6] The larger fund-management firms offering pooled funds tend to have a range of funds: at least one fund with a discretionary management brief, and several with differing specialist briefs (e.g. UK equities, overseas equities, UK fixed interest, property, etc.).

[7] Linklaters & Paines, *Unit Trusts: The Law and Practice* (1989) para. A2.0310.

[8] Goode Committee (n. 5 above), at para. 2.4.27.

[9] See Linklaters & Paines (n. 7 above), at paras. A2.0310, A2.0380–A2.0420. Note that in the case of pooled funds operated by fund managers other than insurers, the investing pension-scheme trustees may actually become unit-holders in a unit-trust scheme. If so, they collectively enjoy beneficial ownership of the assets of the unit trust: see n. 14 below.

[10] Note that a small proportion of the assets of some directly invested pension schemes is invested in pooled funds: it is the practice of some fund managers to invest a portion of each directly invested fund under discretionary management into one or more pooled funds, which invest in the shares of small companies, rather than to make separate direct investments in those small companies on behalf of each client.

equity and other investments are owned by the scheme trustees, rather than an intermediary (insurance company).

Unit trusts are open-ended investment funds which operate under a trust structure. They may be authorized or unauthorized (only the former may be marketed to the public),[11] but most are authorized. Authorized unit-trust schemes must have a trustee independent of a manager.[12] The trustee is responsible for the custody or control of the scheme's assets,[13] and either it or another custodian will be the legal owner of scheme investments. The collective body of unit-holders, however, enjoys beneficial ownership of those assets.[14] Many UK unit trusts invest heavily or exclusively in listed UK equities.

Investment trusts are closed-end investment funds, and despite their name are not trusts at all: they are public companies. They are, therefore, legal entities separate from the parties (i.e. their shareholders) which invest in them.[15] The beneficial ownership (and often also the registered ownership, unless an external custodian is used) of an investment trust's assets rests with the investment-trust company itself. Many investment trusts, like many unit trusts, invest mostly or wholly in listed UK equities.

The two primary causes of the increase in the proportion of listed UK equities held by institutions over the period from World War II until the early 1990s were (a) the growth in long-term saving since World War II, and the resultant massive increase in funds available to the institutions for investment;[16] and (b) the disposition of insurance companies and pension funds towards equities, especially since the 1950s and 1960s. There are several factors behind each of (a) and (b). In relation to (a), demographic trends, inadequate state pensions, and income growth have all contributed.[17] In relation to (b), the concern of institutions to protect their capital bases during periods of inflation, and the relative performance of equities as opposed to gilts and cash since the end of World War I, appear to be the central factors.[18]

---

[11] Financial Services Act 1986, s. 76.
[12] Financial Services Act 1986, s. 78(2).
[13] Financial Services (Regulated Schemes) Regulations 1991, reg. 7.10.2.
[14] *Charles* v. *Federal Commissioner of Taxation* (1954) 90 CLR 598, at 609.
[15] *Salomon* v. *A. Salomon & Co. Ltd.* [1897] AC 22.
[16] See generally P. L. Davies, 'Institutional Investors in the United Kingdom' in D. D. Prentice and P. R. J. Holland (eds.), *Contemporary Issues in Corporate Governance* (1993) 69, at 70–3.   [17] See Davis (n. 2 above), at 5–7.
[18] Over any rolling 20-year period between 1918 and 1990, UK equities produced better returns than gilts and Treasury Bills: WM Company, *UK Pension Fund Service Annual Review* (1990) 4–6. A lesser factor behind (b) was the statutory recognition given to equities as acceptable trust investments by the Trustee Investments Act 1961; equity investments were previously possible only if there was an express power in the trust deed. The person credited with founding 'the cult of the equity' is George Ross Goobey, the internal investment manager of the Imperial Tobacco pension fund from 1947–74: see J. Plender, *That's the Way the Money Goes* (1982) 39–45.

Although the level of long-term saving, and hence institutional cash flow, is expected to remain high in the future,[19] it is questionable as to whether pension funds' penchant for listed UK equities will remain at an internationally high level. There are prudential and other reasons for at least a slight shift away from the extremely high allocation of pension-fund assets (approximately 58%) to local equities which existed at 1993. The two main arguments in favour of a fall in equity weightings are:[20] (a) equities are likely to outperform bonds by less than in the past;[21] and (b) from the perspective of UK pension funds, equities are probably a riskier investment than in the past, because (i) the proportion of retirees to members has risen over time;[22] (ii) net cash flow has fallen over time, thereby leading to a shortening of effective time horizons (and equities become a less risky investment as the time horizon is lengthened); (iii) index-linked gilts, a relatively new instrument, are a potential substitute for equities as a hedge against inflation; and (iv) a minimum solvency standard for defined-benefit schemes will come into effect in the second half of the 1990s.[23]. The fall in the proportion of the UK equity market held by pensions funds, from 32.4% in 1992 to 27.8% in 1994 (see Table 2.1), may indeed reflect an allocational shift away from equities by UK pensions funds.

[19] Note however that the net cash flow of UK pension schemes fell steadily from 15% of assets in 1981 to 2% in 1992: WM Company, ibid., at 13; 'Bonds May Deliver KO', *Fin. Times*, 9 Jan. 1993, sec. II, p. I. The fall in the latter years is explicable largely by the taking of 'contributions holidays' by sponsors of defined-benefit schemes during 1988–92, and by the high level of redundancies in the recession of 1991–2.

[20] S. Wadhwani and M. Shah, *The Equity-Bond Debate in the UK* (1993).

[21] After Sterling entered the European Exchange Rate Mechanism ('ERM') in 1990, and a consensus developed that Britain was entering a decade of low inflation and low growth, many suggested that the relative attractions of equities would decline *vis-à-vis* gilts. Sterling exited the ERM in 1992, however, and equities returned to favour: 'Theory of Bond Investment Culture Comes Unstuck', *Fin. Times*, 19 Sept. 1992, p. 4. However, the March 1993 Budget included a reduction in advance corporation tax ('ACT': the tax on profit distributed as dividends) from 25% to 20%. Equities became less attractive for pension funds with a high level of mature liabilities, because the change to ACT was accompanied by a decrease from 25% to 20% in the tax credit granted to pension funds and other tax-exempt investors. The effect was a decrease of 6.25% in net income from dividends. For a fund with the then typical 58% allocation to UK equities, this meant a fall in cash flow of 3.6%.

[22] Some asset-management consultants were during 1992–5 advising their pension fund trustee clients—especially those with fairly mature schemes—to re-weight their asset allocation towards fixed-interest investments, on prudential grounds: see e.g. 'Too Many Eggs in One Basket', *Fin. Times*, 11 Nov. 1992, p. 20.

[23] See Pensions Act 1995, ss. 56–61. This may lead to switching out of equities and into gilts: see 'The MSS Effect', *Pensions Mgt.*, Sept. 1994, p. 35.

B. AUSTRALIA

There is in Australia no equivalent of the annual survey of beneficial shareholdings conducted by the UK's Central Statistical Office, and thus no direct evidence of an increase over recent decades in institutional share ownership. There is, however, indirect evidence that there was a sizeable increase over 1955–86 in the proportion of Australian equities held beneficially by institutions.[24]

The survey underlying Table 2.2 gives a snapshot at 1991. Table 2.2 shows that the Australian institutions' combined beneficial holding of local equities in 1991 was 36%. This is considerably less than the UK institutions' holding of over 60% of the UK equity market at the same time. Where do the differences lie? First, local industrial and commercial companies held 7% of listed Australian equities, as opposed to only 2–3% in the UK. This is explicable mainly by a greater degree of cross-holdings amongst listed Australian companies than amongst their UK counterparts. Secondly, individuals held a larger proportion of local equities in Australia than they did in Britain, although their proportional holding had declined in Australia as it had over previous decades in the UK. Thirdly, the most significant difference is in the level of foreign holdings—the proportion of the Australian equity market held by foreigners was the highest level of any OECD country at 1993. This was due mostly to the high number of listed Australian companies that either were partly owned subsidiaries of foreign companies, or had a foreign shareholder with a large stake. Two of Australia's five largest listed companies (measured by market capitalization) at the end of August 1993 fell into this category: one was 60%-owned by a listed UK company; the other was 49%-owned by another listed UK company. Foreign institutions would also appear to have had a relatively large share of the Australian equity market at 1993.

Of the *insurance companies* operating in Australia, far fewer are listed companies than in the UK. Australian life offices tend to be mutuals or subsidiaries of overseas-based insurance groups. The remarks made about

---

[24] The two pieces of indirect evidence are: (a) statistics of annual net changes in holdings of ordinary and preference shares by sector, which show that institutions were net purchasers from 1955 until at least 1986, whilst individuals were net sellers for much of that time: see P. Marshman and P. Davies, 'The Role of the Stock Exchange and the Financial Characteristics of Australian Companies' in R. Bruce, B. McKern, I. Pollard, and M. Skully (eds.), *Handbook of Australian Corporate Finance* (4th edn., 1991) 78, at 93; and (b) studies of the top 20 *registered* shareholders of listed Australian companies, which show an increase in the percentage of the issued capital held in the name of institutions and nominee companies (which are used extensively to register the holdings of superannuation funds and unit trusts), and a decrease in the percentage held by individuals: see e.g. G. J. Crough, *Financial Institutions and the Ownership of Australian Corporations* (1981) 3–4.

Table 2.2 Ownership of Australian equities, 1991

Sector of beneficial owner	*Beneficial ownership of listed Australian equities, 1991 (%)*
Individuals	28
Life offices*	10
Superannuation funds*	22
Unit trusts and investment companies	2
Other financial institutions	2
Other companies	7
Overseas	29
	100

* Equities held by life insurers for insured pension schemes and managed funds are attributed to superannuation funds. If those equities were treated as assets of the life offices, the proportion of equities held by life offices and superannuation funds would be approximately 16% apiece: see ABS, *Managed Funds: Australia, September Quarter* (1993) Tables 3, 4 (assets of superannuation funds wholly administered by life offices are included in the category 'statutory funds of life insurance offices' (Australian equities: A$27,054m. at 30 June 1993) rather than 'superannuation funds and approved deposit funds' (Australian equities: A$27,151m. at 30 June 1993)).

Source: Industry Commission, *Availability of Capital* (1991) 140.

the life funds of UK insurance companies are also applicable generally to Australian insurers.

Australian pension funds are more commonly called *superannuation funds*.[25] Funded superannuation schemes are very similar to their UK counterparts: they are mostly trusts; they operate on either a defined-benefit or defined-contribution basis; and their assets are either directly invested, insured, or invested in pooled funds.[26] A 'superannuation guarantee charge' ('SGC') came into operation in Australia in 1992. The effect of the SGC legislation was to force employers to make superannuation contributions on behalf of employees, initially at a rate of at least 3% of 'base earnings', but rising to 9% by 2002.[27] Existing employer-sponsored schemes were adequate for meeting the SGC requirements.

[25] On the history of superannuation provision in Australia, see D. Paatsch and G. Smith, 'The Regulation of Australian Superannuation: An Industrial Relations Law Perspective' (1992) 5 *Corp. & Bus. LJ* 131.

[26] See generally CCH, *Australian Superannuation Law and Practice* (1991) paras. 33-550–33-575.

[27] See Paatsch and Smith (n. 25 above), at 148.

Nevertheless, the SGC legislation (and, before it, the onset of widespread 'award' superannuation[28]) brought about a dramatic increase in the number of industry-wide (or 'multi-employer') superannuation schemes—many of which were set up by trade unions.

Unit trusts in Australia are open-ended investment funds as in the UK. They are required to have a management company and an independent trustee or 'representative' approved by the Australian Securities Commission ('ASC').[29] Either the trustee/representative or the unit-holders themselves must hold the legal title to scheme assets,[30] and in either case the unit-holders collectively enjoy beneficial ownership. Compared to UK unit trusts, a much smaller proportion of Australian unit trusts specializes in equity investments; property and mortgage trusts accounted for about 70% of the Australian unit-trust sector in 1991.[31]

Trustee companies regulated under State legislation manage 'common funds'. A common fund consists of a pool of depositors' moneys invested as one fund. Legal title to investments rests with the trustee company, but depositors retain the beneficial ownership. Some funds specialize in their investments, for instance in Australian equities.

An *investment company* is a company declared as such by the ASC on the basis that it engages primarily 'in the business of investment in marketable securities for the purpose of revenue and for profit and not for the purpose of exercising control'.[32] Most are listed on the ASX, and they are the equivalent of the UK's investment-trust companies. Investors (shareholders) have no interest, legal or beneficial, in the assets of the company.[33] Several large companies invest almost exclusively in Australian equities.[34]

---

[28] Prior to the SGC, there had been a form of compulsory superannuation in operation since 1987 for employees covered by 'awards' under the Australian industrial-relations system. The amount was initially only 1.5% and then 3% of ordinary-time weekly earnings: Paatsch and Smith, ibid., at 140–5.

[29] CL, ss. 1065, 1066. The independence of the trustee/representative is not a statutory requirement, but the guidelines for approval of trustees effectively require it: see National Companies and Securities Commission, *Release 126*. It is likely that the trustee:manager structure will be replaced with one whereby just the management company is responsible for running a unit-trust scheme: see Australian Law Reform Commission, and Companies and Securities Advisory Committee, *Collective Investments: Other People's Money* (1993).

[30] Again, there is no statutory requirement. However, in practice the ASC will not approve a unit-trust deed unless this is the case: see ASC, *Policy Statement 23*.

[31] Industry Commission, *Availability of Capital* (1991) 53.

[32] CL, s. 399(3).

[33] *Salomon* v. *A. Salomon & Co. Ltd.* (n. 15 above).

[34] *Friendly societies* are another Australian institutional investor. They provide health and disability insurance, funeral benefits, and collective-investment schemes. Their equity investments are almost negligible, and they are not therefore of much relevance for present purposes.

Table 2.3 Allocation of assets under management of AIMA members

Asset category	Proportion of total assets under management as at 30 June 1993 (%)
Australian equities	27.6
Overseas equities	10.7
Australian fixed interest	30.3
Overseas fixed interest	4.6
Property	11.1
Cash	12.9
Other	2.8
	100.0

Source: Australian Investment Managers' Group, *December 1993 Half-Year Member Survey* (1994).

The main reasons for the growth in institutional share ownership in Australia, as in the UK, would appear to be (a) a growth in long-term saving, with an accompanying increase in institutional funds available for investment; and (b) an asset-allocation shift towards equities and away from fixed-interest securities (although to a lesser degree than in Britain).

In relation to (a), the assets of Australian life offices and superannuation funds rose from 17.3% to 20.1% of financial-sector assets between 1981 and 1990.[35] Also, between 1984 and 1988 there was rapid growth in real terms in the level of Australian household savings accounted for by superannuation and life-insurance contributions.[36] The introduction of the SGC will almost certainly accelerate this trend. Regarding (b), Australian insurers and superannuation funds re-weighted their portfolios away from government bonds, and towards equities and real property, during 1950–80.[37] Table 2.3 shows the allocation of the assets under management of 45 of the largest Australia-based fund managers, at mid-1993. Despite the allocational change just mentioned, the weighting given to local

---

[35] Industry Commission (n. 31 above), at 52.

[36] Ibid., at 52–3; Reserve Bank of Australia, *Bulletin* (Mar. 1994) Table D.4.

[37] Life offices' holdings of Australian public-sector securities fell from 52% of assets in 1953, to 35% in 1960, to 30% in 1980: Committee of Inquiry into the Australian Financial System, *Final Report* (1981) 174. Note that, until 1984, there was in Australia a '30/20 rule' which provided tax concessions to life offices and superannuation funds which held at least 30% of their assets in Australian public-sector securities.

equities (27.6%) was markedly less than in the UK: the average UK-based fund manager allocated around 50–60% of funds under management to UK equities at mid-1993. The weighting given to fixed-interest securities was much higher in Australia than in Britain in 1993. Whilst UK institutions are likely to re-weight their investment portfolios (at least slightly) away from domestic equities during the mid-to-late 1990s,[38] there would appear to be scope for Australian institutions to increase the weighting given to domestic equities in the future.

[38] See 'Pension Funds in UK "Set to Cut Equities Holdings" ', *Fin. Times*, 20 Sept. 1994, p. 31; and nn. 20–3 above, and accompanying text.

PART II

Institutional Involvement in Corporate Governance in the UK: History and Current Level

3

The Participants in the UK

A. INTRODUCTION

This and the following two chapters look at the history and current level of institutional monitoring of the management of UK quoted companies. The most obvious and important matters to be addressed are the various issues with which the institutions have been concerned, and the manner in which the institutions have gone about their monitoring. Those two matters are dealt with in Chapters 4 and 5, respectively. However, before attention is shifted to those substantive topics, this chapter addresses two subsidiary issues. First, who are the significant institutional players in the UK corporate-governance arena? Are they the pension schemes, insurance companies, unit trusts, and investment trusts (i.e. the bodies which own beneficially about 60% of UK equities)? Alternatively, are they the fund managers (i.e. the outside firms and in-house subsidiaries which provide investment-management services to the pension schemes, insurers, unit trusts, and investment trusts)? Secondly, institutional monitoring some-times occurs through collective-action vehicles—mostly the institutions' trade associations. The second main aim of this chapter is therefore to provide a brief description of the institutions' collective-action bodies.

B. TRADITIONAL INSTITUTIONS OR FUND MANAGERS?

1. THE DISTINCTION OUTLINED

We have seen already that, of the various institutional and non-institutional groups, the occupational pension funds collectively hold the largest proportion of the issued ordinary shares of listed UK companies.[1] It would be natural to assume, therefore, that an inquiry into the role of institutional shareholders in UK corporate governance would focus heavily upon the pension funds themselves. However, whilst the pension funds *have* played a major role in *indirect* monitoring,[2] their role in *direct*

---

[1] See Ch. 2, Sec. A.
[2] Their involvement in indirect monitoring has taken place principally through the Investment Committee of their trade association (the National Association of Pension Funds Ltd.) and through the umbrella body, the Institutional Shareholders' Committee: see Sec. C below.

monitoring has been relatively minor.[3] The same cannot be said of the insurance companies. In the documented institutional interventions at firm level, the names of major UK insurers such as the Prudential and Norwich Union have been to the fore.

The factor responsible primarily for the relatively insignificant role of pension funds in direct institutional monitoring also largely explains the relative prominence of the insurers in that area: in general it is *fund managers* that meet (regularly) with, talk (regularly) to, and engage (occasionally) with the management of companies. A large proportion of the life and general funds of UK insurance companies is managed by investment-management subsidiaries of the various insurers. If it is reported in the press that the Prudential, Norwich Union, and Scottish Amicable have applied pressure for management changes at company X, it is actually Prudential Portfolio Managers Ltd., Norwich Union Investment Management Ltd., and Scottish Amicable Investment Managers Ltd.—the respective fund-management subsidiaries—that would have been involved. In contrast, the reason why pension funds have not often been involved in direct monitoring lies in the fact that most of them have for many years employed external fund-management firms to undertake the investment of their funds. As at 1993, 78% of directly invested UK occupational pension funds[4] used solely external fund managers, whilst only 14% managed their investments wholly 'in-house', and 8% utilized both external and in-house managers.[5] It is these outside fund-management houses, rather than the pension-scheme trustees whose assets they manage, that interact with the management of portfolio companies.[6] And, further, in the case of

---

[3] In this book, monitoring is classified as 'direct' if institutional shareholders (including fund managers) are the bodies involved; and 'indirect' if the participants are bodies other than institutions (the usual indirect monitors are the institutions' trade associations, and non-executive directors).

[4] See Ch. 2, Sec. A, for an explanation of the difference between 'directly invested', 'managed or pooled', and 'insured' pension schemes.

[5] Author's calculations based on information in NAPF, *Annual Survey of Occupational Pension Schemes* (1993) 67. The survey included some unfunded schemes, some insured schemes, and some schemes invested in managed or pooled funds. The author recalculated the NAPF's statistics for management methods by excluding the unfunded, insured, and managed/pooled schemes, so as to give the figures in the text for directly invested schemes.

[6] There are, however, exceptions. As at 1992, British Rail's pension schemes had a corporate trustee: The British Rail Pension Trustee Company Ltd. ('BRPTC'). Although BRPTC delegated the day-to-day management of the schemes' equity portfolios to seven external fund-management firms, it fulfilled a role greater than that carried out by most trustees of externally managed funds. Importantly, all UK equities were registered in the name of nominee companies owned by BRPTC, rather than in the names of nominee companies owned by or selected by the external fund managers (as is usually the case with externally managed funds). This facilitated the exercise by BRPTC of voting rights attached to the equities. BRPTC also met regularly with the management of portfolio companies in which a 3% or larger stake was held; and it had established informal links with other

insured pension schemes and pension schemes invested in managed or pooled funds, the trustees are *never* involved personally in direct monitoring. Once again it is fund managers (of the insurance companies which invest the premiums of insured schemes, and of the insurers and other firms which run the managed/pooled funds) who interact with the management of companies in which shares are held.[7]

It should thus be apparent that a proper analysis of institutional monitoring in the UK requires a reasonably detailed understanding of the major UK-based fund managers. Several features of these firms are discussed in later chapters, where their relevance is more apparent.[8] What is appropriate at this stage is a little detail about the relationship between fund managers and each of the 'traditional institutions': occupational pension funds, insurance companies, unit trusts, and investment trusts. One prefatory matter should, however, first be mentioned.

Fund-management houses (whether or not forming part of a traditional institution such as an insurance company) are often themselves referred to as 'institutions', 'institutional shareholders', and 'institutional investors'. This is understandable given that fund managers manage not their own personal property[9] but that of (usually) a collection of entities such as pension funds, unit trusts, and charities[10] (the funds of many of which are, likewise, an aggregation of the assets of others[11]). In many parts of this book the terms 'institutions', 'institutional shareholders', and 'institutional investors' embrace both fund-management firms and the traditional

---

institutional investors as a means of exchanging information on matters of common concern. See *BR Pension Scheme Annual Report & Financial Statements 1992*; BRPTC, *Corporate Governance: Policy Statement* (1992).

[7] See nn. 36–9 below, and accompanying text.

[8] For instance, Ch. 10 deals with the likelihood of an increased level of institutional monitoring in the absence of major legal reforms. It is shown that, partly due to their being arms of financial conglomerates, some of the largest UK-based investment managers face numerous structural disincentives to a high level of monitoring. Two of the most significant of these disincentives would not affect their clients (such as pension-fund trustees) if those clients managed their funds in-house: see Ch. 10, Secs. B.1.iii, B.1.vi.

[9] Although they often manage some in-house funds (e.g. the fund-management arms of large insurers manage their groups' insurance funds and 'in-house' unit trusts, and (in some cases) the funds of group pension schemes; similarly, fund managers associated with merchant-banking groups commonly manage the funds of group pension schemes and 'in-house' unit trusts).

[10] This is thus a UK illustration of part of the 'fourth stage of capitalism' elucidated in R. C. Clark, 'The Four Stages of Capitalism: Reflections on Investment Management Treatises' (1981) 94 *Harv. L Rev.* 561, at 565–7 ('[P]rofessional savings planners—for example, the sponsors and administrators of large corporate pension plans—rarely perform the active investment function. Most pension plan sponsors and administrators contract with outside trust departments, insurance companies, and investment advisory firms for investment management services.').

[11] This is Clark's 'third stage of capitalism': the 'separation of the decision about how to invest from the decision to supply capital for investment': ibid., at 564.

institutions. It is, though, occasionally necessary to draw a distinction between fund managers (including those which are subsidiaries of traditional institutions, and which also manage external funds) and the traditional institutions. Where such a distinction is necessary, it is made clear in the text.

2. INVESTMENT OF UK INSTITUTIONS' FUNDS

i. Insurance Companies

Virtually every well-known UK company authorized to write life insurance has an investment-management subsidiary which manages the investment of the vast majority, if not all, of the group's life and general insurance funds. As expanded upon below, the insurers' investment-management arms also provide fund-management services to pension funds and unit trusts. For the moment, though, the concern is with the management of insurance funds. Although the insurers' fund-management subsidiaries manage by far the largest proportion of insurance funds, some other fund-management houses also manage insurance assets.[12] In some instances, the fund-management firm is part of a multifaceted financial group which provides, amongst other things, insurance services. In such cases, the insurance assets under management usually include, and sometimes consist entirely of, 'in-house' funds in the sense that the funds are those of the insurance-providing subsidiary of the fund-management firm's corporate group.[13] This does not, however, account for all of the insurance assets managed by outside fund-management firms. Some such assets are the funds of smaller insurance firms which do not have the resources to conduct investment management.[14] Other of those assets represent the funds of insurance companies that lack expertise in specialized areas (for

---

[12] e.g. as at 31 Dec. 1991, the fund-management firms INVESCO MIM Management Ltd. and Phillips & Drew Fund Management Ltd. ('PDFM') had £774m. and £514m., respectively, of insurance funds under management: Hymans Robertson, *Pension Fund Investment Manager Survey: Manager Analysis* (1992). In each instance the funds were 'external': information provided to the author by INVESCO MIM and PDFM.

[13] e.g. as at 31 Dec. 1991, Barclays de Zoete Wedd Investment Management Ltd. ('BZWIM') had £1,477m., and Midland Montagu Asset Management Ltd. ('MMAM') had £345m., of insurance funds under management: Hymans Robertson, ibid. In the former case some, and in the latter case all, of those funds were assets of insurance-providing subsidiaries of BZWIM's and MMAM's ultimate parents (High Street banks): information provided to the author by BZWIM and James Capel Fund Managers.

[14] e.g. in Jan. 1993 it was reported that Crown Financial Services Ltd., the UK life insurance, pensions, and unit-trust subsidiary of Crown Life of Canada, was ceasing to manage its funds in-house. Its funds under management, some £700m., did not amount to the 'critical mass' necessary for high-quality fund management. Crown's funds, including its life-insurance funds, were in future to be managed by an external firm: 'Lazard To Manage Crown Funds', *Fin. Times*, 19 Jan. 1993, p. 21.

example Pacific Basin, ex-Japan equities), and which employ specialist independent managers to manage a portion of their funds to cover the deficiency in the particular area(s).[15]

ii. Occupational Pension Funds

The Pensions Act 1995 gives to the trustees of UK occupational pension schemes wide powers to delegate the investment-management task.[16] In practice, the responsibility for day-to-day investment management is almost invariably delegated to either one or more external managers, an in-house manager, or a mixture of the two. Any external fund managers employed by a pension fund to manage assets in the UK are required to be authorized (or exempted) persons under the Financial Services Act 1986.[17] Any in-house pension-fund managers who do not fall within the Act's definition of carrying on investment business are nevertheless deemed to be doing so,[18] and are thus required to be authorized or exempted.[19]

It was stated earlier that, as at 1993, 78% of directly invested UK pension funds employed external fund managers to undertake the investment of their funds, and that a further 8% used both external and internal managers. It is not the case, however, that external firms managed over 78% of the total assets of directly invested UK pension funds at that time. The reason for this lies principally in the fact that the assets of most of the largest schemes were managed in-house. For example, British Coal Corporation, the electricity-supply companies (jointly), British Gas plc, Imperial Chemical Industries plc, The 'Shell' Transport & Trading Company plc, The British Petroleum Company plc, British Steel plc, British Airways plc, British Aerospace plc, Courtaulds plc, and Blue Circle Industries plc each had a subsidiary company dedicated to the management of most[20] or all of the assets of the respective groups' pension schemes at the end of 1991. And, as shown later in Table 3.1, the internal manager of 85% of the assets of the pension funds of British Telecommunications plc

---

[15] Information supplied to the author by J. Marsh, Director, PDFM.

[16] See Pensions Act 1995, s. 34. The trustees of most UK pension schemes had enjoyed wide powers of delegation prior to the enactment of the Pensions Act, by virtue of widely drawn trust deeds: see Pension Law Review Committee ('Goode Committee'), *Report* (1993) ch. 4.9. There is also a (narrow) statutory power of delegation in s. 25 of the Trustee Act 1925 (substituted by the Powers of Attorney Act 1971).

[17] See Pensions Act 1995, s. 34(2) and (3); Financial Services Act 1986, ss. 1, 3; Sch. 1, para. 14.   [18] Financial Services Act 1986, s. 191(1).

[19] They are most commonly authorized by becoming OPS members of the Investment Managers Regulatory Organisation ('IMRO'): see Goode Committee (n. 16 above), at para. 4.9.21.

[20] Some pension schemes employ both an in-house manager and one or more external managers; even those trustees that employ an in-house manager to manage the entire fund sometimes retain one or more external fund managers on an advisory basis.

and the Post Office (PosTel Investment Management Ltd.) was one of the largest fund managers in the UK in the early 1990s. At 31 March 1992, it had £20,400 million of funds under management. The next largest in-house manager was CIN Management Ltd., which managed the funds of the British Coal pension schemes. It had about £12,500 million under management at the end of 1991.[21] At the same stage, the fund-management arms of the other companies mentioned had total assets under management ranging in value from approximately £500 million to over £9,000 million (with six out of the ten each handling in excess of £4,000 million).[22] It should be noted that most of these in-house fund managers did not provide fund-management services to external bodies.[23]

A number of the pension schemes of large non-financial companies have, however, changed from in-house to external investment management. The first may have been the Ford UK pension fund, which in the mid-1960s wound up its fund-management operation and allocated the management duties amongst four external fund managers.[24] The pension schemes of British Rail and Unilever plc replaced internal with external managers during the 1980s; Imperial Chemical Industries plc and Coats Viyella plc did so in 1995.[25] Whilst some large public-sector schemes actually changed from external to internal investment management during the 1970s,[26] the long-term trend would appear to be the other way around.[27]

The in-house managers discussed in the previous two paragraphs are, of

---

[21] Author's calculations from figures in the 1991–2 annual reports of the Mineworkers' Pension Scheme and the British Coal Staff Superannuation Scheme. Note that CIN Management Ltd. was to be sold in 1995 as a result of the privatization of British Coal.

[22] Information provided to the author by ICI Investment Management Ltd., Shell International Petroleum Company Ltd., BP Pension Fund, British Airways Pension Investment Management Ltd., British Aerospace Pension Funds Investment Management Ltd., Courtaulds Pensions Investment Trustees Ltd., and Blue Circle Group Pension Investment Fund; and information from annual reports of the Electricity Supply Pension Scheme, British Gas Staff Pension Scheme, British Gas Corporation Pension Scheme, and British Steel Pension Scheme.

[23] There were a couple of minor exceptions. One was ESN Pension Management Group Ltd., the in-house manager of the Electricity Supply Pension Scheme. It bought some £100m. of investment-management interests from Manchester Exchange and Investment Bank Ltd. in Aug. 1993. The acquisition resulted in ESN undertaking for the first time the management of external assets.

[24] E. V. Morgan and A. D. Morgan, *Investment Managers and Takeovers: Information and Attitudes* (1990) 11.

[25] M. I. Reid, *All-Change in the City* (1988) 196; 'In House Management Hits the Buffers', *Pensions Mgt.*, Feb. 1995, p. 96.

[26] See R. Minns, *Pension Funds and British Capitalism* (1980) 32–3. Some private-sector schemes have also internalized their investment management: see 'Rowntree Shuffles Pension Fund Team', *Fin. Times*, 3 May 1994, p. 22.

[27] CBI, *Pension Fund Investment Management* (1987) 55 (proportion of large pension schemes using in-house management decreased from 23% to 19% over 1982–7).

course, subsidiaries of non-financial companies. The pension schemes of financial companies (such as insurance companies, High Street banks, and merchant banks) are commonly—indeed, much more commonly than the schemes of non-financial companies—managed in-house. But, of course, unlike their counterparts at non-financial companies, the investment-management arms of financial companies also invariably provide fund-management services to external bodies and persons.

Given this leaning of the largest pension funds towards internal management, it is not surprising that, whilst only 14% of directly invested UK pension *schemes* were managed wholly internally in early 1993, some 38% of the *assets* of directly invested pension funds were then managed in-house.[28] About 62% of assets were managed externally, compared to the figure of 78% for the proportion of schemes managed externally.[29]

At the end of 1991, the dominant *external* managers of the assets of directly invested pension funds were the investment-management arms of financial conglomerates.[30] Independent fund-management houses also managed a sizeable volume of such assets at that time.[31] The fund-

---

[28] Author's calculations from information in NAPF (n. 5 above). Note that the NAPF survey gives figures for proportions of schemes and proportions of scheme members. The author's calculations use the NAPF figures for proportions of scheme *members* as the figures for proportions of scheme *assets* (i.e. the assumption made is that the amount of assets per member is constant for all directly invested schemes). It is also assumed that schemes using both internal and external managers had 50% of their assets under each form of management. See also the remarks in n. 5 above, about the recalculation of the NAPF figures to exclude unfunded schemes, insured schemes, and schemes invested in managed or pooled funds.

[29] Ibid.

[30] e.g. the top five managers of external segregated UK pension funds, at 31 Dec. 1991:

Manager	Total external segregated UK pension funds under management		As proportion of total funds under (%)	Market share (ext. seg. pension fund assets) (%)
	(£million)	(No. of portfolios)		
MAM	27,925	410	70	19
PDFM	16,612	246	89	11
Schroder	13,608	155	75	9
BZWIM	7,928	119	42	5
Fleming	7,306	117	39	5

Sources: Author's compilation and analysis of information in Hymans Robertson (n. 12 above); 'Funds "Back Equities Over Gilts" ', *Fin. Times*, 29 July 1992, p. 6. (Abbreviations: see App. E.) The top three firms in this table, plus Gartmore Investment Management plc, received a very substantial proportion of the pension-fund portfolios, the investment managers of which were changed during 1991–3, such that a 'two-tier' market was hailed: ' "Two-Tier" Fund Market Identified', *Fin. Times*, 12 Mar. 1993, p. 8.

[31] The largest amongst the independent houses at end-1991 were (showing external segregated UK pension-fund assets/number of external segregated UK pension-fund portfolios): Henderson Administration Group plc: £4,158m./100 portfolios; Baillie Gifford & Co.: £2,250m./59 portfolios; M&G Group plc: £2,064m./36 portfolios: Hymans Robertson, ibid.

management arms of some insurance companies were also prominent. Of these, Prudential Portfolio Managers Ltd. managed by far the largest amount of such assets at the end of 1991: some £7,267 million, representing 20% of the total assets managed by it from the UK.[32] Other entities such as firms of stockbrokers and solicitors managed, at that time, comparatively small amounts of external pension-fund moneys on a segregated basis.

Externally managed pension funds do not necessarily employ just one investment-management firm. A 1991 survey of pension funds found that, amongst the 78% of respondents which used external balanced management,[33] the average number of managers was two.[34] For funds with less than £200 million in total assets, it was quite common for there to be only one balanced manager. However, for funds with over £500 million in total assets, the average rose to three managers.

Not all funded pension schemes are directly invested schemes.[35] However, in so far as one is concerned with pension funds as shareholders, and more importantly with the potential for pension funds as shareholders to exercise control over the managers of UK quoted companies, it is directly invested pension funds upon which the focus of attention must be fixed. To explain, it is helpful to look at the two other ways in which the assets of pension funds may be invested. First, there are insured schemes. The trustees of an insured scheme own not the underlying assets purchased by the insurance company, but one or more insurance policies. The insurance company is both the registered and the beneficial owner of equities purchased with the premiums of an insured scheme.[36] An important consequence is that, unlike the case of a directly invested pension fund,[37] there is no possibility of the trustees of an insured scheme

---

[32] Hymans Robertson, ibid. External segregated pension-fund moneys represented a smaller proportion of the total assets managed from the UK by other large insurers at end-1991: e.g. Scottish Widows Investment Management Ltd.: 10%; Legal & General Investment Management Ltd.: 7%; The Standard Life Assurance Company: 3%; Norwich Union Fund Managers Ltd.: 0.4%: author's calculations from information in Hymans Robertson, ibid.

[33] The difference between external balanced (or 'discretionary') management and external specialist management is that, in the former case, the manager has discretion as to (a) in most cases, asset allocation (i.e. the proportion of the portfolio to be devoted to equities, bonds, property, cash, etc.); *and* (b) stock selection. In the latter case, however, the asset-allocation decision is taken separately (sometimes by the pension fund's trustees; sometimes by specialist asset-allocation advisers) and then specialist managers are hired for particular areas of investment. Balanced management is more prevalent than specialized management.

[34] PDFM, *Survey of Investment Management Arrangements* (1991) 2.

[35] See Ch. 2, Sec. A, for a description of the three different ways in which the assets of funded occupational pension schemes may be invested: as insured schemes; in pooled funds; or directly invested.

[36] Contrast a directly invested pension fund using an external investment manager. There, a nominee company of the custodian (which may be related to the fund manager or may be independent) is normally the *registered* owner of equity investments made for the fund, but it holds these on trust for its client: the trustees of the pension fund: see Ch. 5, Sec. B.1.iii.

exercising the voting rights attached to those shares (because this power rests with the insurance company). The other way in which the assets of a pension scheme may be invested is in one or more pooled funds. Most pooled funds are either unit-linked insurance funds[38] or authorized unit trusts. It is not surprising, therefore, that the insurance companies' investment-management arms are prominent amongst the managers offering pooled pension funds. The company managing a pooled pension fund has the power to exercise the voting rights attached to the equity investments of the fund. The trustees of the investing pension schemes have no right to influence that voting power.[39]

iii. Unit Trusts

The funds of the 1,500 or so UK unit trusts were, at mid-1992, managed by about 160 fund-management firms. The great majority of these management companies handled more than one trust, and many managed between 15 and 40. Although individuals collectively hold a large proportion of unit-trust units, the units of some trusts are owned largely or completely by the management company or an associated company. For instance, due to the proliferation of unit-linked insurance policies, insurance companies owned unit-trust units worth about 40% of the total asset value of the unit-trust industry, as at mid-1993.[40]

Nearly all of the fund managers that form part of financial conglomerates or are subsidiaries or divisions of insurance companies have unit trusts under management. Although specialist unit-trust managers also exist, most of the 1,500 or so trusts at mid-1992 were managed by investment-management houses which also managed the assets of other bodies such as pension funds, insurance companies, charities, etc.

iv. Investment Trusts

One of the most striking things upon examining the managers of UK investment trusts is the dearth of the insurance companies' investment-management subsidiaries. Many of the insurers, as mentioned above, manage the assets of pension schemes and unit trusts as well as their own insurance funds. Despite the absence of the insurers, it is rare for the manager of an investment trust not to have several other types of funds, besides investment trusts, under management. There were over 160

---

[37] In the case of a directly invested pension fund, the voting rights attached to equity investments are exercisable by, or on the instruction of, the trustees of the pension fund (unless expressly delegated to the investment manager, external or internal): see Ch. 5, Sec. B.1.iii.

[38] Known as life company 'managed funds'.

[39] See Ch. 5, Sec. B.1.iii.

[40] 'Rule Changes for Open-Ended Funds', *Fin. Times*, 17 June 1993, p. 6.

investment trusts in 1990. Only 14 employed an in-house manager; the rest employed about 50 external fund managers.[41] A 1990 survey found that fund managers involved principally in managing investment trusts had an average of 32 portfolios under management, but the researchers noted that even the largest managers of investment trusts handled no more than about 10 trusts.[42] At the end of 1991, some of the largest managers of investment-trust assets actually had other assets under management which exceeded markedly their investment-trust funds.[43]

Investment trusts are, as mentioned in Chapter 2, listed public companies. Each investment trust is, as a corporate body in its own right, in theory quite distinct from the firm that manages its assets.[44] Nevertheless, an investment trust is commonly very closely associated with the fund-management firm that invests its assets. For instance, a substantial proportion of a trust's share capital may be held by pension funds and other bodies whose assets are managed by the fund-management firm that manages the investment trust's assets.[45]

3. FUND MANAGERS' EQUITY HOLDINGS

Fund-management firms manage not only the assets of the traditional UK institutions; they also manage the assets of private clients, overseas institutions, and charities. At 31 December 1991, overseas holdings accounted for 12.8%, and holdings of private non-profit-making bodies for 2.2%, of the total market value of listed UK equities.[46] It is reasonable to assume that a substantial proportion of those holdings formed part of the funds under management of UK-based investment managers.[47] In many instances these other clients would, like the traditional institutions discussed above, give their external fund managers a 'balanced' or

---

[41] Morgan and Morgan (n. 24 above), at 9.   [42] Ibid., at 15.

[43] e.g. Foreign & Colonial Management Ltd., which takes its name from the UK's largest investment trust (which it manages), had £4,750m. of assets under management from the UK at end-1991. At £1,699m., investment-trust funds represented only 36% of total assets under management: author's calculations from figures in Hymans Robertson (n. 12 above).

[44] Indeed, in 1993 the London Stock Exchange added a listing requirement that 'the board of directors . . . of the investment [trust] must be able to demonstrate that it will act independently of any investment managers of the investment [trust] and a majority must not be employees of or professional advisers to the investment managers or any other company in the same group as the investment managers': *Listing Rules*, paras. 21.9(d), 21.10, 21.20.

[45] See Minns (n. 26 above), at 107–9 (and figs. 4.1–4.3).

[46] See Central Statistical Office, *Economic Trends* (No. 466, 1992) 90, at 94.

[47] This assumption is supported by some of the larger fund managers' figures for charities', non-UK institutions' and private clients' funds under management at end 1991:

'discretionary' management brief.[48] And, in many cases the fund-management agreement would confer upon the investment manager the right to exercise votes attached to UK equity investments. When these additional clients are taken into account, therefore, it is clear that UK-based fund managers spoke for more than 'just' the 60% of listed UK equities which were owned beneficially by the fund managers' better-known clients (viz. the traditional institutions) at the end of 1991. Thus, the fund managers' collective, potential power at the individual-firm level is greater than that which might be inferred from the extent of the traditional institutions' holdings of listed UK equities.

Table 3.1 shows the 10 largest UK-based investment managers at 31 December 1991.[49] The funds under management of these 10 firms accounted for 31% of the UK professionally managed funds market at the end of 1991. The top 10 fund managers comprised, with one exception, the investment-management arms of financial conglomerates and of insurance companies. The exception, PosTel, was owned jointly by, and managed 85% of the assets of, the British Telecommunications plc and Post Office pension funds. It managed no external funds.

The sums of money under management, listed in Table 3.1, were not of course all invested in UK equities. British and overseas bonds (government and corporate), overseas equities, real property and cash are among the assets (other than UK equities) into which funds are invested by UK-based

[47] (continued)

| Manager | (£ million) | | |
	Charities	Non-UK Institutions	Private Clients
Cazenove & Co.	1,141	–	2,141
Hill Samuel Investment Management Ltd.	660	6,105	798
Kleinwort Benson Investment Management Ltd.	256	818	2,093
Mercury Asset Management plc	778	3,919	1,662
Morgan Grenfell Asset Management Ltd.	634	6,530	576
Robert Fleming Asset Management Ltd.	1,047	3,551	1,115
Rothschild Asset Management Ltd.	378	5,219	260
Schroder Investment Management Ltd.	671	2,008	446

Source: Author's compilation of information in Hymans Robertson (n. 12 above).

[48] See n. 33 above.

[49] The figures in Table 3.1 are for funds managed *from the UK*. If funds managed from both within and outside the UK are taken into consideration, Prudential Portfolio Managers Ltd. was the largest manager: on that basis, it had £43,133m. under management at end 1991: 'Survey: Pension Fund Investment', *Fin. Times*, 6 May 1993, sec. III, p. II.

Table 3.1 Ten largest fund-management firms in the UK, 1991

Manager	Total funds managed from the UK at 31 Dec. 1991 (£million)	As proportion of total funds under professional management from UK at 31 Dec. 1991[a] (%)
Mercury Asset Management plc (FC)	39,617	5.28
Prudential Portfolio Managers Ltd. (Ins.)	36,035	4.80
The Standard Life Assurance Company (Ins.)	24,838	3.31
Norwich Union Investment Management Ltd (Ins.)	22,151	2.95
PosTel Investment Management Ltd. (Pens.)	20,400*	2.72
Barclays de Zoete Wedd Investment Mgt. Ltd. (FC)	18,887	2.52
Phillips & Drew Fund Management Ltd. (FC)	18,673	2.49
Robert Fleming Asset Management Ltd. (FC)	18,550	2.47
Schroder Investment Management Ltd. (FC)	18,028	2.40
Legal & General Investment Management Ltd. (Ins.)	17,099	2.28

Note: abbreviations: see App. E.

* At 31 Mar. 1992.

[a] Total funds managed from the UK by investment-management firms at 31 Dec. 1991 is estimated at £750,000m.: author's calculation from estimations in Price Waterhouse, *Investment Management Survey* (1992).

Sources: Author's compilation and analysis of information in Hymans Robertson, *Pension Fund Investment Manager Survey: Manager Analysis* (1992), and in Price Waterhouse, *Investment Management Survey* (1992) 4; information supplied to the author by A. Ross Goobey, Chief Executive, PosTel Investment Management Ltd.

fund managers. The concern of this book is, however, with fund managers' holdings of UK equities.

Table 3.2[50] shows the fund managers which had the 50 largest sums of

---

[50] As with Table 3.1 (see ibid.), the figures given in Table 3.2 are for UK equities managed *from the UK*. Several of the firms in Table 3.2 (in particular, Prudential) had a larger amount

Table 3.2 Fifty largest managers of UK equities, 1991

Manager	Market value of UK equities under management at 31 Dec. 1991 (£million)	As proportion of market value of total quoted UK equities at 31 Dec. 1991[a] (%)
Mercury Asset Management plc (FC)	20,403	3.81
Prudential Portfolio Managers Ltd. (Ins.)	19,063	3.56
PosTel Investment Management Ltd. (Pens.)	11,400*	2.13
The Standard Life Assurance Company (Ins.)	11,326	2.11
Barclays de Zoete Wedd Investment Mgt. Ltd. (FC)	10,501	1.96
Phillips & Drew Fund Management Ltd. (FC)	9,561	1.78
Robert Fleming Asset Management Ltd. (FC)	9,015	1.68
Schroder Investment Management Ltd. (FC)	8,870	1.66
Scottish Widows Investment Management Ltd. (Ins.)	7,395	1.38
Legal & General Investment Management Ltd. (Ins.)	7,267	1.36
CIN Management Ltd. (Pens.)	7,102**	1.33
Norwich Union Investment Mangement Ltd. (Ins.)	7,066	1.32
Commercial Union Asset Management Ltd. (Ins.)	6,890	1.29
AMP Asset Management plc (Ins.)	6,100	1.14
M&G Investment Management Ltd. (Indep.)	5,700	1.06
County NatWest Investment Management Ltd. (FC)	5,577	1.04

of UK equities under management if those managed by their overseas associates were taken into account. The only overseas-based institutions which may have qualified for Table 3.2 were Kuwait Investment Office (which actually manages funds from London as well as Kuwait) and Abu Dhabi Investment Authority ('ADIA'). These two institutions are very secretive, and it was not possible to obtain the relevant information from them. In any event, ADIA employs external (London-based) fund managers to manage some of its UK equity investments.

Table 3.2 (*Continued*)

Manager	Market value of UK equities under management at 31 Dec. 1991 (£million)	As proportion of market value of total quoted UK equities at 31 Dec. 1991[a] (%)
Baring Asset Management Ltd. (FC)	5,387	1.01
Hill Samuel Investment Management Group Ltd. (FC)	5,377	1.00
ESN Pension Management Group Ltd. (Pens.)	5,143*	0.96
Gartmore Investment Management Ltd. (FC)	5,099	0.95
Allied Dunbar Asset Management plc (Ins.)	4,700	0.88
INVESCO MIM Management Ltd. (Indep.)	4,155	0.78
Scottish Amicable Investment Managers Ltd. (Ins.)	4,123	0.77
Provident Mutual Life Assurance Association (Ins.)	4,117	0.77
Henderson Administration Group plc (Indep.)	4,058	0.76
Sun Life Investment Management Services Ltd. (Ins.)	4,005	0.75
Sun Alliance Investment Management Ltd. (Ins.)	4,000	0.75
Co-operative Insurance Society Ltd. (Ins.)	3,760	0.70
Cazenove Investment Management Ltd. (FC)	3,759	0.70
Morgan Grenfell Asset Management Ltd. (FC)	3,737	0.70
British Gas Pension Funds Management Ltd. (Pens.)	3,359*	0.63
Royal Insurance Asset Management Ltd. (Ins.)	3,275	0.61
Lloyds Investment Managers Ltd. (FC)	3,263	0.61
Eagle Star Asset Management Ltd. (Ins.)	3,221	0.60
Friends' Provident Life Office (Ins.)	3,087	0.58

Table 3.2 (*Continued*)

Manager	Market value of UK equities under management at 31 Dec. 1991 (£million)	As proportion of market value of total quoted UK equities at 31 Dec. 1991[a] (%)
Kleinwort Benson Investment Management Ltd. (FC)	3,000	0.56
The Equitable Life Assurance Society (Ins.)	2,743	0.51
Capel-Cure Myers Capital Management Ltd. (FC)	2,703	0.50
ICI Investment Management Ltd. (Pens.)	2,675	0.50
Clerical Medical Investment Group (Ins.)	2,589	0.48
Midland Montagu Asset Management Ltd. (FC)	2,516	0.47
British Steel Pension Fund (Pens.)	2,455*	0.46
BP Pension Fund (Pens.)	2,294	0.43
Shell International Petroleum Company Ltd. (Pens.)	2,243	0.42
GRE Asset Management Ltd. (Ins.)	2,200	0.41
Britannic Assurance plc (Ins.)	2,198	0.41
British Airways Pension Inv. Mgt. Ltd. (Pens.)	2,109*	0.39
Rothschild Asset Management Ltd. (FC)	2,041	0.38
Confederation Life Insurance Company (Ins.)	2,011	0.38
Baillie Gifford & Co. (Indep.)	1,957	0.37

Note: abbreviations: see App. E.

* At 31 Mar. 1992.
** A hybrid figure combining value of UK equities managed for British Coal Staff Superannuation Scheme at 5 Apr. 1992, and the Mineworkers' Pension Scheme at 30 Sept. 1992.

[a] Value of total quoted UK equities (i.e. listed and USM) at 31 Dec. 1991 was £535,867m.: author's calculation from figures in London Stock Exchange, 'Quality of Markets Review' [1991] (Winter) *Stock Ex. Q* 36, at 39 (figure for USM companies adjusted to exclude overseas companies and Irish companies).

Sources: Author's calculations from information in Hymans Robertson, *Pension Fund Investment Manager Survey: Manager Analysis* (1992), and in London Stock Exchange, 'Quality of Markets Review' [1991] (Winter) *Stock Ex. Q* 36, at 39; other sources listed in App. F.

quoted UK equities under management at the end of 1991. The top 50 firms managed equities worth 49.8% of the market value of the total quoted UK equities at 31 December 1991. The figure for the top five fund managers at that time was 13.6%, and for the top 10 it was 21.4%. Gaved gathered similar data for the years 1989 and 1994. His study shows that the market share of the top 50 fund managers grew from 50.2% at the end of 1989 to 55.0% at the end of 1994. This increase was largely a result of the increase in the market share of the top five fund managers: from 11.9% at the end of 1989 to 15.2% at the end of 1994.[51] Table 3.2 reveals the prevalence of the investment-management arms of insurance companies (numbering 21 out of the top 50 managers). The fund-management arms of financial conglomerates were prominent (16 out of 50, including five of the top eight).[52] Firms engaged solely or almost completely in managing the assets of in-house pension funds were also a noteworthy class (nine out of 50). Firms which were dedicated entirely to investment management, and were not part of a larger financial group, made up the remainder (four out of 50). An important statistic is that pension-fund moneys was the largest category of client funds under management for all 16 fund-management arms of financial conglomerates, and all four independent managers. Furthermore, pension-fund moneys represented *more than 50%* of total funds under management for 11 of those 20 managers.[53] The significance of these facts is introduced in the next subsection, and expanded upon in later chapters.

4. CONCLUSION: AN IMPORTANT EARLY OBSERVATION

Trustees of UK pension schemes are collectively the largest category of beneficial owners of quoted UK equities. Fund managers, on the other hand, have the power to sell, and in the majority of cases also to exercise the votes attached to, probably more than two-thirds of all quoted UK equities.

If one calls the party which has the power to sell and vote a share the

---

[51] M. Gaved, *Ownership and Influence* (1995) 21–2.

[52] The 21 insurers led also in terms of the value of their aggregate holding: £111,229m.; compared to the 16 financial conglomerates' aggregate holding of £95,232m. Note that Mercury Asset Management Group plc ('MAM'), the largest manager, was a 75%-owned subsidiary of the listed merchant-banking group, S. G. Warburg Group plc, at the time of Table 3.2. MAM was, nevertheless, itself a listed company. It became a widely held listed company in mid-1995 as part of the deal whereby Swiss Bank Corporation acquired the investment-banking businesses of S. G. Warburg and S. G. Warburg was delisted.

[53] Author's calculations from information in Hymans Robertson (n. 12 above). This is not surprising given that, as Table 2.1 shows, of the various institutional and non-institutional groups, pension funds accounted for the largest proportion of the UK equity market at the end of 1991.

'controller' of the share, it is possible to produce statistics contrasting the beneficial owners of UK equities with the controllers of UK equities. Minns made some estimates of the allocation of the control of UK equities as at the end of 1975.[54] He compared these with official figures for beneficial ownership at the same date. Table 3.3 reproduces Minns' findings.

This table illustrates well the reason for distinguishing between fund managers and the traditional institutions. The ownership-compared-to-control picture for financial conglomerates (and insurance companies) was in 1975 the opposite to that for pension funds (and persons, charities, unit trusts, and investment trusts). It was not possible to obtain a more recent picture of the overall distribution of the control of UK equities, but it is likely that the disparities evident in Table 3.3 would have increased by the 1990s.

Two principal implications arise from the fact that it is fund managers which control the majority of quoted UK equities. First, the formation of manageable, but effective, institutional coalitions to replace the under-performing management of portfolio companies has been possible. If all pension-scheme trustees managed their funds internally, these coalitions would have required too many participants to have been successful in most cases. This is because the fund managers with the five or six largest percentage stakes in any given quoted UK company are each very likely to control a greater proportion of the issued equity capital than the proportion owned beneficially by the trustees of all but (perhaps) one or two of the largest UK pension schemes.[55] Secondly, however, some of the largest UK-based investment managers face numerous structural disincentives to a high level of monitoring, partly due to their being subsidiaries of financial conglomerates. Two of the most significant of these disincentives would not affect their clients (such as pension-fund trustees) if those clients managed their funds in-house.[56]

C. THE TRADE ASSOCIATIONS AND OTHER COLLECTIVE-ACTION VEHICLES

Each of the groups of traditional institutions has its own trade association: the National Association of Pension Funds Ltd. ('NAPF'); the Association of British Insurers ('ABI');[57] the Association of Unit Trusts and Investment Funds ('AUTIF'); and the Association of Investment Trust Companies ('AITC').

[54] Minns (n. 26 above), at 35–41.
[56] See Ch. 10, Secs. B.1.iii, B.1.vi.   [55] See Ch. 5, Sec. B.3.i.
[57] The ABI was formed when the British Insurance Association dissolved in 1986.

Table 3.3 The ownership and control company shares, 1975

Category of beneficial holder/controller	Beneficial ownership of listed UK equities at 31 Dec. 1975 (%)	Control of listed UK equities at 31 Dec. 1975 (%)
Persons	37.5	29.9
Charities and other non-profit-making bodies	2.3	0.2
Financial conglomerates	1.1	23.9
Insurance companies	15.9	17.1
Pension funds	16.8	5.6
Unit trusts	4.1)	11.1
Investment trusts and other financial companies	10.0)	
Industrial and commercial companies	3.0	3.0
Public sector	3.6	3.6
Overseas sector	5.6	5.6
	100.0	100.0

Source: R. Minns, *Pension Funds and British Captialism* (1980) 41 (but note that this table aggregates Minns' categories of 'banks' and 'stockbrokers (and jobbers)' into one category: 'financial conglomerates').

The NAPF and the ABI each have an Investment Committee ('IC') to deal with matters concerning the investment side of their constituents' operations. As UK equities form such an important part of the investment portfolios of most of the constituents of the associations, 'shareholder affairs' is one of the major concerns of the ICs. The ABI IC—known until 1986 as the Investment Protection Committee ('IPC')—has been in existence since 1933. In September 1993 it had a secretariat of 10. At the same time the ABI had 460 members, and the IC was made up of 19 senior investment managers of insurance companies. The Committee meets monthly.[58] The NAPF's IC—known until the mid-1980s as the Investment Protection Committee ('IPC')—was formed in 1963.[59] Its secretariat

---

[58] Information provided to the author by R. D. Regan, Secretary, ABI IC, in interview on 22 Sept. 1993.

[59] From 1947 to 1963 the NAPF operated a less formal Investment Co-operation Service to assist members in the protection of their investments.

consisted of one full-time employee, and three part-time employees, at September 1993. The Committee numbered 14 at that time, and included in-house pension-fund managers, external fund managers, lawyers, and actuaries. It meets around 8–12 times per year.[60]

AUTIF was formed in 1959 as the Association of Unit Trust Managers ('AUTM'). It was renamed the Unit Trust Association ('UTA') in 1976, and became AUTIF in 1993. AUTIF's membership includes managers of UK authorized unit trusts, and firms managing personal equity plans, open-ended investment companies, investment trusts, and UCITS funds set up in other EU member States.[61]

The AITC was formed in 1932, but was known until 1969 as the Association of Investment Trusts ('AIT'). Its membership consists only of investment-trust companies; no fund-management firms are entitled to be members.[62]

Another trade association is the London Investment Banking Association ('LIBA'). It was known until mid-1994 as the British Merchant Banking and Securities Houses Association ('BMBA'); the BMBA was formed in the 1980s out of the Accepting Houses Committee and the Issuing Houses Association. LIBA represents virtually all of the City's major merchant and investment banks—the 'financial conglomerates' or 'integrated houses'. It has an Asset Management Committee which deals with matters concerning the fund-management aspect of its members' businesses.

These trade associations have all, to varying degrees, been active in matters of shareholder protection and corporate governance. The ICs of the ABI and NAPF have, however, been the major players.

In the early 1970s, the Conservative Government of Mr (later Sir) Edward Heath discussed with the Governor of the Bank of England the possibility of the institutions intervening more actively in corporate affairs.[63] The Bank of England then set up a working party 'to examine and report upon a possible structure and method of operation of a central organization through which institutional investors, in collaboration with those concerned, would stimulate action to improve efficiency in industrial and commercial companies where this was judged necessary'.[64]

By December 1972 the NAPF, the AITC, and AUTM had agreed to

[60] Information provided to the author by J. E. Rogers, Secretary, NAPF IC, in interview on 29 Sept. 1993.

[61] Linklaters & Paines, *Unit Trusts: The Law and Practice* (1989) 209.

[62] Information provided to the author by J. W. Rath, Secretary, AITC, in interview on 21 Sept. 1993.

[63] 'The Limits to Institutional Power', *Fin. Times*, 22 May 1990, p. 20.

[64] Press announcement issued by the Bank of England, reproduced in (1973) 13 *Bank Eng. Q Bull.* 148.

establish such a body. However, the British Insurance Association ('BIA'), the predecessor of the ABI, initially declined involvement on the grounds that (a) its members were apprehensive that they would be seen to be accepting the prime responsibility for monitoring and improving the management of companies; and (b) it feared that any such body might operate in a way prejudicial to the control by individual institutions of action at portfolio companies. It was, however, prepared to co-operate with such a body in individual cases.[65] The Accepting Houses Committee and the Issuing Houses Association also refused to participate, on the basis that to do so would conflict with their members' role as corporate advisers.[66]

After some compromising over the structure and method of operation of the proposed organization, the BIA agreed in April 1973 to join with the NAPF, AITC, and AUTM in creating the Institutional Shareholders' Committee ('ISC'). The ISC's terms of reference required it to 'co-ordinate and extend the existing investment protection activities of institutional investors'. Its role was to conduct firm-level monitoring through the mechanism of case committees. It did this for a few years, but probably not to the extent envisaged originally.[67] After a lull in its activities during the mid-1980s, an attempt was made during 1988–90 to revive it through three proposed actions: (a) a broadening of its membership to include the merchant banks' trade association; (b) a reinvigoration of its interventionist role; and (c) a rewriting of its constitution such that it would assume the additional roles of providing a forum for discussion about corporate governance and of identifying and promoting statements of best practice in the area of corporate governance.[68] Proposal (a) was implemented: its membership became the NAPF, ABI, UTA (later AUTIF), AITC, and BMBA (later LIBA).[69] Proposal (b) was

---

[65] (1973) 13 *Bank Eng. Q Bull.* 148.

[66] 'Bank Hails BIA Decision to Join City Investors' "Ginger Group" ', *Fin. Times*, 17 Apr. 1973, p. 1. The structural conflicts of interest inherent in financial conglomerates are discussed in Ch. 10, Sec. B.1.vi.

[67] A detailed account of the operation of the ISC in its early years is given in Ch. 5, Sec. D.1.i.

[68] 'Institutional Investors as Interventionists', *Fin. Times*, 10 Aug. 1990, p. 10.

[69] Although the ISC's membership is the five associations, it is concerned only with the shareholding aspect of the associations' constituents' activities. Therefore, it is in effect the ICs of the NAPF and ABI, and the Asset Management Committee of LIBA, together with AUTIF and AITC, that make up the ISC. Each member body is entitled to nominate three persons to represent it at meetings of the ISC. The bodies have in practice nominated two persons each; in the case of the ABI and the NAPF, the two attendees at ISC meetings are usually the chairman (or deputy chairman), and the full-time Secretary, of the IC. AUTIF and AITC are usually represented by their respective Directors-General. The ISC meets once every three months: information provided to the author by J. Potter, Secretary-General, ISC, in interview on 28 Sept. 1993.

criticized heavily and not implemented.[70] Proposal (c) was effectuated and, due to the abandonment of proposal (b), this industry-wide monitoring role became the ISC's only function.[71]

It should be borne in mind that the formation of the ISC did not lead to a noticeable diminution in the activities of the ABI and NAPF ICs on matters of corporate governance and investor rights. Further, although the range of institutions has acted as one through the ISC, occasionally the two ICs have acted divergently on corporate-governance issues.[72]

The Institutional Fund Managers' Association ('IFMA') is made up of, and represents the interests of, nearly 80 fund-management firms. IFMA's membership includes the investment-management subsidiaries of several merchant banks that are members of LIBA, of numerous insurance companies that are members of the ABI, and of a few internally managed pension funds that are members of the NAPF. Independent fund-management firms are also members. IFMA's concern with corporate governance extends, however, only to its impact upon the day-to-day operations of fund managers (for example the practicalities of the exercise of voting rights).[73]

Another UK body which advises institutional shareholders on matters of corporate governance is Pensions & Investment Research Consultants Ltd. ('PIRC'). It was established in 1986 by a consortium of British local-authority pension funds. At September 1993, PIRC advised 15 UK pension funds with assets of £15,000 million. Some of these pension funds managed their assets in-house, some employed external managers, and a couple did both. It was also retained, at that time, to research and advise on UK companies by two US institutional-shareholder advisory bodies: Institutional Shareholder Services and Investor Responsibility Research Center.[74] PIRC's principal function is the provision of a proxy-voting service for its subscribers.[75]

---

[70] The details of this aspect are in Ch. 5, Sec. D.1.i.

[71] See Ch. 5, Sec. C, for more detail.

[72] e.g., the debate in 1992–3 between the two ICs on the matter of the appropriate measure of management performance in relation to executive share schemes: see 'Shareholder Group Calls for Changes to Stock Option Plans', *Fin. Times*, 6 July 1992, p. 1; a compromise was reached eventually: see 'Boards Face Share Option Pressure', *Fin. Times*, 15 July 1993, p. 9; ABI and NAPF, *Share Scheme Guidance* (1993).

[73] Information provided to the author by J. Le Fanu, IFMA.

[74] Information provided to the author by S. Bell, Research Director, PIRC, in interview on 28 Sept. 1993.   [75] See Ch. 5, Sec. B.1.v.

4

Areas of Involvement in the UK

One aim of this chapter is to bring to light the wide range of shareholder and corporate-governance issues with which UK-based institutions have been concerned (i.e. *what* matters they have been concerned about). Another aim is to analyse these issues and thereby to draw out the features which exist commonly amongst a number of issues, and then to explain the significance of these commonly occurring features. The discussion is divided into two broad sections. First, attention is focused upon procedural and general issues. Secondly, company-specific issues are addressed. A procedural or general issue is one which 'arise[s] in similar form at many companies',[1] whilst a company-specific issue is one peculiar to the company in question. The issues are only touched upon because the more important thing is *how* the institutions have involved themselves in these matters—which is described in detail in the next chapter. It is not possible to divide completely the discussion of *what* and *how*—a degree of overlap is inevitable—but the separation into two chapters allows a detailed coverage in Chapter 5 of the manner of involvement without sidetracking too much into the specific issues concerned.

Throughout this chapter (and some later chapters), there are many references to an interview study involving UK-based institutions. The study referred to was conducted by the author during September and October 1993. It involved interviews in London, Edinburgh, Glasgow, and Norwich, with the chief executive or a senior fund manager of 17 investment-management firms.[2] The 17 institutions managed quoted UK equities worth £136,470 million at 31 December 1991, which represented over 25% of the value of the UK equity market at that date. The institutions included the eight largest, and 10 of the 12 largest, managers of UK equities at the end of 1991.[3] The writer also interviewed the Secretary-General of the ISC, the Secretaries of the ICs of the ABI and the NAPF, the Secretary of the AITC, and the Research Director of PIRC.

---

[1] B. S. Black, 'Agents Watching Agents: The Promise of Institutional Investor Voice' (1992) 39 *UCLA L Rev.* 811, at 822.

[2] They are listed in App. A. Standard questions were asked in the interviews; these are set out in App. B. The author's study was designed to build upon that of Coffee, who interviewed some UK-based fund managers in 1992: see B. S. Black and J. C. Coffee, 'Hail Britannia? Institutional Investor Behavior Under Limited Regulation' (1994) 92 *Mich. L Rev.* 1997.

[3] See Ch. 3, Table 3.2.

A. PROCEDURAL AND GENERAL ISSUES

The procedural and general issues discussed below are classified as either issues of 'investor protection and corporate governance' or 'ethical and political' issues. The opportunity is taken, whilst discussing these issues, to mention features occurring generally amongst the issues. An attempt is made to account for these commonly existing features.

1. INVESTOR PROTECTION AND CORPORATE GOVERNANCE

The institutions have developed a number of policies that have the common characteristic of seeking, directly or indirectly, to protect shareholder rights and interests. All of these policies have impacted, to some degree, upon the management of quoted UK companies.

i. Pre-emption Rights

A right of pre-emption[4] over issues of equity for cash was first conferred upon shareholders of listed companies by way of a London Stock Exchange listing requirement. The introduction of this listing rule in the 1950s has been attributed by a former Stock Exchange executive to institutional pressure upon the Exchange.[5] Indeed, during the 1970s the Investment Protection Committees ('IPCs') of the old British Insurance Association and the NAPF introduced pre-emption guidelines of their own, which were more restrictive than the Stock Exchange rule.[6] A statutory pre-emption right was enacted in 1980, but this was an adoption of the European Community's Second Directive on harmonization of company law.[7] A relaxation of the Stock Exchange's rule in 1986,[8] accompanied by a number of large non-rights issues to overseas investors, resulted initially in a tightening of the guidelines of the ABI and NAPF ICs,[9] and then in the establishment of the Pre-emption Group. The Pre-emption Group, made up of representatives of the ICs, the Stock Exchange, and the corporate

---

[4] A pre-emption rule requires that newly issued shares must be offered first to existing shareholders in proportion to their existing shareholdings.

[5] J. Knight, 'The Role of the Shareholder and the Institutions' in The Corporate Policy Group, *Control of the Corporation: A Review of the British Company in the 1980s* (1980) 11, at 13.

[6] The IPCs' guidelines placed an annual cap on non-rights issues: 5% of authorized share capital or 6.67% of issued capital: Bank of England, 'Pre-emption Rights' (1987) 27 *Bank Eng. Q Bull.* 545, at 546.

[7] See Directive 77/91/EEC, art. 29; CA 1980, s. 17 (see now CA, 1985, ss. 89–96).

[8] See now London Stock Exchange, *The Listing Rules* (referred to hereafter as '*Listing Rules*'), paras. 9.18–9.20.

[9] See 'Institutions Seek Curb on Share Issues', *Fin. Times*, 30 Apr. 1987, p. 1.

sector, issued guidelines which replaced the ICs' guidelines:[10] annual disapplication of the pre-emption right would still be required by the Stock Exchange, but this should be restricted to 5% of issued ordinary share capital; non-rights issues should not exceed 7½% of issued ordinary share capital in any rolling three-year period; any discount should be restricted to 5% of market price; prior consultation with the ICs should be sought before attempting a non-rights issue in excess of these limits;[11] the ICs would be likely to recommend their members to oppose annual disapplications by any company with an unsatisfactory record of compliance with the guidelines. The ICs have also lobbied successfully against a Treasury proposal to remove the statutory pre-emption right in the interests of wider share ownership.[12]

Three general points arise out of the institutional stance on pre-emption rights. First, it is an illustration of the substantial potential of institutional action in areas where the institutions' pecuniary interests are threatened. It is indisputable that 'insistence on pre-emption rights . . . protects the shareholders' equity interest from dilution', and thereby serves 'to maintain the potential for institutional influence over management'.[13] However, a majority of the fund managers interviewed by the author said that the primary concern about non-rights issues was the loss[14] often sustained by existing shareholders as a result of the discounted price at which such issues are usually made.[15] This feature of the pre-emption rights matter is possessed also by the matters of management buy-outs and equality of treatment in takeovers, discussed below.

Secondly, institutional insistence on pre-emption rights has also presented institutions with a procedural device of some importance in cases of extreme sub-optimal performance by management. Institutions have occasionally made their support for a rescue rights issue conditional upon changes in the management team deemed responsible for the company needing the emergency refinancing in the first place.[16]

---

[10] The Pre-emption Group, *Pre-emption Guidelines* (1987).

[11] The institutions have been flexible: between Aug. 1988 and May 1989 the ICs considered 14 requests to act outside the guidelines, and approved them all: S. Wright, *Two Cheers for the Institutions* (1994) 23.

[12] See 'Pre-emption rights "Still on Agenda" ', *Fin. Times*, 4 May 1989, sec. III, p. XIV.

[13] P. L. Davies, 'Institutional Shareholders in the UK' in D. D. Prentice and P. R. J. Holland (eds.), *Contemporary Issues in Corporate Governance* (1993) 69, at 85, 87.

[14] The loss referred to would occur normally as a result of a subsequent lowered market price of the particular class of shares, and possibly of a reduction in the dividend level due to a dilution of earnings per share (due to the expanded shareholder base).

[15] The shareholders' loss may well be short-term only; in the long term, shareholders might benefit from cost savings accruing to the company as a result of the non-rights form of fund-raising. A dilution of earnings per share would not eventuate if, *ceteris paribus*, the company earned a sufficient return on assets.   [16] See Ch. 5, Sec. B.3.vii.(a).

Thirdly, the pre-emption rights matter illustrates the capability of institutional shareholders to exert influence indirectly—through the ICs of the ABI and NAPF. The ICs, and/or the ISC, have in fact been involved in the action taken on almost every other procedural or general issue discussed below. It is submitted that this is because using the ICs allows the costs of, and practical difficulties associated with, collective action amongst many institutions[17] to be reduced materially.

ii. Non-Voting Shares

A majority of the Jenkins Committee concluded in 1962 that it would be 'too drastic a step' to prohibit statutorily the issue of non- or restricted-voting shares.[18] A minority of the Committee, however, which included Mr Leslie Brown, then Chief Investment Manager of Prudential Assurance, supported submissions made by the insurers' and investment trusts' trade associations in favour of restricting the growth of such shares.[19] In the result, no step was taken to prohibit non-voting ordinary shares.[20] Although the London Stock Exchange disapproves of these shares, they are also not prohibited in the *Listing Rules* and are thus able to be listed.[21] However, there have been 'no instances in recent years of a company seeking a listing for any new class of non-voting equity capital',[22] and several companies with non-voting shares enfranchised them during 1992–4 in the face of institutional pressure.[23] A further indication of the institutional influence is that the proportion of domestic listed companies with non- or restricted-voting shares is far lower in the UK than in most other European countries in which they are allowed.[24]

Upon analysis, the matter of non-voting shares has three features which are also possessed by several of the other procedural and general issues

---

[17] See Ch. 10, Sec. B.1.ii.

[18] Company Law Committee, *Report* (1962) para. 136.

[19] Ibid., at 207–10.

[20] There is, however, a statutory presumption of one vote per share: CA 1985, s. 370(6); see also Table A, art. 54, and the proposed Fifth EC Directive on harmonization of company law: 1983 OJ (C 240) 2.

[21] The only restriction imposed is the requirement that the words 'non-voting', 'restricted voting' or 'limited voting' must be included in their designation: *Listing Rules*, ch. 13, App. 1, paras. 2, 3.

[22] L. Rabinowitz, *Weinberg and Blank on Take-overs and Mergers* (5th edn., 1989) para. 3–805.

[23] See e.g. 'Whitbread Gives Equal Rights', *Fin. Times*, 7 Oct. 1993, p. 25; 'Hammerson Share Vote Changes', *Fin. Times*, 20 Oct. 1993, p. 22; 'W H Smith to Change Share Structure', *Fin. Times*, 20 May 1994, p. 20. Since late 1991, it has been an express principle of good practice of the ISC that '[i]nstitutional investors are opposed to the creation of equity shares which do not carry full voting rights': ISC, *The Responsibilities of Institutional Shareholders in the UK* (1991) 5.

[24] K. Rydqvist, 'Dual-Class Shares: A Review' (1992) 8 (3) *Ox. Rev. Econ. Pol.* 45, at Table 2.

with which institutions have been concerned. It (a) is relatively uncomplicated and does not concern the detailed business of a company; (b) has the potential to arise at a large number of companies; and (c) can be addressed relatively easily and inexpensively across a wide range of companies. There is, in fact, a strong correlation between those matters upon which there has been dedicated, systematic, and efficacious institutional monitoring, and those matters which (as well as being of concern to institutions) possess these attributes.

This in turn leads to another general point. Economies of scale are, by definition, all but absent from company-specific issues. But with procedural and general issues—which usually either exist in, or have the potential to arise at, many companies—institutions stand to benefit from economies of scale should any monitoring actions be employed at more than one company. Institutional monitoring is thus more likely to take place in relation to commonly occurring procedural and general issues than company-specific issues.

iii. Enhanced Scrip Dividends

A change to advance corporation tax ('ACT') in the March 1993 Budget led to 'enhanced scrip dividends' being offered by over a dozen companies in the ensuing six months. These comprised a scrip dividend worth 50% more than the alternative cash dividend, which was able to be on-sold at a small discount almost immediately—thereby effectively giving the shareholder a substantially larger cash dividend.[25] Although they were, for obvious reasons, attractive to many shareholders, some companies seemed to be using them to avoid a dividend cut rather than to avoid a structural taxation problem. They were thus considered in some cases to be an indirect capital raising, but with the potential problem of more equity on issue to service by way of cash dividends in the future, and without the disclosure required for normal capital raisings. The ABI IC met with the Confederation of British Industry ('CBI') and other industry bodies, and individual institutions met with company managements, and requested that enhanced scrip dividends be confined to those companies with ACT problems, and that they not be used as an ongoing measure.[26]

The matter of enhanced scrip dividends shares a feature possessed by several other procedural and general issues. It is a matter where institutional influence has been exerted upon quoted companies through the lobbying of third parties: in this case the CBI. In other matters, institutional influence has been brought to bear upon, *inter alia*, the

---

[25] See generally C. Mallin, 'Enhanced Scrip Dividends' [1993] (Autumn) *Stock Ex. Q* 13.
[26] See 'Fashion for the Thinly Veiled Rights Offering', *Fin. Times*, 19 Apr. 1993, p. 17; 'Doubts Rise Over Enhanced Scrips', *Fin. Times*, 13 Oct. 1993, p. 20.

London Stock Exchange, the Accounting Standards Board, and government departments.

iv. Major Transactions/Acquisitions

The proposed takeover by the drinks group Allied Breweries Ltd. of the food group J. Lyons & Co. Ltd. in 1978 led to a confrontation with a case committee of the NAPF IPC. The case committee wanted the proposal to be put to a vote at an extraordinary general meeting, on the basis that the takeover involved a fundamental change in the nature of Allied Breweries' business. A compromise was reached between the board and the case committee, under which shareholders were able to vote on a resolution to 'note with approval' the acquisition.[27] However, the IPCs of the NAPF and the insurers then had extensive discussions with the Stock Exchange, which resulted in a tightening of its listing rules such that shareholders' consent would be required in advance for an acquisition which would alter materially the character of the buyer's business.[28] The insurers' IPC also made representations to the Stock Exchange which were partly responsible for the introduction of the listing requirement under which very large transactions now require prior approval by shareholders in general meeting.[29]

v. Own-Share Purchase

The prohibition of the acquisition by UK companies of their own shares[30] has, since 1981, been tempered by a set of statutory provisions under which, *inter alia*, restricted purchases through the market are permitted. For market purchases, the Companies Act requires that the company's articles authorize buy-backs, and that authority to purchase for a specified period of no more than 18 months be given by the shareholders in general meeting.[31] The London Stock Exchange imposes a further restriction upon listed companies: a maximum of 15% of issued share capital can be purchased through the market per year.[32] In practice, however, listed companies have faced more rigorous restrictions. Informal guidelines of

---

[27] J. Plender, *That's the Way the Money Goes* (1982) 70–1.

[28] M. I. Reid, *All-Change in the City* (1988) 199. See now *Listing Rules*, paras. 10.4(e), 10.39.

[29] Information provided to the author by R. D. Regan, Secretary, ABI IC, in interview on 22 Sept. 1993. These are now called 'Super Class 1 transactions': see *Listing Rules*, paras. 10.4(d), 10.37. See further Ch. 5, Sec. B.3.vii.(b); Ch. 11, Sec. B.1.vi (recommendation for reduction in threshold from 25% to 20%).

[30] Initially a rule of common law: *Trevor* v. *Whitworth* (1887) 12 App. Cas. 409; since 1980, imposed by statute: see now CA 1985, s. 143(1).

[31] CA 1985, ss. 143(3), 159–70 (which implemented part of the Second EC Directive on harmonization of company law: 77/91/EEC).

[32] *Listing Rules*, para. 15.6.

the ABI IC request companies to seek authority from the general meeting every 12 months, as opposed to the 18-month statutory limit, and seek to restrict the level of repurchase to only 10% of issued capital, annually (as opposed to the Stock Exchange's 15% limit).[33]

Amongst the assortment of possible motives for own-share purchase, support of the share price and protection against hostile takeover bidders are two which clearly embody the potential for a conflict to arise between the directors' duties to the company and their personal interests. The ABI IC's policy on buy-backs is designed to protect the interests of shareholders by limiting the scope for any detriment to the company from conflict-influenced buy-back schemes, and putting a limit on the increase in gearing (i.e. debt-equity ratio) which occurs as a result of any own-share purchase.[34]

vi. Management By-Outs

In the case of own-share purchase, conflict of interest is merely a *potential* problem. However, a proposed management buy-out ('MBO') of a listed company—involving a takeover offer made by members of the offeree's executive management—will always involve conflicts of interest for the executive directors who are to have roles in the bought-out company. They are, after all, (a) as members of the offeree's board, required normally to give to shareholders their views on any takeover offer;[35] *and* also (b) as parties to the buy-out plan, naturally supportive of it.[36] In the light of this, in December 1989 the ISC issued guidance notes indicating the circumstances in which institutional shareholders would be likely to receive sympathetically any proposals for buy-outs of listed companies.[37]

Whilst wishing not to prevent 'appropriate' MBOs, the ISC document states that proposals are unlikely to be received favourably unless (a)

---

[33] City Capital Markets Committee, 'Share Repurchase by Quoted Companies' (1988) 28 *Bank Eng. Q Bull.* 382, at 385, 388.

[34] In some circumstances, of course, an increase in gearing may prove beneficial to shareholders by leading to an increase in profits. Note also that institutions encourage own-share purchase in some situations (e.g. a company with a large cash flow but which operates in a mature or declining industry; here, many shareholders would prefer that funds be returned to investors rather than invested in a new line of business: see 'Cash Returns', *Fin. Times*, 27 July 1993, p. 17; M. C. Jensen, 'Agency Costs of Free Cash Flow, Corporate Finance, and Takeovers' (1986) 76 *Am. Econ. Rev.—Papers & Proc.* 323).

[35] Panel on Takeovers and Mergers, *The City Code on Takeovers and Mergers* ('*Takeover Code*'), Rule 25.1. (See also General Principle 4; Rules 3.1, 30.2.)

[36] These conflicts are recognized in the *Takeover Code*: see Note 1 to Rule 3.1; Notes 3 and 4 to Rule 25.1 (directors intended to have a role—executive or non-executive—in either the offeror or offeree company, in the event of the MBO offer being successful, will normally be regarded as having a conflict of interest such that they should not be joined with the remainder of the board in the expression of its views on the offer).

[37] ISC, *Management Buy-Outs* (1989).

'there is, and has been for some time, a strong, independent, non-executive presence' on the board of the offeree company; and (b) the proposals 'were supported and recommended by those independent non-executive directors'.[38]

vii. Pre-Bid Takeover Defences

Pre-bid defensive tactics are outside the scope of the *Takeover Code*, which takes effect only when a takeover bid is 'imminent'.[39] And the common law, Companies Act, and London Stock Exchange listing requirements are not particularly restrictive in this area. There is thus a wide range of pre-bid moves that may in theory be deployed by the management of a potential target company.[40] The close restrictions placed on *post*-bid defensive moves by the *Takeover Code* have not, however, contrary to what one might expect, led to widespread adoption of pre-bid defences by listed UK companies. Institutional opposition to measures which would inhibit the replacement of a management team, should its performance become unsatisfactory, may provide the explanation.[41]

viii. Equality of Treatment in Takeovers

It is the first General Principle of the *Takeover Code* that all offeree shareholders of the same class are to be treated similarly by the offeror.[42] Institutions have in a number of instances taken action in relation to takeover offers, or market activities by the offeror, which appear to infringe this principle.[43] Interestingly, in one such case ('the Bosch/Worcester case') the offeror was a German company, which offered

[38] Ibid., paras. 3.1.1 and 3.3.1. The mettle of these guidance notes was tested by the attempted buy-out of Amstrad plc in late 1992. The company had no non-executive directors, and thus no independent arbiter of the price offered by the offeror executives. Public opposition from institutional and non-institutional shareholders resulted in the defeat of the proposal at the general meeting: see 'Institutions Turn Against Sugar's Bid for Amstrad', *Fin. Times*, 3 Dec. 1992, p. 23; 'Opposition Grows to Sugar's Plans', *Fin. Times*, 8 Dec. 1992, p. 18; 'Amstrad Vote Halts Battle', *Fin. Times*, 11 Dec. 1992, p. 25.

[39] *Takeover Code*, General Principle 7.

[40] See P. L. Davies, 'The Regulation of Defensive Tactics in the United Kingdom and the United States' in K. J. Hopt and E. Wymeersch (eds.), *European Takeovers—Law and Practice* (1992) 195, at 205–14.

[41] Ibid. The institutional policies on pre-emption rights, non-voting shares, and own-share purchase, discussed above, have all served (intentionally or otherwise) to limit pre-bid defences. On takeover defences in the UK, generally, see T. Jenkinson and C. P. Mayer, *Takeover Defence Strategies* (1991); A. Paul, 'Corporate Governance in the Context of Takeovers of UK Public Companies' in Prentice and Holland (n. 13 above), 135.

[42] See generally D. D. Prentice, 'Regulation of Takeover Bids in the United Kingdom' in K. Kreuzer (ed.), *Öffentliche Übernahmeangebote* (1992) 133.

[43] See 'Institutions Demand Fair Shares for All', *Fin. Times*, 30 Apr. 1992, p. 23; 'Own Goals Keep the Underdog in the Game', *Fin. Times*, 5 July 1994, p. 26; R. Minns, *Pension Funds and British Capitalism* (1980) 106–7. Note that the membership of the Panel on Takeovers and Mergers, which administers the *Takeover Code*, includes representatives of the ABI, NAPF, AUTIF, and AITC.

different terms to the target's management and non-management share-holders.[44] The absence of takeover regulations in Germany, and in particular the absence of any prohibition on partial bids,[45] is reflected in the fact that most takeovers in Germany involve the purchase of a majority stake rather than a full acquisition.[46] The Bosch/Worcester case was thus an interesting interface between the insider and outsider systems of corporate control which exist in the UK and Germany, respectively.[47]

ix. Disclosure of Financial Information

UK institutions, as important users of companies' financial statements, were criticized for an allegedly low level of involvement, in the 1970s and 1980s, in the continual process of attempting to improve company reporting.[48] However, in the early 1990s the institutions were involved in several areas of the disclosure debate. This subsection, and the following three subsections, outline four areas of the debate in which UK institutions have been involved.

Since the establishment of the Accounting Standards Board ('ASB') in 1990, the Chairman and Director General of the ASB have met regularly with the NAPF IC, to canvass shareholder opinion on ASB proposals and to seek shareholder views on possible areas for reform.[49] Also, the NAPF IC publicly approached the ASB in 1991 asking that it consider the introduction of a number of additional disclosure requirements for companies.[50] Institutional input into the area of disclosure reform was strengthened in 1994 when Mr Huw Jones, Corporate Finance Director of Prudential Portfolio Managers Ltd., became a part-time member of the ASB.

---

[44] See 'Worcester Holders Angry Over £72m German Offer', *Fin. Times*, 18 Apr. 1992, p. 8; 'Worcester Shareholders at Odds with Takeover Panel', *Fin. Times*, 22 Apr. 1992, p. 22; 'Institutions Demand . . .', ibid.; 'Institutions Fail to Block Bosch's Bid for Worcester', *Fin. Times*, 12 May 1992, p. 22.

[45] These are heavily restricted under the *Takeover Code*, Rule 36. Note that a full bid is required under the proposed Thirteenth EC Directive on harmonization of company law: 1990 OJ (C 240) 7, art. 4.

[46] J. R. Franks and C. P. Mayer, 'Capital Markets and Corporate Control: A Study of France, Germany and the UK' (1990) 10 *Econ. Pol.* 189, at 196–7.

[47] See further Ch. 9, Sec. B.1; Ch. 10, Sec. B.1.i.

[48] See e.g. D. A. Walker, 'Some Perspectives for Pension Fund Managers' (1987) 27 *Bank Eng. Q Bull.* 247, at 251; I. N. Tegner, 'A View from the Board Room' (1993) 1 *Corp. Gov.: Inter. Rev.* 191, at 192.

[49] Information provided to the author by J. E. Rogers, Secretary, NAPF IC, in interview on 29 Sept. 1993. The slight delay in production of the final version of the ASB's *Statement: Operating and Financial Review* (1993) was attributed partly to its 'careful discussions' with the ABI and NAPF: 'Broad-Brush Approach for a Truer Picture', *Fin. Times*, 8 July 1993, p. 12.

[50] 'Institutions Want Fuller Financial Information', *Fin. Times*, 2 Sept. 1991, p. 14.

x. Corporate-Treasury Policy

Following the loss by Allied-Lyons plc of £147 million on foreign-exchange dealings in early 1991, the corporate-treasury policy of listed UK companies became a prominent issue with the institutions. There were two main developments. First, discussions in 1991 between the Association of Corporate Treasurers ('ACT') and the ICs of the NAPF and ABI resulted in the ACT organizing a study of issues of foreign-exchange management which would be of importance to institutions. The resulting document,[51] intended as a guidebook for institutions, sets out some basic information about foreign-exchange management. It also lists questions (and gives pointers to understanding possible answers) appropriate for investors to put 'in a short meeting with company management [so as] to get a useful idea of how well the company itself understands its risks and how appropriately that understanding has come through in actions or systems in the company'.[52]

Secondly, Mr Hugh Jenkins, the Chief Executive of Prudential Portfolio Managers Ltd., called for greater disclosure of corporate-treasury policies in companies' accounts.[53] As a consequence, the ACT set up a working party (involving the NAPF, the ABI, and the ASB) which developed guidelines on the appropriate level of disclosure of treasury-management activities.[54]

xi. Disclosure of R&D Expenditure

The topic of research and development ('R&D') expenditure by UK companies arises in another area in this book.[55] The essence of its relevance is that (a) the level of R&D expenditure by UK companies has for many years been lower than that of many overseas (in particular, Japanese and German) rivals; and (b) institutions have been accused of contributing to this by pressuring companies to increase short-term profits and dividends at the expense of 'discretionary investment' such as R&D (i.e. by engaging in 'short-termism').

One commonly suggested remedy for the alleged failure by institutions to take into account companies' innovation activities has been to improve the communication between companies and institutions about such

---

[51] J. Grout and D. Ross, *Foreign Exchange Management in Non-Financial Corporations: A Checklist of Major Issues for Institutional Investors* (1992).

[52] Ibid., at 1.

[53] 'Pru Chief Issues Plea for Greater Treasury Detail', *Fin. Times*, 16 Oct. 1992, p. 31.

[54] These guidelines are set out in ACT, *The Treasurer's Handbook* (1994) 115–16. A 1994 survey found that only 27% of UK companies provided meaningful disclosure in this area, but this was a considerable increase on the 15% level in 1991: 'Currency Details "Lacking" ', *Fin. Times*, 6 June 1994, p. 9.

[55] See Ch. 9, Sec. B.1.

activities.[56] The Electrical Equipment Association (an industry trade body) approached the ISC in 1991 requesting clarification of the level and type of R&D disclosure desired by institutions.[57] In response, the ISC published a paper which 'attempts to break the impasse by setting out those facts about R&D that it would be useful for institutional investors to know, whether through the accounts or through other channels'.[58] It is too soon to judge the impact of the ISC paper. There is, however, some evidence that companies which have been very open about their innovation plans have, in return, had their long-term growth prospects assessed adequately.[59]

xii. Disclosure of Non-Audit Relationships with Auditors

The provision, by accounting firms, of non-audit services to audit clients has periodically been a contentious matter. Those favouring a prohibition on the provision of non-audit services to audit clients claim that this would (a) eliminate any incentive for the audit department of an accounting firm to be inappropriately accommodating towards the management of client companies (so as not to jeopardize the non-audit work of that accounting firm's other departments); (b) exclude the possibility of one department of an accounting firm (i.e. the audit department) reviewing the figures of another department (for example the corporate finance or taxation department) of the same firm; and (c) eliminate any incentive for an accounting firm to use (inappropriately) its audit services as a 'loss-leader' for other, lucrative, non-audit work. The issue is not only one of auditor independence, but also one of investor protection: the principal underlying purpose of the appointment and work of auditors is to assist the collective body of shareholders in making an informed appraisal of the stewardship of the company's directors and management.[60]

Stopping short of calling for such a prohibition, in 1991 the NAPF IC urged the ASB to introduce an accounting standard requiring companies to disclose all of the services provided by their auditors.[61] At mid-1995 no such standard had been issued, but regulations made in 1991 require companies to disclose the amount of non-audit fees paid to the auditors.[62]

---

[56] See e.g. CBI City/Industry Task Force, *Report: Investing for Britain's Future* (1987) 33–4, 58–9.

[57] 'Institutions Tackle "Short-Termism" ', *Fin. Times*, 30 Apr. 1992, p. 8.

[58] ISC, *Suggested Disclosure of Research and Development Expenditure* (1992).

[59] See e.g. 'The Secret of T&N', *Fin. Times*, 12 Mar. 1993, p. 13.

[60] *Caparo Industries plc* v. *Dickman* [1990] 2 AC 605, at 626 *per* Lord Bridge; 630–1 *per* Lord Oliver; 661–2 *per* Lord Jauncey.   [61] 'Institutions Want . . .' (n. 50 above).

[62] Companies Act 1985 (Disclosure of Remuneration for Non-Audit Work) Regulations 1991 (SI 1991/2128). The relative value of the auditors' total non-audit work can now be gauged by comparing that figure with the audit fee: CA 1985, s. 390A(3) requires 'the amount of the remuneration of the company's auditors in their capacity as such' to be disclosed in the notes to the accounts; cf., however, *Cadbury Report*, para. 5.11.

The NAPF IC highlights this information in its *Voting Issues Service*—a proxy-voting information service provided to subscribers.[63]

xiii. Rotation of Audit Partners

Another suggested measure aimed at strengthening auditor independence is the compulsory rotation of audit firms.[64] A more modest measure was suggested by the NAPF IC to the ASB in 1991: that audit firms be required to change periodically the partner responsible for each corporate account.[65] After submissions from, *inter alia*, the NAPF, the Cadbury Committee later advocated the same requirement,[66] and this led to its introduction.[67]

xiv. Insider Dealing

Lobbying by institutions, amongst others, was partially responsible for revisions made to draft legislation on insider dealing in 1992–3.[68] There was nevertheless some concern in the City about the possible effect of the final legislation[69] upon the openness of company managements in communication with shareholders and analysts. This, together with institutional concern about selective leaking of price-sensitive information,[70] led to IFMA and the ABI IC, amongst others, conducting a revision of the Stock Exchange's guidance on the release of price-sensitive information.[71] It should be borne in mind, however, that the topics of

---

[63] The NAPF *Voting Issues Service* is described in Ch. 5, at nn. 121–3, and accompanying text.

[64] The goal being 'to prevent relationships between management and auditors becoming too comfortable': *Cadbury Report*, para. 5.12. In an Australian case, *AWA Ltd.* v. *Daniels* (1992) 7 ACSR 759, a partner (D) of a firm of auditors, sued successfully in negligence by a corporate client (AWA), had been the audit partner for AWA's accounts for some 12 or 13 years. Rogers CJ (Comm. Div.), at first instance, noted that D and AWA's general manager and internal auditor were friends of long standing (at 766). His Honour continued that if D had reported to AWA's board certain deficiencies known by D to exist in AWA's management (below board level), and more significantly the failure of senior management to rectify the deficiencies after having been notified of them by the auditors, it would likely 'have reflected badly on [D's] two friends' (at 766–7). His Honour concluded: 'The difficulties which may arise from too close a relationship between auditor and management have been recognised in recent proposals to require a change of auditor at least every 7 years.' (at 767). On appeal, the New South Wales Court of Appeal did not comment on this issue: see *Daniels* v. *Anderson* (1995) 16 ACSR 607.   [65] 'Institutions Want . . .' (n. 50 above).

[66] Cadbury Committee, *Draft Report* (1992) para. 5.12.

[67] Chartered Accountants Joint Ethics Committee, *Rotation of Audit Partners* (1993).

[68] See 'Treasury Expands Defences to Insider Dealing Charges', *Fin. Times*, 8 May 1993, p. 10; A. Alcock, 'Insider Dealing—How Did We Get Here?' (1994) 15 *Co. Law.* 67.

[69] Criminal Justice Act 1993, Pt. V (implementing Directive 89/592/EEC).

[70] See e.g. 'Crackdown Over Private Briefings for Analysts', *Fin. Times*, 15 May 1993, p. 1; 'Gartmore Seeks Insider Dealing Review', *Fin. Times*, 7 May 1993, p. 19; 'Calls Grow for Action on Insider Dealing', *Fin. Times*, 8 May 1993, p. 1.

[71] See 'Exchange Will Review Disclosure Guidelines', *Fin. Times*, 6 July 1993, p. 20; London Stock Exchange, *Guidance on the Dissemination of Price Sensitive Information* (1995).

insider dealing and institutional shareholders are normally discussed together in the context of the alleged ability of the latter to engage in the former. That matter is discussed in another chapter.[72]

xv. Election and Removal of Directors

Before discussing the issue of election and removal of directors, a very brief history should be given of the way in which UK institutions have exerted influence on board matters. First, for many years prior to the reconstitution of the ISC in 1988, UK institutions individually promoted their own (similar) views of best practice on matters such as board composition and structure.[73] This continued after the re-emergence of the ISC, but from 1991 the institutions were able to promulgate uniform standards: those set out in an ISC statement.[74] The ISC's *Statement on Directors* was then influential upon the recommendations of the Cadbury Committee.[75] Indeed, compliance by companies with the *Cadbury Code* is, for this reason, a measure—albeit an indirect one—of institutional influence in UK corporate governance. A further reason is that the Cadbury Committee expressly relied upon institutions to ensure compliance with the Code.[76]

Under the Table A articles of association, one-third of the company's directors must, by rotation, retire each year at the annual general meeting.[77] The retiring directors are eligible for re-election by an ordinary resolution of the shareholders. However, article 84 of Table A states that a 'managing director and a director holding any other executive office shall not be subject to retirement by rotation'.[78] The articles contained in Table A at the date of a company's registration apply automatically to a company limited by shares, to such extent that they are not excluded or modified by any articles registered by the company.[79] It is therefore possible for companies to make provision in their articles for all directors (executive as well as non-executive) to be required to seek periodic re-election by the

---

[72] See Ch. 9, Secs. B.4, B.8.

[73] See e.g. L. E. Linaker, 'The Institutional Investor—Investment from M&G's Viewpoint' in Prentice and Holland (n. 13 above), 107.

[74] ISC, *The Role and Duties of Directors—A Statement of Best Practice* (1991) (references below are to the second edition, 1993: cited hereafter as '*Statement on Directors*'). This is based upon a discussion document prepared by the ABI IC: ABI, *The Role and Duties of Directors—A Discussion Paper* (1990).

[75] The then chairman of the ISC, Mr Mike Sandland, was a member of the Cadbury Committee.

[76] *Cadbury Report*, para. 6.16. See Ch. 5, Sec. D.1.ii.

[77] Table A, arts. 73–80. Art. 73 specifies that all the directors shall retire at the first AGM. Note that Table A uses the terms 'appointment' and 'reappointment', rather than 'election' and 're-election'.

[78] See also Companies Act 1948, Sch. 1, art. 107 (the provision in the 'old' Table A).

[79] CA 1985, s. 8(2).

general meeting. Indeed, it is ISC policy that: 'One-third of the directors should be subject to retirement by rotation each year. They can stand for re-election if they so choose.'[80] A survey of 52 of the FT-SE 100 companies, conducted by PIRC in 1992, found that 27 had provisions in their articles whereby some or all of their *executive* directors were not required to retire by rotation, and hence not required to seek periodic re-election by the shareholders.[81] PIRC and the ICs of the ABI and NAPF all called for this 'insulation' of executive directors to be removed by alterations to the articles. It was reported during 1993–5 that several of the 27 companies identified in the PIRC survey were proposing changes to their articles so as to require retirement by rotation for all of their directors.[82]

The Companies Act provides the general meeting with the inalienable right to remove a director before the end of his or her period of office.[83] Neither the Companies Act nor the Table A articles confers upon *the board* a power of dismissal in relation to one of its number.[84] However, ISC policy is that '[t]he Articles should provide that a director may be dismissed from his or her office by written resolution of all co-directors (or at the very least a majority of 75% of co-directors) who should account to shareholders at the next general meeting for their course of action'.[85] This can be contrasted with the position in Australia, where the statute prohibits the removal of a director of a public company by 'any resolution, request or notice of the directors or any of them notwithstanding anything

---

[80] *Statement on Directors*, para. 3.2(a).

[81] Reported in 'Lack of Voting on Directors Attacked', *Fin. Times*, 18 May 1992, p. 11.

[82] 'Directors Size Up New Rules', *Fin. Times*, 10 Apr. 1993, p. 7; 'BA Proposes Changes to Boardroom Election Process', *Fin. Times*, 12 June 1993, p. 12; 'M&S Ends Chief's Insulation from Re-Election', *Fin. Times*, 29 June 1995, p. 18. Interestingly, the *Cadbury Report* did not recommend that all directors should be subject to periodic shareholder vote. Rather, it proceeded on the ill-founded assumption that directors are always subject to periodic endorsement by the shareholders: 'Shareholders are responsible for electing board members . . .' (para. 4.2); 'The formal relationship between the shareholders and the board of directors is that the shareholders elect the directors . . .' (para. 6.1). This is surprising given that the influential Confederation of British Industry (as well as PIRC) drew the matter to the Committee's attention: 'We . . . suggest that *all* directors, executive and non-executive, should be subject to retirement and re-election by rotation at intervals of not longer than 3 years.': CBI, *Response to the Draft Report of the Committee on the Financial Aspects of Corporate Governance* (1992) para. 24 (original emphasis). See Ch. 11, Sec. B.1.v, where there is a recommendation for the introduction of a stock exchange listing requirement that the articles of association of listed companies must require all directors to be subject to retirement and re-election by rotation.

[83] CA 1985, s. 303. Special notice (defined in s. 379) is required: s. 303(2). See also s. 304.

[84] Cf. *Samuel Tak Lee* v. *Chou Wen Hsien* [1984] 1 WLR 1202 (Privy Council upholding the use by directors of a Hong Kong company of a director-dismissal provision in the articles of the company).

[85] *Statement on Directors*, para. 3.2(d). See further Ch. 5, Sec. D.2.ii. (c).

in the articles or any agreement'.[86] Given that it is now recognized widely that an important function of the board is to monitor—and thus, by implication, to make any necessary changes to the composition of— the executive management (which includes executive *directors*),[87] the Australian provision is inappropriate.[88]

In practice, 'boardroom coups' occur not infrequently in the UK. Most often it is the top executive director (who may be the chairman/chief executive, the chief executive, or the executive chairman) who leaves the company as a result. The *substance* of most such incidents is that the director is dismissed from both executive and directorial positions by the board—even where the board concerned does not have a director-dismissal power. *Formally*, however, there is no exercise of any power by the board; the director tenders his or her resignation as a director and officer of the company (after informal pressure from other directors).[89]

xvi. Board Composition and Structure

As outlined above, the ISC's *Statement on Directors* was influential upon the recommendations of the Cadbury Committee. Regarding board composition, the *Cadbury Code* states that the board of a listed company 'should include non-executive directors of sufficient calibre and number for their views to carry significant weight in the board's decisions';[90] and that a majority of the non-executives should be 'independent'.[91] In order to meet the latter recommendation, together with another regarding audit committees, all boards should have a minimum of three non-executive members, two of whom should be independent.[92] Table 5.10 in Chapter 5 shows that the average board of a quoted UK *industrial* company had the minimum three non-executive members from at least 1982 until at least 1993. And Table 5.11 shows that quoted UK *financial* companies have for

---

[86] CL, s. 227(12).

[87] See Ch. 1, Sec. B; Ch. 5, Sec. D.2.ii.(a).

[88] See further Ch. 11, Sec. B.2.ii, where there is a recommendation for the repeal of the Australian provision, and for the introduction of a stock exchange listing requirement that the articles of association of listed companies must empower 75% of the board to dismiss any of its number.

[89] See Sir Adrian Cadbury, *The Company Chairman* (1990) 171–3. Very occasionally, the board needs to formally dismiss the director from executive office, and call a general meeting to remove him or her as a director (if there is no director-dismissal power in the articles): see e.g. 'George Walker Ousted Under Pressure from Banks', *Fin. Times*, 31 May 1991, p. 1. The 'management' article (e.g. Table A, art. 70) probably does not provide the board with power to dismiss one of its number: *Pulbrook* v. *Richmond Consolidated Mining Company* (1878) 9 Ch. D. 610, at 613.

[90] *Cadbury Code*, para. 1.3. This is almost identical to para. 4.5(a) of the ISC's *Statement on Directors*. [91] *Cadbury Code*, para. 2.2.

[92] *Cadbury Report*, para. 4.11.

many years had a majority of non-executive directors.[93] For the period 1993–4, the Monitoring Sub-Committee of the Cadbury Committee found that all or a majority of non-executive directors were independent in 92% of the top 100 listed UK companies.[94] However, the percentage of independent non-executives was smaller for medium-sized and small listed companies.[95]

With regard to board structure for listed companies, the Cadbury Committee recommended that (a) there should be a clearly accepted division of responsibilities at the head of a company, which will ensure a balance of power and authority, such that no one individual has unfettered powers of decision;[96] (b) there should be an audit committee composed solely of non-executive directors—with a minimum of three members and a majority of 'independent' members;[97] (c) there should be a remuneration committee made up wholly or mainly of non-executive directors, and chaired by a non-executive;[98] and (d) non-executive directors should be selected through a formal selection process, which should be a matter for the board as a whole[99] (but the Committee regarded it as 'good practice' for there to be a nomination committee composed of a majority of non-executive directors, and chaired by the chairman or a non-executive director, responsible for proposing new appointments to the board).[100] Recommendation (a) is discussed below. Recommendation (c) was replaced[101] in 1995 by the Greenbury Committee's recommendation that all listed companies should have a remuneration committee consisting 'exclusively of non-executive directors'.[102] The proportion of quoted UK industrial companies operating audit, remuneration, and nomination committees rose markedly between 1988 and 1993: in the case of audit committees, from 35% to 90%; in the case of remuneration committees,

---

[93] See also Cadbury Committee, *Compliance with the Code of Best Practice* (1995) 17, 29 (listed UK companies divided into groups according to size in terms of market capitalization, as at 1993–4, and percentage of companies which had three or more non-executive directors: companies ranked 1–100: 97%; companies ranked 101–250: 91%; companies ranked 500–750: 74%; companies ranked 1,251–550: 39%).   [94] Ibid., at 21, 30.

[95] Ibid. See also Ch. 5, at nn. 287–8 and accompanying text.

[96] *Cadbury Code*, para. 1.2. Whilst the *Cadbury Report* recognizes that the positions of chairman of the board and chief executive officer should 'in principle' be held by separate persons (para. 4.9), the *Code* does not recommend as much. It states merely that, where the roles are combined, 'it is essential that there should be a strong and independent element on the board, with a recognised senior member' (para. 1.2).

[97] *Cadbury Code*, para. 4.3; *Cadbury Report*, para. 4.35(b).

[98] *Cadbury Code*, para. 3.3; *Cadbury Report*, para. 4.42.

[99] *Cadbury Code*, para. 2.4.   [100] *Cadbury Report*, paras. 4.15, 4.30.

[101] See Study Group on Directors' Remuneration ('Greenbury Committee'), *Report* (1995) para. 4.2. The Greenbury Committee's *Report* and *Code of Best Practice* are referred to in the remainder of the book as the *Greenbury Report* and *Greenbury Code*.

[102] *Greenbury Code*, para. A4; *Greenbury Report*, para. 4.8.

from 54% to 94%; and in the case of nomination committees, from 10% to 39%.[103]

As regards (a), about 57% of quoted UK industrial companies separated the roles of chairman and chief executive in 1988, but some 77% did so in 1993.[104] This apparent structural improvement has served to disguise a potentially serious flaw in accountability at the head of quoted UK companies. In many instances where the roles have been split in the light of ISC and/or Cadbury Committee recommendations,[105] the person previously occupying the roles of chairman and chief executive has remained as an executive chairman whilst a new chief executive has been appointed. Indeed, the practice of having an executive chairman and a separate chief executive is not new, although it seems to have grown in popularity. A study by the author of a sample of the top 100 listed UK companies at 31 December 1971, 31 December 1981, and 31 December 1991 found that the proportion of companies with the specified types of structure was as follows: a combined chairman/chief executive: 55% (1971), 47% (1981), 34% (1991); a full-time chairman and a separate chief executive: 17% (1971), 27% (1981), 39% (1991); a part-time chairman and a separate chief executive: 28% (1971), 26% (1981), 27% (1991).[106]

However, the rationale behind having separate persons for these two jobs is that the chairman's role is leader of the board of directors—a primary function of which is to 'monitor the executive management'.[107] The inherent problem with a combined chairman/chief executive is that the chairman, who is supposed to lead the board in ensuring the accountability of executive management, is a member of the executive management. This problem does not disappear if there is an executive chairman and a separate chief executive. In such cases, the reality is often that the executive chairman is the top executive in the company (i.e. effectively the chief executive), and the 'chief executive' is effectively what is known

---

[103] M. J. Conyon, 'Corporate Governance Changes in UK Companies Between 1988 and 1993' (1994) 2 *Corp. Gov.: Inter. Rev.* 97, at 103–5. See also Cadbury Committee (n. 93 above), at 18–20.

[104] Conyon, ibid., at 101. See also Cadbury Committee, ibid., at 16.

[105] Institutional pressure has clearly led to many of these instances: 'Of Hats and Heads', *Fin. Times*, 5 Feb. 1993, p. 10; 'Institutional Concern Over a Top Banker's Dual Role', *Fin. Times*, 6 Aug. 1992, p. 19.

[106] This was part of Study C, described in Ch. 5, Sec. D.2.i, and App. J. These results are consistent with those cited in A. Sampson, *The New Anatomy of Britain* (1971) 600–1 (for the top 200 listed UK companies in 1970); Korn/Ferry International, *Boards of Directors Study* (1980) 8 (for a sample of the top 1000 (quoted and unquoted) UK industrial companies in 1979); and Korn/Ferry International, *Boards of Directors Study UK* (1988) 19 (for a sample of the top 1000 (quoted and unquoted) UK industrial companies in 1987).

[107] *Cadbury Code*, para. 1.1.

in the US as a chief operating officer.[108] In his treatise on the role of the chairman, Sir Adrian Cadbury says: 'It is a great help to the chairman to be able to meet with the independent directors from time to time, with or without the chief executive. . . . Then there are matters concerning the top executives of the company, which the chairman can only discuss with his outside colleagues.'[109] An executive chairman might well meet with non-executive directors to discuss concerns about the 'chief executive'—and there are recent examples of this.[110] But, since the executive chairman is more often than not the real top executive, with whom do the non-executives meet to discuss concerns about the executive chairman? The *Cadbury Code* says that, where the chairman is also the chief executive, there should be 'a recognised senior member' amongst the independent non-executive directors.[111] On the reasoning set out above, there should be a recognized senior non-executive even where there is a separate chairman and chief executive, if the chairman is an executive director. Better still, consideration should be given to paying more than lip-service to the importance of the chairman's role as leader of the board of directors. That would entail ensuring that the chairman was not a full-time officer of the company, reliant upon it for his or her livelihood; and prohibiting the chairman from participating in executive share schemes (as is the usual case for non-executive directors).[112] In summary, for those companies which have an executive chairman and a separate chief executive, a preferable structure would be that shown at the top of page 73.

Companies which have a single chairman/chief executive could adopt the preferred structure by appointing their existing 'recognized senior non-executive' (which they are required to have by virtue of the *Cadbury Code*) to the position of chairman, and leaving the existing chairman/chief executive as chief executive. Under this structure, the position of 'chief executive' would, in substance as well as in name, be the top

---

[108] The executive chairman is commonly the highest-paid director. In a minority of cases the executive chairman is second in command to the chief executive: Korn/Ferry International, *Boards of Directors Study UK* (1993) 18.

[109] Cadbury (n. 89 above), at 114.

[110] There have been several cases where the 'chief executive' has left the company after disagreements with the executive chairman: see e.g. 'Glaxo's Bitter Pill', *Sunday Times*, 14 Mar. 1993, sec. 3, p. 3; 'Tate & Lyle Chief Executive Leaves After 11 Months', *Fin. Times*, 2 Mar. 1993, p. 19; 'British Steel Denies Rift as Chief Executive Resigns', *Fin. Times*, 21 May 1991, p. 19. The substance of such cases is surely that the executive chairman sacked a subordinate executive.

[111] *Cadbury Code*, para. 1.2. The wording used in the Cadbury Committee's *Draft Report* (para. 4.6) and *Draft Code* (para. 1.2) was 'an appointed leader'; this was moderated after criticism from the Confederation of British Industry, and others.

[112] See *Cadbury Report*, para. 4.13.

EXISTING	PREFERRED
Senior Non-Executive Director	Independent Part-time Chairman
Executive Chairman	Chief Executive
Chief Executive	Chief Operating officer (or Divisional Heads)[a]

[a]The role of chief operating officer could be incorporated into that of chief executive (as it is in many medium-sized and small quoted UK companies), with the divisional heads reporting directly to the chief executive.

executive position in the company, and the position of chairman would in substance be the independent leader of the board of directors.[113]

xvii. Executive Remuneration and Service Contracts

The issue of executive remuneration came to a head in the UK in the period from late 1994 until mid-1995. The announcement that the chief executive of British Gas plc, a privatized utility, had received a 75% pay rise and a substantial package of share options, whilst junior staff suffered wage cuts,[114] led to a political uproar,[115] a focusing of the public's attention upon executive remuneration (especially at privatized utility companies),[116] and the formation of the Greenbury Committee.[117] Against this backdrop, the Greenbury Committee handed down a report which seemingly was quite radical. As demonstrated below, however, several of the key elements of the *Greenbury Code* had actually been on the agenda of institutional shareholders for some time. In addition, both the ABI and the NAPF were represented on the Greenbury Committee.

One important point should be noted before examining the aspects of executive remuneration with which institutional investors have been concerned. The 1994–5 debate about executive remuneration at the privatized utilities was, for a majority of UK-based fund managers,

---

[113] It is recognized that, even with the 'best' structures, things can go wrong; and that there have been many very successful companies where the roles of chairman and chief executive have been combined. See further Ch. 11, Sec. B.2.i.

[114] See 'Cabinet Will Seek City Advice on Defusing Executive Pay Row', *Fin. Times*, 17 Dec. 1994, p. 1.

[115] See 'Labour Steps Up Campaign Over Utility Chiefs' Pay', *Times*, 7 Jan. 1995; 'Major Set to Tackle Executive Pay Deals', *Daily Tel.*, 1 Mar. 1995, p. 1.

[116] See 'The Great Utility Scandal', *Times*, 8 Feb. 1995, p. 16.

[117] The terms of reference of the Greenbury Committee were '[t]o identify good practice in determining Directors' remuneration and prepare a Code of such practice for use by UK PLCs': *Greenbury Report*, para. 1.2.

essentially an ethical or political matter. It is mentioned in Section A.2, below, that most UK-based fund managers have traditionally lacked interest in ethical and political issues affecting the corporate sector generally. That this is a case in point is demonstrated by the significant support given by institutional shareholders to the board and management of British Gas plc at its 1995 AGM. Two resolutions (one initiated by PIRC and one initiated by a private shareholder), which criticized the company's policy on executive remuneration, were defeated overwhelmingly when a poll was taken.[118]

The issue of executive remuneration is one in which UK institutions have been interested for many years. The absolute level of executive remuneration, *per se*, has not generally been a concern of institutions.[119] Rather, institutional policies have attempted to ensure that (a) executives' compensation packages are not determined by executives; (b) share incentive schemes reward executives only for improvement in the company's financial performance, and do not involve excessive dilution of the stakes of existing shareholders; and (c) executives removed for poor performance are not 'rewarded for failure'. The reduction of agency costs[120] is clearly at the heart of this issue.

In relation to (a), institutions have supported the establishment of remuneration committees made up solely or mainly of non-executive directors.[121] Regarding (b), guidelines on executive share schemes were introduced first by the predecessor of the ABI IC in the 1960s, and by the NAPF Investment Protection Committee in 1971. The NAPF IC's detailed guidelines ceased to operate from mid-1993, when the ABI and NAPF ICs released a joint statement on the elements normally required in an executive share scheme before the scheme will obtain the approval of ABI and NAPF members.[122] The two basic elements are that (i) the board has a properly constituted remuneration committee which is responsible for the scheme; and (ii) the exercise of executive share options should be subject to 'significant and sustained improvement in the underlying financial

---

[118] See 'British Gas Board Bruised on Pay But Wins the Day', *Fin. Times*, 1 June 1995, p. 1; House of Commons Employment Committee, *Third Report: The Remuneration of Directors and Chief Executives of Privatised Utilities* (1995) para. 23, n. 85 (just over 50% of the issued shares were voted; of the shares voted, 16.9% supported and 83.1% opposed PIRC's resolution, whilst 9.8% supported and 90.2% opposed the private shareholder's resolution). An issue arose of the accountability of the fund managers: see Ch. 9, at n. 166.

[119] This has, however, surfaced on the odd occasion as a company-specific concern: see n. 139 below, and accompanying text.　　　　　　　　　[120] See Ch. 1, Secs. C, D.

[121] See discussion under Sec. A.1.xvi, above.

[122] See ABI and NAPF, *Share Scheme Guidance* (1993). Employee share schemes involving the issue of new shares (as opposed to those in which shares are acquired in the market) require approval by ordinary resolution in the general meeting: *Listing Rules*, para. 13.13 (see also para. 11.7(d)). See also *Greenbury Code*, para. B12.

performance'[123] of the company, in accordance with criteria determined by the remuneration committee and disclosed to shareholders.[124] The ABI IC still maintains more specific guidelines which deal mostly with the maximum acceptable amount of share capital that may be issued under share option and profit-sharing incentive schemes.[125] Regarding (c), institutions have during the 1990s expressed varying degrees of opposition to long-term rolling contracts of service.[126] Most prominent has been the stance of PosTel Investment Management Ltd. (known now as Hermes), which advocated strongly a maximum length of one year for rolling contracts, and then in 1994 began voting against the re-election of directors employed on rolling contracts with terms in excess of two years.[127] The NAPF IC made an unsuccessful recommendation to the Cadbury Committee that rolling service contracts should not exceed one year, and in late 1994 a considerable number of its members would appear to have been supporting the voting stance adopted by PosTel.[128] The views of the NAPF and PosTel, and other institutions, would appear to have influenced the Greenbury Committee. The *Greenbury Code* states that there is a 'strong case' for a maximum term of one year for rolling service contracts, and that the remuneration committee's annual report to shareholders

---

[123] UK empirical studies demonstrate reason for concern about the link between executive remuneration and corporate performance: see M. J. Conyon, P. Gregg, and S. Machin, 'Taking Care of Business: Executive Compensation in the UK' (1995) 105 *Econ. J* 704, and the studies cited therein.

[124] See also *Greenbury Code*, paras. C6–C10; *Greenbury Report*, paras. 6.23–6.40.

[125] See ABI IC, *Share Option and Profit Sharing Incentive Schemes: Guidelines to Requirements of Insurance Offices as Investors* (1987) (as amended).

[126] An x-year rolling contract is one under which the executive concerned has x years of her or his term to run at any time, such that dismissal (other than for fraud, etc.) entitles the executive to an amount equal to x years' remuneration as compensation for breach of contract (ignoring mitigation for the moment). CA 1985, s. 319 permits directors' service contracts with terms of up to five years, without shareholder approval. The *Cadbury Report*, para. 4.41, recommended that s. 319 be amended to reduce the maximum term to three years. Three-year rolling contracts were enjoyed by executive directors of 44 of the top 100 listed UK companies at Aug. 1994, but more than a dozen FT-SE 100 companies at that time had changed, or were planning to change, their directors to shorter contracts: see 'Cut the Strings on the Parachute', *Fin. Times*, 17 Aug. 1994, p. 13.

[127] See 'PosTel Draws Line on Contracts', *Fin. Times*, 25 June 1994, p. 24.

[128] See NAPF, *Investment Committee Briefing—December 1994: Directors' Service Contracts* (1994). Other institutions and institutional trade associations have also criticized three-year rolling contracts: see 'Ifma Attacks Long-Term Contracts for Directors', *Fin. Times*, 10 June 1993, p. 9. In 1993, senior executives of several listed insurance companies had three-year rolling service contracts, which may explain the refusal of the ABI IC to add its voice to the lobby against such contracts: see 'Directors Cool to Plea on Contracts', *Fin. Times*, 14 June 1993, p. 8. (On this type of conflict of interest, see further Ch. 10, Sec. B.2.i.) The ABI IC urged instead that remuneration committees should review annually whether existing service contracts were appropriate, and be tougher in negotiating the pay-offs for dismissed executives: see ABI, *Long Term Remuneration for Senior Executives* (1994) 3–4.

should disclose and explain the reasons for any 'service contracts which provide for, or imply, notice periods in excess of one year'.[129]

xviii. Regulations Affecting General Meetings

In 1991 the NAPF IC urged companies to ensure that their articles of association provided for at least 21 days notice of extraordinary general meetings ('EGMs').[130] This request was made in the light of reports of practical difficulties faced by some investment managers in attempting to vote their UK equity investments.[131] PIRC has made several recommendations for substantial changes to the procedures governing general meetings. Proposals include a reduction in the threshold for the proposing of shareholders' resolutions, and abolition of voting by a show of hands.[132] There does not, however, appear to be any evidence of widespread institutional support for these proposals.[133]

2. ETHICAL AND POLITICAL

Most UK-based fund-management firms have taken little or no interest in ethical and political issues which affect numerous companies. A lack of advice from City investment managers on ethical issues was, in fact, one of the primary reasons behind the founding of PIRC by a group of local-authority pension schemes in the mid-1980s. As well as involving itself in company-specific ethical matters (see Section B, below), PIRC has taken action in relation to ethical and political matters which concern a range of companies. For example, in 1992 it conducted research into, and subsequently publicized, the prevalence of political donations by listed UK companies. It then began a campaign urging companies to refrain from making political donations without shareholder approval.[134] In 1995 PIRC conducted research into, and then publicized, the extent to which non-

---

[129] *Greenbury Code*, paras. B10, D2.
[130] See 'Pension Funds Attacked Over Failure to Vote', *Fin. Times*, 2 Mar. 1991, p. 7. The minimum notice period for EGMs is 14 days: CA 1985, s. 369(1) (and Table A requires at least 14 days: art. 38).
[131] See Ch. 5, Sec. B.1.iii. See also Ch. 11, Sec. B.1.iv, for a recommendation similar to that of the NAPF.
[132] PIRC, *Submission to the Committee on the Financial Aspects of Corporate Governance* (1992) 8–10.
[133] The Cadbury Committee left open the matter of a loosening of the rules governing shareholder resolutions: see *Cadbury Report*, para. 6.4.
[134] See 'Political Payments', *Pensions Mgt.*, May 1992, p. 6; 'Donations Come Under Scrutiny', *Sunday Tel.*, 7 May 1995, City & Bus. sec., p. 6. Note that the GMB trade union announced in mid-1995 that it would commence a legal action (a 'test case') against a company in which GMB held shares, alleging that the company's political donations were made *ultra vires*: see 'Companies Challenged on Political Gifts', *Fin. Times*, 5 June 1995, p. 6.

executive directors of the top 250 listed UK companies held multiple directorships.[135]

Some charities, local authorities (in respect of their pension funds), religious bodies, and educational institutions have ethical policies which their fund managers are required to observe. The most common action taken in relation to such ethical principles is, however, to sell or refrain from buying the shares of 'unethical' companies,[136] rather than to try to change things from the inside.

B. COMPANY-SPECIFIC ISSUES

UK institutions have become involved in a wide range of company-specific issues at their portfolio companies. The most important for current purposes is sub-optimal performance by a company's senior management.[137] The actions which institutions have taken in relation to this issue, and the other company-specific and procedural/general issues with which they have been concerned, are examined in the next chapter. Other company-specific issues with which some UK institutions have become involved include: strong suspicion of impropriety on the part of a company's senior management; deliberate misrepresentations by senior management as to the state of a company's financial health; a proposed major deal, the terms of which were seen as unduly generous to the company's chairman;[138] proposed remuneration packages under which the top executive, who had in each case presided over a very unsuccessful period in terms of shareholder returns, stood to receive millions of pounds over a handful of years;[139] the proposed re-engagement by a fast-growth company of a firm of auditors which had audited a number of other fast-growth companies which had collapsed in the recent past;[140] allegations of a 'dirty tricks' campaign by a quoted airline company against another

---

[135] See 'Non-executive Directors Come Under Fire', *Fin. Times*, 12 June 1995, p. 11.

[136] See Ethical Investment Research Service, *Attitudes to Ethical Investment* (1993) 11. In the case of pension funds, charity funds, and other trusts, this approach is fraught with danger: see *Cowan* v. *Scargill* [1985] Ch. 270; *Harries* v. *The Church Commissioners for England* [1992] 1 WLR 1241.

[137] See e.g. 'Corporate Assassins', *Sunday Tel.*, 17 Oct. 1993, City & Bus. sec., p. 5.

[138] See 'British Land Scraps Restructuring', *Fin. Times*, 21 Dec. 1989, p. 15.

[139] See 'Saatchi Doesn't Work', *Fin. Times*, 14 Jan. 1995, p. 6; ' "Five-year £35m" Package for WPP Chief is Attacked', *Fin. Times*, 17 June 1995, p. 1; 'Shareholders Force WPP to Modify Chief's Pay Package', *Fin. Times*, 22 June 1995, p. 1; 'Sorrell Backdown Appeases Rebels', *Fin. Times*, 23 June 1995, p. 19; 'Sorrell Wins £28m Deal But 26pc Vote Against', *Guardian*, 27 June 1995, p. 17.

[140] See 'City Forces Sacking of Stoy Hayward', *Fin. Times*, 9 Apr. 1991, p. 26.

airline;[141] proposed alterations to a company's articles of association to restrict shareholders' rights at general meetings;[142] the extraction of peat by a pharmaceuticals and horticultural company within a particular county, which attracted the opposition of the local council's pension fund; and the tardiness of the management of Distillers Company Ltd. in reaching agreement with thalidomide victims on compensation terms.[143]

C. CONCLUSION

Although many company-specific matters have been the subject of institutional interest, the most significant for current purposes is the sub-optimal performance of senior management. That matter aside, the impact of institutional shareholders upon the affairs of quoted UK companies has probably been greatest in relation to procedural and general, rather than company-specific, issues. UK institutions have been involved in a wide range of procedural and general issues which concern, directly or indirectly, corporate governance and shareholder interests. These issues invariably possess some or all of the same important features: (a) they are reasonably uncomplicated; (b) they exist in, or have the potential to arise at, a large number of companies; and (c) they can be addressed relatively easily and inexpensively across a wide range of companies.

---

[141] See 'BA Shareholders Concerned at Combined Top Jobs', *Fin. Times*, 20 Jan. 1993, p. 21.
[142] See 'Hanson Power Provokes Concern', *Fin. Times*, 10 June 1993, p. 21; 'Hanson Softens on Voting Rights', *Fin. Times*, 14 June 1993, p. 18; 'Hanson Backs Down Over Proposed Rule Changes', *Fin. Times*, 18 June 1993, p. 17.
[143] See '£12m.–£20m. Thalidomide Offer Likely', *Times*, 5 Jan. 1973, p. 1.

5
Manner of Involvement in the UK

Having now analysed the various areas of corporate affairs with which the institutions have been concerned, the purpose of this chapter is to describe in more detail the actual manner in which the institutions have monitored their portfolio companies. The institutions' manner of participation can be broken down into four types, although each type possesses the same two variables. The first and second categories are 'direct' methods of monitoring, in that it is the institutions themselves[1] that carry out the action(s). The third and fourth categories are 'indirect' methods of monitoring, in that the institutions act through proxies—either collective-action vehicles such as the Institutional Shareholders' Committee, or non-executive directors on portfolio companies' boards. One variable is, therefore, the party that performs the monitoring actions.

The other variable is the target of the monitoring actions. The first and third types of monitoring comprise acts directed at all companies or at a certain category of company, rather than at any particular company ('industry-wide monitoring'). The second and fourth types of monitoring, in contrast, consist of actions undertaken at or in relation to an individual company ('firm-level monitoring'). Industry-wide monitoring consists generally of the devising and promulgating of some kind of recommended practice. It extends to the lobbying of government, the Stock Exchange, and other regulatory bodies for the introduction of new laws and/or regulations and the reform of existing ones. Firm-level monitoring takes a much wider range of forms, including the exercise by institutions of the voting rights attached to their equity holdings; periodic meetings between institutions and company managements; the appraisal of company managements by shareholder-elected non-executive directors; and the attempted replacement of an under-performing management team by a coalition of institutional shareholders.

Combining the two possible types of executant with the two possible targets of institutional activism, the four permutations of the manner in which institutional monitoring takes place are thus (a) direct industry-wide monitoring; (b) direct firm-level monitoring; (c) indirect industry-wide monitoring; and (d) indirect firm-level monitoring. The four sections of this chapter reflect this division.

---

[1] Fund-management firms are included, with the four traditional institutions, as 'institutions' for the purpose of this classification.

Table 5.1 Summary of areas and manner of institutional monitoring

Manner and Area of Monitoring	Procedural & General issues	Company-specific issues
Direct industry-wide	●	
Direct firm-level	●	●
Indirect industry-wide	●	●
Indirect firm-level	●	●

The various areas of institutional involvement discussed in Chapter 4 were grouped as concerning either procedural and general issues or company-specific issues. By definition, all industry-wide monitoring must relate to procedural or general issues rather than company-specific issues. On the other hand, firm-level monitoring may concern a matter peculiar to the company in question (a company-specific issue), or it may involve some kind of specific action in relation to a procedural or general matter.

A. DIRECT INDUSTRY-WIDE MONITORING

Although the vast majority of industry-wide monitoring has been *indirect* (in that it has been undertaken by collective-action bodies acting on behalf of institutional shareholders), a handful of institutions have (individually) conducted industry-wide actions. Bearing in mind that industry-wide monitoring typically comprises the formulation and promulgation by a body of its views on best practice in a particular area, the following are some examples of individual institutions undertaking this task personally.

(i) Disclosure of corporate-treasury policy. Mr Hugh Jenkins, the chief executive of Prudential Portfolio Managers Ltd., proposed in 1992 a number of improvements in the way that companies' treasury-management activities are disclosed and controlled.[2] His proposals led to the establishment of a working party which was to determine the appropriate level of disclosure of such activities.

(ii) Directors' service contracts. Mr Alastair Ross Goobey, the chief executive of PosTel Investment Management Ltd. (known now as Hermes), wrote a letter to the chairmen of all of the FT-SE 100 companies in June 1993, setting out his institution's policy on the length and form of executive directors' service contracts.[3] Although the letter went to 'just'

---

[2] See Ch. 4, Sec. A.1.x, for a full description.
[3] See Ch. 4, Sec. A.1.xvii, for a full description.

100 companies, it received enormous publicity, and PosTel's policy was thereby made known to virtually all listed UK companies. An indication of the reach of Mr Ross Goobey's initial action was that an FT-SE Mid 250 company shortly afterwards employed a new chief executive on a service contract complying with PosTel's policy: 'We are abiding by the wishes of PosTel', said the company's chairman.[4]

Other fund managers have also made public calls on the topic of executive service contracts. Gartmore Investment Management plc expressed publicly in 1993 its opposition to three-year rolling contracts. Mr Paddy Linaker, both in his capacity as managing director of M&G Group plc and as chairman of IFMA, often expressed disfavour with lengthy contracts.[5] Mr Dick Barfield, chief investment manager of The Standard Life Assurance Company, proposed greater disclosure of the contents of service contracts in the annual report.[6]

(iii) Insider dealing. Mr Paul Myners, chairman of Gartmore Investment Management plc, in May 1993 criticized the thoroughness of past investigations of possible cases of insider dealing in the UK. He called for a radical review of the entire investigatory process.[7] The attendant publicity resulted in supportive statements from other fund managers.[8]

Another way in which individual institutions have engaged in industry-wide monitoring has been through their senior executives sitting on government and private-sector committees, and on the boards of less transient bodies,[9] reviewing matters related to corporate governance. Fund managers on such committees are commonly there in their capacity as, for example, chairman of the ISC or of the Investment Committee of the ABI.[10] In this case, their involvement is properly classified as *indirect* industry-wide monitoring—since they represent the relevant collective-action vehicle. However, senior investment managers are sometimes appointed to committees in their capacity as such.[11] Indeed, as long ago as 1962 it was reported that Mr Leslie Brown, who was then the Prudential's

---

[4] 'Booker Meets Postel Concern on Pay-Offs', *Fin. Times*, 18 June 1993, p. 17.

[5] See e.g. L. E. Linaker, 'The Institutional Investor—Investment from M&G's Viewpoint' in D. D. Prentice and P. R. J. Holland (eds.), *Contemporary Issues in Corporate Governance* (1993) 107, at 110.

[6] 'Shareholders Wage War', *Fin. Times*, 6 Nov. 1991, p. 14.

[7] See 'Letters to the Editor', *Fin. Times*, 7 May 1993, p. 16.

[8] 'Calls Grow for Action on Insider Dealing', *Fin. Times*, 8 May 1993, p. 1.

[9] e.g. Mr Huw Jones, Corporate Finance Director of Prudential Portfolio Managers Ltd., became a member of the ASB in Aug. 1994. See also Ch. 4, Sec. A.1.ix.

[10] e.g. Mr Mike Sandland, chairman of the ISC, was a member of the Cadbury Committee; the chairmen of the ABI and NAPF ICs were members of The Pre-emption Group (see Ch. 4, Sec. A.1.i).

[11] e.g. the CBI City/Industry Task Force (which issued the report *Investing for Britain's Future* (1987)) had senior executives from five institutional investors amongst its membership.

chief investment manager, had 'been one of the most active members of the Jenkins Committee on Company Law'.[12] In these cases, their involvement should be regarded as *direct* industry-wide monitoring. Of course, one of the ways in which an individual institution can promulgate its views on matters of corporate governance is by making submissions to these inquiries—and some institutions have done this—although it is clear that most fund managers prefer to leave it to the ABI, NAPF, IFMA, and LIBA to make such submissions.

B. DIRECT FIRM-LEVEL MONITORING

This important section examines the ways in which the institutions have monitored the managers of individual UK companies. Most of the methods of firm-level monitoring can be categorized as (a) actions performed regularly; or (b) actions effected only in extraordinary circumstances. These are addressed in Sections B.2 and B.3, respectively. The exercise by institutions of the voting rights attached to their ordinary shareholdings is discussed separately, in Section B.1, because voting is a form of monitoring which some institutions perform regularly and others perform only in exceptional situations.

1. EXERCISE OF VOTING RIGHTS

The right to vote which is attached to the ordinary shares of most quoted UK companies is a central element of the Anglo-Saxon system of corporate governance. The vast majority of quoted UK companies have only one class of ordinary shares, with each ordinary share carrying one vote on a poll at a general meeting of the company.[13] There are, of course, two types of general meetings: (a) the annual general meeting ('AGM'); and (b) all other general meetings—known commonly as extraordinary general meetings ('EGMs').[14] This subsection deals with the exercise of voting rights by institutions at both AGMs and EGMs.

---

[12] A. Sampson, *The Anatomy of Britain* (1962) 408.

[13] In most companies, this is prescribed in the articles of association, memorandum of association, or the terms on which the ordinary shares were issued. There is nevertheless a presumption of one vote per share on a poll: Table A, art. 54; CA 1985, s. 370(6). Non-voting and restricted-voting ordinary shares do exist, although they are rare, and becoming rarer—largely due to the institutions' opposition to them: see Ch. 4, Sec. A.1.ii. Preference shares also usually carry voting rights. Those voting rights are, however, restricted almost invariably to meetings which affect the rights of the preference shareholders. The present discussion relates, therefore, to the exercise of voting rights by the owners—or controllers—of ordinary shares.   [14] See e.g. Table A, art. 36.

Under the nexus-of-contracts model of the company,[15] '[v]oting exists in corporations because someone must have the residual power to act (or delegate) when contracts are not complete'.[16] That someone is the body of ordinary shareholders because they 'are the residual claimants to the firm's income. . . . The gains from abnormally good or bad performance are the lot of the shareholders, whose claims stand last in line.'[17]

The exercise—or rather the apparent non-exercise—of voting rights by institutional shareholders has been a matter of concern in some quarters over recent years.[18] One object of this section is to present, through empirical evidence, a picture of the extent of voting by institutional shareholders up until 1993. The other main object of this section is to bring to light some practical difficulties which can inhibit the exercise of voting rights by fund managers. Before those two issues are addressed, a couple of preliminary matters are dealt with. First, there is a brief review of the matters which the UK regulatory system requires to be put to a shareholder vote. Secondly, there is an examination of an argument that pension-fund trustees and their fund managers have a legal obligation to exercise the voting rights attached to their funds' equity investments.

i. Matters on which Shareholders are Entitled to Vote

It has already been mentioned that under the standard articles of association the general meeting of shareholders has very little power to interfere with the directors' and executives' day-to-day exercise of managerial powers.[19] There are, however, numerous matters which, to be effected, require shareholder approval.[20] These matters can be construed as things which either the Companies Act, the company's articles, the London Stock Exchange, or the general law deems to be more appropriate for determination by the shareholders rather than the directors.

Things which the shareholders have the power to effect or which, from a

---

[15] See M. C. Jensen and W. H. Meckling, 'Theory of the Firm: Managerial Behavior, Agency Costs and Ownership Structure' (1976) 3 *J Fin. Econ.* 305, at 310–11.

[16] F. H. Easterbrook and D. R. Fischel, 'Voting in Corporate Law' (1983) 26 *J Law & Econ.* 395, at 403.

[17] Ibid. This analysis incorporates situations where ordinary shareholders lose their position of ultimate control (for instance, where the company becomes insolvent): 'The right to vote . . . follows the residual claim. . . . When the firm is insolvent, the bondholders and other creditors eventually acquire control [through the terms of debt agreements and insolvency legislation]': ibid., at 404.

[18] See e.g. Sir Francis Tombs, 'The Inter-relationship Between Institutional Investors, the Company in which they Invest, and Company Management' in NAPF, *Creative Tension?* (1990) 79, at 83. [19] See Ch. 1, Sec. B.

[20] There are several kinds of approval which may be required where a public company is concerned: an ordinary, extraordinary, or special resolution of all or a class of shareholders who cast a vote.

different perspective, require shareholder approval, include:[21] (i) alteration of the memorandum and articles of association;[22] (ii) changing of the
company's name;[23] (iii) certain alterations to the capital structure;[24] (iv)
purchase by the company of its own shares;[25] (v) allotment of shares;[26]
(vi) disapplication of the statutory pre-emption right;[27] (vii) declaration of
a dividend, after a recommendation by the board;[28] (viii) determination of
the number of directors;[29] (ix) re-election of directors;[30] (x) removal
of directors;[31] (xi) appointment, remuneration, and removal of the
auditors;[32] (xii) determination of the directors' remuneration;[33] (xiii)
gratuitous payments to directors on loss of office;[34] (xiv) directors' service
contracts with a term exceeding five years;[35] (xv) 'substantial property
transactions' between directors or their associates and the company;[36] (xvi)
transactions between the company and parties related thereto;[37]
(xvii) transactions which involve the acquisition or disposal of assets worth
25% or more of the company's net assets (or a similar criterion);[38]
(xviii) employee share schemes involving the issue of new shares;[39] (xix)
reconstructions and schemes of arrangement;[40] and (xx) a voluntary
winding up.[41] The general meeting is also able (xxi) to ratify certain
breaches of directors' duties;[42] (xxii) by *special* resolution, to issue
directions to the board regarding the management of the business of the
company;[43] (xxiii) to exercise a residual power of management where
the board is deadlocked or unable to act;[44] and (xxiv) *arguably*, to resolve

---

[21] Several of these examples presume that the Table A articles of association apply. See
CA 1985, s. 8(2).   [22] CA 1985, ss. 4, 9, 17.   [23] CA 1985, s. 28(1).
[24] CA 1985, ss. 121, 135.   [25] CA 1985, ss. 164, 166.   [26] CA 1985, s. 80.
[27] CA 1985, s. 95; *Listing Rules*, para. 9.20.
[28] Table A, art. 102. Art. 103 leaves interim dividends within the preserve of the directors.
[29] Table A, art. 64.
[30] Table A, arts. 73–80. But see Ch. 4, Sec. A.1.xv.
[31] CA 1985, s. 303.   [32] CA 1985, ss. 385(2), 390A(1), 391(1).
[33] Table A, art. 82; cf. art. 84, which gives the board the power to determine the
remuneration of the executive directors.   [34] CA 1985, ss. 312–13.
[35] CA 1985, s. 319.   [36] CA 1985, s. 320.   [37] *Listing Rules*, ch. 11.
[38] *Listing Rules*, para. 10.37 ('Super Class 1 transactions'). See Sec. B.3.vii.(b), below.
[39] *Listing Rules*, para. 13.13. See also *Greenbury Code*, para. B12: 'Shareholders should be
invited specifically to approve all new long-term incentive schemes (including share option
schemes) whether payable in cash or shares in which Directors and senior executives will
participate which potentially commit shareholders' funds over more than one year or dilute
the equity.' The Greenbury Committee recommended that the London Stock Exchange
should require listed companies to comply with this provision, amongst others: see *Greenbury
Report*, para. 2.4.
[40] Insolvency Act 1986, s. 110; CA 1985, ss. 425–7A, sch. 15B.
[41] Insolvency Act 1986, s. 84(1).
[42] See e.g. *Regal (Hastings) Ltd.* v. *Gulliver* [1967] 2 AC 134; *Bamford* v. *Bamford* [1970]
Ch. 212.
[43] Table A, art. 70.
[44] *Barron* v. *Potter* [1914] 1 Ch. 895; *Foster* v. *Foster* [1916] 1 Ch. 532.

that the company commence litigation against the directors.[45] Finally, it is common for a resolution to be proposed that the accounts and directors' and auditors' reports be received and adopted, even though there is no requirement for this to occur.[46]

Chapter 4 shows that, in regard to (iv), (vi), and (xviii), institutional shareholders have in fact bolstered the provisions of the Companies Act and/or *Listing Rules* with their own more restrictive requirements—by which all listed UK companies have, in practice, abided. Chapter 4 also shows that there have also been moves by some institutions and institutional collective-action bodies to impose extra requirements in relation to matters (ix) and (xiv).

When resolutions concerning the great majority of the above matters are proposed at general meetings of quoted companies, they are management- or board-initiated proposals, for which requisite shareholder support is being sought. Shareholder-initiated resolutions are, however, also a possibility.[47] These can be proposed for adoption at the AGM[48] (which occurs only very rarely in quoted companies), or a shareholder or group of shareholders representing at least 10% of the paid-up voting capital can requisition the directors to convene an EGM to consider the proposal(s).[49] The latter option has occasionally been utilized where a small group of institutional shareholders has been attempting to remove a director or directors of a quoted company. It has tended to be a tactic of last resort but, when attempted, it has usually been successful.[50]

ii. Do Pension-Fund Trustees have a Duty to Vote?

The Companies Act, and the constitutional documents of probably every UK public company do not actually *require* the holders of voting shares to exercise their votes. It has been argued, however, that the trustees of a pension scheme have a legal obligation to take an interest in the way in

---

[45] On the basis that, where the directors themselves are implicated in the alleged wrongdoing, there is no board in existence capable of determining whether or not to litigate: L. S. Sealy, *Cases and Materials in Company Law* (5th edn., 1992) 462; *Foster* v. *Foster* [1916] 1 Ch. 532; cf. *Breckland Group Holdings Ltd.* v. *London & Suffolk Properties Ltd.* [1989] BCLC 100.

[46] CA 1985, s. 241(1) merely requires that a copy of the balance sheet, profit and loss account, directors' report, and auditors' report must be laid before the general meeting.

[47] Such resolutions must, of course, concern matters within the province of the general meeting; they must not concern matters falling within the directors' powers: *John Shaw & Sons (Salford) Ltd.* v. *Shaw* [1935] 2 KB 113; but cf. CA 1985, s. 376(6).

[48] Under CA 1985, ss. 376–7, one or more members representing at least 5% of the total votes (or 100 members holding an average paid-up capital of £100 each) can require the company to give notice to members of the resolution(s) which they intend to propose at the AGM. The company's expenses for so doing must, however, be paid by the requisitioning shareholders unless the general meeting resolves otherwise.

[49] CA 1985, s. 368.

[50] See Sec. B.3.(6), below.

which portfolio companies are managed, and to exercise the voting rights attached to the shares of portfolio companies.[51] That is, in order to fulfil their duty to act in the interests of the beneficiaries (and contingent beneficiaries) under the trust, they are required to, *inter alia*, exercise their voting rights.[52] This obligation is said to extend, indirectly, to any investment managers appointed by the trustees. The reasoning is that an investment adviser appointed under a fund-management agreement is an agent of the trustees, and is thus in the position of 'a quasi trustee or constructive professional trustee' *vis-à-vis* the scheme's beneficiaries.[53]

If this proposition were correct, two serious ramifications would follow: (a) a majority of the trustees and investment managers of UK pension schemes would for many years have been breaching (by omission) their fiduciary/quasi-fiduciary duties; and (b) the trustees and investment managers of charity trusts (and possibly also the managers of authorized unit trusts[54]) would, arguably, be under a similar obligation to vote their trusts' shareholdings.[55]

It would appear, however, that there is no authority for the proposition. Further, it is submitted that the proposition is ungrounded in principle. In regard to authority, it is established that it is the duty of a trustee 'to conduct the business of the trust in the same manner as an ordinary prudent man [or woman] of business would conduct his [or her] own'.[56] Where a trustee (for example a trust corporation) holds itself out as a specialist in the business of trust management, a higher standard of care applies.[57] Where a trustee has a *controlling* interest[58] in the share capital of

---

[51] See 'Survey: Pension Fund Investment: Focus on Investors' Behaviour', *Fin. Times*, 6 May 1993, sec. III, p. VII, citing John Quarrell of Nabarro Nathanson, solicitors.

[52] There are clear parallels with the US Department of Labor's rulings under the Employee Retirement Income Security Act ('ERISA'), 29 USC §§ 1001–468 (1988), which applies to US non-public pension funds. See generally: E. B. Rock, 'The Logic and (Uncertain) Significance of Institutional Shareholder Activism' (1991) 79 *Georgetown LJ* 445, at 476–8. See also *Cadbury Report*, para. 6.12: 'Voting rights can be regarded as an asset . . .'

[53] See 'Survey: Pension Fund . . .' (n. 51 above); see also J. J. Quarrell, *The Law of Pension Fund Investment* (1990) 54.

[54] But see Financial Services (Regulated Schemes) Regulations 1991, reg. 7.11: All rights of voting conferred by any of the property (besides shares or units in related collective-investment schemes) of an authorized unit-trust scheme are exercisable 'at the direction of the manager' (i.e. the regulations expressly make voting optional).

[55] Contrast the position of directors and fund managers of investment-trust companies (*vis-à-vis* the shareholders), and of insurance companies (*vis-à-vis* the policyholders): the existence of an interposed separate legal entity (the company) would in each case preclude any such duty: *Percival* v. *Wright* [1902] 2 Ch. 421; cf. *Coleman* v. *Myers* [1977] 2 NZLR 225.

[56] *Speight* v. *Gaunt* (1883) 22 Ch. D 727, at 739–40; see also *Re Whiteley* (1886) 33 Ch. D 347, at 355.

[57] *Bartlett* v. *Barclays Bank Trust Co. Ltd. (No. 1)* [1980] 1 Ch. 515, at 534.

[58] In the two main cases, the shareholding of the trustee(s) was substantially in excess of 50% of the issued share capital. However, the courts may well extend the 'controlling interest' rule to situations where a trustee with a stake of less than 50% is, nevertheless, *effectively* in a controlling position.

a company, the courts have held that the trustee must (as an ordinary prudent person of business would) place him- or herself in a position to make an informed decision as to whether it is appropriate to take any action for the protection of the shareholding.[59] This duty may in some instances necessitate board representation.[60] It certainly necessitates action in addition to the mere consideration of information revealed at general meetings.[61] However, most if not all UK pension schemes have no controlling interests in operational quoted companies. And there seems to be no case requiring a trustee with a non-controlling interest to take these additional types of measures.[62]

Turning to legal principle, it is submitted that the trustees of a pension fund[63] can fulfil their fiduciary[64] and statutory[65] duties regarding the equity investments of the fund by regularly reviewing and assessing the shareholdings, and taking whatever of a *range* of possible actions (which sometimes would include doing nothing) is appropriate in the circumstances. It would commonly be suitable to pursue any of a number of different courses of action in any given set of circumstances. Exercising the voting rights or seeking to influence the management would sometimes be amongst the appropriate actions, but there would often be alternative courses of action available which would also satisfy the relevant duties. Selling the shares in a particular company may well be a quite satisfactory exercise of power by the trustees, where there are problems with the company's management. It is considered unlikely that a court would hold that the trustees, in such a situation, were under a duty to remain shareholders and to exercise their rights of ownership.[66] Doing nothing at

---

[59] *Bartlett* (n. 57 above), at 532–4.

[60] See *Re Lucking's Will Trusts* [1968] 1 WLR 866, at 874.

[61] *Bartlett* (n. 57 above), at 532.

[62] But note *Butt* v. *Kelson* [1952] Ch. 197, where it was held that trustees holding shares in a company could be compelled by the beneficiaries to vote the shares according to the wishes of the beneficiaries (or of the court, if the beneficiaries were not unanimous). This decision is difficult to reconcile with *Re Brockbank* [1948] Ch. 206, and other authorities which state that beneficiaries are not entitled to compel trustees to exercise a discretionary power in a certain way. See also *Re George Whichelow Ltd.* [1954] 1 WLR 5, at 7–9.

[63] This paragraph assumes that the trustees themselves, as an OPS member of the Investment Managers Regulatory Organisation ('IMRO'), manage the scheme's investments (see Financial Services Act 1986, s. 191; *IMRO Rules*, chs. XI, XII).

[64] See *Learoyd* v. *Whiteley* (1887) 12 App. Cas. 727, at 733 (the prudence test); trustees also have a duty to consider whether their powers should be exercised, and thus to review the investments periodically.

[65] See particularly Pensions Act 1995, s. 36; Trustee Investments Act 1961, s. 6(1).

[66] Even if they were under such a duty, it would often be extremely difficult to establish the necessary causative link between the trustees' lack of voting and any losses incurred by the trust funds on the shareholding in question. See A. F. Conard, 'Beyond Managerialism: Investor Capitalism?' (1988) 22 *U Mich. J Law Ref.* 117, at 151–2.

all may even be appropriate sometimes.[67] Equally, where a company is performing well, and has a management with a good track record, it is surely implausible that the trustees of a pension fund with a holding in that company could be found to be in breach of their duty to the beneficiaries through not exercising their voting rights on uncontroversial or unexceptional resolutions.[68] And it follows that, if the submissions made in this paragraph are correct, any fund managers appointed by the trustees would not have any obligation under the general law to exercise voting rights.

Whether trustees *are* obliged, and whether they *ought to be* obliged, to exercise their voting rights are, however, two entirely different questions. A case can be made for the introduction of a regulatory requirement that the trustees of pension funds must exercise, or procure the exercise (by their fund managers) of, the voting rights attached to equity investments. It is submitted, however, that the likely practical benefits of such a requirement would be minimal.[69]

iii. Practicalities of Institutional Voting

The incidence of voting by institutional shareholders in quoted UK companies is revealed below to have been fairly low, in the period to 1994. One reason cited commonly by fund managers for either never voting or voting only occasionally is that there are practical difficulties associated with exercising votes on behalf of *external* clients. This subsection explains the practical issues involved in the exercise of voting rights by fund-management firms. A few assumptions are made in the following discussion. First, although public companies may be limited either by shares or by guarantee,[70] what follows relates solely to public companies limited by shares. Secondly, it is assumed that the Table A articles apply. Thirdly, it is assumed that, for companies with more than one class of shares, the ordinary shares are the only ones carrying the right to attend and vote in all circumstances at general meetings.

Those eligible to attend and vote at a company's general meetings are the 'members' upon whom such rights are conferred, and their proxies or representatives. With the above-mentioned assumptions, the members are

---

[67] e.g. if the trustees reasonably believed that a takeover bid might soon be made. Trustees are, however, under a duty to *consider* whether their powers should be exercised: *McPhail* v. *Doulton* [1971] AC 424, at 449, 456.

[68] A duty to exercise the voting right may arise where there is a resolution or series of resolutions which, if passed, would have a sizeable impact upon the value of the shareholding (e.g. a proposed reconstruction or scheme of arrangement). Even here, though, it would often be very difficult to establish causation (see n. 66 above).

[69] See Ch. 11, Sec. B.1.i, where this issue is discussed in detail.

[70] In the latter case, only if formed before 22 Dec. 1980: CA 1985, s. 1(3) and (4).

the *registered shareholders* (ordinary and preference (if there are any)), and the members entitled to vote are the registered *ordinary* shareholders. Equity investments of directly invested, externally managed pension funds are often registered in the name of a nominee company of the custodian appointed under the fund-management agreement.[71] It is this nominee company—which is the member of the portfolio companies—to which those portfolio companies send AGM and EGM notices and proxy-voting materials,[72] and which has the right to exercise voting rights or to appoint a proxy to do so on its behalf.[73] However, the nominee company holds the shares as a bare trustee, and as such it is required under equitable principles (and usually also by an express contractual provision) to exercise the voting rights as instructed by the pension fund's trustees, or somebody specified by them. The latter is the usual case. Thus, modern fund-management agreements often provide that the fund manager may, at its discretion, give voting instructions to the custodian (subject always to any specific instructions from the trustees).[74]

The fact that it is the registered shareholder which receives AGM and EGM notices, and proxy-voting materials, creates the potential for a couple of practical difficulties to accompany the exercise of voting rights by managers of external funds. (These are, however, much less of a problem than the major problem discussed in the next paragraph.) First, where the custodian is independent of the fund manager, the notices and proxy forms would be sent to an address other than that of the fund manager. This may lead to a delay before the fund manager becomes aware of an important proposed resolution. Any delay of more than two or three days may in some cases be crucial,[75] because the minimum notice period prescribed by

---

[71] Some custodians use a 'pooled nominee system' under which the shareholdings of all clients are registered in just one nominee name (with reliance on internal records to differentiate the different underlying holdings); others use a 'designated nominee system' under which each client's holding is registered in a unique name: see Securities and Investments Board, *Custody Review Discussion Paper* (1993) ch. 6.

[72] Table A, art. 38; CA 1985, s. 370(1) and (2).

[73] CA 1985, s. 360 states that no notice of any form of trust shall be entered on the register for companies registered in England and Wales. See also Table A, art. 5.

[74] See e.g. IFMA and BMBA, *Terms and Conditions for Discretionary Fund Management* (1991) para. 14. Express provisions dealing with the delegation or otherwise of the voting right became common in fund-management agreements only in the early 1990s. Until at least the late 1970s, the matter was 'not made explicit': R. Minns, *Pension Funds and British Capitalism* (1980) 103; and by the mid-1980s it was still 'rarely made explicit': J. Scott, *Capitalist Property and Financial Power* (1986) 25. Voting was, however, widely regarded 'as an indivisible aspect of investment management': Scott, ibid. Pensions Act 1995, s. 34 gives trustees the authority to delegate the voting right; cf. the position in Australia: see Ch. 8, Sec. B.1.ii; Ch. 11, Sec. B.1.ii.

[75] Whether or not delays are common in practice is unclear. However, a 1993 study of custodians' collection of dividends found that dividends received from UK companies were forwarded to pension funds, on average, 3 days late (the worst case being 56 days late): 'Measuring Up', *Pensions Mgt.*, Mar. 1993, p. 43.

the Companies Act for EGMs is just 14 days, and most companies require that proxy forms must reach them at least 48 hours before the meeting.[76] This would normally only give rise to an actual problem if the scenario outlined in the next paragraph also existed. Secondly, a few major UK-based fund managers register the equity investments of segregated clients in the name of one nominee company (for example 'ABC Nominees Ltd.'), rather than in the clients' own names or in designated nominee names (for example 'ABC Nominees Ltd. a/c 001', 'ABC Nominees Ltd. a/c 002', etc.). This is known as a 'pooled nominee system' of registration.[77] The practical obstacle to voting which is discussed in the next paragraph could be exacerbated by the use of a pooled nominee system, because determining how many votes were able to be cast in the nominee company's name could involve a large administrative task if there were a large number of clients.[78]

The most significant practical obstacle to the exercise of voting rights by fund managers is a requirement to consult with or obtain the blessing of the client before voting.[79] There are two ways in which this situation may arise. First, some pension-fund trustees do not delegate the voting right to their external fund manager (but do not normally themselves exercise the votes either), such that the fund manager must obtain express approval every time it wishes to vote the relevant shares. It should be noted that, where the voting right is 'retained' in this way by the trustees, it would not necessarily have been the trustees who proposed the arrangement. Some major UK fund managers tell their clients that they do not want voting discretion, and seek to have a clause in the fund-management contract

[76] CA 1985, s. 369(1); Table A, art. 62(a) (see also CA 1985, s. 372(5)). Boards of quoted companies often, however, give their shareholders more than the minimum 14 days' notice: 'Pension Funds Attacked Over Failure to Vote', *Fin. Times*, 2 Mar. 1991, p. 7. See also Ch. 4, See A.1.xviii; and Ch. 11, Sec. B.1.iv (recommendation that the minimum notice period for EGMs be increased to 21 days).

[77] See n. 71 above.

[78] Note CA 1985, s. 374: 'On a poll taken at a meeting . . . a member entitled to more than one vote need not, if he votes, use all his votes or cast all the votes he uses in the same way.' This provision 'is designed to enable trustees or nominees to give effect to the directions of the beneficial owners': L. C. B. Gower, *Gower's Principles of Modern Company Law* (5th edn., 1992) 523.

[79] Contrast the position of managers of 'internal' funds—such as the fund-management arms of insurance companies in respect of policyholders' funds, and investment managers of internally managed pension funds. The absence of external clients means that the exercise of voting rights is, for such fund managers, much less difficult than for managers of predominantly external funds. Note also the case of a manager of unit trusts. Although the assets of authorized unit trusts must be in the custody or under the control of the trustee (Financial Services (Regulated Schemes) Regulations 1991, reg. 7.10.2), which must be independent of the manager (Financial Services Act 1986, s. 78(2)), it is the manager which has control over voting: Financial Services (Regulated Schemes) Regulations 1991, reg. 7.11.1.

stating that they may exercise voting rights only with the approval, or on the specific instructions, of the client.[80] The second way in which the problem situation may arise is that some pension-fund trustees, despite delegating to their external investment manager the power to vote, require that they be consulted on contentious or momentous resolutions. If either of these two scenarios exists, there is a potential problem because it may be quite time-consuming if an investment manager has to consult with many clients in order to be able to amass its potential voting power. The minimum (14-day) notice period for EGMs may prove too short. On the other hand, as a Working Party of the CBI City/Industry Task Force stated:

> The extent of any administrative task involved would clearly depend on the arrangements made for deciding how and when voting rights should be exercised. The task would be relatively straightforward if . . . the powers to take voting decisions were vested exclusively in the chairman of the trustee body, but far more complex if views had to be sought from all trustees and perhaps from all advisers as well.[81]

Further, the two scenarios are relatively unusual. In regard to the first, a 1987 survey which included 199 directly invested, externally managed pension schemes found that in only 11% of cases was the external fund manager required to consult the trustees or the trustees' investment advisory body before voting.[82] In relation to the second scenario, the same survey revealed that the trustees of only 10% of externally managed funds had issued guidelines to their external fund manager(s) regarding the exercise of delegated voting rights.[83] A fund manager interviewed by the present author said: 'Out of 170 pension-fund clients, only 10 have 'bring to us any controversial issues' clauses in their [fund-management] agreements.' Nevertheless, a majority of fund managers interviewed by the author deemed it proper to consult on contentious resolutions even with those pension-fund trustees who had made an unrestricted delegation of the voting right. This is not to say, though, that the fund managers stumble in looking for ideas:

---

[80] This was motivated in part by regulations which, until Sept. 1993, allowed a fund manager to avoid having to disclose a 3% or larger shareholding under its management if (a) it was not the registered holder; *and* (b) its interest in the shares consisted only of a power over their disposal (and did not include the power to vote them): see P. L. Davies and G. P. Stapledon, 'Corporate Governance in the United Kingdom' in M. Isaksson and R. Skog (eds.), *Aspects of Corporate Governance* (1994) 55, at 63 (n. 16). In Sept. 1993 the disclosure threshold for fund managers changed to 10%: see CA 1985, s. 199(2), (2A)(a) and (b); The Disclosure of Interests in Shares (Amendment) Regulations 1993 (SI 1993/1819) (which implemented Directive 88/627/EEC).

[81] CBI, *Pension Fund Investment Management* (1987) 18.

[82] CBI, ibid., at 54–5 (author's calculation from figures in Table 18).

[83] Ibid., at 59 (Table 22).

> If there is something which we think might be a bit sensitive or indeed is of a
> very public nature then I would anticipate that we would at least consider
> whether or not we should communicate what we are doing to the trustees. When
> I say we would communicate, we would not seek to ask them what we should do;
> we would tell them what we were doing or had done or were proposing to do.
> The distinction has some importance, not least from the timing point of view
> because trustees can be slow to respond and time is not always on one's side.

The author's interview study gave the impression that in the vast majority
of such cases the trustees give their approval to whatever action is deemed
appropriate by the fund manager.[84]

It should be borne in mind that the practical obstacles just discussed
constitute by no means the only—or even the main—reason for the fairly
low level of voting by managers of external funds. Economic theory[85]
suggests, and the interview studies of Coffee[86] and the present author have
shown, that external fund managers face numerous disincentives to the
performance of detailed monitoring of the managements of portfolio
companies. These economic disincentives reflect an agency problem at the
level of fund manager:client. They are detailed in Chapter 10, Section B.

iv. Evidence on Institutional Voting

A couple of points should be borne in mind when looking at the evidence
on the exercise of voting rights by institutional shareholders. First, UK
institutions on the whole have a tradition of not attending general
meetings.[87] The present issue is, therefore, the extent to which the
institutions have exercised, and currently do exercise, their proxies.[88] The

---

[84] Cf., however, 'Big Investors Threaten to Revolt on Pay', *Guardian*, 26 June 1995, p. 14
(pension-fund trustees expressing regret, after the event, in regard to the failure of their fund
managers to consult in detail with them prior to voting in support of management at the 1995
AGM of British Gas plc—the AGM at which the executive-pay scheme of British Gas was
under scrutiny: see generally Ch. 4, at nn. 114–18, and accompanying text). On this issue of
the accountability of fund managers exercising delegated voting rights, see further Ch. 9, Sec.
B.3.i; Ch. 11, Sec. B.1.viii.

[85] See e.g. Rock (n. 52 above); J. C. Coffee, 'Liquidity Versus Control: The Institutional
Investor as Corporate Monitor' (1991) 91 *Colum. L Rev.* 1277.

[86] Reported in B. S. Black and J. C. Coffee, 'Hail Britannia? Institutional Investor
Behavior Under Limited Regulation' (1994) 92 *Mich. L Rev.* 1997.

[87] There are a couple of exceptions to this: (a) where an institution or institutional coalition
has itself requisitioned an EGM to attempt to remove one or more directors, the institution(s)
concerned would of course be in attendance at the EGM (see Sec. B.3.vi, below); and (b)
one of the fund managers interviewed by the author said: 'We tend to go to as many AGMs as
we can, because that is one time you *can* talk to non-execs.'

[88] Note that, unless the articles provide otherwise, a proxy is entitled to vote only on a poll
(not on a show of hands): CA 1985, s. 372(2). (The Table A articles do not provide otherwise:
see art. 54.) A proxy is, however, able to demand or join in demanding a poll: CA 1985,
s. 373(2). The articles usually provide that resolutions at general meetings are to be decided
on a show of hands unless a poll is demanded (see e.g. Table A, art. 46). Much routine
business at the AGMs of quoted companies is decided on a show of hands, and therefore
many 'proxy votes' are never actually cast.

second thing to note is that the exercise of voting rights by institutional shareholders really only surfaced as a prominent issue in the UK in the late 1980s. Indeed, as recently as 1991, 'the way in which discretionary managers use the votes attached to their clients' investments' was described as 'a previously unnoticed corner of institutional fund management'.[89] That probably explains why there is very little information on institutional voting prior to 1987. Bearing in mind those two points, there are basically two types of empirical evidence on institutional voting. First, there have been a handful of studies showing the percentage of issued ordinary shares actually voted by way of proxy at the general meetings of large listed UK companies. Secondly, there is a growing body of evidence on the voting policies of the largest fund managers, and of all fund managers in respect of the shares which they manage for pension funds.

(a) The Overall Level of Proxy Voting

There seems to have been four publicly reported studies of proxy voting in UK companies. The earliest study is that of Midgley.[90] His study dealt with the exercise of votes by all types of shareholders, not just institutional shareholders. From a sample of large UK companies, he found that the proxy forms returned for the period 1960–9 represented less than 11% of the total possible votes for 39% of sample companies, between 11–30% of potential votes for a further 50% of sample companies, and over 30% of possible votes for only 11% of sample companies.[91] Although there was no breakdown for institutional and non-institutional shareholders, a later work reporting research conducted during the 1970s disclosed that, '[o]n most occasions where the financial institution could vote, the ability to use the voting proxies [was] not exercised'.[92]

The second study involved a survey by the ISC of the level of proxy voting at the 1990 AGMs of about 50 of the FT-SE 100 companies. It found that, '[o]n average, the total [institutional and non-institutional] proxy vote received by companies amount[ed] to about 20% of the total shareholding'.[93] This figure would probably be fairly similar to, or perhaps a little higher than, the overall figure from Midgley's study of 1960–9.[94] This

---

[89] IFMA, *Voting by Institutional Shareholders* (1991) 1.

[90] K. Midgley, 'How Much Control Do Shareholders Exercise?' (1974) 14 *Lloyds Bank Rev.* 24.

[91] Ibid., at 31. Midgley also reported that shareholders in that period virtually never used the general meeting to initiate proposals: ibid., at 32.

[92] Minns (n. 74 above), at 105.

[93] ISC, *Report on Investigation of Use of Voting Rights by Institutions* (1993) para. 4.1.

[94] Midgley (n. 90 above) did not give an overall figure, just the breakdown cited in the text above.

ISC study was not published, and its finding on the extent of voting by institutions is unknown.

The third study was also conducted by the ISC. This survey covered 20 large listed UK companies which had AGMs in April or May 1993. It found that an average of 34% of the issued ordinary shares of the sample companies were voted at those AGMs.[95] This is appreciably higher than the 20% recorded in the earlier ISC survey,[96] and would certainly be higher than the overall figure from Midgley's survey. The 1993 ISC study focused on *registered* shareholdings. Each sample company identified its 20 largest registered *institutional* shareholdings. The study found that, on average, proxies were lodged in respect of 49.5% of the shares in those 20 largest registered institutional shareholdings. This is well in excess of the figure (25.6%) for all other registered shareholdings (which were held by or on behalf of both non-institutions and institutions).[97]

The fourth study, which was conducted by Mallin, covered 101 of the largest 250 listed UK companies.[98] It examined the lodgement of proxies for AGMs occurring between November 1993 and September 1994. It found that an average of 35% of the issued ordinary shares of the surveyed companies were voted at those AGMs—a figure very similar to that of the 1993 ISC study. Interestingly, however, Mallin's study found that, on average, proxies were lodged in respect of over 70% of the shares in the 20 largest registered institutional shareholdings. That represents an appreciable increase on the 49.5% figure from the 1993 ISC survey.

It is clear from other studies (including the interview study of the present author) that most institutions have for many years lodged proxies in two types of situation. First, most institutions have voted where a company or a company's stockbroker has explicitly requested that the institution exercise its votes in relation to a particular resolution or meeting.[99] Secondly, a majority of institutions has for many years voted where a resolution is either controversial or of major importance. Examples include resolutions concerning proposed takeover bids, reconstructions, and the removal of board members. Other examples relate to matters (such as executive share schemes, disapplication of the pre-emption right, and management buy-outs) where institutional-shareholder guidelines are in place but have not been observed.[100]

---

[95] ISC (n. 93 above), at Table A.
[96] The results of the two ISC surveys are comparable as the sampling frame was the same in each case.   [97] ISC, (n. 93 above), at Table A.
[98] C. Mallin, *Voting: The Role of Institutional Investors in Corporate Governance* (1995) 21–30.   [99] See Minns (n. 74 above), at 105.
[100] See Midgley (n. 90 above), at 31–2; Minns, ibid., at 105–7; and Ch. 4, Secs. A.1.i, A.1.vi, A.1.xvii, B.

(b) Voting Policies of Fund Managers

There was by 1993 considerable evidence of the voting policies of the major UK fund managers.[101] The picture at late 1993 was as follows. Some managers (for example PPM; PosTel; and CIN) had for many years lodged proxies in respect of all of their UK equity holdings. Other managers (for example BZWIM; PDFM; and Scottish Amicable) began voting at all times during the early 1990s, after having previously voted only on major or controversial issues. Still other managers (for example Fleming; and M&G) voted wherever they held more than a specified proportion of a company's issued share capital. Then there were managers (for example MAM; Baring; Baillie Gifford; and Framlington) which voted only on contentious or major issues, the rationale of at least one of them being that 'routine voting may give company managers blanket endorsement'.[102]

Of the two main types of UK-based fund manager—those linked to insurers and those linked to financial conglomerates—it was evident that a far greater proportion of the former voted at all times, as at 1993. This was a finding of the author's interview study, but there is additional evidence. Jackson, who interviewed (*inter alia*) five fund managers from both categories in early 1987, found that none of the financial-conglomerate investment managers voted routinely, whilst two of the insurers always voted and a third always did so where it had a 'significant holding'.[103] A survey conducted by the ISC in early 1991 found that 11 out of 13 insurance-company fund managers voted at all times, whilst only one out of seven financial-conglomerate investment managers did so.[104] In the mid-1980s, the ABI IC started monitoring its members' use of proxies. It asked quoted companies to inform it if they were receiving an unacceptably low number of proxy forms from insurance companies. Where this was the case, the IC encouraged the insurers concerned to make use of their votes. By 1993, the IC claimed to have 'a 90% success rate' with its members.[105] The insurers' greater propensity to vote is not surprising in the light of the discussion above about the practical difficulties associated with institutional voting, which affect particularly the external managers of pension funds. The 'internal' shareholdings of insurance-company fund managers

---

[101] The information in this paragraph is derived from the following sources: author's interviews with fund managers; 'Punters' Progress', *Econ.*, 7 Sept. 1991, p. 112; 'Survey: Pension Fund Investment: Focus on Investors' Behaviour', *Fin. Times*, 6 May 1993, sec. III, p. VII; Linaker (n. 5 above), at 110. (For abbreviations of fund managers' names, see App. E.) [102] 'Punters' Progress', ibid.

[103] P. D. Jackson, 'Management of UK Equity Portfolios' (1987) 27 *Bank Eng. Q Bull.* 253, at 257. [104] See IFMA (n. 89 above).

[105] Information provided to the author by R. D. Regan, Secretary, ABI IC, in interview on 22 Sept. 1993.

can obviously be voted without terribly much practical difficulty. Also, many of the economic disincentives mentioned earlier affect only the managers of external funds; managers of internal funds, such as the investment-management arms of insurance companies, face far fewer economic disincentives to detailed monitoring.

The voting practices of investment managers in respect of UK equities managed for pension funds is of special interest, because pension funds' holdings account for almost one-third of the listed UK equity market. Table 5.2[106] shows the voting *policy*[107] of directly invested pension UK pension schemes over 1990–4. For 1990, 1991, and 1992, the party determining this policy was the investment manager(s) in about 50% of cases; and the trustee(s), the chairman of the trustees, the pensions manager, or other persons in about 50% of cases. In 1993 and 1994, the party determining the voting policy was the investment manager(s) in 58% of cases; and the trustees, etc., in only 42% of cases.[108] This moderate change may reflect the recent movement towards the insertion of an express clause, in the fund-management agreements of externally managed pension schemes, under which the investment manager is given full or qualified discretion over the exercise of voting rights.[109] Given that roughly 80% of the pension schemes whose responses underlie Table 5.2 used external, as opposed to internal, fund managers, the table would appear to bear out what was said earlier about the practical difficulties associated with, and the economic disincentives affecting, the exercise of voting rights by external managers of pension funds.

The only significant changes in Table 5.2 over the five-year period were the increase in schemes whose shareholdings were voted routinely (either by the trustees or by the investment manager(s)), and the decrease in schemes answering 'other'. Virtually all schemes answering 'other'

[106] The table is based on the following question: 'What is the policy of the fund and its investment manager(s) as regards voting at company meetings?': NAPF, *Annual Survey of Occupational Pension Schemes* (1990, 1991, 1992, 1993, 1994) qu. 8.3(g). There were in each year several hundred respondents to this question, all of them directly invested pension funds—with about 70–80% using external managers, 15–20% using internal managers, and about 10% using both internal and external managers. (These figures were calculated by excluding all unfunded, insured, and pooled pension schemes from the table corresponding to qu. 7.3, so as to leave only directly invested schemes.)

[107] It seems that the stated policy does not always translate into practice. It was reported in 1991 that a company had approached the trustees of 46 pension funds which held its shares, and sought their vote on a contentious issue. Twenty said that they or their investment managers had a policy of not voting—and none of them voted. Nine said they (or their managers) might vote—but only one actually did so (and its proxy form arrived too late). Seventeen said they (or their managers) would vote—but only six eventually did so: 'Squandering the Potential of Annual Meetings', *Indep.*, 10 June 1991, p. 23.

[108] See NAPF (n. 106 above), at table corresponding to qu. 8.3(h).

[109] See n. 74 above.

Table 5.2 Voting policy of UK pension schemes

Policy	Proportion of schemes (over the period 1990–4)				
	1990	*1991*	*1992*	*1993*	*1994*
Vote at all times if practicable	20%	21%	26%	26%	28%
Vote only on contentious issues	33%	34%	34%	31%	32%
Not vote	23%	24%	22%	24%	21%
Other	24%	21%	18%	19%	19%

Source: NAPF, *Annual Survey of Occupational Pension Schemes* (1990, 1991, 1992, 1993, 1994) Table corresponding to question 8.3(g).

apparently specified that they had no policy or did not know whether or not their manager(s) voted.[110] The decrease in this response coupled with the increased incidence of routine voting is probably attributable to (a) an increased awareness amongst pension-fund trustees of matters of corporate governance as the debate on that broad topic progressed through the late 1980s and early 1990s; and (b) a wide-ranging call for institutional shareholders to make more use, or at least consider making more use, of their voting rights. In regard to (b), the proponents included (i) 'neutral' parties such as the Bank of England,[111] the City/Industry Task Force,[112] and the Cadbury Committee;[113] (ii) industrialists[114] and their peak body— the Confederation of British Industry;[115] and (iii) the institutions' own trade associations—the ABI,[116] NAPF,[117] ISC,[118] and IFMA.[119] The urgings of the four institutional trade associations can probably be ascribed

[110] 'Squandering the Potential . . .' (n. 107 above); 'Survey: Pension Fund Investment: Investors Urged to Behave Like Owners', *Fin. Times*, 7 May 1992, sec. III, p. VIII.
[111] See D. A. Walker, 'Some Perspectives for Pension Fund Managers' (1987) 27 *Bank Eng. Q Bull.* 247.
[112] CBI City/Industry Task Force (n. 11 above), at 37–8, 60.
[113] *Cadbury Report*, para. 6.12.
[114] See e.g. Sir Francis Tombs (n. 18 above); cf. Sir Hector Laing, 'The Balance of Responsibilities' in NAPF, *Creative Tension?* (1990) 59, at 66; House of Lords Science and Technology Committee, *First Report: Innovation in Manufacturing Industry* (1990–1) (recommending restrictions on voting rights in the interests of 'long-termism').
[115] CBI, *Response to the Draft Report of the Committee on the Financial Aspects of Corporate Governance* (1992) para. 54.
[116] ABI, *The Responsibilities of Institutional Shareholders—A Discussion Paper* (1991) 2, 4.
[117] See A. W. Matheson, 'The Institutional Investor's Viewpoint' (1993) 1 *Corp. Gov.: Inter. Rev.* 178.
[118] ISC, *The Responsibilities of Institutional Shareholders in the UK* (1991) 2, 5.
[119] IFMA (n. 89 above).

largely to a desire to forestall regulatory intervention.[120] But, in view of Table 5.2, it is fair to say that mere urgings had by 1994 failed to bring about a substantial change in the voting of the shareholdings of the largest class of institutions. Therefore, if the regulators were to perceive institutional voting as highly desirable, the trade associations' attempted forestalment of regulatory intervention would probably prove to be a failure. This matter is discussed further in the final chapter.

v. Voting-Information Services for Institutions

The NAPF, the ABI, and PIRC have, since 1992, 1993, and 1991 respectively, operated services which provide material to assist institutional investors in making an informed use of their voting rights.

The NAPF's *Voting Issues Service* initially covered the largest 125 listed UK companies, then from the beginning of 1993 it covered the top 250 companies, and as at mid-1995 it embraced the top 300 companies.[121] It was run by a team of five NAPF employees, and it had 95 subscribers, at June 1995. At that time, the subscribers included the trustees of externally managed private-sector pension schemes, the administering authorities of externally managed local-authority pension schemes, in-house pension-fund managers, nearly all of the dozen largest financial-conglomerate investment managers,[122] and a few pensions advisers and US proxy-voting advisers. The *Voting Issues Service* provided the following as at mid-1995: (a) a report on each forthcoming AGM or EGM setting out the proposed resolutions, explanatory details where necessary, and whether each particular resolution was viewed as non-contentious or worthy of closer examination by the investor; (b) a check-list showing whether the company met certain recommendations of the Cadbury Committee, the ISC, and PRO NED; and (c) a three-month rolling calendar of AGM dates and locations to assist with forward planning. In relation to (a), the NAPF service did not make recommendations on how subscribers should vote on any resolution, that being regarded as 'entirely the province of the institutional investor concerned'. The NAPF IC was, however, 'always happy to talk about [apparent breaches of best practice] with subscribers

---

[120] See Black and Coffee (n. 86 above), at 2040. Another influence upon the trade associations was probably a fear of loss of voting control to US institutions, given that US institutions increased markedly their voting of foreign (including UK) equity investments over the period 1991–4: see Black and Coffee, ibid.; 'US Investors Use Foreign Voting Rights', *Fin. Times*, 29 Nov. 1994, p. 30 (the average large US institution voted at 71% of foreign portfolio companies in 1994, up from 24% in 1991).

[121] The sources of these details are: (a) information provided to the author by J. E. Rogers, Secretary, NAPF IC, in interviews on 29 Sept. 1993 and 30 June 1995; and (b) sample *Voting Issues Service* documents provided to the author by the NAPF IC.

[122] Including a couple that have a policy of normally not voting (i.e. of voting only on contentious or major matters).

and with the companies covered by [the] Service'. Further, the reports were sent to the companies concerned at the same time that they were sent to subscribers, so that there was time for informed discussion between both prior to the meeting in question. Regarding (b), the check-list was 'intended as an aide-memoire for investment managers in their conversations with [the] management' of portfolio companies.[123]

The ABI established a proxy-voting service, available only to ABI members, in September 1993.[124] It covered the top 500 listed UK companies, and 20% of all other listed UK companies. As at mid-1995, the service included a report showing contentious proposed resolutions—with contentiousness assessed according to ABI and Cadbury Committee principles of best practice. The report also informed the subscribers about the action, if any, that was being taken by ABI members and/or the ABI IC in relation to contentious proposed resolutions.

PIRC's *Corporate Governance Service* was, at September 1993, provided to the administering authorities of 15 local-authority pension schemes which had total assets of £15,000 million, and to the two main US institutional-shareholder proxy-voting advisers.[125] About half of the subscribing local-authority schemes used internal investment managers, and half employed external fund managers. At that time, the *Corporate Governance Service* consisted of, *inter alia*, a voting-information service similar—except in two main respects—to those of the NAPF and the ABI. The first major difference was that only the FT-SE 100 companies (plus those companies on the FT-SE 100 'reserve list') were covered. Secondly, and importantly, the PIRC service provided voting recommendations— either 'for', 'abstain', or 'against'—based on Cadbury, ISC, and PRO NED best practice, together with PIRC's own principles on and views of best practice in corporate governance. PIRC's own agenda included things like political donations, environmental policy, and the level of executive remuneration. All of PIRC's reports were sent to the companies concerned ahead of the meeting in question, and PIRC also spoke each year to the chairman and/or a senior executive of about 25% of the companies covered by its service.

As mentioned, the trustees (and administering authorities, in the case of local-authority schemes) of *externally managed* pension schemes (amongst others) subscribed to the NAPF and PIRC services. In some of these cases the trustees had retained the right to vote (i.e. had not delegated it to the

---

[123] Matheson (n. 117 above), at 181. See Sec. B.2, below.

[124] These details were provided to the author by R. D. Regan, Secretary, ABI IC, in interviews on 22 Sept. 1993 and 29 June 1995; and by J. Weld of the ABI IC, in telephone conversation on 24 June 1994.

[125] These details were provided to the author by S. Bell, Research Director, PIRC, in interview on 28 Sept. 1993.

external fund managers(s)). Here, the trustees would utilize the NAPF/ PIRC service in deciding how (or if) to vote. However, some such subscribers had delegated the voting right. Here, the NAPF/PIRC service would be used to give guidance to the external manager on the exercise of its discretion. One of the large fund managers interviewed by the author said that some of its local-authority clients had given it 'strict guidelines on how to exercise voting rights—namely, according to the recommendations of PIRC'.

2. ROUTINE ACTIONS

i. Analysis of Information Concerning the Company

Analysis of information regarding portfolio companies has, as one would expect, always been a routine function of institutions which manage equities. Until the early 1960s, it was common for this analysis to consist largely of a review of the many research reports sent to institutions by stockbroking firms. That is, the primary analysis was conducted externally. The institutions did, of course, carry out a limited amount of analysis internally, in that they had access to annual reports and other information disclosed by companies to the market. During the 1960s and 1970s many larger institutions carried out an increasing amount of research in-house. Thus, the Wilson Committee reported in 1980 that:

> Most of the larger institutions usually maintain small staffs of financial analysts, actuaries, accountants and economists—though the great majority have little industrial, as distinct from financial, expertise. . . . The smaller institutions, and some of the larger ones, find it more cost-effective to rely more on outside analysis, particularly stockbrokers' reports and commentaries by financial journalists.[126]

The trend towards in-house research continued in the 1980s and early 1990s. A survey conducted in 1990 investigated, *inter alia*, the degree to which fund managers relied upon in-house research and brokers' research in making investment decisions.[127] Only one respondent relied entirely on internal research, and none relied entirely on brokers' recommendations. In-house research was relied upon 'largely' by 62%, 'a little' by 26%, and not at all by 7% of respondents. Brokers' research was relied upon 'largely' by 54%, and 'a little' by 44% of respondents; no respondents ignored

---

[126] Committee to Review the Functioning of Financial Institutions ('Wilson Committee'), *Report* (1980) para. 899.
[127] E. V. Morgan and A. D. Morgan, *Investment Managers and Takeovers: Information and Attitudes* (1990) 18–21. The percentage figures given in the text are calculations from Morgan and Morgan, Table 2.3a.

altogether the research of brokers. The annual surveys conducted by Extel showed that 46% (in 1990), 48% (in 1991), and 43% (in 1992) of UK-based investment managers increased their in-house research, whilst only 3% (in 1990), 3% (in 1991), and 4% (in 1992) decreased their internal research (and the remainder maintained the same level).[128]

The information analysed by stockbrokers' and institutions' research staffs is of two broad types. First, there is published information. This embraces annual reports and preliminary and interim statements produced by the companies themselves, and other information disclosed to the market under the provisions of the *Listing Rules*,[129] as well as information contained in trade journals, official statistics, newspapers, etc. Secondly, there is information obtained from dialogue with companies' executives. This dialogue takes the form of company presentations to large groups of analysts and/or fund managers (at post-results presentations, 'road shows', brokers' lunches, site visits, and the like), and one-to-one conversations (either in person or by telephone) between analysts/fund managers and companies' senior executives. The regular dialogue that fund managers have with company executives is of sufficient importance to merit separate treatment.

ii. Regular Meetings and Dialogue with Management

It is the policy of the ISC that '[i]nstitutional investors should encourage regular, systematic contact [with portfolio companies] at senior executive level to exchange views and information on strategy, performance, board membership and quality of management'.[130] This was endorsed by the Cadbury Committee.[131] The CBI recommends that an institutional shareholder should receive annually from company managements: (a) a meeting after the final figures have been released; (b) a one-to-one meeting with senior management, if a large shareholder; (c) a site visit to factory or plant, if interested; and (d) at least one presentation providing a full update on current trading and strategic thinking.[132] Given that the peak bodies of the institutions and the corporate sector (and also the Cadbury Committee) each champion the holding of regular meetings and

---

[128] Extel Financial Ltd., *Survey of Investment Analysts* (1992) 17. The main reason for financing in-house research would seem to be concern about brokers' conflicts of interest (brokers have an interest in generating sales and purchases of shares, from which they receive commission): 'Continental Firms Pose Threat to UK Brokers, Study Says', *Fin. Times*, 29 Oct. 1992, p. 27.

[129] See e.g. *Listing Rules*, para. 9.1 (information necessary to avoid creation of a false market in securities, and information on major new developments); ch. 10 (large transactions). [130] ISC (n. 118 above), at 5.

[131] *Cadbury Report*, paras. 4.59, 6.11, 6.15.

[132] NAPF, *Corporate Relations: Reminder on Good Investor Relations* (1994) (citing CBI National Manufacturing Council).

dialogue between the management and major institutional shareholders of quoted companies, what has been the incidence of, and what are the characteristics of, these discussions?

It would seem that, prior to the early 1960s, fund managers met with the management of their portfolio companies only irregularly—when some sort of extraordinary circumstances arose.[133] It is clear, however, that by 1970 senior investment managers from the largest insurance companies, such as the Prudential, were meeting periodically with the management of portfolio companies.[134] The large insurers were, at that time, reported to be 'interested in becoming known to the [portfolio] company and in obtaining from it sufficient information to assess both the standard of management and the long-term prospects of the company'.[135] Regular meetings were more common by the late 1970s. Evidence submitted by the British Insurance Association to the Wilson Committee showed that, of 994 listed UK companies each capitalized at over £3 million, 76% of the largest 50 companies, and 43% of the largest 600 companies, had periodic dialogue with some of their major institutional shareholders.[136] Only 17% of the smallest 394 companies, however, had regular contact of this sort.[137] The Wilson Committee cited one large internally managed pension scheme whose managers visited 300 companies at least annually, although the Committee thought that this was exceptional.[138] By the late 1980s, however, that level of direct contact between fund managers and the management of their portfolio companies was by no means exceptional. The 1988 Korn/Ferry survey of UK boards of directors asked respondents to specify how many days were spent annually by the chief executive communicating with institutions.[139] It was found that 10% of chief executives spent under 5 days, 29% devoted 5–9 days, 33% devoted 10–19 days, and 19% spent 20 or more days; 9% of respondents provided no information for this question, perhaps indicating that their chief executives did not meet with institutional shareholders. A survey of finance directors from a large sample of the top 750 quoted UK companies, in early 1992, found that in 87% of companies there were regular meetings between senior executives and institutional shareholders.[140] Further, all of the fund

---

[133] See A. Sampson, *The New Anatomy of Britain* (1971) 526–7.

[134] 'A Special Report: Insurance: Institutional Investors Make Their Mark', *Times*, 8 Feb. 1971, p. V.

[135] G. Griffith, 'The Role of the General Meeting in the Conduct of Business in the Registered Company' (1971) 196.

[136] Reported in Lord Carr, 'The Function of Ownership and the Role of Institutional Shareholders' in K. Midgley (ed.), *Management Accountability and Corporate Governance* (1982) 91, at 97.   [137] Ibid.

[138] Wilson Committee (n. 126 above), para. 900.

[139] Korn/Ferry International, *Boards of Directors Study UK* (1988) sec. III.

[140] 3i plc, *Plc UK: The Role of the Finance Director: Part 3—Corporate Governance* (1992) 24.

managers interviewed by the present author said that they communicated regularly with the management of portfolio companies. Some of the main features of this dialogue, derived from the author's interview study and other sources, are set out below.[141]

First, most fund managers meet with company managements in several locations: (a) in the company's offices or on site at a factory, sales centre, etc.; (b) in the fund manager's offices; and (c) at a luncheon or presentation held either at the offices of the company's broker or at a meeting venue. They also have telephone contact, and in some cases communicate by letter. Meetings of type (a) may be one-to-one or may include several institutions; those of type (b) are obviously one-to-one; and those of type (c) involve numerous institutions, and possibly also brokers' analysts. During the 1980s and early 1990s company managements became more inclined to visit their institutional shareholders for one-to-one meetings, rather than having the institutions come individually to see them. As a rough rule of thumb, however, the larger the shareholding, the more likely it is that the company's management will visit the institution.

Secondly, most investment managers like to see the management of their portfolio companies, in one way or another, at least once each year. Nearly all of the larger institutions aim to have a one-to-one meeting with the management of each portfolio company at least once per year.[142] Most, but not all, institutions have more one-to-one meetings with the management of smaller portfolio companies than with the management of medium-sized and larger portfolio companies, because smaller companies are researched much less thoroughly by brokers' analysts.

Thirdly, the executives with whom the institutions usually meet are the chief executive (and/or the executive chairman, if there is one) and/or the finance director. Fund managers visiting a larger company may sometimes speak to divisional heads either in addition to or instead of the chief executive and finance director. Specialist investor-relations executives are becoming common in large listed companies. The vast majority of fund managers are not, however, content to see just the investor-relations executive; most wish to see the chief executive or finance director on a one-to-one basis at least once per year.

Fourthly, it is impossible to generalize about the persons who represent

---

[141] Lest it be thought that it is the institutions that always take the major role in initiating and organizing this dialogue, it should be pointed out that many large and medium-sized listed companies spend a great deal of time and effort on their investor-relations programmes. See e.g. Sir David Plastow, 'Corporate Strategy and the Institutional Shareholder' in NAPF, *Creative Tension?* (1990) 70, at 75–6.

[142] It is also the aim of many company managements to meet their major institutional investors in person at least once a year: Plastow, ibid.; 'An Art That Deserves a High Priority', *Fin. Times*, 15 Nov. 1993, p. 14.

the institutions in their meetings and other dialogue with company managements. Some institutions have in-house analysts separate from their fund managers, and the UK equity analysts devote their entire time to researching UK companies. In some such cases the analysts carry out most of the meetings with company managements, but in other cases both the fund managers and the analysts meet company executives, although with different aims:

> In any given week our senior investment managers and specialist support staff will have contact with a dozen or more companies and their professional advisers, concerned with the relationship between companies and their shareholders, and quite distinct from the programme of meetings with our analysts which aims at improving our understanding of company operations, their management strategies and of the investment merits of companies at current prices.[143]

In other institutions the roles of fund manager and analyst are, to a greater or lesser extent, fused. In the case of these institutions, the one-to-one meetings with company managements might be attended by the fund manager responsible for the sector or sub-sector in which the company operates, together with other interested fund managers. Some institutions have a policy of the (or one of the) senior investment director(s), or the investment manager with responsibility for UK equities, being present at all one-to-one company meetings.

Fifthly, the one-to-one meetings usually last for about an hour. The issues covered at the meetings vary according to the type of meeting. If the institution's in-house analysts, or fund manager/analysts are involved, then standard analysts' topics may arise: the latest financial results; current trading; operations; trends in pricing; capital expenditure; cash flow; gearing; etc. However, many fund managers interviewed by the author stressed that they use one-to-one meetings with company managements not to explore 'short-term' issues such as current trading,[144] but to discuss more general topics (such as 'long-term strategy'; 'the company's philosophy and its strategy'; investment; and R&D) so as to gain a better understanding of the company, and to assess the quality of the management. One way of assessing management was described by a senior investment manager:

> You are always looking and asking yourself: 'What are they telling us is happening, and is that supported by the factual information?' If they've told you

---

[143] R. E. Artus, 'Tension to Continue' in NAPF, *Creative Tension?* (1990) 12 (describing the arrangement at Prudential Portfolio Managers Ltd.).

[144] It is, of course, a belief of many UK company managements that institutions and brokers' analysts focus too much on short-term issues: see Ch. 9, Sec. B.1. On this matter, see also City/Industry Working Group, *Developing a Winning Partnership* (1995).

three times that something is going to happen, and it doesn't happen, then you know the next time you take it with a pinch of salt. But if there's somebody who tends to always deliver on what they say, then it gives you more confidence.

Most institutions are prepared to voice their opinions on the general strategy expressed to them at these meetings. For instance, five interviewees said that their institutions had on a number of occasions encouraged company managements to slow down or stop their companies' growth by acquisition, and to concentrate on digesting the acquisitions already made. Procedural and general issues relating to corporate governance and shareholders' rights (in particular, things like the number and calibre of non-executive directors on the board; separation of the roles of chairman and chief executive; service contracts of executive directors; and non-voting shares) are also raised where the institution believes that there are shortcomings. Another topic, brought up commonly by company managements at one-to-one meetings, is the company's competitors. Several fund managers interviewed said that they learn a lot about their portfolio companies from what competitors (in which they are also shareholders) say about them in one-to-one meetings.

Sixthly, most regular one-to-one meetings (and indeed many presentations to groups of institutions and brokers' analysts) are held soon after an announcement of results. One of the reasons for this is to minimize the possibility of undisclosed price-sensitive information being released at these private meetings. The potential problem of insider dealing arising out of a close relationship between company managements and institutional shareholders is a topic which is discussed in detail in a later chapter.[145]

Seventhly, company managements can be loath to discuss certain information (including general strategies as well as more specific information of a commercially sensitive nature) with their main institutional shareholders, given that those institutions might well be shareholders in competitor firms.[146] This is covered in a later chapter.[147]

Eighthly, private meetings between institutions and company managements raise concerns about a lack of parity between the treatment of large and small shareholders.[148] This too is discussed later.[149]

Ninthly, it was mentioned earlier tsome institutions communicate regularly with the management of portfolio companies by way of letter. The large 'independent' fund manager, M&G, writes a letter annually to the chairmen of companies in which it has a significant holding.[150] Matters

---

[145] See Ch. 9, Sec. B.4.
[146] See A. Cosh, A. Hughes, and A. Singh, *Takeovers and Short-Termism in the UK* (1990) 16 (evidence from interviews with company managements).
[147] See Ch. 9, Sec. B.5.   [148] See *Listing Rules*, para. 9.16.
[149] See Ch. 9, Sec. B.8.   [150] See Linaker (n. 5 above), at 108–10.

of corporate governance, shareholder rights and interests, and capital raising have been covered. It is not a unilateral statement, but 'part of [M&G's] continuous dialogue' with the management of its portfolio companies.[151]

3. EXTRAORDINARY ACTIONS

In addition to the firm-level monitoring performed routinely by UK institutions, there are several types of firm-level monitoring which the institutions have carried out on an *ad hoc* basis. Each of these 'extraordinary actions', which are discussed below, has been executed in isolation, and some of them have been carried out either successively or jointly. For example, each—and in some cases all—of the actions described in Sections B.3.iii (viz. extraordinary meetings and dialogue with the management of a portfolio company), B.3.iv (viz. meetings and dialogue with the non-executive directors of a portfolio company), and B.3.v (viz. meetings and dialogues with other institutions concerning a company in which all have a holding) has sometimes been a precursor to, or part of, the remedy described in Section B.3.vi (viz. the procurement of changes in the management of a portfolio company).

Section B.3.i examines a preliminary issue. Several UK-based fund managers interviewed by the author stated that the most serious form of institutional intervention at a portfolio company—the attempted replacement of an under-performing or otherwise unacceptable management team—normally requires for its success a group of institutions (a) controlling (between them) at least 20–30% of the equity; and (b) numbering no more than three or four (due to the practical difficulties associated with co-ordinating a larger group). One determinant of successful institutional activism is, therefore, the percentage of the equity controlled by the few largest institutions in the company concerned. Section B.3.i comprises an identification and analysis of the few largest institutional stakes in the issued share capital of individual listed UK companies. This is a useful precursor to the subsequent analysis of current methods and levels of extraordinary monitoring. It is also, however, a *precondition* of any sensible forecast of the future level of such monitoring (which is a topic addressed in Chapter 10, Section B).

i. Preliminary: The Size of the Stakes

At the end of 1991 there were 1,852 listed UK companies and over 300 USM-quoted UK companies with equity securities trading on the London Stock Exchange. It is widely known that institutional holdings accounted

---

[151] See Linaker (n. 5 above), at 108.

for about 60% of that equity market.[152] It is also reasonably well known that, as at the early 1990s, 'Prudential Portfolio Managers manage[d] . . . British equities amounting to over 3½% of the entire [listed UK equities] market'.[153] There is, however, a lack of publicly available information as to the proportion of the issued ordinary share capital of individual quoted UK companies which was, as at the early 1990s, *controlled* by the fund managers with the 6–10 largest stakes in those companies. For present purposes, 'control' of a share rests with the party which has power to control the exercise of the right to vote attached to the share. It was noted earlier that, by the early 1990s, it was very common for UK fund managers to control the voting right attached to their clients' equity investments.[154] One way of determining the identity of the persons/bodies having control over the largest chunks of the equity of a particular company is to ascertain the identity of the persons/bodies having the largest 'interests' in its issued ordinary share capital, within the meaning of the Companies Act 1985. Section 208(2) of the Companies Act 1985 states that '[a] reference to an interest in shares is to be read as including an interest of any kind whatsoever in the shares'. Section 208(4) deems a person to have an interest in shares if, 'not being the registered holder, [the person] is entitled to exercise any right conferred by the holding of the shares or is entitled to control the exercise of any such right'. Fund managers to whom the voting right has been delegated clearly have an interest in the relevant shares.

It was the aim of Study B, described below, to discover the size of the interest of each of the few largest 'interest-holders' in a sample of listed UK companies. This is a very important set of data because, as mentioned earlier, the success of a major institutional intervention at the individual-firm level usually depends upon (a) the institution(s) concerned controlling at least 20–30% of the equity; and (b) the number of participating institutions being four or less. It should be noted that the participants in an institutional intervention are not always the institutions with the largest three or four institutional stakes in the company, because each institution has a range of options only one of which is to join an institutional group pushing for management changes. So, given that, for example, the third- and fourth-largest institutions may decide to sell their shares, it is desirable to have a picture of at least the six largest institutional interest-holders.

The author actually conducted two studies: Study A and Study B. Study A involved an analysis of the annual reports of the 100 listed UK

---

[152] See Ch. 2, Sec. A.

[153] Artus (n. 143 above). See also Table 3.2.

[154] See n. 74 above, and accompanying text. The usual situation was that the fund manager had discretion to vote as it saw fit, subject to any express instructions from the client.

companies which composed the FT-SE 100 index at the end of 1991.[155] When those reports were filed, the disclosure threshold for fund managers was still 3%.[156] A 3% (or greater) interest in the issued ordinary share capital of medium-sized and large listed companies is generally regarded, in the fund-management industry, as carrying a particularly significant weight in dealings with a company's management. The notifiable interests revealed in the surveyed annual reports provide, therefore, a good picture of the institutions whose views might be expected to have held particular sway in the top 100 companies at the end of 1991.

Study B involved a stratified sample (10%) of the 695 companies which composed the FT-A All Share index (excluding investment trusts) at September 1993.[157] From each sample company was obtained a list of the bodies/persons having the 10 largest interests in their issued ordinary share capital, and the percentage size of those interests.

Studies A and B did not seek to address identical objectives. Study A was concerned with obtaining information about the equity holdings of a few well-known UK institutions, rather than with examining the 'institutional-shareholder profile' of the sample companies. The second objective could not be met using Study A data, because not every company in Study A had institutions with notifiable interests in its equity, and even those that did have such institutional interest-holders did not have the same number of institutional interest-holders. However, Study B was devised precisely for the purpose of addressing that second objective. Within the confines of the 10 largest interest-holders, the information gathered in Study B allows an examination of the relative position of the dominant institutions in large, medium-sized, and small companies. Study B was also concerned with the first objective.

(a) Study A

Ninety-four of the top 100 companies had at least one body/person with a notifiable interest in their issued ordinary share capital. Upon further examination of those 94 companies, the body with the largest, or the only, notifiable interest was *an institution* in 66 cases (i.e. 70.2% of the 94). Table 5.3 presents a breakdown of those 66 companies.

The largest institutional interest comprised, as implied by the upper parameter of the last band, about one-third of the equity of the investee company (this being the 33.17% interest of The Standard Life Assurance

---

[155] The companies had, of course, a variety of accounting reference dates (see CA 1985, s. 224). The annual reports used in the study were for financial years ending between 1 July 1991 and 30 June 1992.

[156] It changed to 10% in Sept. 1993: see CA 1985, s. 199(2), (2A)(a) and (b); Disclosure of Interests in Shares (Amendment) Regulations 1993 (SI 1993/1819) (which implemented Directive 88/627/EEC).

[157] The methodology used in Study B is set out in App. I.

Table 5.3 FT-SE 100 companies in which an institution had the largest or only notifiable interest, 1991–2

Size band of largest institution's interest (% of issued ordinary share capital)	No. of companies
3% ⩽ × <4%	17
4% ⩽ × <5%	20
5% ⩽ × <6%	10
6% ⩽ × <7%	8
7% ⩽ × <8%	5
8% ⩽ × <34%	6

Source: Author's analysis of annual reports and accounts.

Company in the issued ordinary stock of Bank of Scotland, which was actually a 'corporate' holding as opposed to a portfolio investment holding). There were only three other double-figure institutional interests: Mercury Asset Management plc's 17.97% interest in Blue Circle Industries plc; Co-operative Insurance Society Ltd.'s 16.76% interest in MEPC plc; and Kuwait Investment Office's 10% interest in Midland Bank plc. This indicates the rarity of *extremely large*, individual institutional stakes in the equity of *large* listed UK companies. Table 5.4 shows, however, that institutional stakes in the range 3–7% were not uncommon. The institutions listed in Table 5.4 are those which had notifiable interests in at least three FT-SE 100 companies at the time of the study.[158]

An interesting comparison can be made between Table 5.4 and Table 3.2. Three of the top 10 managers listed in Table 3.2 do not even appear in Table 5.4. PosTel Investment Management Ltd. (ranked number 3 in Table 3.2) had just one notifiable interest in an FT-SE 100 company at the time of Study A; The Standard Life Assurance Company (ranked number 4 in Table 3.2) had only two such notifiable interests; and Legal & General Investment Management Ltd. (ranked number 10 in Table 3.2) had none. In contrast, GRE Asset Management Ltd.—ranked a mere number 45 in Table 3.2—had five notifiable interests in FT-SE 100 companies at the time of Study A.[159]

---

[158] There were a further six institutions which had notifiable interests in two FT-SE 100 companies, and seven institutions which had a notifiable interest in one FT-SE 100 company—these make up the 'Others' category in Table 5.4.

[159] The apparent discrepancy between the number of notifiable interests of Mercury Asset Management plc ('MAM') and Prudential Portfolio Managers Ltd. ('PPM')—the managers ranked numbers 1 and 2 in Table 3.2—is simply a result of the fact that MAM was not required to disclose many of its 3%+ interests at the time of Study A: see Davies and Stapledon (n. 80 above), at 63 (n. 16).

Table 5.4 Institutions' stakes in FT-SE 100 companies, 1991–2

Institution	No. of FT-SE 100 companies in which a notifiable interest held, 1991–2 (with breakdown by interest size)						
	3% ≤ x < 4%	4% ≤ x < 5%	5% ≤ x < 6%	6% ≤ x < 7%	7% ≤ x < 8%	8% ≤ x < 34%	Total
PPM (Ins.)	28	16	3	6	3	1	57
Schroder (FC)	13	5	2	–	–	–	20
Fleming (FC)	9	2	1	2	–	–	14
BZWIM (FC)	11	1	–	–	–	–	12
Scot. Wid. (Ins.)	9	2	1	–	–	–	12
MAM (FC)	–	–	4	1	–	2	7
PDFM (FC)	2	3	1	1	–	–	7
GRE (Ins.)	1	2	1	1	–	–	5
Norwich (Ins.)	1	2	–	–	–	1	4
Morg. Gren. (FC)	2	1	1	–	–	–	4
Prov. Mut. (Ins.)	3	1	–	–	–	–	4
Abu Dhabi (O/S)	1	–	–	1	2	–	4
Gartmore (FC)	3	–	–	–	–	–	3
Sun Life (Ins.)	3	–	–	–	–	–	3
Others	9	3	3	–	–	4	19
Total	95	38	17	12	5	8	175

Note: abbreviations: see App. E.

Source: Author's analysis of annual reports and accounts.

There is not, therefore, a strong correlation between the leading fund managers in Table 3.2, and those in Table 5.4. The main reason for this is that some of the institutions followed widely differing investment policies for UK equities, at the time of Study A. For instance, some[160] either explicitly or loosely 'indexed' their holdings (or the bulk of their holdings) in FT-SE 100 companies (normally as part of a wider index of companies)— and thereby had a similar percentage holding in all FT-SE 100 companies. Others[161] (and this was more common) exercised stock-selection judge-ment and had substantially overweight positions in some FT-SE 100 companies and only minor holdings (or even none at all) in others. Further, some institutions were underweight in many FT-SE 100 companies, and considerably overweight in a large number of medium-sized and/or smaller companies.[162] This was a contributing factor behind

[160] e.g. Barclays de Zoete Wedd Investment Management Ltd. and PosTel Investment Management Ltd.

[161] e.g. Mercury Asset Management plc and Phillips & Drew Fund Management Ltd. But see also 'Tracking the Behaviour of Stock Pickers', *Fin. Times*, 6 Dec. 1993, p. 16 (many supposed stock-pickers are really 'closet indexers').

[162] e.g. M&G Investment Management Ltd. and Scottish Amicable Investment Managers Ltd.

the decision to conduct Study B, which covered a much wider spread of companies than did Study A in terms of the companies' market capitalizations.

(b) Study B

Due to the wide spread of companies and the stratified nature of the sample, in Study B, statistics could be calculated for different types of companies: large, medium-sized, and small. Table 5.5 provides information about the entire sample of companies together with comparable information for the 10 large companies, the 25 medium-sized companies, and the 34 small companies within the sample. It gives an impression of the prominence, amongst the bodies and persons having the 10 largest interests in companies' issued ordinary share capital, of institutional investors *vis-à-vis* non-institutional investors.

One-tailed t-tests were performed on the various pairs of sample means in Table 5.5. The t-statistics reveal that:

(a) in regard to the collective holding of the top 10 interest-holders, at a 1% level: (i) the small-companies sample mean is significantly greater than the medium-sized companies sample mean; (ii) the small-companies sample mean is significantly greater than the large-companies sample

Table 5.5 The relative position of institutions amongst companies' 10 largest interest-holders

Category of company	Ave. (mean) collective holding of top 10 interest-holders (% of issued ord. shares)	Ave. (mean) number of institutions amongst top 10 interest-holders	Ave. (mean) collective holding of 'top' institutions[a] (% of issued ord. shares)
Large	27.47% (*sd*: 4.36)	9.70 (*sd*: 0.60)	26.22% (*sd*: 4.90)
Medium-sized	44.92% (*sd*: 14.23)	9.20 (*sd*: 2.02)	38.49% (*sd*: 7.47)
Small	59.10% (*sd*: 12.26)	7.90 (*sd*: 2.01)	40.63% (*sd*: 14.17)
All	49.38% (*sd*: 16.54)	8.64 (*sd*: 2.01)	37.76% (*sd*: 12.15)

Note: '*sd*': standard deviation.
   [a] For the purposes of the last column, the 'top' institutions for a sample company means the institutions which were amongst the 10 largest interest-holders of that company.

Source: Author's calculations from information provided by the sample companies.

mean; and (iii) the medium-sized companies sample mean is significantly greater than the large-companies sample mean;

(b) in regard to the number of institutions amongst the top 10 interest-holders, at a 1% level: (i) the small-companies sample mean is significantly less than the medium-sized companies sample mean; and (ii) the small-companies sample mean is significantly less than the large-companies sample mean; but (iii) the difference between the medium-sized companies sample mean and the large-companies sample mean is not significant;

(c) in regard to the collective holding of the 'top' institutions, at a 1% level: (i) the difference between the small-companies sample mean and the medium-sized companies sample mean is not significant; (ii) the small-companies sample mean is significantly greater than the large-companies sample mean; and (iii) the medium-sized companies sample mean is significantly greater than the large-companies sample mean.

Further to Table 5.5, only one of the 69 companies surveyed did not have at least one institution amongst its 10 largest interest-holders. An institution was the largest interest-holder in nine (90%) of the large companies; in 21 (84%) of the medium-sized companies; in 22 (65%) of the small companies; and in 52 (75%) of all the sample companies.

Table 5.6 gives a more detailed view of the potential voting strength of the few largest institutional interest-holders in large, medium-sized, and small listed UK companies. It addresses what was referred to at the

Table 5.6 Profile of companies' largest institutional interest-holders

Category of company	Average (mean) collective holding of the largest n institutions amongst the 10 largest interest-holders (% of issued ordinary share capital)					
	One	Two	Three	Four	Five	Six
Large	5.55%	9.19%	12.07%	14.73%	17.06%	19.25%
	(sd: 2.13)	(sd: 2.51)	(sd: 2.79)	(sd: 3.00)	(sd: 3.29)	(sd: 3.67)
Medium-sized	9.67%	15.45%	20.09%	23.82%	27.16%	29.99%
	(sd: 4.31)	(sd: 5.19)	(sd: 5.99)	(sd: 6.07)	(sd: 6.20)	(sd: 6.41)
Small	10.73%	17.54%	22.95%	27.84%	32.30%	36.44%
	(sd: 3.85)	(sd: 5.82)	(sd: 7.22)	(sd: 8.17)	(sd: 8.97)	(sd: 9.18)
All	9.59%	15.58%	20.34%	24.08%	28.19%	31.33%
	(sd: 4.21)	(sd: 5.94)	(sd: 7.30)	(sd: 8.23)	(sd: 9.04)	(sd: 9.63)

Note: 'sd': standard deviation.

Source: Author's calculations from information provided by the sample companies.

beginning of this subsection as the 'second objective' of this subsection's empirical studies: to examine the institutional-shareholder profile of large, medium-sized, and small listed UK companies. This is, as mentioned earlier, of importance in relation to assessing the likelihood that a small group of institutions in any given company could if necessary seriously challenge the management of that company.

One-tailed t-tests were performed on the various pairs of sample means in Table 5.6. The t-statistics reveal that:

(a) for the top 1, top 2, top 3, top 4, top 5, and top 6 institutions amongst the 10 largest interest-holders, at a 1% level: (i) the small-companies sample mean is significantly greater than the large-companies sample mean; and (ii) the medium-sized companies sample mean is significantly greater than the large-companies sample mean;

(b) for the top 1, top 2, top 3, and top 4 institutions amongst the 10 largest interest-holders, at a 1% level,[163] the difference between the small-companies sample mean and the medium-sized companies sample mean is not significant;

(c) for the top 5 and top 6 institutions amongst the 10 largest interest-holders, at a 1% level, the small-companies sample mean is significantly greater than the medium-sized companies sample mean.

An analysis of Table 5.6 reveals that, even if the top three or four institutions are assumed to compose the institutional coalition, as at 1993 it was only in small and (to a lesser extent) medium-sized listed UK companies that an ideal coalition could have been formed.[164] One further point is worth making at this stage. The well-known thesis of Berle and Means[165] was formulated in the US in the late 1920s when a mass of diffuse small holdings characterized the shareholding structure of those numerous quoted public companies which lacked a significant 'founding family' or corporate shareholding, and in which senior management and their associates had a negligible stake. Tables 5.5 and 5.6 show that that shareholding structure clearly did not prevail in most such listed UK companies in 1993.[166]

---

[163] At a 2.5% level, however, the small-companies sample mean is significantly greater than the medium-sized companies sample mean for the top 4 institutions amongst the 10 largest interest-holders.

[164] An 'ideal' coalition is, as mentioned earlier, one comprising no more than four institutions which together control at least 20–30% of the equity.

[165] A. A. Berle and G. C. Means, *The Modern Corporation and Private Property* (rev. edn., 1968) 82: 'Where ownership is sufficiently sub-divided, the management can . . . become a self-perpetuating body even though its share in the ownership is negligible.'

[166] However, even though the structural background to the Berle and Means thesis did not exist in Britain in 1993, it does not necessarily follow that the thesis itself (self-perpetuating management, lack of control by shareholders, etc.) was thereby null as well. This is because a

Table 5.7 Institutions' stakes in the large companies

Institution	Number of the 10 large, sample companies in which a top 10 interest held (with breakdown by interest size)						
	1% ≤ x < 2%	2% ≤ x < 3%	3% ≤ x < 4%	4% ≤ x < 6%	6% ≤ x < 8%	8% ≤ x < 11%	Total
MAM (Ins.)	1	2	3	2	–	1	9
Stan. Life (Ins.)	2	6	–	1	–	–	9
BZWIM (FC)	3	5	–	–	–	–	8
L&G (Ins.)	8	–	–	–	–	–	8
PPM (Ins.)	–	1	2	2	1	1	7
PDFM (FC)	–	3	1	3	–	–	7
Schroder (FC)	1	2	3	1	–	–	7
PosTel (Pens.)	6	–	–	–	–	–	6
Scot. Wid. (Ins.)	1	3	–	1	–	–	5
CIN (Pens.)	1	4	–	–	–	–	5
Allied Dun. (Ins.)	–	2	1	–	–	–	3
Norwich (Ins.)	1	1	1	–	–	–	3
AMP (Ins.)	3	–	–	–	–	–	3
Others	9	6	2	–	–	–	17
Total	36	35	13	10	1	2	97

Note: abbreviations: see App. E.

Source: Author's analysis of information provided by the sample companies.

Tables 5.7, 5.8, and 5.9 show—for the 10 large companies, the 25 medium-sized companies, and the 34 small companies, respectively—the institutions whose names appeared at least three times in the lists of top 10 interest-holders provided by the sample companies.

A comparison of (on the one hand) Tables 5.8 and 5.9, and (on the other hand) Table 3.2, shows that even fund managers with a relatively small share of the overall UK equity market occasionally hold a relatively large percentage of a *medium-sized* or *small* listed company's issued ordinary capital. Consider, for instance: Baillie Gifford (ranked 50th in Table 3.2; two interests of between 5–7%, and one of 7–10%, in medium-sized sample companies); Britannic Assurance (ranked 46th in Table 3.2; two interests of 5–7% in medium-sized sample companies, and one of 7–10% in a small sample company); and the substantial interests held by Framlington,

highly dispersed shareholder body is not a precondition to the thesis. If a substantial part of the shareholder body of a listed UK company were a small group of institutions, it would still be perfectly possible for the management to be self-perpetuating, and for there to be negligible shareholder influence, if those institutional shareholders were very passive and aloof. Nevertheless, Ch. 4 and the current chapter seek to demonstrate that the Berle and Means thesis itself would not have described accurately the state of governance in most quoted British companies in the early 1990s.

Table 5.8 Institutions' stakes in the medium-sized companies

Institution	Number of the 25 medium-sized, sample companies in which a top 10 interest held (with breakdown by interest size)						
	1% ≤ x < 3%	3% ≤ x < 5%	5% ≤ x < 7%	7% ≤ x < 10%	10% ≤ x < 13%	13% ≤ x < 25%	Total
PPM (Ins.)	2	4	5	3	1	–	15
Norwich (Ins.)	5	6	3	–	–	–	14
Schroder (FC)	5	3	1	1	3	–	13
M&G (Indep.)	–	4	–	1	3	2	10
MAM (FC)	1	4	3	1	–	1	10
AMP (Ins.)	4	3	2	–	–	–	9
Allied Dun. (Ins.)	2	7	–	–	–	–	9
Gartmore (FC)	4	2	1	–	1	–	8
Stan. Life (Ins.)	3	4	1	–	–	–	8
BZWIM (FC)	3	2	2	–	–	–	7
Co-op. (Ins.)	2	4	–	–	–	–	6
J. Capel (FC)	4	2	–	–	–	–	6
Sun Life (Ins.)	5	–	1	–	–	–	6
CIN (Pens.)	5	1	–	–	–	–	6
Fleming (FC)	1	1	1	–	1	1	5
Britannic (Ins.)	1	2	2	–	–	–	5
Sun All. (Ins.)	2	3	–	–	–	–	5
L&G (Ins.)	3	2	–	–	–	–	5
Henderson (Indep.)	4	1	–	–	–	–	5
Conf. Life (Ins.)	1	2	1	–	–	–	4
Prov. Mut. (Ins.)	1	2	1	–	–	–	4
PDFM (FC)	2	1	1	–	–	–	4
Scot. Wid. (Ins.)	2	2	–	–	–	–	4
Scot. Amic. (Ins.)	3	1	–	–	–	–	4
Royal Ins. (Ins.)	4	–	–	–	–	–	4
Baillie (Indep.)	–	–	2	1	–	–	3
Equit. Life (Ins.)	1	2	–	–	–	–	3
Morg. Gren. (FC)	1	2	–	–	–	–	3
Cler. Med. (Ins.)	3	–	–	–	–	–	3
Framling. (FC)	3	–	–	–	–	–	3
PosTel (Pens.)	3	–	–	–	–	–	3
Others	21	13	2	–	–	–	36
Total	101	80	29	7	9	4	230

Note: abbreviations: see App. E.

Source: Author's analysis of information provided by the sample companies.

Edinburgh, Scottish Mutual, and 3i, all of which were outside the top 50 managers of quoted UK equities at the end of 1991.

A wide range of UK-based fund managers thus filled the position of largest institutional interest-holder (which in many instances was also the position of largest interest-holder of any description) in medium-sized and small listed UK companies at the time of Study B. (The largest institutional

Table 5.9 Institutions' stakes in the small companies

Institution	Number of the 34 small, sample companies in which a top 10 interest held (with breakdown by interest size)						
	1% ≤ x < 3%	3% ≤ x < 5%	5% ≤ x < 7%	7% ≤ x < 10%	10% ≤ x < 13%	13% ≤ x < 20%	Total
PPM (Ins.)	–	5	6	5	–	–	16
Scot. Amic. (Ins.)	3	7	3	1	1	–	15
M&G (Indep.)	1	3	–	1	1	6	12
PDFM (FC)	1	4	–	3	3	1	12
BZWIM (FC)	5	4	2	–	–	–	11
Schroder (FC)	1	2	4	1	1	–	9
Framling. (FC)	1	3	2	1	1	–	8
MAM (FC)	2	1	2	1	–	1	7
PosTel (Pens.)	–	4	–	3	–	–	7
Stan. Life (Ins.)	1	2	2	2	–	–	7
Cler. Med. (Ins.)	2	2	3	–	–	–	7
Norwich (Ins.)	2	4	1	–	–	–	7
Gartmore (FC)	–	–	1	3	1	1	6
Edinburgh (Indep.)	–	3	–	3	–	–	6
Hill Sam. (FC)	–	3	2	1	–	–	6
Britannic (Ins.)	2	3	–	1	–	–	6
Friends' (Ins.)	1	3	1	–	–	–	5
Scot. Wid. (Ins.)	2	3	–	–	–	–	5
Morg. Gren. (FC)	3	2	–	–	–	–	5
3i (†)	–	2	1	–	1	–	4
Allied Dun. (Ins.)	–	2	–	2	–	–	4
Fleming (FC)	–	2	1	1	–	–	4
Equit. Life (Ins.)	2	–	1	1	–	–	4
L&G (Ins.)	–	3	1	–	–	–	4
Lloyds (FC)	1	2	1	–	–	–	4
Scot. Mut. (Ins.)	–	2	–	1	–	–	3
Prov. Mut. (Ins.)	1	2	–	–	–	–	3
Baring (FC)	1	2	–	–	–	–	3
Brit. Gas (Pens.)	–	3	–	–	–	–	3
Brit. Air. (Pens.)	–	3	–	–	–	–	3
County (FC)	1	2	–	–	–	–	3
Co-op. (Ins.)	2	1	–	–	–	–	3
Others	24	35	6	1	–	1	67
Total	59	119	40	32	9	10	269

Note: abbreviations: see App. E.

Source: Author's analysis of information provided by the sample companies.

interest-holders in Top 100 companies came, as Table 5.4 shows, from a much narrower group of institutions.) The relevance of this for present purposes is that institutional interventions to change under-performing management teams at portfolio companies have, generally, been led by the largest institutional interest-holder in the company concerned. This, and the other information contained in the tables above is analysed and interpreted further in the remainder of this section, and in Chapters 9 and 10—which examine the desirability, and likelihood, of a greater level of institutional monitoring in the future.[167]

ii. Detailed Systematic Review

A very large institution may from time to time conduct an in-depth analysis of a company in which it has an overweight holding, and which it sees as a long-term constituent of its equity portfolio. This involves, in a sense, just a much more thorough and detailed version of the routine analysis, meetings, and dialogue described in Section B.2, above. For example, Prudential Portfolio Managers Ltd. carried out 'an exhaustive six-month study' of The General Electric Company plc ('GEC') during 1991–2.[168] Prudential had had an overweight holding in GEC for many years,[169] and it had a stake of about 7% at the end of 1991, which was then worth around £380 million (equivalent to roughly 2% of the total value of Prudential's UK equity holdings at that time).

These detailed reviews are exceptional because only a small minority of institutions conducts them, and because those few institutions that do conduct them do so only in relation to certain holdings—where they are carried out infrequently and at irregular intervals.

iii. Extraordinary Meetings and Dialogue with Management

Occasionally, institutions have meetings and dialogue with the management of portfolio companies in addition to the routine meetings described earlier. These additional meetings may be initiated by the company management or by the institution(s).

One type of company-initiated extraordinary meeting arises where the management decides to 'pre-market' a possible (a) capital raising; (b) restructuring; (c) large transaction; or (d) unusual course of action. Here, one or more of the company's senior executive directors, and/or the company's broker or merchant-bank adviser, visits (or sometimes just telephones) the larger institutional shareholders on a one-to-one basis shortly before the date on which the management plans to announce the event. The idea is to get a feel for whether the proposal has the support of the holders of a sizeable proportion of the company's share capital. The following is a good illustration of (a):

---

[167] A final point to note about the tables is that the institutions covered in the author's UK interview project held 308 of the 690 'top 10 interests' in the 69 sample companies in Study B, which is more than half of the 596 interests that were held by institutions.

[168] 'The Shape of Things to Come', *Fin. Times*, 10 July 1992, p. 15.

[169] It had a holding of 4.8% in 1957: G. Clayton and W. T. Osborn, *Insurance Company Investment: Principles and Policy* (1965) 177; and a holding of 6.5% in 1976: J. Scott, *The Controlling Constellations* (1984).

S. G. Warburg . . . has dropped plans to raise £80m of new equity after sounding out its leading institutional shareholders. [Warburg] had been considering raising the new equity although there has been no formal stock exchange announcement. In the middle of the week . . . Warburg's stockbroker took soundings from [Warburg's] institutional shareholders about whether they would be prepared to buy £80m of new convertible preference shares. . . . The broker took the view that the institutions were not keen to subscribe, and so the share sale plans were dropped.[170]

An example of (b) is:

[L]ast week . . . Babcock International announced a three-year plan which will give a new look to the engineering contracting and materials handling group. . . . Babcock's managing director had spent the last few days before [the] announcement on a punishing schedule of 37 meetings with institutions. . . . Winning the City's approval is crucial . . . for a plan which hinges on a larger than expected £78.6m rights issue, and a restructuring of the company's energy division that—along with the division's losses—will produce an estimated group pre-tax loss of £41.2m in the year ended March 31.[171]

An example of (c) is:

Shares in Amber Day fell 9p to 41p after In Shops [plc] . . . said it had decided against proceeding with any offer for the discount retailer. In Shops halted the recent slide in Amber Day's share price on Monday when it said it might make a bid. However, it decided against proceeding 'after consultation with advisers and having taken account of the views of shareholders'. . . . The potential bidder's institutional shareholders were reluctant [for the company] to pursue Amber Day.[172]

An example of (d) is: '[Thames Water plc] decided against offering an enhanced scrip dividend alternative[173] after sounding out some of its larger shareholders.'[174]

The author's interview study revealed a number of points about pre-marketing. First, it usually involves the company's largest six or so

---

[170] 'Warburg Gives Up £80m Equity Plan', *Fin. Times*, 5 June 1993, p. 26. Note, however, that Warburg was some six weeks later able to launch a £91m. convertible bond issue, 'targeted more to continental investors than the City institutions who snubbed it in the first place': 'Lex: S. G. Warburg', *Fin. Times*, 22 July 1993, p. 20. (The convertible bonds would, if all converted, have represented just under 5% of Warburg's issued ordinary capital ('Warburg Seeks £91m Via Bond Issue', *Fin. Times*, 22 July 1993, p. 22), and the issue was thus within the limit set by the *Pre-Emption Guidelines* for non-rights issues: see Ch. 4, Sec. A.1.i.

[171] 'City Sets Sights on a Less Exciting Future', *Fin. Times*, 28 Apr. 1994, p. 30.

[172] 'In Shops Drops Plans to Bid for Amber Day', *Fin. Times*, 2 July 1992, p. 24. See also A. D. Cosh, A. Hughes, K. Lee, and A. Singh, 'Institutional Investment, Mergers and the Market for Corporate Control' (1989) 7 *Int. J Indust. Org.* 73.

[173] See generally Ch. 4, Sec. A.1.iii.

[174] 'Price Increase Behind Rise at Thames Water', *Fin. Times*, 3 June 1993, p. 24.

institutional shareholders.[175] Secondly, pre-marketing is very common, for obvious reasons, in case (a). It is also common in cases (b) and (c) *if* the proposed restructuring or transaction requires a capital raising. Case (c) (i.e. large transactions) can be divided into those which require general-meeting approval (i.e. Super Class 1 transactions and reverse takeovers),[176] and those which do not (i.e. transactions smaller than Super Class 1). The former are, as one would expect, much more likely to be pre-marketed than the latter. Several fund managers said that, in relation to the latter sort of transactions (and where a capital raising is not required), they are not normally consulted. Others said that they generally do get pre-marketed on these sort of deals in the case of small and medium-sized companies in which they have a holding of about 3% or more, whereas 'large companies are almost a law unto themselves'. Thirdly, especially in relation to transactions not requiring a capital raising, institutions are often consulted late in the day, when 'quite a momentum has built up'. Fourthly, most pre-marketed proposals elicit a diversity of views—some favourable, some unfavourable (to varying degrees), and some indifferent. Some proposals are, therefore, carried into effect in spite of the strong opposition of a major shareholder. This is especially the case with larger companies.[177] Where there is this diversity of views, the courses of action available to an aggrieved shareholder are limited—essentially to 'lumping it', selling the shareholding, or voting against the proposal (if general-meeting approval is required); there is by definition little chance of any effective collective action by large institutional shareholders.[178] Fifthly, even where institutional opposition causes management to abandon a proposal, that is not necessarily the end of the matter: 'there are several ways to skin a cat and, just because the institutions say no to such and such, it is not to say that the management is not able to find another way of achieving that objective'.[179] Finally, and importantly, pre-marketing very often involves the imparting of undisclosed price-sensitive information. Although company managements sometimes just put 'hypotheticals' to their largest institutional shareholders, it is fairly common for pre-marketing to consist of an exposition of the precise proposal. Institutions insist on being warned in advance if a company management wishes to make them an insider; this is also a requirement of the *Listing Rules*.[180]

---

[175] But cf. the text accompanying n. 171 above (37 separate meetings).

[176] See *Listing Rules*, ch. 10; and Sec. B.3.vii.(b), below.

[177] Five of the fund managers interviewed cited examples of where their institutions had objected vehemently to proposals made by the management of large companies (three proposals were takeover bids, and one was a rights issue to finance expansion by way of, *inter alia*, takeovers), but where the proposals had nevertheless been effected.

[178] This is discussed in Ch. 10, Sec. B.1.ix.

[179] Comment of an interviewee. See also n. 170 above.

Most are unwilling to be made insiders, and put in a position of being unable to trade, for more than six or seven days. This topic is dealt with in a later chapter.[181]

A second type of company-initiated extraordinary meeting involves the management (with or without its broker/adviser) explaining its reasons for having a rights issue, or making an acquisition, etc., *after* it has been announced publicly. This might occur where the institution concerned was not pre-marketed.

A third kind of company-initiated extraordinary meeting involves the management, or occasionally a senior non-executive director, explaining the resignation, removal, or unexpected retirement of a senior executive. For example, the chief executive of Glaxo Holdings plc was forced by the company's executive chairman to resign in March 1993. A report of the incident said: 'On Thursday morning, as soon as the [Stock Exchange] announcement was made, Glaxo's broker contacted the institutions to arrange meetings with [the executive chairman and new chief executive], a tactic perfected last year when another key company, BP, ousted its chairman, Bob Horton. Even so, the shares took a terrible battering.'[182]

Shareholder-initiated extraordinary meetings and dialogue arise where an institution is (a) seriously dissatisfied with the management of a portfolio company; or (b) concerned about some other matter (either company-specific or procedural/general) existing at a portfolio company. In case (a), the dialogue may, if it does not produce a satisfactory outcome from the institution's viewpoint, be followed or attended by one or more of: (i) meetings/dialogue with some of the company's non-executive directors; (ii) meetings/dialogue with other institutional shareholders; and/or (iii) an attempted ousting of some or all of the impeached management.[183] In case (b), the meetings/dialogue with management may occasionally be accompanied by dialogue with other institutional share-holders (perhaps together with, or under the auspices of, one of the institutional collective-action vehicles), but only rarely[184] would the company's non-executive directors be involved. The writer's interview study indicated that case (b) often involves the institution communicating its concern by way of letter or telephone rather than there being an actual meeting. In contrast, case (a) commonly involves face-to-face meetings due to the greater urgency and significance of the issue involved. In each type of case,

---

[180] See *Listing Rules*, para. 9.3.
[181] See Ch. 9, Sec. B.4.
[182] 'Glaxo's Bitter Pill', *Sunday Times*, 14 Mar. 1993, sec. 3, p. 3.
[183] See Secs. B.3.iv, v, vi, below. There are of course other possible courses of action, such as disposal of the shareholding: see Ch. 10, Secs. B.1.i, B.1.ii.
[184] See Sec. D.2.ii(d), below.

it is not unusual for some of the communication to be effected through the company's broker or financial adviser.

The interviews also revealed that there have been many more instances of case (b) than case (a). As to the average level of each, it is not possible to generalize. In regard to case (a), this is because some institutions have a much greater disposition than others to, for example, sell a shareholding rather than try to exert pressure if serious management problems occur. In regard to case (b), this is because some institutions put more resources into, and/or attach greater importance to, proactive firm-level monitoring on matters such as the adequacy in number and calibre of a company's non-executive directors, separation of the roles of chairman and chief executive, executive service contracts, etc. It is reasonably clear, however, that the late 1980s and early 1990s witnessed an increased level of proactive monitoring by a significant minority of the 17 institutions covered in the interview project. At the time of the interviews, two of the institutions had a senior executive (called the Director of Corporate Finance in one case) devoted full time to matters of corporate governance and problem companies; another had employed a Corporate Finance Director until early 1992.[185] Another had a 'Shareholders' Affairs' executive who, together with its chief executive, devoted a substantial amount of time to proactive discussions with company managements. And one interviewee, who managed a specialist fund investing in 'recovery' stocks, also spent a considerable proportion of his time on problem companies and pushing for improvement in areas of corporate governance at portfolio companies.

iv. Meetings and Dialogue with Non-Executive Directors

A majority of the institutions covered in the interview project met with or otherwise entered into dialogue with the non-executive directors of a portfolio company only where there was perceived to be an extreme problem at the company. A small number of institutions communicated with non-executives on a wider range of topics. This liaison between institutions and non-executive directors is examined later.[186]

v. Meetings and Dialogue between Institutions

The fund managers interviewed by the author said that in their experience dialogue between a number of a company's largest institutional share-holders ranged from several bilateral telephone conversations to an organized meeting at the offices of one institution. Such dialogue usually

---

[185] His position had, interestingly, been discontinued because 'his actions had received too much adverse publicity': 'Tough Tactics Behind the Unit Trusts', *Fin. Times*, 5 Aug. 1992, p. 15. See further Ch. 10, Sec. B.1.
[186] See Secs. B.3.vi and D.2.ii.(d), below.

occurred after the failure of, or in conjunction with, discussions between individual institutions and the company's management regarding a serious management problem or another issue of concern. Where a serious management problem was at issue, the dialogue between the institutions led sometimes to an attempted ousting of the impeached management by a coalition of some or all of the institutions. On the other hand, the dialogue sometimes produced no consensus of opinion for collective action. In the latter case, the courses of action taken by institutions included disposing or attempting to dispose of the shares, attempting to engineer a takeover bid for the company, and doing nothing at all. The interviewees said that where institutional shareholders had acted collectively at any one company, in relation to something other than a serious management problem, their aim had generally been something other than replacement of the management. For example, the major institutional shareholders of Distillers Company Ltd. had extensive dialogue amongst themselves regarding the tardiness of the company's management in reaching agreement with thalidomide victims on compensation terms. A secret meeting was eventually held between the company's chairman and executive directors, and seven institutions, at the offices of the company's financial adviser, after which a substantially increased—and ultimately successful—offer of settlement was made by the company.[187]

vi. Procurement of Management Changes by an Institution or Institutional Coalition

> Scarcely a week goes by without some chairman or managing director resigning or being publicly pushed out before the end of his term [which is due partly to] the increasingly active role the insurance companies and [fund-management arms of] merchant banks are taking when their investments turn sour. They are now sometimes stirred to take action, either behind the scenes or occasionally in public, to remove the boss.[188]

> Bad managers have been eying their shareholders with anxiety recently. Over the last 18 months the big institutional investors have shown themselves willing to remove managements which are not performing well.[189]

It may be surprising to some readers that only the second of these statements was made during the UK recession of the early 1990s. The first was made in 1970, which demonstrates that the ultimate form of institutional monitoring is far from nascent in the UK. In fact, the first case of this nature appears to be that of the Birmingham Small Arms Company Ltd., where the Prudential's chief investment manager played a pivotal

---

[187] See '£12m–£20m. Thalidomide Offer Likely', *Times*, 5 Jan. 1973, p. 1.
[188] 'How the Mighty are Falling', *Times*, 3 July 1970, p. 25.
[189] 'A Coalition Versus a Dictator', *Fin. Times*, 27 May 1992, p. 13.

role in the ouster of the chairman way back in 1956.[190] The Prudential's fund managers also played a major part in a number of cases of institutional removal of an under-performing management (hereafter 'intervention') during the 1960s,[191] 1970s,[192] and 1980s.[193] During the four years 1990–3, however, Prudential Portfolio Managers was just one of numerous institutions which participated in interventions at a number— dozens—of quoted UK companies. It was a major part of the author's interview project to probe into a series of interventions which occurred during 1990–3, and which were reported (with identification of the institutions involved) in the press.[194] The interviewees' descriptions of those cases, supplemented by (a) the newspaper descriptions of the cases; (b) interviewees' comments about other interventions; (c) fund managers' published descriptions of various features of interventions;[195] and (d) reports of other interview studies involving UK fund managers,[196] provided the source material for the following overview of interventions which occurred in the early 1990s.[197]

Why the interventions occurred. The matter which gave rise to seemingly every intervention was that the company's management had been completely discredited—interventions occurred 'where there [was] no doubt as to the lack of ability of the existing management'. An important reason for this is that the institutions' 'strength increases the weaker the company's position is. Until the company's strategy has been proved wrong all one is doing is simply exchanging opinions.'[198] The one thing that

---

[190] See Sampson (n. 12 above), at 409–10.

[191] For a few examples, see Griffith (n. 135 above), at 197–205.

[192] For a few examples, see S. Nyman and A. Silberston, 'The Ownership and Control of Industry' (1978) 30 *Ox. Econ. Papers* 74, at 94–6.

[193] See e.g. 'Outsider for Rank in Board Changes', *Fin. Times*, 18 Mar. 1983, p. 22.

[194] The interventions focused upon by the author were those where at least some of the institutions involved were identified in the *Financial Times*: Bunzl plc (2 Nov. 1990, p. 23); Savage Group plc (26 Nov. 1990, p. 17; 20 Dec. 1990, p. 21); Budgens plc (1 May 1991, p. 21); Tace plc (19 Jan. 1991, p. 10; 4 May 1991, p. 10; 20 June 1991, p. 23); Brown & Jackson plc (10 Oct. 1991, p. 24; 23 Oct. 1991, p. 24; 11 Feb. 1992, p. 22); MTM plc (1 May 1992, p. 20); Pegasus Group plc (16 Dec. 1992, p. 24); Whitecroft plc (28 June 1993, p. 18); Alexon Group plc (23 Apr. 1993, p. 19); Spring Ram plc (1 Apr. 1993, p. 23; 10 July 1993, p. 24; 14 July 1993, p. 20; 28 July 1993, p. 19; 23 Sept. 1993, p. 19). Further cases are described (with institutions named) in 'Corporate Assassins', *Sunday Tel.*, 17 Oct. 1993, City & Bus. sec., p. 5.

[195] See 'A Coalition . . .' (n. 189 above); 'How to Replace the Board—By Stealth', *Governance*, Aug. 1993, p. 8; House of Commons Trade and Industry Committee, *Minutes of Evidence: Takeovers and Mergers* (1991) paras. 907–11, 925–34; Artus (n. 143 above); P. E. Moody, 'A More Active Role for Institutional Shareholders', *Banker*, Feb. 1979, p. 49.

[196] See Black and Coffee (n. 86 above); 'Corporate Assassins' (n. 194 above); M. Gaved, *Ownership and Influence* (1995).

[197] Where a source is not cited, quotations are of fund managers interviewed by the author.

[198] 'Why the Ideal Board Remains So Elusive', *Fin. Times*, 4 July 1990, p. 10. There are other reasons why it has proved difficult for institutions to intervene effectively until late in the day: see Ch. 10, Sec. B.

contributed most often to the complete discrediting of a company's management was the company's terrible financial performance—both in absolute terms and relative to competitors. In a few cases the fact that an institution had been deliberately misled, in one-to-one meetings with management, as to the financial health of the company was also a contributing factor. And a strong suspicion of some form of impropriety on the part of management[199] played a part in it being discredited in a handful of cases.[200]

How the interventions occurred. There is some variation in the manner in which the interventions were carried out, but most began with a large institutional shareholder having exceptional meetings with the impugned management and voicing grave concerns.[201] That institution (hereafter 'the proactive institution') was in most cases the largest institutional share-holder in the company, and in all cases it had an overweight holding in the company. The company's advisory merchant bank or broker was commonly involved in some of these meetings. In some cases the proactive institution was rebuffed bluntly at that stage; in other cases the management took some action[202] aimed at placating the institution, but did not do enough to restore its credibility. At least three interventions began when a director (who was in two cases an executive director, and in one case a non-executive director) resigned or was sacked and then approached one of the company's largest institutional shareholders with concerns about the management. That institution then commenced dialogue with the management. In none of the cases reported in the press did the management make sufficient changes at this stage to satisfy the proactive

[199] Impropriety was suspected in cases where (a) two directors placed a large parcel of their shares with institutions only a very short time before a profits warning was issued by the company; (b) a company had purchased a suspect business from a group with which its executive chairman was associated; and (c) there had been grossly excessive payments to directors and their associates.

[200] Therefore, virtually all interventions involved *ex post* absolute failure or *ex post* relative failure on the part of management, in the terminology of J. R. Franks and C. P. Mayer, 'Capital Markets and Corporate Control: A Study of France, Germany and the UK' (1990) 10 *Econ. Pol.* 189, at 211. Note that PosTel's campaign of voting against the re-election of directors with long-term rolling service contracts (see Ch. 4, Sec. A.1.xvii) during 1994 may appear exceptional given that most, and probably all, of the executive directors with such contracts had not been 'completely discredited' as referred to in the text. In reality, however, PosTel was not attempting to 'intervene' in those companies; it could not seriously have expected to remove the 'offending' directors (since many institutions did not support its campaign of voting against the re-election of such executive directors). It seems, therefore, that PosTel's action was designed simply as a form of protest and to draw attention to its view on the undesirability of long-term rolling service contracts.

[201] Some interventions began with more than one institution having extraordinary meetings with the impeached management; the institutions were acting independently at that stage.

[202] e.g. undertook to appoint extra non-executive directors; or agreed to split the roles of chairman and chief executive.

institution, but one interviewee said that he had on several occasions 'hint[ed] to [a] company that other shareholders [were] likely to feel the same way, and then the thing [was] resolved quietly with a discreet resignation'.

Returning to the reported interventions, the second main step taken by the proactive institution in several instances was contacting one or more of the company's non-executive directors. In some unreported cases, dialogue between the proactive institution and some of the non-executives, without anything else, led to management changes. However, in all of the reported cases where the second step was contacting the non-executives, a third step—dialogue with other large institutional shareholders—was required at some stage. One fund manager said that 'it's hugely difficult often in these situations to get the non-executives to stand up against the chief executive'. Indeed, in three of the reported cases, the intervening institutions and the non-executive directors were diametrically opposed,[203] and the non-executives were eventually forced to resign. In a fourth case, the non-executives grudgingly supported the institutions in removing the impugned executive directors, but successfully opposed the appointment of a new management team backed (originally) by all of the intervening institutions.

The second main step in some other reported interventions was that the proactive institution made contact with one or more of the other large institutional shareholders. One interviewee said that the reason why his institution had sometimes contacted other institutions prior to contacting a non-executive director was that 'we don't want to be in a minority of one'. Contact with non-executives was commonly the third step in these cases.

Appointing a good replacement management team is, of course, just as important as removing a bad existing one. In some cases an alternative management team already existed in the form of a team assembled by an ex-director who had been sacked by the impugned directors, and whose subsequent approach to a large institutional shareholder marked the start of the intervention. In other cases it was necessary for the proactive institution, sometimes with and sometimes without its coalition partners, to find a potential replacement management team. In a couple of cases an independent merchant bank was employed to assist in so doing. It was necessary in at least one case for the intervening institutions to indemnify

---

[203] In two cases this was because the non-executives supported the impugned executive directors. The other case was unusual in that the institutions sided with the executive directors who wanted to bring in a new chief executive and try to trade the company out of its difficulties. The non-executive directors and the company's merchant-bank adviser had a rival plan to revive the company by selling key assets to reduce debt. The institutions and the executives prevailed; the non-executives and the adviser resigned.

the new management team because the company was close to trading insolvently.

Thus, at some stage in all of the reported interventions there was dialogue between the proactive institution and other large institutional shareholders. Although in some cases some of the institutions approached by the proactive institution declined to provide support, in every reported intervention the proactive institution was able to form a coalition[204] of between two and six institutions. The input of these other institutions often comprised a mere undertaking to support, or to use best endeavours to support,[205] the action proposed by the proactive institution. Still, in some cases two or three coalition members all played a fairly active part in further negotiations with the company's management, advisers, and non-executive directors, and in finding a replacement management team.

In each case negotiations with the impugned management were conducted against the background of an implicit, if not explicit, threat that the institutions would if necessary requisition an EGM and attempt to vote the impugned directors off the board. In the majority of reported interventions the institutions succeeded in securing management changes without the need to requisition a general meeting, but in four cases that final step was taken. In each of those four cases, some or all of the impugned directors resigned before the actual EGM, when it became clear that the institutions would prevail on the contested resolutions.

Number of institutions in, and percentage of equity held by, the coalitions. Membership of coalitions varied in number between two and six institutions. Six was exceptional—most coalitions comprised either two, three, or four members. The coalitions represented between roughly 20% to roughly 40% of the issued share capital of the companies concerned.[206] Interviewees commented that the ideal coalition would have two or three members, and that four is the maximum for a workable group: 'beyond that it becomes very difficult to act quickly and to speak with one voice'. These institutions should, ideally, represent somewhere between 20–30% of the equity. If reference is made to Table 5.6, it can be seen that, even if the top three or four institutions are assumed to compose the coalition,[207]

---

[204] 'Coalition' is a very appropriate term to describe these institutional groups. It is defined in *The Concise Oxford Dictionary of Current English* (8th edn., 1990) 215 as 'a temporary alliance for combined action'.

[205] Institutions managing the assets of external pension funds, and which are required to refer controversial voting matters to their clients (the trustees) (see nn. 79–84 above, and accompanying text), can only pledge to use their best endeavours to vote their clients' shares in a certain way.

[206] In one company one of the impugned directors had a 23% stake, and in another case an impugned director controlled 16% of the equity. The institutional coalition was nevertheless successful in each case.

[207] The qualification to this assumption is that sometimes one (or more) of the top 3–4 institutions refuses to join the coalition.

as at 1993 it was only in small and (to a lesser extent) medium-sized UK companies that an ideal coalition could have been formed. This may explain partly why none of the reported interventions involved Top 100 companies.[208]

Secrecy of coalitions' operations. In most of the reported interventions the institutions operated behind the scenes, such that the first press reports were of an EGM being requisitioned or even of a group of directors being replaced.[209] This is because 'complete discretion is usually necessary for the success of these operations'.[210] Any leak 'could jeopardise the share price and any hope of a future fund-raising'.[211] Institutions sought publicity, exceptionally, during the course of a couple of the reported interventions. This was done largely as a defensive measure, in response to public statements of the impugned management.

Length of interventions. Several of the interventions lasted for over a year, from the time of the proactive institution's first extraordinary dialogue with the impeached directors until the date of their replacement. Other cases took as little as a couple of months. One interviewee calculated that he had spent a total of 48 hours (not including travel time) in meetings relating to one intervention. The length of the process is important both in terms of 'rais[ing] the cost of building and maintaining a coalition [and because] once an institution joins a coalition, it will be expected to stand fast and not liquidate its stake in the company'.[212]

Pressure from the company's advisers. In most of the interventions the impeached directors obtained legal advice at an early stage, and in some cases the company's solicitors attempted to intimidate the intervening institutions into ceasing their actions. Several coalitions incurred legal expenses obtaining general advice as to the legality of their proposed actions. In one unreported case, a company's merchant bank approached the clients (pension-fund trustees) of the proactive institution and asked questions like 'Should an institutional investor be allowed to ask for changes like this?', 'What authority do they have?', and 'Are you in favour of this action?' The fund manager's clients all told the merchant bank that they preferred to accept the fund manager's judgement on such cases.

General. A few general points should be mentioned. First, it was noted

---

[208] Note, however, that 'Corporate Assassins' (n. 194 above) cites an institutional intervention at BET plc in 1991. BET plc was an FT-SE 100 constituent at that time. It should also be borne in mind that the Top 100 companies represented less than 5% by number of all quoted UK companies as at the end of 1993.

[209] There is a consensus amongst fund managers that a majority of interventions never surfaces in the press.

[210] *Inquiry into Corporate Takeovers in the United Kingdom: Evidence from the Association of British Insurers (& ors.)* (1990) 3.

[211] 'Corporate Assassins' (n. 194 above).

[212] Black and Coffee (n. 86 above), at 2047.

earlier that fund managers say that more interventions are completed without any public knowledge than those which crop up in the press. The author concentrated on ten interventions which occurred during 1990–3, and where the institutions involved were identified in press reports. There were at least a dozen other interventions reported during that period, but where the institutions involved were not identified. That gives an average of roughly half a dozen interventions per year which reached the public eye. A leading fund manager made an estimate in mid-1991 of 'the numbers of serious or possibly robust discussions which [had] not surfaced in the press or wider public' over the previous year: 'I find it very difficult [to estimate], maybe a dozen.'[213] That suggests a combined total of about 18 interventions per year. The UK economy was for much of the 1990–3 period either in recession or in a relatively subdued state. Several fund managers believe that there was 'a cyclical element' in the number of interventions during that time, and that there were considerably less interventions during the 1985–9 period (when there was a high level of takeover activity). This suggests that interventions are, to an extent, substitutes for takeovers.[214] If so, it is likely that the number of full-blown interventions will peter out somewhat as the UK economy becomes more vibrant and takeover activity increases.

Secondly, most institutions consider it preferable to sell their shareholding where possible rather than undertake an intervention. This means that most institutions sell out of problem companies more often than they intervene.[215] Such a sale would normally be in the market, but quite a few interviewees mentioned that they frequently tried (often successfully) to 'engineer a takeover bid' for a problem company. This might involve the institution talking directly to the management of another of its portfolio companies, and suggesting that they bid for the problem company. Alternatively, the institution might let a number of merchant banks know that it would support a reasonable takeover bid for the problem

---

[213] Trade and Industry Committee (n. 195 above), para. 933.

[214] See T. Jenkinson and C. P. Mayer, 'The Assessment: Corporate Governance and Corporate Control' (1992) 8 (3) *Ox. Rev. Econ. Pol.* 1, at 4. US empirical studies provide some support for the hypothesis that monitoring by non-executive directors, on the one hand, and either takeovers or ownership concentration, on the other hand, are substitute control mechanisms: see J. A. Brickley and C. M. James, 'The Takeover Market, Corporate Board Composition, and Ownership Structure: the Case of Banking' (1987) 30 *J Law & Econ.* 161; A. Shivdasani, 'Board Composition, Ownership Structure, and Hostile Takeovers' (1993) 16 *J Acc. & Econ.* 167; O. Kini, W. Kracaw, and S. Mian, 'Corporate Takeovers, Firm Performance, and Board Composition' (1995) 1 *J Corp. Fin.* 383. See also D. Hirshleifer and A. V. Thakor, 'Managerial Performance, Boards of Directors and Takeover Bidding' (1994) 1 *J Corp. Fin.* 63 (demonstrating the importance of the board of directors even where there is an active takeover market).

[215] One fund manager said in 1992 that there was 'at least a 10:1 ratio' of sale over intervention at his institution: Black and Coffee (n. 86 above), at 2053.

company.[216] The possibility of an alternative course of action to intervention is the greatest disincentive to an institution intervening. The interviews (and other sources) revealed that there are a number of other strong disincentives to interventions to change management. There are, on the other hand, a few factors which, if they exist, serve as incentives to engage in intervention as opposed to other courses of action. These are all discussed in another chapter.[217]

The final general point is that, in the mid-1990s, US institutions were showing signs of increasing their involvement in interventions at UK companies and other non-US companies. A Chicago-based fund-management firm was instrumental in the removal of the executive chairman of Saatchi & Saatchi plc in late 1994. The US fund manager had a shareholding of 9.8% (an unusually large stake in a UK company for a US institution), and was supported by several other US institutions as well as some UK institutions.[218] Also, California Public Employees' Retirement System ('CalPERS'), one of the largest US public-sector pension schemes, announced in June 1995 that it intended to take overseas its highly publicized campaign of confronting the management of underperforming portfolio companies. The UK, Germany, and Japan were cited as the possible countries in which it would start its overseas campaign.[219]

vii. Two Especially Important Actions

The following two actions which have been taken occasionally by institutions are of special importance. Actually, the importance lies not so much in the action taken but in the two regulatory structures—the various rules setting out the pre-emption right, and the shareholder-approval provisions of the Stock Exchange's *Listing Rules*—which enable the actions to be taken. There is further discussion of this topic in the final chapter.

(a) Conditional Exercise of Rights Entitlement

One interviewee said that 'the time you really get a chance to have an influence on the company is if they want money'. Another said: 'If we are asked to provide money, our due diligence is to be satisfied that it's going to the right place.' A company in urgent need of fresh equity capital would,

---

[216] Note that the engineering of a takeover bid in such circumstances should not be construed as evidence of short-termism on the part of institutions. The threat of this occurring would be felt only by seriously underperforming management teams; it would not impact upon the thinking of the vast majority of company managements. In regard to the alleged connection between institutions, takeovers, and short-termism, see Ch. 9, at nn. 42–51, and accompanying text. 　　　　　　　　　　　　　　　　　　　　[217] See Ch. 10, Sec. B.

[218] See 'Saatchi Doesn't Work', *Fin. Times*, 14 Jan. 1995, p. 6.

[219] See 'Calpers to Track Foreign Groups', *Fin. Times*, 8 June 1995, p. 27.

due to the fairly tight restrictions imposed upon non-rights issues,[220] normally attempt to launch a rights issue. The following situation sometimes ensues. The company's merchant-bank adviser, whilst pre-marketing the proposed issue with the main institutional shareholders,[221] receives the message that the poor state of the balance sheet is attributed to the existing management, and that investors are unwilling to throw good money after bad. One or more institutions may also contact a non-executive director and express their concerns directly. The message flowing back to the company's management and board is that the capital raising will not be supported at a reasonable price, or even at any price, without management changes. This has in a number of cases in the 1990s led to some quite significant board and management shake-ups.[222] The institutions' successful campaign to preserve their rights of pre-emption in regard to new equity issues, although driven mainly by financial motives,[223] thus also ensured that they maintained a significant, potential lever of power over company managements.

One of the main virtues of this type of extraordinary action is that many of the problems associated with collective intervention by institutions[224] do not arise. This is because the onus is on the management team to satisfy the bulk of the major shareholders that it is deserving of further funds, and the institutions can therefore in effect wait for the management to approach them—rather than the other way around. But this is something of a double-edged sword, because the very fact that the institutions do not need to take the initiative means that the problem of a lack of homogeneity amongst institutional viewpoints[225] is exacerbated. Unless the major institutional shareholders go to the effort and expense of getting together and determining common ground so that the views expressed to the company management are consistent, it is likely that a mixed message will result.[226]

(b) Rejection of 'Super Class 1 Transactions' and Other Major Deals

Some important provisions which assist direct firm-level monitoring are those in the London Stock Exchange's *Listing Rules* under which certain

---

[220] These restrictions are largely a result of institutional pressure: see Ch. 4, Sec. A.1.i.

[221] See n. 170 above, and accompanying text.

[222] See 'Institutions Force Management Change at Alexon Group', *Fin. Times*, 23 Apr. 1993, p. 19; 'Sacrifice to Woo the Franchise Gods', *Fin. Times*, 11 May 1991, p. 10; 'Tougher at the Top', *Fin. Times*, 28 Sept. 1991, p. 7; 'The Institutions Get Militant', *Fin. Times*, 11 June 1991, p. 18. A variation occurred at Lloyds Bank in 1978: see Scott (n. 74 above), at 99.

[223] See Ch. 4, Sec. A.1.i.   [224] These are discussed in Ch. 10, Sec. B.

[225] See Ch. 10, Sec. B.1.ix.

[226] e.g. in the Granada case, some institutions wanted the executive chairman to resign, some wanted the chief executive to resign, and some wanted both to resign; in the end just the chief executive went: 'Granada Loses Chief, Gains Cash', *Indep.*, 11 May 1991, p. 15.

transactions (Super Class 1 transactions, reverse takeovers, and related-party transactions) require general-meeting approval.[227] A proposed large transaction very rarely gets to the stage of a shareholder vote at a general meeting if the bulk of the company's main institutional shareholders are opposed to it. In such cases, things do not normally even reach the stage of a meeting being convened, because the proposal (at least in the opposed form) would be abandoned at the pre-marketing stage. This simply illustrates, however, the importance of the shareholder-approval provisions in the *Listing Rules*: as mentioned already,[228] pre-marketing occurs much more frequently for transactions which require general-meeting approval than for those which do not. And there will of course always be cases where, for one reason or another, a proposed transaction gets to the EGM stage despite strong shareholder opposition.

For example, in 1989 British Land plc proposed to carry out a major restructuring involving the formation and transfer of assets to a new company.[229] Most of its institutional shareholders were in favour of the basic plan, but there were some aspects of the proposal to which they were strongly opposed (these were mostly related to the balance of rewards between management and shareholders), and many were also aggrieved at the extremely short timetable given for consideration of it (the EGM was called with the minimum 14 days' notice). The management met with at least eight institutions, who collectively represented 30% of the equity, in the days leading up to the EGM. However, an institution with a 7.4% stake decided publicly, two days before the meeting, to vote against the proposal. The ABI IC had also, by that time, circulated its members with information that a number of insurers were proposing to vote against the proposal.[230] A decision was then made on the day before the EGM that the relevant resolutions would not be put to a vote; the plan was effectively abandoned.[231]

viii. Litigation

Judging by what was said to the author by the fund managers interviewed, the vast majority of UK institutions would never have taken, or seriously considered taking, legal action against company directors or officers for

---

[227] See *Listing Rules*, Ch. 10, 11. See also Ch. 4, Sec. A.1.iv; and Ch. 11, Sec. B.1.vi, of this work. [228] See n. 176 above, and accompanying text.

[229] See 'Opposition to British Land Reconstruction', *Fin. Times*, 16 Dec. 1989, p. 8. For an earlier example, see 'Aer Lingus-Kingsley Hotel Deal Strongly Opposed', *Fin. Times*, 11 Feb. 1970, p. 30.

[230] 'Fleming Votes Against British Land Scheme', *Fin. Times*, 20 Dec. 1989, p. 19.

[231] 'British Land Scraps Restructuring', *Fin. Times*, 21 Dec. 1989, p. 15. Many institutions actually hoped that the plan could be revived with a more equitable balance of rewards between management and shareholders, but this did not occur.

breach of their fiduciary duties or duties of care and skill.[232] Interviewees were unanimous that there is an overwhelming financial disincentive to litigation of that sort, and mentioned the following specific components of that disincentive: (a) an indeterminable amount of senior fund managers' (expensive) time would be tied up; (b) in the case of managers of external funds, the cost could not in reality be passed on to the clients for whose benefit the action was taken; (c) in any derivative action,[233] all other shareholders would be able to free-ride on any benefits obtained. In addition to those factors, the absence of a US-style contingency-fee system coupled with the English 'loser pays all' rule of costs is an enormous deterrent to litigation by any shareholder—institutional or otherwise—in the UK.[234] Also, there is the rule in *Foss* v. *Harbottle*,[235] and associated case-law,[236] which provides significant practical difficulties for shareholders wishing to sue directors for breach of duty.

There would appear to be only one reported case of a UK institution bringing such an action against directors of a portfolio company. In the 1970s, Prudential Assurance sued two directors of a listed company in which it held a 3.2% stake, alleging that they had caused the company to purchase property at an inflated price from a company with which they were associated, and had deceived the shareholders in the related circular.[237] The Court of Appeal was far from enthusiastic about a policy argument put by counsel for the plaintiff institution:

> We were invited to give judicial approval to the public spirit of the plaintiffs who, it was said, [were] pioneering a method of controlling companies in the public interest without involving regulation by a statutory body. In our view voluntary regulation of companies is a matter for the City. The compulsory regulation of companies is a matter for Parliament.[238]

---

[232] Contrast the position in the US, where there were in 1994 quite grave concerns about the effect of shareholder lawsuits upon disclosure of information by company managements to analysts and institutional shareholders: 'Growing Concern Over Investor Lawsuits', *Fin. Times*, 18 May 1994, p. 30.

[233] A derivative action is one brought by a shareholder or shareholders on behalf of the company: Gower (n. 78 above), at 647. Any recovery must go to the company and not to the shareholder(s) bringing the action: *Stokes* v. *Grosvenor Hotel Co.* [1897] 2 QB 124, at 128.

[234] See D. D. Prentice, 'Some Aspects of the Corporate Governance Debate' in Prentice and Holland (n. 5 above), 25, at 39–40. Note, however, that the Lord Chancellor introduced a limited system of 'conditional' fees in late 1993—mainly for personal-injury cases.

[235] (1843) 2 Hare 461. One effect of the rule is to restrict considerably the circumstances in which a minority shareholder can bring legal proceedings against a director or directors for breach of duty; cf. the proposed Fifth EC Directive on harmonization of company law (1983 OJ (C 240) 2), arts. 16–18, which would bolster the ability of minority shareholders to bring derivative actions.

[236] See *Pavlides* v. *Jensen* [1956] Ch. 565; cf. *Daniels* v. *Daniels* [1978] 1 Ch. 406; G. P. Stapledon, 'The AWA Case: Non-Executive Directors, Auditors, and Corporate Governance Issues in Court' in Prentice and Holland (n. 5 above), 187, at 204–14.

[237] *Prudential Assurance Co. Ltd.* v. *Newman Industries Ltd. (No. 2)* [1982] Ch. 204.

[238] Ibid., at 224.

Although UK institutions in their role as *ordinary* shareholders have not generally sued company directors, they have brought actions to protect their rights as *preference* shareholders[239] and bondholders. They have also provided information to regulatory authorities which has led to the prosecution of company directors.[240]

C. INDIRECT INDUSTRY-WIDE MONITORING

To recapitulate, industry-wide monitoring consists of the devising and promulgating of some kind of recommended practice. It was mentioned earlier that a small amount of industry-wide monitoring has been performed by institutions personally—this was termed *direct* industry-wide monitoring.[241] Most industry-wide action has, however, been carried out *indirectly*—that is, by collective-action vehicles on behalf of the institutions. The main collective-action vehicles in this respect have been the institutional trade associations, but PIRC has also conducted some industry-wide monitoring.

The most prominent of the institutional trade associations have been the ABI and the NAPF, or specifically the Investment Committees (ICs) thereof. As shown in Chapter 4, the ICs have produced and promoted statements of, and guidelines on, best practice in areas such as employee share schemes, the pre-emption right, and own-share purchase. Chapter 4 also shows that the ICs have liaised with and/or lobbied (a) government departments (on issues such as own-share purchase and executive share-option schemes); (b) the London Stock Exchange (on matters such as the pre-emption right, large transactions, management buy-outs, own-share purchase, disclosure of price-sensitive information, and enhanced scrip dividends); (c) the CBI (on matters including enhanced scrip dividends and corporate-treasury activities); (d) the Accounting Standards Board (on various disclosure matters);[242] (e) the Association of Corporate Treasurers (on corporate-treasury matters); and (f) the Institute of Chartered Accountants in England and Wales (on corporate-treasury matters). In addition, the ICs are represented on 'permanent' bodies (such as the Panel

---

[239] See 'Legal Briefs: Rolls-Royce Defeated by Shareholders', *Fin. Times*, 31 May 1994, p. 12.

[240] See 'Former Electronics Chief Cleared', *Fin. Times*, 12 Nov. 1993, p. 8 (unsuccessful prosecution of a company director under Financial Services Act 1986, s. 47, regarding a statement made to two fund managers). Note also the announcement by the GMB trade union, in mid-1995, that it was planning to take legal action against companies in which it held shares and which had made political donations without shareholder approval: see 'Companies Challenged on Political Gifts', *Fin. Times*, 5 June 1995, p. 6.

[241] See Sec. A, above.

[242] The NAPF IC meets regularly with the ASB Chairman and Director General: Matheson (n. 117 above).

on Takeovers and Mergers,[243] the Pre-Emption Group, the Stock Exchange's Investors Advisory Group, and the Bank of England's City/ EEC Committee), and have been represented on many *ad hoc* bodies over the years.[244] Finally, the ICs (and AUTIF, AITC, LIBA, and PIRC) have made submissions to bodies inquiring into various aspects of corporate governance.

From the late 1980s, the ICs were joined as prominent industry-wide monitors by the ISC. As mentioned in Chapter 3, Section C, the ISC was formed in 1973 to carry out firm-level monitoring, but it abandoned that role in 1991.[245] Since 1989, the ISC has sought 'to provide a channel of communication and a forum for discussion of current issues between institutional shareholders and corporate management' and 'to facilitate the identification of areas of common ground amongst [its] members and thereafter to promulgate the jointly held opinions'.[246] The change from its original role of firm-level monitor could barely have been greater: since 1991 the ISC has 'not normally become involved in matters concerned with particular investments or companies, as it believes that here any dialogue should be between the company and the shareholders concerned (or the Investment Committee of the relevant member-Association of the ISC)'.[247]

PIRC has also played a role in industry-wide monitoring. As Chapter 4 shows, PIRC has conducted research into, publicized the prevalence of, and called for shareholder approval of, political donations by listed UK companies; and has researched and publicized the arguably excessive number of non-executive directorships held by some senior executive directors of listed UK companies.

D. INDIRECT FIRM-LEVEL MONITORING

Firm-level monitoring has been performed on behalf of institutions (i.e. indirectly) by two types of monitor: collective-action vehicles and non-executive directors.

---

[243] LIBA, AUTIF, and AITC are also represented on the Panel on Takeovers and Mergers.

[244] e.g. the ABI IC was represented on the Working Party on Price Sensitive Information, as was IFMA: see Ch. 4, Sec. A.1.xiv; Ch. 9, Sec. B.4; the chairman of the ISC was a member of the Cadbury Committee; the ABI and the NAPF were sponsors of Cadbury Mark II, and were represented on the Greenbury Committee.

[245] See further Sec. D.1.ii, below.

[246] ISC, *Newsletter No. 1* (1992). On the latter, the ISC has produced and promulgated statements of best practice on management buy-outs, the role and duties of directors, and disclosure of expenditure on research and development, as well as on the responsibilities of institutional shareholders (see Ch. 4).

[247] ISC, yellow brochure titled 'Institutional Shareholders' Committee' (undated).

1. COLLECTIVE-ACTION VEHICLES

i. Case Committees of the Trade Associations

The ABI and NAPF ICs, the ISC, the AITC, and AUTIF have all at some stage formed 'case committees' of institutional shareholders to deal with concerns or problems at individual companies. Of those bodies, the ABI and NAPF ICs, which were formerly called Investment Protection Committees (IPCs), have been the most prominent in setting up case committees.

The Wilson Committee described, in 1980, the way in which the IPCs established and operated their case committees:

> The IPCs generally act by setting up case committees consisting of representatives of the main institutions with substantial shareholdings in the relevant company. The existence of a case committee will be known only to the consulted institutions[248] of the relevant IPC and there is no obligation on all those holding shares in the company to join or support it. Institutions who take a different view can stay aloof so as to maintain their freedom to deal.[249]

It was confirmed to the present author that this remained an accurate description of the way that the ABI IC created and operated its case committees as at 1993.[250] Case committees were described in 1993 by the chairman of the NAPF IC as 'usually involv[ing] conversations with management and its advisers [in order to] understand what may be happening, offer help where possible . . . express shareholder concerns [and] influence . . . management decisions'.[251] It is common for case committees to arise out of approaches made by company managements to the IC with the aim of ensuring that proposals required to be put to the shareholders in general meeting will be supported, or at least will not be opposed, by most institutional shareholders.[252] Where a shareholder vote is required, case committees normally make a voting recommendation which is communicated by the IC to the interested members of the parent trade association.[253]

---

[248] The ABI IC ring-fences the issue to the extent of liaising only with a specified individual(s) at each participating insurance company; these individuals are the only persons made 'insiders': Regan (n. 105 above). The NAPF IC has 'very specific procedures to cover' the likely eventuality of case-committee members obtaining inside information: Matheson (n. 117 above), at 179.   [249] Wilson Committee (n. 126 above), para. 911.

[250] Regan (n. 105 above).   [251] Matheson (n. 117 above), at 179.

[252] Regan (n. 105 above).

[253] Until the mid-1950s, it was common for companies whose proposals had been approved by the Association of Investment Trusts and/or the IPC of the British Insurance Association to state this in the circular explaining the proposed resolution(s). This practice was viewed favourably by Greene MR in *Re Selfridge's (Holdings) Ltd.* (unreported; cited in 'Protection

As for the frequency of occurrence of case committees, and the issues with which they have dealt, the Wilson Committee reported the following for the 1970s:

> [T]he insurance IPC . . . averaged about 200 cases a year for the last 10 years. These cases are of three main kinds. A substantial majority are concerned with technical issues such as the revision of lending contracts or capital re-arrangements and are frequently initiated as a result of approaches by the company concerned. A second, somewhat smaller group, involves points of principle such as the issue of non-voting shares or the establishment of the rights of shareholders to be consulted on major changes in the structure of a business. Finally there have been a small number of cases, between 10 and 20 a year for the insurance IPC, where consideration by several institutions collectively has been thought necessary to deal with a management problem by exercising joint pressure to improve matters.[254]

During the early 1990s, the ABI IC was still forming about 200 case committees annually.[255] The vast majority still concerned procedural/general issues rather than company-specific issues such as under-performing management, although there had been a shift during the 1980s away from issues concerning fixed-interest securities towards issues concerning equities (for example disapplication of the pre-emption right; own-share purchase; executive share-option schemes; etc.).[256]

The ISC was set up in 1973 as a collective-action vehicle to 'function through case committees composed of members of the constituent associations [which were] shareholders in the companies concerned'.[257] It was intended that the case committees would, 'where appropriate, be assisted by experienced industrialists or financial consultants', and it was envisaged that they might 'encourage companies to enlist the help of professional advisers'.[258] It is quite apparent, despite the lack of information at the time about the activities of its case committees,[259] that the ISC in operation during the 1970s fell short of its initial aims. The

---

in the City: Safeguards for the Small Investor', *Times*, 17 Apr. 1964), but criticized severely by Evershed MR in *Re Old Silkstone Collieries Ltd.* [1954] Ch. 169, at 191–2. After the latter judgment, the practice ceased due to the possibility of 'undue influence on outside shareholders': 'Protection in the City: Safeguards for the Small Investor', *Times*, 17 Apr. 1964.

[254] Wilson Committee (n. 126 above), para. 910. Six companies made board changes in 1970 after representations from the NAPF's IPC: 'Men and Matters: What They Get for £50', *Fin. Times*, 28 Apr. 1971, p. 20.   [255] Regan (n. 105 above).

[256] Ibid.

[257] Press announcement of Bank of England, 16 Apr. 1973, reproduced in (1973) 13 *Bank Eng. Q Bull.* 148.   [258] Ibid.

[259] The ISC decided from the beginning to act discreetly: 'The [ISC] is very conscious that the co-operation of company managements will depend on the absence of publicity and no public statements will therefore be made about any of the activities of the case committees': ibid.

Wilson Committee, reporting in 1980, disclosed that the ISC's first six-and-a-half years yielded only seven formal case committees.[260] A former adviser to the Governor of the Bank of England has commented that, nevertheless, on the rare occasions when an ISC case committee 'intervened in regard to the composition of [a company's] board . . . success was often spectacular'.[261] The ISC had an active period in the early 1980s, 'when British industry was . . . going through a period of enforced restructuring brought about by economic forces beyond its control'.[262] It was at that stage 'dealing with four or five cases at a time of companies in difficulty. Knowledge that the ISC was concerned about a company was often sufficient for remedial action—such as senior management changes—to take place.'[263]

With the economic and stock-market recovery in the mid-1980s, the ISC became virtually dormant as 'the incidence of obvious managerial failure diminished'.[264] It was reconstituted in late 1988.[265] Under the reconstituted body's first chairman (Mr Donald Brydon of Barclays de Zoete Wedd Investment Management Ltd.) the ISC looked set to recommence its interventionist function. Mr Brydon proposed that the ISC should take a proactive stance in relation to some problem companies: 'It would be appropriate [for the ISC] to appoint an independent consultant [for example McKinsey & Co] to advise shareholders on the strategies open to [a problem] company';[266] 'It is not for shareholders to tell a company how to run itself. . . . But it is their role to present a company they are concerned about with alternatives and to get its reaction. The response of management would be the best clue as to whether it was going to take the company forward successfully or not.'[267] These proposals were, however, criticized widely in the fund-management industry, and never implemented. They were considered objectionable for a variety of reasons: institutions in competition with one another did not want to co-operate in that way;[268] no one really wanted to pick up the costs associated with such an intervention; and some institutions would have refused to hand over their proxies.[269]

---

[260] Wilson Committee (n. 126 above), para. 912. The ISC actually dealt with 37 cases during that time. However, 19 were referred elsewhere (either to one of the old IPCs of the BIA or NAPF, or to an individual institution), whilst 11 'had either already gone too far for anything to be done or were resolved in some other way, for example by the company concerned becoming the subject of a successful takeover bid': ibid.

[261] J. P. Charkham, 'Are Shares Just Commodities?' in NAPF, *Creative Tension?* (1990) 34, at 41.

[262] 'Institutional Investors as Interventionists', *Fin. Times*, 10 Aug. 1990, p. 10.

[263] Ibid.   [264] Ibid.   [265] See Ch. 3, Sec. C.

[266] D. Brydon, 'More Dialogue Between Boards and Shareholders is Needed', *Indep.*, 11 Feb. 1991, p. 21.

[267] 'Institutional Investors . . .' (n. 262 above).

[268] Information provided to the author by Mr Brydon in interview on 22 Sept. 1993.

[269] Black and Coffee (n. 86 above), at 2020.

After the abandonment of Mr Brydon's proposals, the ISC became a body confined to industry-wide action.[270]

ii. The Investment Committees and PIRC

The ABI and NAPF ICs sometimes carry out firm-level monitoring without establishing formal case committees. The Secretary of the IC sometimes just communicates with member institutions with large holdings in the company concerned, and then negotiates with the company's management (on both procedural/general and company-specific issues). For example, in September 1993 the ABI IC set up a monitoring service, covering the top 500 (and 20% of all other) listed UK companies, to test qualitatively the level of compliance with the *Cadbury Code*.[271] This service was established in response to the Cadbury Committee's call for 'institutions . . . to use their influence as owners to ensure that the companies in which they have invested comply with the Code'.[272] It was supplied to the members of the ABI.[273] Although those insurance companies were free to take matters up with the boards of portfolio companies which were not complying with the *Code*, the ABI IC's officers were sometimes asked to make representations to company managements on behalf of ABI members.

PIRC also conducts firm-level monitoring on behalf of its subscribers. As part of its proxy-voting service,[274] PIRC has lobbied individual companies on matters of corporate governance and shareholders' rights, and on ethical and political issues.[275] In the early-to-mid 1990s, PIRC was talking each year to the management of about a quarter of the 125 companies which it researched.[276]

2. NON-EXECUTIVE DIRECTORS

Until the mid-1980s, it would appear that institutional shareholders had very little involvement with the non-executive directors on the boards of portfolio companies. But the late 1980s through early 1990s seems to have been a period during which the relationship became somewhat closer. During that period there appears to have been a gradual increase in the

---

[270] See Sec C, above.   [271] Regan (n. 105 above).

[272] *Cadbury Report*, para. 6.16.

[273] Information provided to the author by J. Weld of the ABI IC, in telephone conversation on 24 June 1994.   [274] See Sec. B.1.v, above.

[275] e.g. PIRC waged a vigorous campaign against the 1993 proposal by Hanson plc to alter its articles of association so as to restrict shareholders' rights at general meetings (see Ch. 4, at n. 142); it also organized the requisitioning of a shareholders' resolution at the 1995 AGM of British Gas plc (see Ch. 4, at n. 118, and accompanying text).

[276] Bell (n. 125 above).

amount of dialogue between institutions and 'traditional' non-executives, and a very small increase in the number of 'institutional' non-executives. The distinction—which is not a legal one—between 'traditional' and 'institutional' non-executives is that the latter owe their presence on the board, to a greater or lesser extent, to a large institutional shareholder or group of institutions, whilst the former are normally appointees of the existing chairman, chief executive, or a board committee. These two types of non-executive director, and their role as shareholder representatives who conduct firm-level monitoring, are analysed below. But, because the ability of non-executives to monitor executive management is partly a function of the ratio of non-executive to executive directors on the board, there is first a presentation of evidence on the composition of boards of quoted UK companies.

i. Board Composition: The Evidence

Table 5.10 summarizes the findings of several studies of the boards of quoted UK industrial companies.[277] There was a fairly steady increase in the proportion of non-executive directors on boards during 1979–93. Nevertheless, even at 1993 the average board of a quoted industrial company had only a minority of non-executive directors. Indeed, in 1985 only 22% of quoted industrial companies had a board with a majority of

Table 5.10 Composition of boards of quoted UK *industrial* companies, 1979–93

	1979	1982	1985	1988	1993
Average size of board	9.8	9.4	9.0	8.9	8.7
Average proportion of non-executive directors	30%	33%	35%	38%	44%

Sources: For 1979 and 1982: Bank of England, 'The Composition of Company Boards in 1982' (1983) 23 *Bank Eng. Q Bull*. 66, at 68 (Table C); for 1985: Bank of England, 'The Boards of Quoted Companies' (1985) 25 *Bank Eng. Q Bull*. 233, at 235 (Table D); for 1988 and 1993: M. J. Conyon, 'Corporate Governance Changes in UK Companies Between 1988 and 1993' (1994) 2 *Corp. Gov.: Inter. Rev*. 97, at 103 (Table 2).

[277] 'Industrial companies' is used in a broad sense to mean non-financial companies. The sampling frame used by the studies reflected in Table 5.10 was *The Times 1000* (various years), which comprises the 1000 largest UK industrial companies ranked by turnover—banks, insurance companies, and other financial companies are not included. *The Times 1000* includes unquoted as well as quoted companies, but the studies underlying Table 5.10 all gave separate figures for quoted companies.

non-executive directors;[278] in 1993 the figure was only 25% (although a further 24% of companies had a board with equal numbers of executives and non-executives).[279]

A leading UK fund manager said at a conference in 1992: '[I]f one casts one's mind back twenty five years, many large UK companies were run by boards of non-executive directors with the general manager in attendance.'[280] On the other hand, Sargant Florence wrote in the early 1970s that

> academic views on the structure and activities of the board of directors have been ill-informed, partly due to . . . concentration of attention on the boards of large banking, insurance and the now defunct railway companies, many of them swollen with 'big name', guinea-pig, directors. . . . Probably in most large companies a majority of directors are full-time executives . . .[281]

In the light of the above, and because the surveys reflected in Table 5.10 did not encompass any financial companies, a study ('Study C') of the boards of large listed companies—industrial and financial—was conducted by the present author for 1971, 1981, and 1991.[282] The results of Study C are presented in Table 5.11.

Further to Table 5.11, non-executives were in the majority on the boards of 12 (92%) of the 13 financial companies in the 1971 sample; at 12 (92%) of the 13 financial companies in the 1981 sample; and at 15 (94%) of the 16 financial companies in 1991. They were in the majority at a mere 6 (10%) of the 59 industrial companies in the 1971 sample; at only 10 (17%) of the 59 industrial companies in the 1981 sample; and at 23 (27%) of the 84 industrial companies in 1991. It is thus quite plain that large listed UK financial companies (mainly banks and insurers) have generally had bigger boards, with a much higher proportion of non-executive directors, than large listed industrial companies (although the difference had narrowed by 1991).

An important qualification must be made to all of the above figures: not all of the non-executive directors identified were 'independent' of the company on whose board they sat. There is a distinction between 'independent' and 'affiliated' non-executives.[283] The two principal determinants of affiliation are (a) that the non-executive director is a former executive of the company; or (b) that he or she is a professional adviser to,

---

[278] Author's analysis of figures in Bank of England, 'The Boards of Quoted Companies' (1985) 25 *Bank Eng. Q Bull.* 233, at 235 (Table C).

[279] Author's analysis of figures in Korn/Ferry International, *Boards of Directors Study UK* (1993) 20, at 58.   [280] Linaker (n. 5 above), at 108.

[281] P. Sargant Florence, *The Logic of British and American Industry* (3rd edn., 1972) 244.

[282] The methodology used in Study C is set out in App. J.

[283] M. L. Mace, 'Directors: Myth and Reality—Ten Years Later' (1979) 32 *Rutgers L Rev.* 293, at 304.

Table 5.11 Composition of boards of large listed UK companies,
1971–91

		1971	*1981*	*1991*
All companies	Average size of board	14.8	14.2	13.0
	Average proportion of non-executive directors	42%	45%	48%
Financial companies	Average size of board	20.9	20.2	16.6
	Average proportion of non-executive directors	76%	72%	66%
Industrial companies	Average size of board	13.5	12.9	12.3
	Average proportion of non-executive directors	31%	36%	43%

Source: Author's calculations from annual reports and information provided by the sample companies.

or a significant supplier or customer of, the company.[284] In the 1985 survey underlying Table 5.10, some 16% of non-executives were former executives of the company, and a further 16% were professional advisers to the company.[285] A 1993 survey of boards of UK industrial companies found that only 7% of non-executives were former executives.[286] Finally, the Monitoring Sub-Committee of the Cadbury Committee, which examined the level of compliance with the *Cadbury Code* during the period from September 1993 until December 1994, found that all or a majority of non-executive directors were independent in 92% of the top 100 listed companies.[287] However, the percentage of independent non-executives was smaller for medium-sized and small listed companies. For example, all or a majority of non-executives were independent in 80% of companies ranked between the 251st and the 500th largest, measured by market capitalization; whilst all or a majority of non-executives were independent

[284] See *Cadbury Code*, para. 2.2; ISC, *The Role and Duties of Directors—A Statement of Best Practice* (1991); PRO NED, *Code of Recommended Practice on Non-Executive Directors* (1987).
[285] Author's analysis of figures in Bank of England (n. 278 above), at 235 (Table E). (The survey did not reveal the number of non-executives in a customer or supplier relationship with the company.)
[286] Author's analysis of figures in Korn/Ferry (n. 279 above), at 33, 58. The survey did not reveal the number of non-executives in a professional, customer, or supplier relationship with the company. But note that it did find that, amongst the largest sample companies (those with turnovers above £1,000m. per annum) which had non-executive chairmen, the non-executive chairman was a former executive of the company in one-third of cases: ibid, at 32.
[287] Cadbury Committee, *Compliance with the Code of Best Practice* (1995) 21, 30.

in only 58% of companies ranked between the 1,251st and the 1,550th largest, measured by market capitalization.[288]

ii. 'Traditional' Non-Executives

(a) Role in Theory

There have long been directors on the boards of British companies who have been 'part-time' and without executive office.[289] However, the Companies Act refers only to directors: it does not differentiate between executive directors and non-executive directors.[290] Whilst all directors have the same legal duties[291] and statutory responsibilities,[292] the very existence of non-executives implies that their role is in some ways different to that of executive directors.

It is accepted widely that the boards of virtually all large public companies do not manage their companies' day-to-day business.[293] Their role has instead been referred to by the Cadbury Committee as one of 'direction and control of the company'.[294] Whether 'direction' should be or is part of the role of modern boards is subject to some debate, but most agree that 'control' (or 'monitoring') should be a major part of a board's role.[295] It is in the exercise of this monitoring function that a central difference between the roles of executive and non-executive directors becomes clear: executive directors 'are responsible (as managers) for activities which it is the duty of the board as a whole to monitor. . . . This means that the nature of the monitoring role is *ipso facto* different for non-executive directors'.[296] It has thus been said that:

> Non-executive directors have two particularly important contributions to make to the governance process as a consequence of their independence from executive responsibility. . . . The first is in reviewing the performance of the board and of the executive. . . . The second is in taking the lead where potential conflicts of interest arise.[297]

During the 1980s and early 1990s, structural support for the second of these functions was given by the introduction—materially as a result of

---

[288] Ibid.

[289] See e.g. *Re Denham & Co.* (1883) 25 Ch. D 752.

[290] But see the proposed Fifth EC Directive on harmonization of company law: 1983 OJ (C 240) 2.

[291] e.g. all are under a fiduciary duty to act bona fide in the interests of the company.

[292] e.g. all are responsible for the preparation of the annual accounts: CA 1985, ss. 226–8.

[293] See Ch. 1, Sec. B.   [294] *Cadbury Code*, para. 1.4.

[295] See e.g. ISC (n. 284 above), at 3; PRO NED (n. 284 above); American Law Institute, *Principles of Corporate Governance: Analysis and Recommendations* (1992) 112–13; cf. C. S. Axworthy, 'Corporate Directors—Who Needs Them?' (1988) 51 *MLR* 273.

[296] J. P. Charkham, *Corporate Governance and the Market for Control of Companies* (1989) 13.   [297] *Cadbury Report*, paras. 4.4–4.6.

institutional influence[298]—of audit, remuneration, and (less commonly) nomination committees of the board.[299] The first function is in theory more likely to be performed effectively if the non-executives are independent of, rather than affiliated with, management. There is some evidence that a growing proportion of non-executives is independent in this sense.[300] Institutional urging has been a contributory factor behind this development too.[301]

(b) Shortfalls in Practice

There is direct and indirect evidence of several impediments to the exercise by traditional non-executive directors of their monitoring function.

First, many traditional non-executives are too 'close' to management. Being an affiliated non-executive rather than an independent one (as defined earlier) poses obvious problems, but even independent non-executives are often closely enough allied to management that detached monitoring may be difficult. For instance, commonly they owe their positions to the chairman. In virtually all listed UK companies, the appointment of all non-executive directors (whether traditional or institutional) must be confirmed by an ordinary resolution of the general meeting, and they are then subject to periodic re-election by the shareholders.[302] Nevertheless, a large proportion of UK non-executive directors has traditionally been *selected* by the chairman of the board,[303] and indeed as recently as early 1994 about 50% of non-executives of UK industrial companies had been chosen by the chairman.[304] The Cadbury Committee recognized this problem and recommended that non-executives 'should be selected through a formal process and both this process and their appointment should be a matter for the board as a whole',[305] and regarded it as good practice for a nomination committee—composed

---

[298] The influence of institutional shareholders consisted initially of individual institutions pressing their own views of best practice, then of institutions pushing for the adoption of ISC recommendations, and finally of institutions and their trade associations pushing for the implementation of the *Cadbury Code* (itself largely a reflection of institutional policies): see Ch. 4, Sec. A.1.xv.

[299] See M. J. Conyon, 'Corporate Governance Changes in UK Companies Between 1988 and 1993' (1994) 2 *Corp. Gov.: Inter. Rev.* 97.

[300] See nn. 285–8 above, and accompanying text.

[301] See n. 298 above.

[302] Nothing is prescribed in the Companies Act, but most companies' articles probably contain provisions similar to Table A, arts. 73–80; cf. the position in regard to executive directors: see Ch. 4, Sec. A.1.xv.

[303] And it was common during the 1980s and early 1990s for the chairman to be also the chief executive officer, or the leading executive where there was a separate chief executive officer: see Ch. 4, Sec. A.1.xvi.

[304] KPMG Peat Marwick, *Survey of Non-Executive Directors* (1994) 12. The survey found that only a small proportion of non-executives was found via consultants (such as PRO NED).

[305] *Cadbury Code*, para. 2.4.

of a majority of non-executive directors and chaired by the board chairman or a non-executive director—to carry out the selection process and make proposals to the board.[306] Another factor allying non-executives to management is that many traditional non-executives are themselves senior executives of other listed companies.[307] As fellow business leaders, it is not uncommon for them to socialize in the same circles as—or to serve on other boards as fellow non-executives with—the senior executives who they are supposed to monitor.[308] This kind of relationship presumably represents some sort of barrier to vigorous monitoring.[309] There is also the possibility that such non-executives may 'pull their punches . . . out of an innate fear of encouraging non-execs on their own boards to rock the boat too often'.[310] A final factor which may ally the interests of non-executives too closely with those of management is an excessively lengthy presence on the board. A 1992 survey found that less than one in five UK public companies had any policy (formal or informal) limiting the number of terms that a non-executive might serve.[311] The Cadbury Committee recognized this problem also, and recommended that non-executives 'should be appointed for specified terms and reappointment should not be automatic'.[312]

A second impediment to effective monitoring by non-executives is executive dominance on the board. Non-executive directors are—in non-financial companies at least—commonly outnumbered by the executive directors.[313] A marketing executive who was one of just two non-executive directors of a UK company whilst it went through a financial and managerial crisis is amongst the proponents of the view that non-executives should be in the majority on the boards of quoted companies.[314] The position of non-executives *vis-à-vis* executives is further weakened where the chairman of the board is not an independent non-executive (or part-time) chairman. This occurs where (a) the chairman is also the chief

---

[306] *Cadbury Report*, paras. 4.15, 4.30. As at 1993, only 39% of quoted UK companies had nomination committees, although this had increased from just 10% in 1988: Conyon (n. 299 above), at 104; see also Cadbury Committee (n. 287 above), at 19.

[307] In 1993, 54% of non-executives of UK industrial companies were main-board executive directors of other unconnected companies: author's analysis of figures in Korn/Ferry (n. 279 above), at 33, 58.

[308] 'Inner City Circle Holds the Key to Top Boardrooms', *Sunday Times*, 14 June 1992, sec. 3, p. 8.

[309] See B. G. M. Main, 'The Governance of Remuneration for Senior Executives' (1995).

[310] 'Knives Are Out in the Boardroom', *Fin. Times*, 1 May 1992, p. 11.

[311] PRO NED, *Research into the Role of the Non-Executive Director: Executive Summary* (1992) 6. But note that there has to be a trade-off here with the need for non-executives to 'get to know' the company's business before being able to perform an adequate monitoring role.

[312] *Cadbury Code*, para. 2.3.   [313] See Sec. D.2.i, above.

[314] 'Confessions of a Non-Executive', *Fin. Times*, 15 July 1991, p. 11. See also the proposed Fifth EC Directive on harmonization of company law: 1983 OJ (C 240) 2, art. 21a.

executive officer; (b) there is a chief executive separate from the chairman, but the chairman is an executive; or (c) the chairman, although part-time or non-executive, is a former executive director of the company. Although there was a significant increase between 1988 and 1993 in the proportion of quoted UK industrial companies in which the roles of chairman and chief executive were separated,[315] as at 1993 a substantial proportion (26%) of 'separate chairmen' were the leading executive (with the chief executive below them),[316] and a substantial proportion of the non-executive chairmen of larger listed companies were former executives. This is of concern given that over 70% of UK non-executives surveyed in 1994 said that a major inhibitor to their effectiveness was a dominant chairman or chief executive.[317]

A third barrier to effective monitoring is the limited time available to a non-executive to spend on any one directorship.[318] It is interesting though that in crisis situations non-executives inevitably spend an enormous amount of time working on the one company. A fourth inhibitor, which flows partly from the third, is that independent non-executives generally lack detailed knowledge of the company's business.[319] The problem is compounded by the fact that their main source of information is the very management which they are monitoring.[320] The dramatic increase in the incidence of audit committees at quoted industrial companies[321] is a positive development in that auditors have become a significant informational source for non-executives.[322] A fifth barrier is the lack of a strong legal incentive to engage in detailed monitoring.[323] And finally there is the fact that even 'independent' traditional non-executives are 'merely . . . independent of management, rather than *dependent* on shareholders'.[324] Given the 'closeness' of many 'independent' non-executives to the

---

[315] From 57% to 77%: Conyon (n. 299 above), at 101; see also Cadbury Committee (n. 287 above), at 16.

[316] Author's analysis of figures in Korn/Ferry (n. 279 above), at 18, 58. A further 6% were an executive but second-in-command to the CEO: ibid. The Cadbury Committee seems to have thought that a separation of the roles of chairman and CEO denotes an acceptable 'division of responsibilities at the head of a company': *Cadbury Report*, para. 4.9. However, where the 'separate chairman' is also an executive (which usually means that he or she is the leading executive), it is submitted that this is not the case: see Ch. 4, Sec. A.1.xvi.

[317] BDO Binder Hamlyn, *Non-Executive Directors—Watchdogs or Advisers?* (1994) 11.

[318] Ibid. [319] Ibid.

[320] KPMG (n. 304 above), at 11, identified 'executive directors of the company' as the principal informational source of the surveyed non-executives.

[321] The incidence was 35% in 1988 and 90% in 1993: Conyon (n. 299 above), at 104; see also Cadbury Committee (n. 287 above), at 18.

[322] KPMG (n. 304 above), at 11, found that 58% of non-executives received information from the auditors.

[323] See Ch. 1, at nn. 55–7, and accompanying text; and Sec. B.3.viii, above.

[324] R. J. Gilson and R. Kraakman, 'Reinventing the Outside Director: An Agenda for Institutional Investors' (1991) 43 *Stan. L Rev.* 863, at 881. (Original emphasis.)

management which they are supposed to monitor,[325] it is even arguable 'that [true] independence of management *can only be achieved* in a reliable way by making the non-executives dependent on another powerful group within the company'[326]—viz. the institutional shareholders. This argument is reinforced by the apparent rarity with which non-executives have performed spontaneously (i.e. unprompted by institutional shareholders) the ultimate monitoring action—the removal of an under-performing chief executive or executive chairman—which is a matter discussed forthwith.

(c) Evidence on Monitoring

Procurement of a change in management personnel is not only the most extreme, but also the most easily detectable, monitoring action performed by non-executives. Due to the publicity inevitably associated with departures of leading executives from quoted companies, there is ample anecdotal[327] and *ad hoc*[328] evidence, and even some systematic evidence,[329] suggesting that 'boardroom coups' occur relatively frequently in the UK. These usually involve the dismissal[330] or forced resignation of the leading executive director—who is normally either the chairman and chief executive, the executive chairman (where there is a separate chief executive), or the chief executive (where the chairman is part-time or non-executive). The author's interview study revealed, however, that several of the high-profile board dismissals of top executives that occurred in the early 1990s, and which were described in the press as instances of non-executives taking the lead, were in fact accompanied or at least preceded by significant institutional pressure for change.[331] The impression gained

---

[325] See nn. 302–12 above, and accompanying text.

[326] P. L. Davies, 'Institutional Investors in the United Kingdom' in Prentice and Holland (n. 5 above), 69, at 93 (original emphasis). Similar reasoning has been applied in relation to the independence of auditors: see e.g. D. Hatherly, 'The Future of Audit: The Case for the Shareholder Panel' (1994). See further Ch. 11, Sec. B.2.iii.

[327] See e.g. 'Knives . . .' (n. 310 above).

[328] See e.g. 'Plysu Managing Director Quits', *Fin. Times*, 13 Nov. 1992, p. 31; 'Horton is Ousted as Chairman of British Petroleum', *Fin. Times*, 26 June 1992, p. 1; 'Ricardo Chief Quits After Pressure from Directors', *Fin. Times*, 4 June 1992, p. 30; 'Barclays Chairman to Stand Down', *Fin. Times*, 25 Apr. 1992, p. 1.

[329] Franks and Mayer (n. 200 above), at 202–4 (of 55 leading executives of UK public companies dismissed during the first six months of 1988, a boardroom dispute was causative in 18 cases). There does not appear to have been a UK empirical study of the relationship between company performance and board-initiated management changes, or of the difference between executive-dominated and non-executive-dominated boards in terms of their monitoring activity. For US studies, see K. E. Scott and A. W. Kleidon, 'CEO Performance, Board Types and Board Performance: A First Cut' in T. Baums, R. M. Buxbaum, and K. J. Hopt (eds.), *Institutional Investors and Corporate Governance* (1994) 181, and the other studies cited therein; M. S. Weisbach, 'CEO Turnover and the Firm's Investment Decisions' (1995) 37 *J Fin. Econ.* 159. [330] See Ch. 4, Sec. A.1.xv.

[331] Franks and Mayer (n. 200 above), at 204, recognized this as a possibility.

was that it is quite rare for non-executives to take action spontaneously to oust an under-performing top executive.

(d) Liaison with Institutions

Dialogue with the non-executive directors of portfolio companies was, for 15 of the 17 fund managers interviewed by the writer, confined almost exclusively to 'problem situations'. The problem situation most likely to result in dialogue between institutions and non-executive directors was substantially sub-optimal performance at a portfolio company which was attributed to the company's management. As discussed earlier,[332] in this type of situation (a) it is not common for non-executives to be contacted before there has been substantial, and unsuccessful, dialogue with the executive management; (b) the non-executives do not always side with the institutions; and (c) in a minority of cases, it is a non-executive(s) who contacts the institutions with concerns—rather than the other way around. Apart from extremely sub-optimal performance, a variety of other serious problems (usually of a company-specific rather than procedural/ general nature) has given rise to meetings and dialogue between institutions and non-executive directors. Such dialogue is almost invariably initiated by the institution(s) concerned, rather than by the non-executives. For example, a listed newspaper-publishing company, which was majority-owned by a foreign company, entered a price war with its main rival only five weeks after its majority shareholder had placed a large parcel of its shares with institutions. The price war caused a sharp drop in the publisher's share price, and one of its institutional shareholders said: 'This is a serious matter which we will be taking up with the non-executive directors.'[333]

Of the two fund managers interviewed who did not restrict their dialogue with non-executives to problem situations, one said:

> We tend to go to as many AGMs as we can, because that is one time you *can* talk to non-execs. I've been to numerous AGMs, purely to talk to non-execs; not just [at] the problem companies. Quite often execs of one company are non-execs in another. We will occasionally . . . have a quick word about their other companies. . . . Sometimes they'll talk about it and sometimes they feel they can't.[334]

---

[332] See Sec. B.3.vi, above. See also A. Pettigrew and T. McNulty, 'Power and Influence in and Around the Boardroom' (1995) 48 *Human Relations* 845.

[333] 'Times Drops to 20p in Price War with Telegraph', *Fin. Times*, 24 June 1994, p. 1. The Stock Exchange investigated the matter and found no evidence that the cut in the newspaper's price was contemplated at the time of the share placement: 'When Price Cuts Prove Price Sensitive', *Fin. Times*, 25 June 1994, p. 10.

[334] The reluctance of some executives to talk about the companies at which they are non-executives was put down to apprehension about insider dealing, which was cited by a couple

The second fund manager—one of the executives mentioned earlier[335] who were involved full-time in matters of corporate governance and problem companies—said:

> There are a number of ongoing governance-type issues nowadays [on] which I will liaise with non-executives when appropriate, irrespective of the performance of the company. One of the helpful things now in accountability is that it is now in many companies a little clearer to see who are the chairman and members of the audit committee and remuneration committee. So if one is, for example, making a particular issue of one of those points you can now say [to the executives, in your correspondence on the matter of concern] that you are sending a copy of the letter to XYZ, in his capacity as chairman of the remuneration committee or whatever. The other method of seeking to address this is, for broader issues, to actually ask the executive concerned (if one is doing it in writing as is so often the case on non-time-sensitive matters): 'Please would you convey the substance of this letter to your board?'—so that there is a degree of communication to directors in totality, and that thereby . . . the non-executive directors are at least made aware of your views.

It is considered likely that dialogue of this sort will increase throughout the 1990s, due to the onus that has been placed, by the ABI and NAPF ICs, in the first instance, and subsequently by the Greenbury Committee, upon remuneration committees for overseeing companies' executive remuneration schemes. By leaving to the remuneration committee the setting of performance criteria for executive share schemes,[336] and for performance-based remuneration schemes generally,[337] the ABI and NAPF ICs established a framework for contact between institutions and non-executive directors, and indeed encouraged such contact:

> The [*Share Scheme Guidance*] document provides that details [of the performance criteria adopted by the remuneration committee] should be disclosed at the time a scheme is adopted, and shareholders will have the opportunity of discussing any apparent shortcomings . . . with the directors through the Remuneration Committee.[338]

> [R]emuneration committees have a central role and responsibility in requiring that demanding targets be set in [performance-based remuneration] schemes. . . . If the remuneration committee appears to fail to measure up to their responsibilities, shareholders should quite properly ask for comment or explanation.[339]

of other interviewees as a reason why their institutions do not have any contact with non-executive directors at non-problem companies.

[335] See n. 185 above, and accompanying text.
[336] ABI and NAPF, *Share Scheme Guidance* (1993) para. 3.
[337] ABI, *Long Term Remuneration for Senior Executives* (1994) 1, 2.
[338] Letter titled 'Joint ABI and NAPF Guidance on Share Scheme Performance Criteria' from R. D. Regan, Secretary, ABI IC, to members of the ABI (dated 15 July 1993).
[339] ABI (n. 337 above), at 1.

Similarly, the Greenbury Committee, which placed the remuneration committee at the heart of its recommendations on directors' remuneration, stated that '[t]he investor institutions should use their power and influence to ensure the implementation of best practice as set out in the [*Greenbury Code*]'.[340]

Finally, several fund managers interviewed thought that regular dialogue between institutions and non-executive directors would be beneficial and was desirable. Mr Donald Brydon, when chairman of the ISC, said that if non-executives 'are to act efficiently as the guardians of the share-holders' interests they must first understand the attitudes of their shareholders. Separate discussions of strategy with non-executives would be most desirable.'[341] A few interviewees were, however, opposed ideologically to speaking in everyday circumstances to non-executive directors separately from executives, due to a perception that this would conflict with the notion of a unitary board.

iii. 'Institutional' Non-Executives

'Institutional' non-executives are those directors who owe their presence on the board, to a greater or lesser extent, to a large institutional shareholder or group of institutions. They may, therefore, be either (a) fund managers, or (b) persons selected by fund managers.

(a) Fund Managers

As at the early 1990s, it was extremely rare for a fund manager or other full-time executive of an institution to serve as a non-executive director of an unrelated *quoted* company, whether or not the institution had a holding in that company.[342] In two of the three cases of which the author was aware as at mid-1993,[343] the institution concerned had only a small shareholding in the company concerned, the senior fund manager was not on the company's board because of that shareholding,[344] and he was not therefore

---

[340] *Greenbury Report*, para. 3.4.   [341] Brydon (n. 266 above).

[342] There was, not unexpectedly, a reasonable number of *non-executive* directors of listed insurance companies and investment trusts who also served as non-executives on the boards of companies in which those institutions had holdings: see B. G. M. Main and J. Johnston, *The Remuneration Committee as an Instrument of Corporate Governance* (1992) 29–34.

[343] Mr Paul Myners, chairman and chief executive of Gartmore Investment Management plc, was a non-executive director of PowerGen plc; and Mr Paul Whitney, then chief executive of CIN Management Ltd., was a non-executive at MFI Furniture Group plc. (Note that Mr A. Scott Bell, managing director of The Standard Life Assurance Company, was a non-executive at Bank of Scotland; however, Standard Life's 33% stake in Bank of Scotland was a 'corporate' holding as opposed to a portfolio investment.)

[344] Mr Whitney's institution, CIN, had provided equity finance for the management buy-out of MFI in Nov. 1987, but CIN's stake became very small upon MFI's floatation in June 1992.

an 'institutional' non-executive within the above definition![345] The third case was that of Budgens plc, where there was an institutional intervention in April 1991 which resulted in the removal of the chairman/chief executive and the appointment of three new executive directors, a new non-executive chairman, and another new non-executive. The new non-executive chairman was an executive director of Electra Investment Trust plc, an internally managed investment trust and 6% shareholder which had been one of the institutions involved in ousting the former chairman/chief executive.[346] The other new non-executive director was an industrialist who was nominated by Gartmore Investment Management plc, a 5% shareholder which was another of the intervening institutions.[347]

The position was quite different in the case of *un*quoted companies, as at the early 1990s: it was very common for institutions to have their executives serving as non-executive directors on the boards of unquoted companies for which they had provided 'venture' or 'development' capital. Institutional representation on unquoted companies has a fairly long history.[348]

What, then, are the reasons why fund managers were found only rarely on the boards of quoted companies but relatively frequently on the boards of unquoted companies to which equity finance had been provided? In relation to the former, the reasons mentioned most commonly by fund managers interviewed by the author were: (a) fund managers are ill-qualified to be non-executive directors of industrial companies ('We're portfolio managers, not industrialists'); (b) it would limit freedom of action ('We don't want to feel tied in to a long-term holding'; 'It makes you an insider'); (c) non-executives should represent the interests of *all* share-holders, not those of a large institution or even institutions generally; conflicts of interest might arise; (d) fund managers lack the time to go onto more than one or two boards each; thus, the senior fund-management staff of any one institution could conceivably go onto the boards of only a small proportion of the companies in the institution's portfolios; (e) the cost: the standard fund-management fee charged by managers of external funds is

[345] Nevertheless, those two men as non-executives would surely, because of their background, have been far less likely to suffer from being too close to the executive management, as discussed at nn. 302–12 above, and accompanying text.

[346] See 'Budgens Meets to Set Terms for Fletcher Departure' *Fin. Times*, 1 May 1991, p. 21; *Annual Report and Accounts of Budgens plc* (1991) 1, 2, 8.

[347] See 'How to Replace . . .' (n. 195 above). Note also that a few former senior executives of institutions have taken up non-executive directorships at industrial companies after retiring as fund managers.

[348] See Committee on the Working of the Monetary System, *Minutes of Evidence* (1960) paras. 7474–96.

insufficient to allow senior fund managers to spend much time as non-executives.

Are these points applicable to unquoted companies? Point (a) is obviously equally applicable, but the fact that managers of venture-capital funds go onto company boards largely contradicts point (a)—which is based on the false premise that the board of a large public company actually manages the company's business. Point (b) does not apply in the case of institutional shareholdings in unquoted companies, because there is not ordinarily a ready market in such shares. (An institution normally holds the shares of an unquoted company with a view to an eventual floatation or trade sale.) It is this lack of a market for the shares that chiefly explains why board representation is obtained. Point (c) is inapplicable in regard to most venture capital-backed unquoted companies because there would usually be only a handful of external shareholders, each of which would be represented on the board. Point (d) is similarly inapplicable, because the managers of venture-capital funds are not portfolio managers in the usual sense—they have less individual investments, and they do not spend time trading shares. In relation to point (e), institutions charge external clients a much larger fee for money invested in their venture-capital funds than for money invested in 'normal' equity portfolios.

Two interviewees were, however, favourable about fund managers acting as non-executives. The first said that if a company was prepared to give his institution a board seat he would be happy for one of his senior fund managers to be a non-executive director. This stance was influenced by the fact that his institution mostly indexed its UK equity holdings, and it would not therefore be selling out of a company whilst that approach remained.[349] The relevant fund manager would be 'ring-fenced' within the institution so that other fund managers would not be made insiders.[350] His only concern was 'finding the right people within the organization who have got the time to do it'. The second interviewee said that he had made two suggestions regarding institutional non-executives. First, he had raised with the managements of some portfolio companies the possibility that one of his institution's fund managers might go onto their boards. His rationale was that it might 'add value' to the board and the company; he did not intend that the fund manager would be his institution's 'representative' on the board—his institution's holdings were mostly about 1.3% of a company's issued capital, and it was thus nowhere near the largest shareholder in most cases. This suggestion was 'not received well'.[351]

---

[349] Of importance, although not mentioned by the interviewee, is the fact that his institution managed *internal* funds—managers of *external* funds that index their equity investments actually have a strong economic incentive to not perform any form of close monitoring: see Ch. 10, Sec. B.1.v. [350] Cf. Point (b) above.

[351] This accords with the results of the survey of finance directors in 3i (n. 140 above).

Secondly, he had suggested to IFMA that they set up a directory of fund managers who would be prepared to go onto boards—'kind of like the PRO NED service'. The intention was that managements 'could get an idea of what an institutional shareholder's feelings were on a matter at the earlier stage of board consideration'. IFMA had 'not taken up' this proposal as it thought that there were problems with conflicts of interest and that fund managers were too busy.

(b) Persons Selected by Fund Managers

Nearly all of the fund managers interviewed said that their institution had occasionally been involved to some extent in the selection process for portfolio companies' non-executive directors. This involvement was thought generally to have increased over the 1980s and early 1990s.[352] The most common form of involvement comprised an institution giving an opinion on possible candidates identified by a company's board. Less commonly, an institution would suggest names of persons it considered suitable—either after being asked for suggestions by the management, or, infrequently, on the initiative of the institution where it was seriously dissatisfied with some aspect of the company's management or with its governance structure. Then, of course, there is the extreme case of a full-blown institutional intervention.[353] It is common in such an institutional intervention for at least one new non-executive director to be brought onto the board (one of them often as non-executive chairman) in addition to new executive directors. Several of the interviewees had, during the 1980s and early 1990s, effectively placed onto the board of an ailing portfolio company a 'company doctor' such as Sir Lewis Robertson, Mr Roy Barber, or Mr David James, or a 'very independent' non-executive director like Mr Michael Beckett; as one interviewee put it: 'someone that we know who's sorted out a company or [is] well respected'.

Returning to the involvement of institutions in the selection of non-executives for non-problem companies, there have been several calls for institutions to take a closer interest in the appointment of non-executives,[354] and for formal structures to be established under which

---

[352] Approximately 12% of non-executives of listed UK industrial companies had, in 1994, been 'recommended by [an] investment institution': KPMG (n. 304 above), at 12. Of those institutional non-executives, 41% cited institutional shareholders as a source of information and/or advice prior to appointment (compared to only 7% for all other non-executives), and 38% cited institutional shareholders as a source of information and/or advice since appointment (compared to 17% for all other non-executives): author's analysis of additional information provided to the author by A. Dean, Market Research Officer, KPMG Peat Marwick.   [353] See Sec. B.3.vi, above.

[354] See e.g. House of Commons Trade and Industry Committee, *First Report: Takeovers and Mergers* (1991) paras. 214, 218; Innovation Advisory Board, *Promoting Innovation and Long Termism* (1990) 5.

institutions could nominate or even appoint a number of a company's non-executive directors.[355] Such proposals have, however, been unpopular with company managements,[356] most institutions,[357] and the Cadbury Committee.[358] There is further discussion of these proposals in the final chapter.[359]

E. SUMMARY AND CONCLUSION

It is clear that the bulk of firm-level monitoring in the UK has been carried out directly (i.e. by fund managers themselves), whilst most industry-wide monitoring has been conducted indirectly (by trade associations of the traditional institutions). In regard to the firm-level monitoring, routine dialogue with company managements has a long history and is widespread; exercise of voting rights increased a little during the early 1990s from a fairly low base, but voting remains problematic for some managers of external funds; a significant minority of the major UK fund managers in 1993 had senior staff engaged full-time in taking a proactive stance on 'problem companies' and companies with inadequacies in their corporate governance; institutional interventions to change the management of problem companies have occurred since the 1950s, but their prevalence in the early 1990s gives weight to the theory that they are a substitute for takeovers; successful institutional interventions are likely only at small and medium-sized quoted companies, because the percentage stake held by the largest handful of institutional shareholders in most large listed companies is too small for an effective coalition to be formed; litigation by institutions as a means of monitoring company managements is virtually non-existent; there are signs that in the late 1980s to early 1990s the relationship between institutions and non-executive directors of non-problem companies became closer (but from an extremely low base); and 'institutional' non-executives are rare, but becoming less so.

When the last UK takeover boom was drawing to a close, an adviser to the Governor of the Bank of England commented:

> [S]hareholders have all but abdicated. As a rule the only time they do anything
> that matters is when they assent, or refuse to assent, their shares when a bid is

---

[355] See e.g. A. Sykes, 'Proposals for a Reformed System of Corporate Governance to Achieve Internationally Competitive Long-Term Performance' in N. H. Dimsdale and M. Prevezer (eds.), *Capital Markets and Corporate Governance* (1994) 111; Gilson and Kraakman (n. 324 above). There have been parallel calls for some form of 'shareholder panel' to nominate and monitor the auditors: see e.g. Hatherly (n. 326 above); Auditing Practices Board, *The Future Development of Auditing* (1992) 11.
[356] See 3i (n. 140 above): 78% of finance directors considered 'consultation with institutions on new board appointments' to be 'not desirable'.
[357] Finding of author's interview study.   [358] *Cadbury Report*, paras. 6.2–6.3.
[359] See Ch. 11, Sec. B.2.iii.

made. It was said of Charles I that there was nothing truly kingly in his life except the leaving of it. So it is with UK shareholders: their only kingly act is when they sell out.[360]

The material presented in this chapter indicates that the amount of firm-level monitoring conducted in the UK in the early 1990s was greater than that suggested in the above passage. Although there were fewer reported institutional interventions to replace under-performing managements during 1985–9, fund managers say that more institutional action occurred behind the scenes than that which was reported in the press. Considering also the regular meetings and dialogue which have been common since the 1970s, institutional monitoring during the latter part of the 1980s was not, as suggested, confined to 'exit' rather than 'voice'.

---

[360] J. P. Charkham, *Corporate Governance and the Market for Companies: Aspects of the Shareholders' Role* (1989) 8.

PART III

*Institutional Involvement in Corporate
Governance in Australia:
History and Current Level*

6

The Participants in Australia

This and the following two chapters examine the involvement of institutional shareholders in corporate governance in Australia. The structure of the analysis mirrors that used in Part II. Thus, Chapters 7 and 8 examine, respectively, the issues with which the institutions have been concerned and the manner in which they have conducted their monitoring. Being the parallel of Chapter 3, the present chapter looks, first, at the significant institutional players in the Australian corporate-governance arena. It then introduces the Australian institutions' collective-action vehicle: the Australian Investment Managers' Association. Chapters 6, 7, and 8 are significantly shorter than their counterparts in Part II. This is evidence of the relatively smaller role (*vis-à-vis* the position in the UK) played to date in Australian corporate governance by institutional investors.

A. THE TRADITIONAL INSTITUTIONS AND THE FUND MANAGERS

The two largest categories of institutional shareholder in Australia, as in the UK, are the occupational pension funds (more commonly called superannuation funds) and the insurance companies. It is important when examining the Australian scene, as demonstrated already for that in the UK, to appreciate the distinction between the 'traditional institutions' and fund managers. It is *fund managers* in Australia—as it is in the UK—which meet with, talk to, and occasionally engage with the management of companies.

1. INVESTMENT OF AUSTRALIAN INSTITUTIONS' FUNDS

i. Insurance Companies

It has been shown that most UK insurance companies have fund-management subsidiaries that manage all or at least the vast proportion of their parents' assets. This is true too for the Australian insurance sector,[1] with the notable exception of the third-largest life insurer, MLC Life Ltd.

---

[1] See Australian Investment Managers' Group ('AIMG'), *December 1993 Half-Year Member Survey* (1994) Table 9.

As at 30 June 1993, there were 54 life offices in Australia.[2] There was, however, enormous concentration in the largest three offices. The Australian assets in the statutory funds[3] of The Australian Mutual Provident Society ('AMP')[4] and The National Mutual Life Association of Australasia Ltd.[5] (both mutual companies),[6] and in those of MLC Life Ltd.[7] (a wholly owned subsidiary of Lend Lease Corporation Ltd., one of Australia's largest listed companies) accounted for 53.18% of the total Australian assets held in the statutory funds of Australian life offices at 30 June 1993.[8] At that time, AMP and National Mutual managed all of the assets of their statutory funds internally. In contrast, about half of the assets of MLC Life's statutory funds were then managed by 28 outside managers.[9] MLC Life made the decision to make use of external fund managers in the mid-1980s, a decision which 'raised eyebrows at the time because it had never been tried in Australia'.[10]

ii. Occupational Superannuation Funds

Chapter 3 revealed that, as at the end of 1991, a fairly large proportion of the assets of directly invested UK pension funds were managed externally. Nevertheless, there were at that time some very significant in-house managers of some of the UK's largest corporate pension schemes. A similar situation existed in Australia at mid-1993: of the A$94,900 million of assets of directly invested Australian superannuation funds at 30 June 1993, A$60,735 million (64.0%) was managed by external fund managers, and A$34,165 million (36.0%) was managed in-house.[11]

A great deal of that internally managed figure was accounted for by three large government-owned managers of public-sector superannuation funds: State Superannuation Investment & Management Corporation of New South Wales (A$12,338 million under management at 30 June 1993),

---

[2] Insurance and Superannuation Commission ('I&SC'), *Quarterly Statistical Bulletin* (June 1993) xi–xii

[3] The Life Insurance Act 1945 (Cth.) requires every company to establish and maintain a statutory fund or statutory funds in respect of its life insurance business. Section 38(1) states that '[a]ll amounts received by a company in respect of any class of life insurance business, after the establishment by the company of a statutory fund in respect of that class of life insurance business, shall be carried to, and become assets of, that fund'.

[4] A$26,076.9m. (Equal to 28.4% of Australian assets of Australian life offices.)

[5] A$13,194.4m. (Equal to 14.37% of Australian assets of Australian life offices.)

[6] Note that National Mutual began demutualizing in 1995.

[7] A$9,555.7m. (Equal to 10.41% of Australian assets of Australian life offices.)

[8] I&SC (n. 2 above), at Table 14C.

[9] 'Pioneering MLC has the Formula Right', *Weekend Aust.*, 12 Feb. 1994, p. 31.

[10] Ibid.

[11] Australian Bureau of Statistics ('ABS'), *Assets of Superannuation Funds and Approved Deposit Funds, September Quarter* (1993) Tables 3, 3A, 3B.

manager of the assets of the New South Wales government and semi-government superannuation funds; Queensland Investment Corporation (A$8,885 million at 30 June 1993), the investment manager of Queensland's public-sector superannuation funds and some other public-sector assets; and Commonwealth Funds Management Ltd. (A$6,569 million at 30 June 1993),[12] the government-owned investment manager of the two main Commonwealth public-sector superannuation schemes.[13]

A handful of corporate superannuation funds also had their assets managed internally at 30 June 1993. At that date, some of Australia's largest industrial companies, such as The Broken Hill Proprietary Company Ltd. (A$1,810 million of superannuation-fund assets under management); Shell Australia Ltd. (A$841 million); CSR Ltd. (A$773 million); and ICI Australia Ltd. (A$642 million) operated internally managed superannuation schemes for their employees.[14] The super-annuation funds of several Australian financial companies (such as insurers and banks) were then also managed in-house.

At early 1994, Australia's industry-wide (or 'multi-employer') super-annuation schemes (which were all trade union-related) delegated the investment of their assets to external fund managers. It was expected, however, that some of the largest industry schemes, having reached the critical mass necessary to be able to cost-effectively manage their investments internally, would soon set up internal teams to do so. The largest industry scheme at the start of 1994 was the Construction and Building Unions Superannuation Fund (C+BUS), which had assets of A$1,100 million.[15]

The A$60,735 million of assets of directly invested superannuation funds that was managed externally at 30 June 1993[16] was distributed amongst an array of fund-management firms—some linked to insurance companies, some linked to banks or merchant banks, and some independent. Many of the larger Australian schemes, like those in the UK, employ two or more external managers (each of whom may have a balanced brief and/or one or more specialist briefs).

In comparison to UK pension schemes, a greater proportion of the total assets of all Australian superannuation funds was invested as insured schemes and in the managed funds of life offices, in the early 1990s. At 30

---

[12] Most, but not all, of this figure consisted of the assets of public-sector superannuation funds—Commonwealth Funds Management ('CFM') was reconstituted in July 1991, and thereafter offered its investment-management services to the market generally: CFM, *Annual Report 1992–93* (1993) 2.

[13] All figures for funds under management provided to the author by I. Matheson, Executive Director, Australian Investment Managers' Association.

[14] Ibid.   [15] 'Billion Dollar Men', *The Bulletin*, 1 Mar. 1994, p. 67, at 70.

[16] See ABS (n. 11 above), at Table 3B.

June 1993, Australian superannuation funds and approved deposit funds had total assets of A\$169,592 million.[17] Of this, A\$74,692 million was held in the statutory funds of life offices. That is, insured schemes and schemes invested in life-company managed funds accounted for A\$74,692 million (44.04%) of the total assets of superannuation funds. Directly invested schemes accounted for the remaining A\$94,900 million (55.96%) of assets.[18]

iii. Unit Trusts

As in the UK, unit trusts in Australia are managed by a variety of fund-management entities. Australian unit trusts had total assets of A\$28,406 million, and Australian equity investments of A\$4,649 million, at the end of June 1993.[19] The general comments made in Chapter 3 about the management of unit-trust assets in the UK are also applicable to the Australian industry.

iv. Other

Trustee companies and listed investment companies are the other main types of Australian institutions with equity investments. There were 14 trustee companies operating 100 common funds at the end of June 1993, and they had Australian equity investments of A\$975 million out of total assets of A\$4,573 million.[20] Virtually all of those assets were managed in-house by the trustee companies. The assets of Australia's two largest listed investment companies—Australian Foundation Investment Company Ltd. and Argo Investments Ltd.—consisted very largely of listed Australian equities at the end of 1993. They had Australian equity investments of A\$955 million and A\$716 million, respectively, at 31 December 1993, and managed these internally.[21] Other prominent listed investment companies operating in 1993 were administered by, and had their assets managed by, major Australia-based fund-management firms.

2. Fund Managers' Equity Holdings

Australia-based fund managers had, in addition to the funds of Australian 'traditional institutions', a not inconsiderable amount of non-institutional funds under management at 30 June 1993. Their funds under management from overseas sources, government, charities, other trusts, and 'other

---

[17] See ABS (n. 11 above), at Table 1.   [18] Ibid., at Tables 2, 3.
[19] ABS, *Managed Funds: Australia, September Quarter* (1993) Table 5.
[20] Ibid., at Table 7.
[21] Information provided to the author by B. J. Tiernan, Secretary, Australian Foundation Investment Company Ltd., and R. J. Patterson, Managing Director, Argo Investments Ltd.

sources'[22] amounted to A$21,113 million at that time.[23] The total funds managed from Australia by professional fund-management firms at the end of June 1993, excluding superannuation assets managed by in-house fund managers, was A$227,633 million.[24] The value of superannuation assets managed internally at 30 June 1993 was A$34,165 million,[25] and thus the total funds managed by Australia-based fund managers at 30 June 1993 was A$261,798 million. An illustration of the difference in the size of the UK and Australian markets is that the equivalent figure for UK-based fund managers 18 months earlier was £750,000 million (about A$1,600,000 million).[26]

Table 6.1 sets out the 10 largest fund managers operating in Australia at the end of June 1993. There was even greater concentration amongst the largest few Australia-based fund managers than amongst their UK-based counterparts. The top 10 UK-based managers represented 31% of the market at the end of 1991,[27] which was a high level of concentration compared to the United States, for instance, but the top 10 Australia-based firms managed assets worth a striking 56% of the Australian professionally managed funds market at 30 June 1993. AMP Investments Australia Ltd., the investment-management subsidiary for the Australian funds of Australia's giant mutual life company, The Australian Mutual Provident Society, alone accounted for 12.6% of the Australian market. That was a market share which was more than one-and-a-half times that of its nearest rival, Bankers Trust Australia Ltd.: a subsidiary of the US commercial bank, Bankers Trust Corporation of New York.

Table 6.2 shows the fund managers which had the 30 largest sums of listed Australian equities under management at the end of 1993. The investment-management arms of financial conglomerates (13 out of the top 30) and insurance companies (10 out of the top 30) were predominant, as in the UK.[28] Interestingly, a handful of overseas-based institutions had fairly large stakes in the Australian equity market at 31 December 1993. From its offices in San Francisco and other overseas locations, the Capital Group Inc. managed listed Australian equities worth about 1% of the Australian market capitalization.[29] At least two other large US mutual-fund managers,

---

[22] Which presumably included funds from private clients.

[23] ABS (n. 19 above), at Table 9.

[24] Ibid. That this figure does not include funds managed by in-house managers of superannuation funds was revealed to the author by D. Baynes, Director, Financial Survey Section, ABS.   [25] ABS (n. 11 above), at Table 3A.

[26] See Table 3.1.   [27] Ibid.

[28] The 10 insurers led marginally in terms of their aggregate holding: A$31,970m.; compared to the 13 financial conglomerates' aggregate holding of A$31,091m.

[29] Capital Group's holdings of UK equities at 31 Dec. 1991 were worth about £1,000m. (information provided to the author by A. Watson, Marketing Statistician, Capital International Ltd., London) which represented only 0.18% of the UK market capitalization. Even this figure did not really represent a holding managed wholly from overseas, because Capital has fund managers in London who managed part of this amount.

Table 6.1 Ten largest fund-management firms in Australia, 1993

Manager	Total funds managed from Australia at 30 June 1993 (A$million)	As proportion of total funds under professional mgt. from Aust. at 30 June 1993 (%)
AMP Investments Australia Ltd. (Ins.)	32,979	12.60
Bankers Trust Australia Ltd. (FC)	21,013	8.03
National Mutual Funds Management (Ins.)	17,783	6.79
CBA Financial Services (FC)	13,917	5.32
State Superannuation Investment & Mgt. Corp. (Pub.)	12,338	4.71
Westpac Investment Management Pty. Ltd. (FC)	11,744	4.49
Lend Lease Corporate Services Ltd. (FC)	10,283*	3.93
Queensland Investment Corporation (Pub.)	8,885	3.39
Macquarie Bank Ltd. (FC)	8,785	3.36
ANZ Funds Management (FC)	8,270	3.16

Note: abbreviations: see App. G.
   * Lend Lease group companies had a further A$8,346m. under external management.

Sources: Information supplied to the author by I. Matheson, Executive Director, AIMA; W. A. H. Webster, Investment Director, Lend Lease Corporate Services; author's calculations of market shares.

Franklin Resources Inc. (through its affiliate Templeton Worldwide Inc.) and Fidelity Investments, also had fairly large sums of Australian equities under management from the US, Hong Kong, and elsewhere, at the end of 1993.

A comparison of Table 6.2 with Table 3.2 shows that, whereas 18 firms managed UK equities worth 1% or more of total domestic market capitalization, only 9 fund managers were in an equivalent position in the Australian market. In all, 39 fund managers had a 0.5% or greater share of the UK equity market, whilst only 17 managers had an equivalent share of the Australian equity market. The market share, in this sense, of the top five managers was 13.6% (UK) compared to 11.9% (Australia); the market share of the top 10 managers was 21.4% (UK) compared to 17.6% (Australia); and the market share of the top 30 managers was 40.1% (UK) compared to 27.1% (Australia). The discrepancy between the positions in the UK and Australia is largely explained by the following factors (which

Table 6.2 Thirty largest managers of Australian equities, 1993

Manager	Market value of Australian equities under management at 31 Dec. 1993 (A$million)	As proportion of market value of total listed Australian equities at 31 Dec. 1993[a] (%)
AMP Investments Australia Ltd. (Ins).	13,161	4.37
Bankers Trust Australia Ltd. (FC)	6,686	2.22
State Superannuation Invest- ment & Mgt. Corp. (Pub.)	6,243	2.07
National Mutual Funds Management (Ins.)	5,334	1.77
County NatWest Australia Investment Mgt. Ltd. (FC)	4,275	1.42
Queensland Investment Corporation (Pub.)	4,088	1.36
Lend Lease Corporate Services Ltd (FC)	3,819	1.27
Westpac Investment Management Pty. Ltd. (FC)	3,722	1.24
The Capital Group Inc. (USA) (O/S)	3,000*	1.00
CBA Financial Services (FC)	2,734	0.91
Colonial Mutual Investment Management (Ins.)	2,506	0.83
Rothschild Australia Asset Management Ltd. (FC)	2,339	0.78
NRMA Investment Pty. Ltd. (Ins.)	2,300	0.76
Mercantile Mutual Investment Management Ltd. (Ins.)	2,058	0.68
Prudential Portfolio Managers Australia Ltd. (Ins.)	1,799	0.60
Commonwealth Funds Management Ltd. (Pub.)	1,704**	0.57
GIO Investment Services Ltd. (Ins.)	1,606	0.53
Potter Warburg Asset Management Ltd. (FC)	1,354	0.45
Fidelity Investments (O/S)	1,350***	0.45
Maple-Brown Abbott Ltd. (Indep.)	1,259	0.42

Table 6.2 (*Continued*)

Manager	Market value of Australian equities under management at 31 Dec. 1993 (A$million)	As proportion of market value of total listed Australian equities at 31 Dec. 1993[a] (%)
Suncorp Insurance Investments (Ins.)	1,140	0.38
Zurich Australia Insurance Group (Ins.)	1,096	0.36
J. P. Morgan Investment Management Australia Ltd. (FC)	1,095	0.36
National Australia Financial Management (FC)	1,070	0.36
Perpetual Funds Management (FC)	1,030	0.34
Macquarie Bank Ltd. (FC)	1,019	0.34
Armstrong Jones Portfolio Management (FC)	995	0.33
Legal & General Investment Management Ltd. (Ins.)	970	0.32
Australian Foundation Investment Company Ltd. (Indep.)	955	0.32
Wardley Investment Services (Australia) Ltd. (FC)	953	0.32

Note: abbreviations: see App. G.
   * At 31 Oct. 1993.
  ** At 30 June 1993.
 *** At 31 Aug. 1994.
 [a] Value of total listed Australian equities at 31 Dec. 1993 was A$301,235m.: information provided to the author by P. M. Pinnock, Corporate Relations Officer (Sydney), Australian Stock Exchange.

Sources: Information supplied to the author by I. Matheson, Executive Director, AIMA; P. M. Pinnock, Corporate Relations Officer (Sydney), Australian Stock Exchange; other sources listed in App. H; author's calculations of market shares.

are detailed in Chapter 2): (a) there is a much higher level of inter-corporate holdings (in particular, those of overseas-based companies) in the Australian quoted corporate sector compared to the UK quoted corporate sector; (b) UK-based fund managers generally allocate a far greater proportion of funds under management to domestic equities than do Australia-based managers; and (c) largely because of (a) and (b), UK institutions control a much higher proportion of total quoted domestic equities than do Australian institutions.

B. THE COLLECTIVE-ACTION VEHICLE: THE AIMA

The trade associations representing Australian life insurers (the Life Insurance Federation of Australia Inc.) and superannuation funds (the Association of Superannuation Funds of Australia ('ASFA')) did not, at the date of writing, perform shareholder-affairs activities like the ICs of the ABI and the NAPF.[30] Other trade bodies include the Investment Funds Association of Australia Ltd. (mainly for unit-trust managers), and the Australian Institute of Superannuation Trustees (most of whose members are trustees of industry-wide superannuation schemes). Neither of these bodies had an organized shareholder-affairs agenda, as at the date of writing.

It was, in fact, only in the early 1990s that Australia-based fund managers established a trade association to, *inter alia*, provide a mechanism for collective action on matters relating to members' shareholdings. The Australian Investment Managers' Group ('AIMG') was formed in December 1990, but it did not have a full-time secretariat until May 1993. It changed its name to the Australian Investment Managers' Association ('AIMA') in mid-1994.[31] At that time, the AIMA had one full-time executive director, a board made up of fund managers from a variety of types of fund-management organizations, and seven committees—one of which was the Corporate Governance Committee, and another of which was the Accounting Standards/Disclosure Committee.

The AIMA has been involved not only in industry-wide monitoring, but also in firm-level monitoring. In fact, one of the express objectives of the AIMA is 'to facilitate investors taking action when warranted by circumstances'.[32] There is a more detailed discussion of the role of the AIMA in Chapters 7 and 8.

---

[30] Note, however, that ASFA announced in Oct. 1995 that it would 'support [its] members with education and research on corporate governance issues [and] facilitate a bit more debate within the association on corporate governance': 'Super Funds Beef Up Scrutiny', *Aust.*, 6 Oct. 1995, p. 21. Also, at the date of writing the Life Insurance Federation had an Investment Committee, but its role did not approach that performed by the ABI IC.

[31] For convenience, the abbreviation 'AIMA' is used throughout the remainder of the book, regardless of whether the organization was known as the AIMA or the AIMG at the relevant time.

[32] AIMG, grey brochure titled 'Australian Investment Managers' Group' (undated).

7

Areas of Involvement in Australia

The following discussion of the various areas of known institutional involvement in the affairs of listed companies in Australia is divided into procedural/general issues and company-specific issues. It will be seen that institutional involvement has a shorter history, and has been considerably narrower in scope, in Australia than in the UK.

The are several references in this chapter and later chapters to an interview study involving Australia-based institutions. This study was conducted by the author in Melbourne and Sydney in February 1994. It was designed as a comparative one *vis-à-vis* the author's UK interview study. The interviewees were the senior executive or a senior fund manager of 13 investment-management firms.[1] The 13 institutions managed listed Australian equities worth A\$52,170 million at 31 December 1993, which represented 17.3% of the value of the Australian equity market at that date. The institutions included the five largest, and seven of the eight largest, managers of Australian equities at 31 December 1993.[2] The writer also had several discussions with the Executive Director of the AIMA, in Sydney, Melbourne, and Adelaide, during 1993, 1994, and 1995.

A. PROCEDURAL AND GENERAL ISSUES

For ease of comparison with Chapter 4, the procedural and general issues discussed below are subdivided into the same two broad categories used in Chapter 4: issues of 'investor protection and corporate governance'; and 'ethical and political' issues.

1. INVESTOR PROTECTION AND CORPORATE GOVERNANCE

i. Differential Voting Rights

The Australian Corporations Law, like the Companies Act 1985 (UK), does not prohibit non-voting or restricted-voting ordinary shares. However, the listing requirements of the ASX include a rule (LR 3K(2)) that '[v]oting rights in respect of fully paid shares shall be on a one for one

---

[1] They are listed in App. C. The questions asked of each interviewee are set out in App. D.
[2] See Table 6.2.

basis'.[3] Due to LR 3K(2), non-voting shares were until 1990 non-existent amongst listed Australian companies. The ASX can, however, waive compliance with any of its Listing Rules in individual cases,[4] and in 1990 News Corporation Ltd. sought such a waiver to enable it to issue non-voting ordinary shares (hereafter 'News Corp.'s 1990 proposal'). It was granted a waiver by the ASX, and it obtained the requisite general-meeting approval, but as at late 1995 it had not issued any non-voting shares. The AIMA was not in existence at the time of News Corp.'s 1990 proposal and it would appear that, the AMP excepted, there was no substantial institutional resistance to the proposal.

In October 1993, the chairman of News Corp. announced at the AGM that the company proposed to issue a new class of shares with 'super' voting rights (hereafter 'News Corp.'s 1993 proposal'). The AIMA had by this time been established for nearly three years, and its secretariat had been in existence for five months. It conducted a well-organized and highly publicized campaign against News Corp.'s 1993 proposal for a one-off waiver of LR 3K(2), and against the possible amendment or deletion of LR 3K(2). The latter option was raised as a possibility in the ASX's discussion paper which followed News Corp.'s 1993 proposal.[5] News Corp. eventually withdrew its application for a one-off waiver of LR 3K(2), and the ASX later decided not to amend or delete LR 3K(2).[6]

ii. Major Corporate Changes

A notable difference between the listing requirements of the London Stock Exchange and the ASX is that only those of the London Stock Exchange include provisions under which corporate transactions above a certain size must be affirmed by the general meeting.[7] The *ASX Listing Rules* simply state that any sale or disposal of a company's 'main undertaking' must be conditional upon ratification by the general meeting; and give the ASX a discretion to order in a particular case that the general meeting must ratify 'a change in activities' by a company.[8] In its *Corporate Governance* document, released in mid-1995, the AIMA recommended that 'major

---

[3] *ASX Listing Rules*, LR 3K(2). See also CL, s. 249(1)(c).

[4] See the Foreword to the *ASX Listing Rules*; *Harman* v. *Energy Research Australia Ltd.* (1985) 9 ACLR 897.

[5] See ASX, *Differential Voting Rights* (1993).

[6] See Ch. 8, Sec. D.1, for a more detailed discussion of the AIMA's role in the forestalment of News Corp.'s 1993 proposal.

[7] See *Listing Rules*, ch. 10.

[8] *ASX Listing Rules*, LR 3S. See Ch. 11, Sec. B.1.vii, where there is a recommendation for the introduction into the *ASX Listing Rules* of London-style material-transactions provisions.

corporate changes which in substance or effect may erode share ownership rights should be submitted to a vote of shareholders'.[9]

iii. Continuous Disclosure

The AIMA made submissions to the Attorney-General's Department, in 1993, in regard to a proposed statutory system of continuous disclosure for listed companies.[10] Criticism by the AIMA and other bodies of the proposed statutory system resulted in the withdrawal of the original Bill[11] and the enactment of a set of provisions which, as regards listed companies, effectively give statutory force to the continuous-disclosure rule in the *ASX Listing Rules*.[12] During 1993 and 1994 the AIMA also made public calls for company managements to improve the flow of information to institutional shareholders,[13] and to consult more with their largest institutional shareholders on potentially controversial matters.[14]

iv. Disclosure of Directors' Share Dealings

In Australia there was not, until late 1995, any requirement for disclosure to the ASX of dealings by directors in the shares of their companies.[15] Following submissions from the AIMA and others, the ASX had raised the possibility in 1992 of the insertion of such a requirement into the *ASX Listing Rules*.[16] It decided not to do so in the face of strong opposition from the corporate sector.[17] The AIMA continued, however, to push for this reform. In its original Practice Note dealing with employee share schemes, the AIMA included a guideline that '[d]irectors should fully declare their . . . holdings . . . and trading activities to the ASX'.[18] It also took up the matter again with the ASX.[19] The efforts of the AIMA were rewarded in late 1995 when the Corporations Law was amended to require

---

[9] AIMA, *Corporate Governance: A Guide for Investment Managers and a Statement of Recommended Corporate Practice* (1995) para. 3.13. The background to this document is set out at nn. 21–8 below, and accompanying text.

[10] See 'AIMG Opts for a More Open Role', *Aust. Fin. Rev.*, 18 May 1993, p. 33.

[11] Corporate Law Reform Bill (No. 2) 1992 (Cth.).

[12] See CL, ss. 1001A, 1001C, 1001D; *ASX Listing Rules*, LR 3A(1).

[13] 'Companies Urged to Talk to Shareholders', *Aust. Fin. Rev.*, 23 Mar. 1994, p. 27.

[14] 'AIMG Moves to Help Restore Our Credibility', *Aust. Fin. Rev.*, 15 July 1993, p. 27.

[15] However, prior to the introduction of the requirement for disclosure to the ASX, the Corporations Law required directors to disclose their share dealings to *the company*, and the company was required to maintain a register of directors' shareholdings (see former ss. 235; 236(1)(a) and (b); 236(2)(a) and (b)). Compare CA 1985 (UK), ss. 324–9; *Listing Rules*, paras. 16.13—16.17, 12.43(k).

[16] ASX, *Exposure Draft: Proposed Listing Rule Amendments and Other Issues* (1992) 54–5.

[17] 'Why No News Would be Bad News for ASX', *Aust. Fin. Rev.*, 26 Nov. 1993, p. 28.

[18] AIMG, *Corporate Governance Practice Note No. 1: Guide to Employee Share Schemes* (1993).

[19] See 'Institutions' Firm Line on Exec Share Plans', *Aust. Fin. Rev.*, 18 June 1993, p. 11.

directors to notify the ASX within 14 days of any change to their holdings of shares in their own companies.[20]

v. Board Composition and Structure

For many years prior to the formation of the AIMA, some of the larger Australia-based institutions (in particular the AMP) expressed their views on matters of board composition and structure in their regular meetings with company managements.[21] It was not until after the establishment of the AIMA in late 1990, however, that Australia-based institutions became involved publicly in the debate about board composition and structure.[22] And, whereas UK-based institutions were a driving force behind moves for improvements in board composition and structure in quoted UK companies, the institutions in Australia were not key players in the development of the first Australian statement of best practice in this area: the Bosch Committee's *Corporate Practices and Conduct*.[23] This document was initiated by the corporate sector itself, amid concerns about damage caused to the reputation of the Australian business community by the highly publicized misconduct of some Australian entrepreneurs during the late 1980s.[24] Nevertheless, one of the first actions of the AIMA upon its formation was the release of a public statement supporting *Corporate Practices and Conduct* and advising that AIMA members would 'give preference in their investment decisions to those corporations which compl[ied] with the principles in "Corporate Practices and Conduct" '.[25] Also, when it was decided in early 1992 that a second edition of *Corporate Practices and Conduct* was required, the AIMA was invited to—and did— join the Bosch Committee to produce the new edition.[26] The AIMA took a major step in 1995, however, when it released its own guidelines on best practice in corporate governance.[27] The *AIMA Corporate Governance Guidelines* were 'issued by the AIMA for the benefit of its members (and indeed for all investors) and for the information of the companies in which they invest'.[28] They include guidelines for investment managers (on

---

[20] See First Corporate Law Simplification Act 1995 (Cth.), s. 26, replacing s. 235 of the Corporations Law.   [21] Finding of author's interview study.

[22] No institution made a written submission or gave oral evidence to the Australian Senate Standing Committee on Legal and Constitutional Affairs ('Cooney Committee'), when it inquired into 'the social and fiduciary duties and responsibilities of company directors' in 1988–9: see the Cooney Committee's report: *Company Directors' Duties* (1989) App. I, II.

[23] Working Group of the Business Council of Australia, et al. ('Bosch Committee'), *Corporate Practices and Conduct* (1991).

[24] See H. Bosch, ' "Corporate Practices and Conduct": Setting Standards for Corporate Governance in Australia' (1993) 1 *Corp. Gov.: Inter. Rev.* 196.

[25] Ibid., at 197.

[26] See Bosch Committee, *Corporate Practices and Conduct* (2nd edn., 1993).

[27] See AIMA (n. 9 above). The document is cited in the remainder of the book as *AIMA Corporate Governance Guidelines*.   [28] Ibid., para. 1.4.

communication with the senior management and directors of portfolio companies; exercise of voting rights; and reporting to clients), as well as recommended corporate practice (on, amongst other things, board composition and structure).

The *AIMA Corporate Governance Guidelines* recommend that 'the board of directors of every listed company should be constituted with a majority of individuals who qualify as independent [non-executive] directors'.[29] Board composition has not been as big an issue in Australia compared to the UK, however, because the average board of large and medium-sized listed Australian companies has for a long time had a majority of non-executive members.[30] The incidence of *independent* non-executives is, unfortunately, unclear. The only piece of evidence of which the author is aware is a study which revealed that, in the case of 46 of the top 300 listed Australian companies (measured by market capitalization) in 1994, there was a non-executive director who represented a legal firm utilized by the company.[31]

As regards board structure for listed companies, the AIMA's guidelines recommend that (a) 'the chairperson should be an independent director or, if the chairperson is not an independent director . . . the independent directors should appoint one of their number to be lead director and to monitor and report to them on issues falling within the normal purview of a non-executive chairperson';[32] (b) there should be an audit committee, chaired by an independent non-executive director and composed entirely of non-executive directors;[33] (c) there should be a remuneration committee

[29] Ibid., para. 3.2.

[30] J. F. Corkery, *Directors Powers and Duties* (1987) 3, cites a study which found that the average board size for the largest 500 listed companies (measured by market capitalization) in 1983 was seven directors, with 30% being executive and 70% being non-executive. These proportions were 'about the same' in 1975. The Cooney Committee (n. 22 above), at 117, cited a study which showed that the figures in 1988 were: 9.3 directors; 31% executive; 69% non-executive. At 1992, the figures were: 8 directors; 25% executive; 75% non-executive: Korn/Ferry International, *Boards of Directors in Australia: Twelfth Study* (1993) 3. Note, however, that there is anecdotal evidence that 400–500 of the smallest listed Australian companies have only the minimum three directors required by law (CL, s. 221(1)), or slightly more, with these being executives, representatives of major shareholders, and consultants: 'Chanticleer: Boards Must Learn to Shape Up or Starve', *Aust. Fin. Rev.*, 9 Aug. 1994.

[31] Reported in 'Board Law Links Pay $20m', *Aust. Fin. Rev.*, 4 Oct. 1995, p. 3.

[32] *AIMA Corporate Governance Guidelines*, para. 3.3. The influence of the *Cadbury Report* is obvious.

[33] Ibid., para. 3.5. Note that the Cooney Committee (n. 22 above), at paras. 8.15—8.16, recommended that audit committees be made mandatory for listed companies, as did the Australian House of Representatives Standing Committee on Legal and Constitutional Affairs, in its report on *Corporate Practices and the Rights of Shareholders* (1991) para. 5.5.22. *ASX Listing Rules*, LR 3C(3)(i) requires listed companies to state in their annual reports whether or not they have an audit committee and, if not, why not.

and a nomination committee, each chaired by an independent non-executive director and made up of a majority, at least, of non-executive directors.[34] As for (a), 84% of a sample of listed and unlisted Australian companies in 1992 had a non-executive chairman separate from the chief executive or managing director.[35] Regarding (b), 48% of a wide sample of listed companies in 1992 had an audit committee, although the proportion amongst larger companies was 63%.[36] By 1994, some 75% of the top 150 listed Australian companies (measured by market capitalization) had an audit committee.[37] In regard to (c), a survey in 1993 of the 100 largest listed Australian companies (measured by market capitalization) found that 73% had a remuneration committee (on 91% of which, non-executive directors were in the majority), but only 17% had a nomination committee (all of which were made up entirely of non-executive directors).[38] There appeared to be a lack of formality in the operation of these committees: less than half of the remuneration committees, and just over half of the nomination committees, had written terms of reference; and less than half of each type of committee presented written minutes to the full board.[39] In the light of these findings, the AIMA called for greater consideration to be given to the establishment *and functioning* of remuneration and nomination committees.[40]

vi. Disclosure of Corporate-Governance Standards

During early 1994 the AIMA encouraged the ASX to adopt a listing rule (along the same lines as the rule adopted by the London Stock Exchange in relation to the *Cadbury Code*)[41] under which companies would be required to disclose the extent of their compliance with the principles in the Bosch Committee's document, *Corporate Practices and Conduct*.[42] In mid-1994 the ASX announced plans to specify in the *ASX Listing Rules* a list of corporate-governance practices, require companies to disclose the extent to which they had adopted such practices, and require companies to give

---

[34] *AIMA Corporate Governance Guidelines*, para. 3.5.
[35] Korn/Ferry International (n. 30 above).
[36] Arthur Andersen, *Audit Committees in the 1990s: Results of the 1992 Arthur Andersen Survey of Audit Committees* (1993) 13–14.
[37] AIMA and Minter Ellison, *Board Committees in Australia* (1995) 7.
[38] AIMG, ASX, and Business Council of Australia, *Survey on Structure and Operation of Board Remuneration and Nomination Committees* (1993). Cf. the somewhat lower figures for the top 150 companies as at 1994, reported in AIMA and Minter Ellison, ibid., at 12–15.
[39] Ibid.
[40] AIMG, 'Media Release: Call for More Formalised Approach to Board Remuneration and Nomination: New Peak Body Survey', 4 Nov. 1993. See also *AIMA Corporate Governance Guidelines*, para. 3.5.
[41] See *Listing Rules*, para. 12.43(j).
[42] Finding of author's interview study.

reasons for any practices not followed.[43] The AIMA announced immediately that it 'strongly supported' this initiative.[44] In mid-1995, a new listing rule was introduced under which companies will be required to include in annual reports, for periods ending on or after 30 June 1996, 'a statement of the main corporate governance practices that the company has had in place during the reporting period'.[45] An 'indicative list of corporate governance matters' is set out in an appendix.[46] Unlike the *Cadbury Code*, and unlike the proposal announced by the ASX in 1994, this list does not recommend any practices. It is merely a list of topics which companies might choose to discuss (for example 'Whether individual directors . . . are executive or non-executive directors').[47] Importantly, however, the *AIMA Corporate Governance Guidelines* do specify minimum standards, and the AIMA document states that the guidelines 'set the appropriate standard for disclosure by Australian listed companies'.[48]

vii. Executive Remuneration

The AIMA issued a 'Practice Note' on employee share schemes in June 1993.[49] It sought 'to articulate a set of guidelines[50] by which employee share schemes [could] be judged by members of [the AIMA] and by companies when deliberating over the structure of these schemes'. It encouraged company managements 'to consult with their institutional shareholders on these schemes prior to their release and voting on by shareholders'.[51] The Practice Note was an attempt to draw together the views of a collection of institutions, which had been formed over a lengthy period. All but one of the fund managers interviewed by the author said that their institutions had, for several years before the release of the Practice Note, discussed executive share-option schemes and employee share schemes with company managements.[52]

In 1994 the AIMA issued two new documents in place of the original

---

[43] ASX, 'Media Release', 1 June 1994; ASX, *Disclosure of Corporate Governance Practices by Listed Companies: ASX Discussion Paper* (1994).

[44] 'Institutions Back ASX Reform Plans', *Fin. Times*, 6 June 1994, p. 27.

[45] *ASX Listing Rules*, LR 3C(3)(j).   [46] See *ASX Listing Rules*, App. 33.

[47] Ibid., para. 1.

[48] *AIMA Corporate Governance Guidelines*, para. 1.5; cf. para. 3.1: '[I]t is recognised that companies may develop alternatives which are also sound. If alternatives are developed, they should be explained [in the annual report].'

[49] AIMG, *Corporate Governance Practice Note No. 1: Guide to Employee Share Schemes* (1993).

[50] The two main underlying themes were ensuring that share options served as an incentive rather than a gift; and avoidance of excessive dilution of the interests of existing shareholders.

[51] See further Ch. 8, Sec. D.1.

[52] And see 'Goodman Revises Option Scheme', *Aust. Fin. Rev.*, 21 Nov. 1990, p. 22; 'Poor Showing from Goodman Comes Under Fire', *Aust. Fin. Rev.*, 27 Nov. 1990, p. 16, for a case in 1990 where institutions forced a large company to revise an executive option scheme.

Practice Note: one dealing with executive share-option schemes,[53] and the other (issued jointly with the Australian Institute of Company Directors) dealing with employee share schemes generally.[54] The new documents share a theme of avoiding excessive dilution of the interests of existing shareholders. The document dealing with executive option schemes has two additional major themes: ensuring that the ability of executives to exercise options is linked to improvements in company performance; and disclosure to shareholders. In relation to disclosure, the *AIMA Corporate Governance Guidelines* also recommend that the annual report should disclose the board's policies for remuneration of board members and senior executives; the justification for these policies and their relationship to the performance of the company; the quantum and components of the remuneration of each director and each of the five highest-paid executives; and the existence and length of any service contract for the chief executive.[55]

viii. Regulatory Restrictions on Voting by Institutional Shareholders

In early 1994 the AIMA asked the Australian Securities Commission, the Insurance and Superannuation Commission (the regulator of Australian occupational superannuation funds), and the State attorneys-general to take action to remove regulatory obstacles to the exercise of voting rights by fund managers.[56] The nature of these obstacles is described in the next chapter.[57] The Australian Securities Commission subsequently recommended, in a submission to the Parliamentary Joint Committee on Corporations and Securities, that one of these regulatory barriers be removed by legislative amendment.[58]

ix. Reform of the Proxy-Voting Process

The AIMA played a pivotal role in the formation in 1995 of the Proxy Voting Reform Working Party. The Executive Director of the AIMA and a senior executive from AMP Investments Australia Ltd. were members of the Working Party. The Working Party produced a model proxy form in September 1995, which incorporated features aimed at improving the efficiency and accuracy of proxy voting.[59]

---

[53] AIMA, *Executive Share Option Schemes Guidelines* (1994).

[54] AIMA and Australian Institute of Company Directors, *Employee Share Schemes* (1994).

[55] *AIMA Corporate Governance Guidelines*, paras. 3.10, 3.11.

[56] See 'Investors Seek Clear Proxy Law', *Aust. Fin. Rev.*, 24 Jan. 1994, p. 19; 'Chanticleer: Directors Face More Pressure', *Aust. Fin. Rev.*, 11 Feb. 1994, p. 64.

[57] See Ch. 8, Sec. B.1.ii.

[58] Parliamentary Joint Committee on Corporations and Securities, *Issues Paper: Inquiry into the Role and Activities of Institutional Investors in Australia* (1994), para. 4.26.

[59] Proxy Voting Reform Working Party, *Model Proxy Form: Explanatory Memorandum* (1995).

x. 'Bundling' of General-Meeting Resolutions

One of the resolutions proposed (and passed) at a 1991 extraordinary general meeting of Westpac Banking Corporation was a 'bundled' resolution. It provided for the removal of restrictions on voting rights, and for a large share placement to the AMP, Australia's largest institutional investor. Several other institutions were aggrieved by this tactic. The *AIMA Corporate Governance Guidelines* now recommend that 'separate issues should not be combined and presented for a single vote by shareholders'.[60] The AIMA document states that '[a]n important purpose of this guideline is to outlaw the sugar coated pill, where a company asks shareholders to approve a contentious matter by combining it with an unconnected beneficial matter'.[61]

2. ETHICAL AND POLITICAL

The evidence suggests that Australia-based institutions have had very little involvement in ethical and political issues. Almost none of the 20 fund managers interviewed in a 1994 study had raised the issue of corporate political donations in their dialogue with company managements. Only one manager considered that issue to be 'a matter of importance'.[62] Nevertheless, the *AIMA Corporate Governance Guidelines* recommend that 'every listed company should have a company Code of Ethics that is adopted by the board and all employees and is available to shareholders on request'.[63]

B. COMPANY-SPECIFIC ISSUES

Institutional shareholders have become involved in the affairs of listed Australian companies in relation to a variety of company-specific issues. The most important of these issues is, as in the UK, sub-optimal performance by a company's senior management.[64] Other issues which have led to institutional action of one form or another include: an apparent lack of effective monitoring by non-executive directors;[65] a proposed

---

[60] *AIMA Corporate Governance Guidelines*, para. 3.12.   [61] Ibid.

[62] Australian Institute of Superannuation Trustees, *Corporate Governance in Australia: The Attitudes and Practices of Funds Managers* (1994) 105.

[63] *AIMA Corporate Governance Guidelines*, para. 3.14.

[64] See e.g. 'Shareholder Revolt Rocks Darrell James', *Aust. Fin. Rev.*, 9 Aug. 1991, p. 16; 'Bloodbath at Goodman', *Aust. Fin. Rev.*, 15 Dec. 1993, p. 1; ' "Perform or Get the Chop" ', *Aust. Fin. Rev.*, 15 Dec. 1993, p. 36.

[65] See e.g. 'Bennett Election Balked by Court', *Aust. Fin. Rev.*, 2 Dec. 1991, p. 23; 'New Bennett Board Promises Stability', *Aust. Fin. Rev.*, 16 Dec. 1991, p. 24; 'Westpac: Neal and Four Directors Go', *Aust. Fin. Rev.*, 2 Oct. 1992, p. 1; ' "Still a Long Way to Go" for Westpac', *Aust. Fin. Rev.*, 2 Oct. 1992, p. 26.

takeover which appeared potentially detrimental to the interests of the bidder's shareholders;[66] a property deal between a company and the spouse of its chairman/managing director;[67] strong suspicion of misuse of company funds by a managing director;[68] and allegations of improper related-party transactions at a retailing company whose board included representatives of major suppliers.[69] The actions taken by institutions in relation to these company-specific matters, and in relation to the procedural and general matters set out earlier, are discussed in the next chapter.

C. CONCLUSION

The issues with which Australian institutional shareholders have been concerned cover a substantially narrower field than those addressed by their UK counterparts. Nevertheless, the issues which have attracted attention in Australia are very similar to some of the matters with which UK institutions have been involved. Further, the procedural and general matters mentioned in this chapter have some or all of the same important features possessed by the procedural and general matters set out in Chapter 4: (a) they are reasonably uncomplicated; (b) they exist in, or have the potential to arise at, a large number of companies; and (c) they can be addressed relatively easily and inexpensively across a wide range of companies.

[66] 'Chanticleer: Kiwi Hijacking May Spark War With Australia Inc', *Aust. Fin. Rev.*, 8 June 1989, p. 104; 'Goodman Fielder Bid for IEL Runs Foul of NCSC', *Aust. Fin. Rev.*, 13 June 1989, p. 16.

[67] 'AMP Says No to Property Deal with Company Chairman's Wife', *Aust. Fin. Rev.*, 23 Nov. 1990, p. 28; 'B&F Dissension Over Property Deal Vote', *Aust. Fin. Rev.*, 30 Nov. 1990, p. 23.

[68] 'Summers Sacked as Bennett's MD', *Advertiser*, 9 May 1992; 'B&F May Sue Summers', *Advertiser*, 5 June 1992; 'Former Bennett Chief Finally Heeds the Call', *Aust. Fin. Rev.*, 5 June 1992, p. 21.

[69] See 'Scandal Rocks Coles Myer', *Aust. Fin. Rev.*, 5 Sept. 1995, p. 1; 'Corporate Coup Begins', *Aust. Fin. Rev.*, 15 Sept. 1995, p. 1; 'AMP Declares War on Coles', *Aust.*, 12 Oct. 1995, p. 1.

8
Manner of Involvement in Australia

This chapter adopts the same fourfold classification of the manner of institutional monitoring that was employed in Chapter 5 (for the UK situation), and there is the same general structure within the four sections.

A. DIRECT INDUSTRY-WIDE MONITORING

There would appear to have been even less industry-wide monitoring carried out directly (i.e. by institutions personally) in Australia than the fairly small amount in the UK. The formation of the AIMA in 1990 certainly led to a substantial reliance upon it to formulate and promulgate institutional views on best practice in matters of corporate governance and investor protection. Nevertheless, there was an instance of direct industry-wide involvement in 1993, when several institutions each made a submission to the ASX in relation to its discussion paper on equity voting rights.[1] Also, Mr Leigh Hall, a senior investment manager at AMP, was a member of the Australian Law Reform Commission until the end of 1992, and a member of the Companies and Securities Advisory Committee ('CASAC') at mid-1994.[2]

B. DIRECT FIRM-LEVEL MONITORING

1. EXERCISE OF VOTING RIGHTS

i. Matters on which Shareholders are Entitled to Vote

Things which shareholders of a listed Australian company have the power to effect or which require their approval include:[3] (i) alteration of the memorandum and articles of association;[4] (ii) changing of the company's

---

[1] ASX, *Differential Voting Rights* (1993).
[2] CASAC is a statutory body charged with advising the government on the operation and possible reform of the Corporations Law: Australian Securities Commission Act 1989 (Cth.), s. 148.
[3] In these examples, it is assumed that the articles applicable are those in Table A (Aust.). See CL, s. 175(2).
[4] CL, ss. 171–3, 176, 197, 198.

name;[5] (iii) certain alterations to the capital structure;[6] (iv) purchase by the company of its own shares;[7] (v) a non-rights issue of shares which, taken together with other shares issued during the previous 12 months, exceeds 10% of the nominal value of those shares on issue at the commencement of the 12-month period;[8] (vi) an issue of shares in the three-month period following receipt by the company of notice of a takeover offer;[9] (vii) a non-pro-rata issue of shares to a director;[10] (viii) alteration of certain terms of issued options;[11] (ix) declaration of a dividend, after a recommendation by the board;[12] (x) increase or reduction of the number of directors;[13] (xi) re-election of directors;[14] (xii) removal of directors;[15] (xiii) appointment and removal of the auditors;[16] (xiv) determination of the directors' remuneration;[17] (xv) certain benefits to directors and officers for loss of, or retirement from, office (including service contracts with a term exceeding seven years in the case of executives);[18] (xvi) service agreements providing for termination benefits above a certain level;[19] (xvii) certain transactions between the company and parties related thereto;[20] (xviii) acquisition or disposal of assets amounting to more than 5% of shareholders' funds where the vendor or purchaser is associated with the company;[21] (xix) provision by the company of financial assistance in connection with the purchase of its shares;[22] (xx) employee incentive schemes;[23] (xxi) sale or disposal of the company's main undertaking;[24] (xxii) a change in the activities of the company, if the ASX orders shareholder consideration;[25] (xxiii) an acquisition of a large shareholding in the company without a formal takeover offer;[26] (xxiv) a voluntary administration;[27] and (xxv) a voluntary winding up.[28] The general meeting is also able: (xxvi) to ratify certain breaches of directors' duties;[29] (xxvii) to exercise a residual power of management where the board is deadlocked or unable to act;[30] and (xxviii)

---

[5] CL, s. 382.   [6] CL, ss. 193, 195.   [7] CL, Pt. 2.4, Div. 4B.

[8] *ASX Listing Rules*, LR 3E(6).   [9] *ASX Listing Rules*, LR 3R(3).

[10] *ASX Listing Rules*, LR 3E(8).   [11] *ASX Listing Rules*, LR 3G(2).

[12] Table A (Aust.), reg. 86. The directors may authorize the payment of interim dividends: reg. 87.   [13] Table A (Aust.), reg. 57(2).

[14] Table A (Aust.), regs. 58–61.   [15] CL, s. 227; Table A (Aust.), reg. 62.

[16] CL, ss. 327–9.

[17] Table A (Aust.), reg. 63(1); *ASX Listing Rules*, LR 3L(7)(c); cf. Table A (Aust.), reg. 80, which gives the directors the power to determine the remuneration of the managing director(s).   [18] CL, ss. 237, 740(4); see also s. 243K(7).

[19] *ASX Listing Rules*, LR 3J(16).   [20] CL, Pt. 3.2A.

[21] *ASX Listing Rules*, LR 3J(3).   [22] CL, s. 205(10).

[23] *ASX Listing Rules*, LR 3W.   [24] *ASX Listing Rules*, LR 3S(2).

[25] *ASX Listing Rules*, LR 3S(3)(b).   [26] CL, s. 623.   [27] CL, Pt. 5.3A.

[28] CL, s. 491.

[29] See e.g. *Winthrop Investments Ltd.* v. *Winns Ltd.* [1975] 2 NSWLR 666.

[30] *Barron* v. *Potter* [1914] 1 Ch. 895; *Foster* v. *Foster* [1916] 1 Ch. 532.

arguably, to resolve that the company commence litigation against the directors.[31]

As in the UK, when resolutions concerning the great majority of the above matters are proposed at general meetings of listed companies, they are management- or board-initiated proposals for which requisite shareholder support is being sought. However, shareholders of Australian companies can, like those of UK companies, propose resolutions for adoption at the AGM[32] (which is extremely rare in Australia as in the UK), and can requisition the directors to convene an EGM to consider shareholder proposals.[33] The latter option has sometimes been used in Australia (as in the UK) where a small group of institutions has been attempting to remove a director or directors of a listed company. This has occurred more rarely in Australia than in the UK.[34]

ii. Legal and Practical Issues

The comments made in Chapter 5 refuting the existence of a fiduciary duty upon trustees of UK pension funds to exercise their voting rights are of equal application in regard to trustees of Australian superannuation funds.

The exercise of voting rights by institutional investors became a prominent issue even later in Australia than in the UK. Prior to the formulation by the AIMA of a standard investment-management agreement in late 1993, which delegates the voting right to the fund manager subject to any specific direction from the trustees,[35] the great majority of fund-management agreements were silent on the matter of voting. Voting was, nevertheless, presumed to be a matter for the fund manager in most such cases. The AIMA standard agreement was being adopted widely by mid-1994.[36]

There has, however, been some concern in Australia about whether trustees actually have the authority to delegate the voting right to the fund

---

[31] See Ch. 5, at n. 45; cf. *Kraus* v. *J. G. Lloyd Pty. Ltd.* [1965] VR 232, at 236–7.

[32] CL, s. 252. The threshold requirements are very similar to those in the UK: one or more members entitled to at least 5% of the total voting rights, or at least 100 members holding shares on which there has been paid up an average sum, per member, of at least A$200.

[33] CL, s. 246. The threshold is lower in Australia than in the UK: under s. 246(1)(c), a member or group of members entitled to at least 5% of the total votes can lodge a requisition (the threshold is 10% in the UK: CA 1985, s. 368(2)). At least 100 members holding shares paid up on average to at least A$200 can also lodge a requisition: CL, s. 246(1)(a). See also CL, s. 247(1), which gives to any two or more members holding at least 5% of the issued share capital the power to convene (as opposed to the power merely to requisition the convening by the directors of) a general meeting. This power is, however, subject to the company's articles: see s. 247(1) and *L. C. O'Neil Enterprises Pty. Ltd.* v. *Toxic Treatments Ltd.* (1986) 10 ACLR 337.   [34] See Sec. B.3.ii, below.

[35] AIMG, *Standard Investment Management Agreement and Commentary* (1993) cl. 12.

[36] Australian Institute of Superannuation Trustees ('AIST'), *Corporate Governance in Australia: The Attitudes and Practices of Fund Managers* (1994) 37–43.

manager.[37] The concern stems from the narrowness of the powers of delegation contained in the Trustee Acts of the Australian States.[38] In practice, this would be a real issue for only a very small minority of superannuation schemes if, as seems likely, the trustees of Australian superannuation schemes are given considerably greater powers in their trust deeds than by the relevant Trustee Act.[39] It is likely that the Australian scene is similar to that in the UK, where '[m]ost, if not all, modern pension scheme trust deeds contain wide powers for the appointment of advisers and agents. Further, trustees are given powers to delegate many of their functions such as investment management.'[40] The AIMA was sufficiently worried about the situation that it made submissions to the State attorneys-general—seeking the insertion of a wider delegatory power into the State Trustee Acts—and to the Insurance and Superannuation Commission (the regulatory body for Australian occupational superannuation funds)—seeking clarification of the voting-right matter by way of either an amendment to the Superannuation Industry (Supervision) Act 1993 (Cth.) or a regulation thereunder.[41] The approach of the AIMA would appear to mirror that of the UK's Goode Committee, which said in relation to the unsatisfactory delegation provisions in the Trustee Act 1925 (UK): although any 'difficulties will be avoided by a properly drawn trust deed . . . it [is] unsatisfactory for the law to be so unresponsive to the needs of modern fund management that it requires supplementation by scheme rules as a matter of course'.[42] This is sensible, and a recommendation for reform of the law is made in the final chapter.[43]

The practical difficulties faced by some external managers of UK pension funds, in regard to the exercise of voting rights, are also faced by some external managers of Australian superannuation funds. The statutory

[37] This concern arose out of a paper prepared by Professor John Farrar for the AIMA: *Legal Restraints on Institutional Investor Involvement in Corporate Governance* (1993) 4–5, 8–11.

[38] See e.g. Trustee Act 1958 (Vic.), s. 28; Trustee Act 1925 (NSW), s. 53. Concerns about the narrowness of the powers of delegation in the Trustee Act 1925 (UK), in regard to the hiring of an investment manager, and matters incidental thereto, were detailed in a report to IMRO and SIB: see D. Hayton, 'Trustees and the New Financial Services Regime' (1989) 10 *Co. Law.* 191. See now Pensions Act 1995 (UK), s. 34.

[39] The statutory powers and discretions conferred by the Trustee Acts are subject to any express provisions in the trust instrument: see e.g. Trustee Act 1958 (Vic.), s. 2(3).

[40] J. J. Quarrell, *The Law of Pension Fund Investment* (1990) 26. See also Pensions Act 1995 (UK), s. 34.

[41] See 'Investors Seek Clear Proxy Law', *Aust. Fin. Rev.*, 24 Jan. 1994, p. 19; 'Chanticleer: Directors Face More Pressure', *Aust. Fin. Rev.*, 11 Feb. 1994, p. 64.

[42] Pension Law Review Committee, *Report* (1993) para. 4.9.25. The UK position has been remedied with the enactment of s. 34 of the Pensions Act 1995 (UK).

[43] See Ch. 11, Sec. B.1.ii.

minimum notice period for the AGM and EGMs in Australia is just 14 days[44] (compared to 21 days for the AGM, and 14 days for EGMs, in the UK), and most companies' articles require that proxy forms must reach the company at least 48 hours before the meeting.[45] This time frame can be too short where a fund manager has to consult with, or obtain the blessing of, many external clients before voting.[46] It is, however, unusual in Australia (as it is in the UK) for the trustees of externally managed superannuation funds to either expressly retain the voting right or require that they be consulted before the fund manager votes. This was a finding of the author's interview project, and of a contemporaneous study.[47] In addition, a 1994 survey of externally managed superannuation funds found that only 6.8% of schemes' trustees either expressly retained the voting right or required the fund manager to consult with them before voting.[48] The AIMA recommends that fund managers should report to their clients, on the exercise of voting rights, 'as a part of the regular reporting process' (and at least annually)—that is, *after* the event.[49]

Managers of UK unit trusts control the exercise of voting rights of their trusts' equity investments.[50] In contrast, managers of Australian unit trusts face a serious legal obstacle to the exercise of voting rights. Section 1069(1)(k) of the Corporations Law requires that a unit-trust deed must contain covenants binding the trustee and manager not to vote the trust's shareholdings on any election of directors, without the prior consent of a majority of unit-holders.[51] The Australian Securities Commission ('ASC'), under its discretionary powers, allows managers and trustees to vote without having to obtain the prior consent of unit-holders, but only in fairly restrictive circumstances. One requirement for an exemption is that neither the trustee, the manager, nor any of their associates holds shares in the company in a capacity other than as a trustee, or as a trustee or

---

[44] CL, s. 247(2); cf. *Exposure Draft—Second Corporate Law Simplification Bill* 1995 (Cth.).   [45] Table A (Aust.), reg. 55; see also CL, s. 248(1)(c).

[46] See AIST (n. 36 above), at 135–43 (some Australia-based fund managers interviewed in 1994 cited difficulties in lodging proxies within this short period, and a few said the situation was compounded by the inefficiency of some custodians in forwarding notices, proxy forms, etc.: see also Ch. 5, at n. 75, and accompanying text).

[47] AIST, ibid., at 45–7, 51–3.

[48] Only 4.1% of schemes' trustees required the fund manager to act as directed by the trustees, whilst 2.7% required that they be consulted before the manager exercised the voting right. A further 5.4% of schemes' trustees required the fund manager to advise them of any action taken: Association of Superannuation Funds of Australia Ltd. ('ASFA'), *Corporate Governance Survey* (1994).

[49] *AIMA Corporate Governance Guidelines*, para. 2.4.

[50] See Ch. 5, at n. 79.

[51] This provision was introduced after the court in *Australian Fixed Trusts Pty. Ltd.* v. *Clyde Industries Ltd.* [1959] SR (NSW) 33, held that a trustee need not consult with beneficiaries before exercising its voting rights on an election of directors in a portfolio company. It was feared that a trustee might exercise its voting rights to benefit associates at the expense of unit-holders.

manager of a unit trust. Another requirement is that the trustee, the manager, and their associates are not entitled to more than 10% of the voting shares.[52] These requirements, especially the first, are unnecessarily restrictive. Indeed, there is little justification for section 1069(1)(k) itself,[53] and a recommendation for its repeal is made in Chapter 11.[54]

iii. Evidence on Institutional Voting

Like their UK counterparts, almost all Australian institutions have a tradition of not attending general meetings. Apart from the obvious exception where a group of institutions has itself requisitioned the general meeting (to remove one or more directors, for instance), there is one main exception: the AMP, Australia's largest institutional shareholder, has a long tradition (and a policy) of being represented in person at every AGM of all the major listed Australian companies.[55] Given that this practice of the AMP is exceptional, the important issue is the extent to which proxies are lodged.[56]

(a) The Overall Level of Proxy Voting

There would appear to have been only two publicly reported studies of the level of proxy voting at the AGMs of listed Australian companies. The first study was conducted by Coopers & Lybrand for the AIMA in 1993.[57] It covered only a small sample of companies (eight), and its results should therefore be treated cautiously. It looked at the 40 largest registered shareholders (institutional and non-institutional) in each company, and found that on average 8.6 had lodged a proxy form, and that the average percentage of the issued voting capital covered by the proxies submitted was 29.8%. The second study was carried out by ISS Australia, and covered proxies lodged in respect of the 1994 and 1995 AGMs of 23 of the top 50 listed Australian companies (measured by market capitalization).[58]

---

[52] ASC, *Policy Statement 55* (1994) paras. 112–14.

[53] Following submissions from the AIMA, the ASC came to this same conclusion: see Parliamentary Joint Committee on Corporations and Securities, *Issues Paper: Inquiry into the Role and Activities of Institutional Investors in Australia* (1994), para. 4.26.

[54] See Ch. 11, Sec. B.1.iii.   [55] Finding of author's interview study.

[56] Indeed, the AMP lodges a proxy form as well as sending a representative to the meeting: ibid. The legal rules governing proxy voting are the same in Australia as in the UK. Unless the articles provide otherwise, a proxy is entitled to vote only on a poll (and not on a show of hands): CL, s. 250(2). (The Table A (Aust.) articles do not provide otherwise: see reg. 49.) A proxy is, however, allowed to demand or join in demanding a poll: CL, s. 248(2). As in the UK, much routine business at the AGMs of listed Australian companies is decided on a show of hands (see Table A (Aust.), reg. 46), and therefore many 'proxy votes' are never cast.

[57] AIMG, *Incidence of Proxy Voting by Major Shareholders: Preliminary Statistics from a Sample of 8 Major Publicly Listed Companies* (1993).

[58] See ISS Australia, *Major Australian Public Companies: Proxy Voting Statistics: September 1994 to March 1995* (1995).

It revealed that, on average, the proxies lodged by both institutional and non-institutional shareholders represented about 40% of the issued voting capital. Neither of these two studies provided a breakdown showing the incidence of proxy voting by institutional shareholders. It is, therefore, important to examine the voting policies of Australia-based institutions.

(b) Voting Policies of Fund Managers

Of the 13 fund-management firms covered in the author's interview project, four had a policy of voting all or the bulk[59] of their shares (two had voted routinely for many years; one had adopted this policy in 1992, and the other one had done so in 1993). The other nine had a policy or practice of voting only on major or contentious issues, or where specifically requested to do so by a company.[60] Three of the routine voters were fund-management arms of insurance companies and one was a government-owned investment manager of public-sector superannuation funds. Notably, none of the investment-management arms of financial conglomerates voted routinely at the time of the interview study. That is not surprising given that their funds under management comprised mostly the assets of external pension funds and unit trusts—for each of which there were, at the time of the study, both practical and legal obstacles to the exercise of the voting right.[61]

The major trade associations representing UK institutions—the ABI, NAPF, ISC, and IFMA—were amongst many bodies which, from the late 1980s through to the mid-1990s, called for a greater use of voting rights by UK institutional investors.[62] It was noted in Chapter 5 that the exhortations of the UK institutional trade associations were explicable largely by a desire to avoid regulatory intervention.[63] Several Australia-based fund managers interviewed by the author believed that the Australian government was considering the desirability of legislation to require the exercising of voting rights by or on behalf of superannuation funds. Most of the interviewees were, however, opposed to any formal regulation in this area.[64] Not surprisingly, therefore, the *AIMA Corporate Governance Guidelines* recommend that AIMA members should 'vote on all material issues at all Australian company meetings where they have the voting

---

[59] One large insurance-company fund manager voted all of the shareholdings of its insurance funds, and all other funds under its management except some which were registered in the clients' names.

[60] These findings are broadly similar to those in AIST (n. 36 above).

[61] It should be borne in mind that economic disincentives are probably even more significant than the practical and legal obstacles to voting. These economic disincentives reflect an agency problem at the level of fund manager:client. They are detailed in Ch. 10, Sec. B.   [62] See Ch. 5, at nn. 111–20, and accompanying text.

[63] See Ch. 5, at n. 120, and accompanying text; and Ch. 11, Sec. B.1.i.

[64] See also AIST (above n. 36).

authority and responsibility to do so [and] have a written policy on the exercising of proxy votes . . . and formal internal procedures to ensure that such a policy is implemented and applied consistently.'[65]

iv. Voting-Information Service for Institutions

There was only one Australian voting-information service in operation as at late 1995. It was provided by ISS Australia, an associate of Institutional Shareholder Services Inc., the large US proxy-advisory organization.[66] The ISS Australia service, which commenced in August 1994, initially covered just the top 50 listed Australian companies, but by October 1995 it had expanded to cover the top 100. The subscribers to the service during its first year of operation were large fund-management firms. At late 1995, the service comprised (a) a preliminary report following the announcement to the ASX of each company's preliminary annual results; (b) a commentary on each forthcoming general meeting (covering not only the proposed resolutions but also the corporate-governance practices and structure of the company concerned); and (c) a post-general meeting report. Voting recommendations were provided only where requested by a subscriber. The corporate-governance analysis included, amongst other things, a table setting out 'the cost of the agents' (i.e. the total remuneration paid to the board and senior executives); and a comparison of the company's structures, practices, and disclosure *vis-à-vis* the *AIMA Corporate Governance Guidelines*. (Incidentally, the principals of ISS Australia assisted in the production of the AIMA document.) Subscribers also received, on an *ad hoc* basis, material relating to current corporate-governance issues.

2. ROUTINE ACTIONS

The author's interview study confirmed that the routine monitoring actions taken by institutional shareholders in Australia reflect closely those carried out by institutions in the UK. There is reliance upon both in-house and external (stockbrokers') analysts; there are regular one-to-one meetings with the senior management of portfolio companies,[67] as well as meetings (such as brokers' lunches, and factory or mine visits) attended by numerous institutions; some institutions have one-to-one meetings at least

---

[65] *AIMA Corporate Governance Guidelines*, paras. 2.2, 2.3.

[66] These details were provided to the author by S. Easterbrook, principal, ISS Australia.

[67] Two institutions covered in the interview study did not conduct meetings with company managements, because to do so would have conflicted with their style of fund management: they were index-based managers, and any moves away from the index were based on quantitative, as opposed to fundamental, analysis of stocks.

twice per year, but most do so annually; it is normally the company's chief executive or managing director, and the finance director, with whom the portfolio managers and/or in-house analysts meet; although there has been a trend towards company managements visiting fund managers, in Australia (compared to the UK) a greater proportion of one-to-one meetings are held at the company's premises; the issues discussed cover the same broad range as in the UK;[68] and there are the same potential problems of disclosure of price-sensitive information and confidential information.[69]

3. EXTRAORDINARY ACTIONS

i. Preliminary: The Size of the Stakes

Tables 8.1 and 8.2 present the results of a study ('the Australian Study') which is similar to Study A described in Chapter 5. The Australian Study involved an examination by the author of 'substantial [5%+] shareholder' information for 234 of the 276 companies which composed the All Ordinaries Index at 31 August 1993. All substantial shareholders that were custodians—whether bank-nominee companies or trustee companies— were ignored.[70]

Of the 234 companies surveyed, 224 had at least one substantial shareholder other than a custodian company. An institution was the largest or only substantial shareholder in 57 cases (i.e. 25.4% of the 224). Table 8.1 gives a breakdown of those cases.

In Study A, described in Chapter 5, it was found that 94 of the top 100 UK companies had at least one notifiable interest-holder. In those 94 companies, the body with the largest or only notifiable interest was an institution in 66 cases (i.e. 70.2% of the 94). To enable a comparison to be made with the UK study, an analysis was made of just the 100 largest Australian companies. It was found that 96 of the top 100 Australian companies had at least one substantial shareholder (other than a custodian company), and that the largest or only substantial shareholder was an institution in 34 cases (i.e. 35.4% of the 96). This is roughly half the figure for the UK. At the time of the Australian Study, however, the top 50 Australian companies accounted for approximately the same proportion of the total market capitalization of all listed Australian companies as did the

---

[68] The AIMA recommends one-to-one meetings to deal with 'performance, corporate governance or other matters affecting shareholders' interests': *AIMA Corporate Governance Guidelines*, para. 2.1.

[69] The position of the AIMA on this matter is that '[w]here, exceptionally, there are compelling reasons for a board to consult shareholders on issues which are price sensitive, those shareholders will have to accept that [the information] will have to be strictly safeguarded and insulated': ibid.   [70] See App. K for details.

Table 8.1 All Ordinaries Index[a] companies in which an institution was the
largest or only 'substantial shareholder', 1993

Size band of largest institution's entitlement (% of issued ordinary share capital)	No. of companies
5% ≤ × <6%	3
6% ≤ × <7%	5
7% ≤ × <8%	6
8% ≤ × <9%	5
9% ≤ × <10%	13
10% ≤ × <12%	6
12% ≤ × <14%	7
14% ≤ × <16%	6
16% ≤ × <18%	2
18% ≤ × <20%	1
29% ≤ × <32%	2
44% ≤ × <45%	1

[a] Modified as described in App. K.

Source: Author's analysis of information in ASX, *All Ordinaries Index Companies Handbook*
(4th edn., 1993).

top 100 listed UK companies *vis-à-vis* all listed UK companies. The
Australian top 50 (rather than top 100) may therefore be a better group to
compare with the UK top 100. Forty-seven of the top 50 Australian
companies had at least one substantial shareholder, and the largest or only
substantial shareholder was an institution in 19 cases (i.e. 40.4% of the 47).
This is still well short of the UK figure. It is no coincidence that UK
institutions owned over 60% of listed UK equities at the time of Study A,
whilst Australian institutions owned only about 36% of listed Australian
equities at the time of the Australian Study.[71]

Table 8.2 shows that institutional stakes in the range 5-14% were not
uncommon at the time of the Australian Study.[72] There were, in fact, 60
institutional substantial shareholdings of 10% or greater in the companies
included in the study. In 32 of those cases, however, there was a *non*-
institutional substantial shareholder with a stake larger than the double-
digit institutional holding. Furthermore, in 23 of those cases, the non-
institutional substantial shareholding was of 30% or more of the issued

[71] See Ch. 2.

[72] The institutions listed in Table 8.2 are those which had substantial shareholdings in at
least three of the sample companies. Note that several of the holdings of above 14% were
'corporate' holdings as opposed to portfolio investments (and most of these were holdings of
insurance companies in other financial companies).

Table 8.2 Institutions' Stakes in All Ordinaries Index[a] companies, 1993

Institution	No. of All Ordinaries Index companies in which a 'substantial shareholding' held, 1993						Total
	5% ≤ x <8%	8% ≤ x <11%	11% ≤ x <14%	14% ≤ x <17%	17% ≤ x <20%	20% ≤ x <45%	
AMP (Ins.)	26	15	3	3	2	–	49
NRMA (Ins.)	9	6	7	1	2	–	25
BT (FC)	8	7	1	2	–	–	18
County (FC)	10	2	5	1	–	–	18
NMFM (Ins.)	8	6	1	–	–	2	17
PPMA (Ins.)	7	2	2	–	–	–	11
SSIMC (Pub.)	4	7	–	–	–	–	11
Pott. War. (FC)	3	3	–	–	1	–	7
Suncorp (Ins.)	–	2	–	1	–	2	5
CBA (FC)	2	–	–	1	1	1	5
Lend Lse. (Ins.)	2	1	2	–	–	–	5
J.P. Morg. (FC)	3	2	–	–	–	–	5
FAI (Ins.)	1	1	1	1	–	–	4
Indosuez (O/S)	–	1	2	–	–	–	3
Rothschd. (FC)	2	1	–	–	–	–	3
Capital (O/S)	3	–	–	–	–	–	3
Tyndall (Ins.)	3	–	–	–	–	–	3
QIC (Pub.)	3	–	–	–	–	–	3
Others	14	9	2	2	–	–	27
Total	108	65	26	12	6	5	222

Note: abbreviations: see App. G.
  [a] Modified as described in App. K.

Source: Author's analysis of information in ASX, *All Ordinaries Index Companies Handbook* (4th edn., 1993).

ordinary capital. Where there is one non-institutional shareholder with a stake of 30% or greater, the chances of a successful institutional intervention to change management are very slight indeed.[73] In the light of this, consideration was given also to all 167 companies in the Australian Study in which a non-institution was the largest or only substantial shareholder. It was found that in 98 companies the largest non-institutional holder had a stake of at least 30%, and in a further 26 companies the largest non-institutional holder had a stake of between 20–30%. Therefore, in 98 (41.9%) of the 234 sample companies, the largest stakeholder was a non-institution with a stake of 30% or more; and in a further 26 (11.1%) of the sample companies, the largest stakeholder was a non-institution with a stake of between 20–30%. These large non-institutional 'controlling' shareholdings were mainly shareholdings of founding families, entrepreneurs, overseas companies, and other listed Australian companies. A

[73] See Ch. 10, Sec. B.1.xi.

large proportion (about 40–50%) of the Australian quoted company sector was thus either effectively immune from, or in most circumstances immune from, serious institutional intervention, and indeed from hostile takeover, at the time of the Australian Study.[74]

How does this compare with the UK? An institution was the largest interest-holder in 52 (75.4%) of the 69 UK companies in Study B. As shown above, the equivalent figure in Australia was only about 25%. In just six (8.7%) of the 69 UK sample companies, the largest stakeholder was a non-institution with a stake of 30% or more; and in a further five (7.2%) of the UK sample companies, the largest stakeholder was a non-institution with a stake of between 20–30%. Thus, whilst roughly 40–50% of the Australian quoted corporate sector was insusceptible (or in most circumstances insusceptible) to institutional intervention or hostile take-over, only about 10–15% of the UK quoted company sector was thus immune. This is empirical support for what was said in the opening chapter about the difference between the systems of corporate governance in the quoted corporate sectors of Australia and the UK.[75] For all but a small proportion of quoted UK companies, an 'outsider' system of corporate governance operates. In contrast, only about half of the Australian quoted company sector is subject to an outsider system of corporate governance. The other half operates under a system which is a mixture of an insider and an outsider system of corporate governance.[76]

There are two final points. First, a comparison between Table 8.2 and Table 6.2 shows that there was not a strong correlation between the leading fund managers in terms of the overall Australian equity market and the fund managers with the largest stakes in All Ordinaries Index companies. A similar finding was made in relation to the UK, and the same factors seem to explain the Australian situation.[77] Secondly, the author attempted

---

[74] It should also be borne in mind that several of the largest institutional stakes in All Ordinaries Index companies at the time of the Australian Study were actually 'corporate' holdings rather than portfolio investments: see n. 72 above. Some of these holdings composed 20–45% of the issued ordinary capital. If these companies were included, the proportion of companies immune from institutional intervention and hostile takeover would have been even greater.   [75] See Ch. 1, Sec. A.

[76] Note that, in the early 1990s, the quoted corporate sectors of Canada and New Zealand contained an even larger proportion of controlled companies. As at 1990, 60.3% of companies in the TSE 300 Composite Index (a Toronto Stock Exchange index) had a single shareholder which controlled more than 50% of the voting shares, and a further 25.4% of TSE 300 companies had either a single shareholder which controlled between 20–49.9% of the voting shares, or two or three shareholders each of which controlled between 10–20% of the voting shares: see R. J. Daniels and J. G. MacIntosh, 'Toward a Distinctive Canadian Corporate Law Regime' (1991) 29 *Osgoode Hall LJ* 863, at 884. As at 1992, 72.7% of listed New Zealand companies had one shareholder with a 30% or larger stake, and a further 9.7% of companies had a shareholder with a stake of between 20–30%: A. Mandelbaum, 'Efficiency and Equity Implications of the Proposed New Zealand Takeovers Code' (1994) 12 *C&SLJ* 489, at 491.   [77] See Ch. 5, at nn. 160–2, and accompanying text.

to conduct a study in Australia equivalent to Study B, described in Chapter 5. It was, unfortunately, impossible to do so using the methodology employed in Study B.[78] This chapter does not, therefore, include a picture of the institutional-shareholder profile of listed Australian companies like that illustrated in Table 5.6 for listed UK companies.

ii. Manner of Extraordinary Involvement

Most of the types of extraordinary action which have been carried out by UK institutions have also been performed by Australian institutions. Extraordinary meetings and dialogue with the management of portfolio companies occur, but probably not as often as in the UK. Company-initiated meetings to pre-market capital raisings, restructurings, large transactions, and unusual courses of action, are a feature of the Australian corporate sector, with the company's broker usually being involved in communicating with the company's largest few institutional share-holders.[79] Shareholder-initiated extraordinary meetings and dialogue also occur in Australia—where there is dissatisfaction with the management of a portfolio company, concern about a procedural or general matter such as the terms of a proposed executive share scheme,[80] or concern about a company-specific matter other than the performance of the senior management.[81] None of the institutions covered in the interview study had, though, reached the stage of four of the institutions covered in the UK interview study, which had staff devoted full-time to matters of corporate governance and problem companies.[82]

Other extraordinary actions taken by Australian institutions include

---

[78] The reasons for this are set out in App. K.

[79] See e.g. 'Central to Spin Off Diamonds', *Aust. Fin. Rev.*, 15 Feb. 1994, p. 20: 'Great Central Mines NL is poised to announce a major reconstruction which will see the company's diamond interests spun off into a separate, publicly listed company. . . . Some institutional shareholders in Great Central are understood to have been sounded out on the details of the restructuring in recent days. The looming diamond spin-off, according to some institutional investors, was one of the attractions behind Great Central's recent capital raisings, which have seen the group raise about $100 million in the last two months.'

[80] See e.g. 'Goodman Revises Option Scheme', *Aust. Fin. Rev.*, 21 Nov. 1990, p. 22; 'Poor Showing from Goodman Comes Under Fire', *Aust. Fin. Rev.*, 27 Nov. 1990, p. 16.

[81] See e.g. 'BHP Acts on Beswick Shareholding', *Fin. Times*, 25 Aug. 1994, p. 22 (announcement by Australia's largest listed company, BHP, that it had revised the procedures for the exercise of voting rights by its 18% major shareholder, Beswick (which was half-owned by BHP), 'to quell unease among some of its institutional shareholders over the group's share structure'); 'Chanticleer: Kiwi Hijacking May Spark War With Australia Inc', *Aust. Fin. Rev.*, 8 June 1989, p. 104; 'Goodman Fielder Bid for IEL Runs Foul of NCSC', *Aust. Fin. Rev.*, 13 June 1989, p. 16 (a takeover bid which appeared potentially detrimental to the interests of the bidder's shareholders led to meetings between AMP (a 9% shareholder) and the bidder's management, at which AMP expressed its strong disapproval of the bid—which was later withdrawn when a rival bidder seized control of the target: 'Goldberg Leads IEL Buy-Out', *Aust. Fin. Rev.*, 4 July 1989, p. 1).

[82] See Ch. 5, at n. 185, and accompanying text.

meeting with one or more of the non-executive directors of a portfolio company, and meeting with or speaking by telephone to other large institutional shareholders.[83] These actions have been taken in relation to dissatisfaction with a company's management, and in regard to an assortment of issues of serious concern. Neither of these steps has been taken unless dialogue with the company's management has proven fruitless. In some cases, these actions have been a precursor to an attempted ousting of an impeached chief executive or a group of ineffective non-executive directors (hereafter 'intervention').

Institutional interventions appear to have a much shorter history in Australia than in the UK (where, as shown in Chapter 5, they date back to 1956). There seems to be no public record of any interventions earlier than the 1980s, and none of the fund managers interviewed by the author mentioned any interventions earlier than the Bell Resources/Bond Corporation matter of 1988.[84] There would, in fact, appear to have been only a handful of full-scale institutional interventions in Australia. Five interventions that have been detailed in the press are described below.[85]

Bennett & Fisher Ltd.[86] In November 1990 a number of institutions attempted unsuccessfully to vote down a resolution ratifying the purchase by Bennett & Fisher Ltd. from its chairman/managing director's wife of a property for twenty-three times the price at which she had bought it just five years earlier. Over the course of the next year a group of three

---

[83] On the latter, see AIST (n. 36 above), at 117–20.

[84] The Bell/Bond case was the genesis of the AIMA. In 1988, when Bond Corp. was attempting to gain control of the Bell Resources board, four or five institutions, which were wary about Bond Corp.'s intentions for Bell's substantial reserves, tried to persuade the late Mr Robert Holmes a Court to remain on the Bell board in order to protect the interests of minority shareholders. In spite of that, Mr Holmes a Court resigned. There was then an institutional attempt to vote the AMP state manager for Western Australia onto the board. This failed. The local institutions then sold out of the company at a loss. However, that left private shareholders and overseas institutions to suffer an even greater loss when Bond Corp. diverted A\$1,500m. from Bell. The local institutions were subsequently criticized severely for bailing out at the 'half-way' stage: 'Wielding the Institutional Club', *Aust. Fin. Rev.*, 9 Aug. 1993, p. 15.

[85] Note that the press reports have in some instances been supplemented by information provided to the author during the interview study. Note also that institutional shareholders played a key role in the board change at Seven Network Ltd. in May 1995: see 'Deveson Courts Institutions', *Aust. Fin. Rev.*, 28 Apr. 1995, p. 32; 'Big Guns Back Stokes, But Not as Chair Apparent', *Aust. Fin. Rev.*, 2 May 1995, p. 1; 'Showdown Near as Stokes Lifts Seven Stake', *Aust. Fin. Rev.*, 17 May 1995, p. 22.

[86] See 'AMP Says No to Property Deal with Company Chairman's Wife', *Aust. Fin. Rev.*, 23 Nov. 1990, p. 28; 'B&F Dissension Over Property Deal Vote', *Aust. Fin. Rev.*, 30 Nov. 1990, p. 23; 'Bennett Election Balked by Court', *Aust. Fin. Rev.*, 2 Dec. 1991, p. 23; 'Trio Clear to Contest B and F Board Poll', *Aust. Fin. Rev.*, 9 Dec. 1991, p. 24; 'New Bennett Board Promises Stability', *Aust. Fin. Rev.*, 16 Dec. 1991, p. 24; 'Sacked Boss Refuses to Go Quietly', *Aust. Fin. Rev.*, 11 May 1992, p. 1; 'Former Bennett Chief Finally Heeds the Call', *Aust. Fin. Rev.*, 5 June 1992, p. 21; 'Huge Claim Alleges Fraud by Summers', *Advertiser*, 6 June 1993.

opponents of the incumbent board met with institutions, and gained institutional support for a purge of the board at the AGM. A month before the AGM, the chairman/managing director relinquished the position of chairman, but to an ally. At the AGM in December 1991, the three dissidents were voted onto the board and the new chairman and four incumbent non-executive directors were, effectively, removed. This only occurred after the chairman had challenged the eligibility of the dissidents to stand as directors, which forced the taking of legal proceedings to clarify the matter. The following May, the new board dismissed the managing director from his position as an executive officer. He refused to resign as a director, and the Corporations Law prevents a board from removing any of its number,[87] so an EGM was called to remove him. He eventually resigned a day or so before the EGM when it was obvious that institutional proxies were heavily in favour of his removal. The company was put into receivership a year later, at which time a large fraud suit was filed against the former managing director.

Darrell James Ltd.[88] This case involved a company that had initially run duty-free stores and latterly turned to property development. It had a three-person board: the executive chairman, his wife, and the finance director. Some institutions were concerned about the company's declining earnings—from A\$9.13 million in 1988 to just A\$0.1 million in the six months to December 1990—in spite of a large cash pool and low gearing. Four institutions and one large private investor, which collectively accounted for 30% of the equity, requisitioned an EGM at which it was proposed to remove the chairman's wife and the finance director (but leave the executive chairman in place), and appoint two new non-executive directors. At the time of the requisition, the chairman and his family controlled 33% of the equity. However, prior to the EGM, the chairman's family company bought a further 3% of the shares in the market (taking their stake to 36%), and a company controlled by a private investor loyal to the chairman purchased 1% to take its holding to 6.75%. Prior to the EGM, the chairman organized a slate of five new non-executive directors to stand against the requisitionists' nominees. In addition, the chairman also secured the support of an institutional shareholder which held 4% of the equity. At the EGM, over 90% of the equity was voted, with 54% supporting the existing board and 38% supporting the dissident institutions. The chairman's five nominees were elected to the board, and the

---

[87] CL, s. 227(1). See the reform proposal in Ch. 11, Sec. B.2.ii.
[88] See 'Shareholder Revolt Rocks Darrell James', *Aust. Fin. Rev.*, 9 Aug. 1991, p. 16; 'Photo Finish for Darrell James', *Aust. Fin. Rev.*, 9 Sept. 1991, p. 64; 'Darrell James Coup Blocked', *Aust.*, 14 Sept. 1991, p. 43; 'Darrell James Board on Notice', *Aust. Fin. Rev.*, 16 Sept. 1991.

institutions' resolutions were not passed. This case illustrates the difficulty with achieving a successful institutional intervention where there is a *non-institutional* shareholder with a stake of 30% or more.[89]

Westpac Banking Corporation.[90] In this case one of Australia's largest banks, which had suffered very badly as a result of a focus on growth during the 1980s, had the ignominy of a shortfall of A$883 million on a A$1,200 million rights issue. At a board meeting a week later, the bank's non-executive chairman and four non-executive directors resigned 'in the interests of the bank and to show board responsibility for the disastrous . . . rights issue which flowed from the costly lending mistakes of the 1980s'.[91] There had been considerable institutional pressure, together with pressure from a private-shareholder lobby group and the media, for the chairman and several directors to resign.[92] The new board consulted extensively with institutional investors regarding the appointment of two new non-executive directors in the aftermath of this affair.

Goodman Fielder Ltd.[93] This company—Australia's largest food company—has been on the receiving end of more interference by institutional shareholders than any other company in Australia.[94] Its management was criticized strongly over a takeover bid in 1989 (which was eventually withdrawn), and was then forced to alter and later defer an executive option scheme in 1990. But it has been in relation to the composition of management and the board that institutions have had most

[89] Over 40% of listed Australian companies have such a stakeholder: see Sec. B.3.i, above. See also Ch. 10, Sec. B.1.xi.

[90] See 'How It All Went Horribly Wrong', *Syd. Morn. Herald*, 25 Sept. 1992, p. 25; 'Editorial: Time for the Westpac Board to Declare', *Aust. Fin. Rev.*, 1 Oct. 1992, p. 17; 'Westpac: Neal and Four Directors Go', *Aust. Fin. Rev.*, 2 Oct. 1992, p. 1; ' "Still a Long Way to Go" for Westpac', *Aust. Fin. Rev.*, 2 Oct. 1992, p. 26.

[91] 'Westpac: Neal . . .', ibid. This still left a board of eight non-executives and two executives.

[92] Interestingly, Australia's largest institutional investor, AMP, had 15 months earlier formed a strategic alliance with Westpac which involved AMP taking a 14.9% stake in Westpac (as well as commercial links and joint ventures). AMP was one of few large shareholders to take up its rights in full. Clearly, however, its role in this case was not as a portfolio investor, because its holding was a 'corporate' holding. AMP's chairman, one of two AMP appointees on the Westpac board, was promoted to the position of deputy chairman at the board meeting.

[93] See 'Chanticleer: Storm Clouds Gather', *Aust. Fin. Rev.*, 14 Dec. 1993, p. 44; 'Bloodbath at Goodman', *Aust. Fin. Rev.*, 15 Dec. 1993, p. 1; 'Chanticleer: "Perform or Get the Chop" ', *Aust. Fin. Rev.*, 15 Dec. 1993, p. 36; 'Chairman of Goodman Fielder to Stand Down', *Fin. Times*, 17 Aug. 1994, p. 19; 'Goodman Fielder EGM Call', *Fin. Times*, 18 Aug. 1994, p. 20; 'Goodman Fielder Board Studies Call for Overhaul', *Fin. Times*, 20 Aug. 1994, p. 11; 'Goodman Sets Date to Face Music', *Fin. Times*, 23 Aug. 1994, p. 22; 'Goodman Fielder Bows to Rebel Investors to Head Off Proxy Battle', *Fin. Times*, 8 Sept. 1994, p. 31.

[94] Significantly, the company did not, during the relevant period, have any large non-institutional shareholders.

influence. This has stemmed from seven years of poor shareholder returns between 1988–94.

In early 1990, after the resignation of the then chief executive, institutions ensured that the executive chairman did not go ahead with a plan to combine the roles of chairman and chief executive. They brought heavy pressure to bear for the appointment of several independent non-executive directors—which occurred. This new board then appointed a new chief executive in April 1990, at which time the executive chairman reduced his role to that of a non-executive chairman. In June 1992 the chairman resigned after the company's own investor-relations consultants revealed almost universal institutional displeasure with his performance. He was replaced with a new non-executive chairman. From then until December 1993 several institutions expressed concerns to the chief executive and chairman about the group's poor performance, depressed share price, and failure to live up to its own forecasts. The resignations of competent divisional heads in late 1993, apparently after a conflict of management styles with the CEO, added to institutional pressure upon the board to remove the chief executive. Institutional dialogue with the non-executive chairman and other non-executive directors eventually led to the board sacking the chief executive at the end of 1993. A new chief executive was appointed, but things had not improved by August 1994 when a businessman with a 3.5% shareholding approached three large institutions, which collectively controlled 16% of the equity, and proposed an assault upon the board. When the board did not agree to the shareholder group's call for a vote on the removal of all seven non-executive directors (including the non-executive chairman), and the consideration of four new specified non-executives, the dissident shareholders requisitioned an EGM seeking these changes. The board convened a general meeting, but some two weeks later (and over a month before the meeting was to take place) the matter was settled when the board agreed to appoint three of the dissidents' nominees as new non-executives, and to search for a new non-executive chairman, and stated that two existing non-executives would stand down.

Coles Myer Ltd.[95] This case involved a retailing company whose board included representatives of major suppliers. The intervention began

---

[95] See 'Scandal Rocks Coles Myer', *Aust. Fin. Rev.*, 5 Sept. 1995, p. 1; 'Corporate Coup Begins', *Aust. Fin. Rev.*, 15 Sept. 1995, p. 1; 'Lew Offers to Stand Down', *Aust. Fin. Rev.*, 19 Sept. 1995, p. 1; 'ASA Joins Clamour for Lew's Scalp', *Aust.*, 20 Sept. 1995, p. 41; 'Coles Activist Plans Move to Force Lew Off Board at AGM', *Aust.*, 4 Oct. 1995, p. 48; 'AMP Declares War on Coles', *Aust.*, 12 Oct. 1995, p. 1; 'Myer Family Dumps Lew', *Aust. Fin. Rev.*, 13 Oct. 1995, p. 1; 'Chanticleer: Even PM Can't Save Lew Now', *Aust. Fin. Rev.*, 17 Oct. 1995, p. 52; 'Institutions Unite Against Lew', *Aust. Fin. Rev.*, 18 Oct. 1995, p. 1; 'Lew Succumbs in Coles Purge', *Aust.*, 20 Oct. 1995, p. 23.

shortly after allegations were made of an improper related-party transaction, through which the company lost about A$18 million. Importantly,
though, only a few weeks before those allegations surfaced, the board had
promoted the chairman (who controlled some 13% of the equity, and
whose private companies in 1994 supplied to the company goods worth
A$95 million) from a non-executive role to that of executive chairman.
This move had been opposed by several institutional investors and the
AIMA.[96]

In early September 1995, the Australian Securities Commission began
an investigation into the allegedly improper related-party transaction, and
shortly thereafter it was reported that several unnamed institutions were
calling for substantial board changes. Interestingly, the AIMA was utilized
as a spokesperson to identify the areas of common ground amongst the
institutions.[97] The embattled chairman began meeting with the company's
largest institutional shareholders, and then made an offer consisting of him
vacating his executive office and reverting to the position of non-executive
chairman, and the company making greater disclosure of related-party
dealings. This offer was rejected outright by most if not all institutions.
Again, the AIMA was used as a vehicle for publicizing the institutions'
basic position. On 19 September, a small-shareholder lobby group (the
Australian Shareholders' Association) announced that it would attempt to
have resolutions included on the agenda for the company's AGM on 21
November. In early October, a private shareholder made a similar
announcement.

The major development occurred on 11 October, when the company's
three largest institutional shareholders—which controlled 10.5% of the
equity—released a joint statement announcing their intention to 'propose a
number of independent non-executive directors to replace some of the
existing directors at the . . . annual general meeting . . . or if necessary, at
an extraordinary general meeting'. This move was made after the trustee of
the Myer family trust (an 8% shareholder) announced that it supported the
institutional views on the structure of the company's board. At the same
time, the board announced a plan under which the company's main
businesses would be spun off into five separate listed companies, and some
new non-executive directors would be appointed in the interim (but no
existing directors were to leave). This plan received the public support of
the Prime Minister, but failed to placate the institutions. On 17 October,
barely one week after the announcement of the proposed proxy battle, the
AIMA reported that 96% of its members—which collectively held 23.9%

---

[96] See 'Lew Appointment Under Fire', *Age*, 24 July 1995, p. 35.
[97] This enabled individual institutions to avoid the possibility of losing business through
being identified publicly in the matter: see Ch. 10, Sec. B.1.vi.

of the equity—favoured the appointment of a new, independent, non-executive chairman. The AIMA expected that overseas institutional shareholders—accounting for another 8% of the equity—would support the local institutions. Counting the Myer family's holding, support for the three intervening institutions was therefore about 40% of the share register, without including any private shareholders who might vote with the institutions. The chairman and his associates could, at this stage, count on only about 20% of the votes.[98] Not surprisingly, therefore, the intervention concluded on 19 October (more than a month before the AGM) when the chairman resigned from the chair (but he remained a non-executive director),[99] and two non-executive directors resigned from the board. An independent non-executive chairman and several new non-executive directors—who had been assembled by the three intervening institutions—were appointed to the board shortly afterwards.

Those then are the main cases of institutional intervention in Australia which have been reported in the newspapers. The author's Australian interview project found that, in contrast to the situation in the UK, behind-the-scenes interventions have not been a feature of the Australian corporate-governance system. Australia-based institutions *have* conducted other forms of detailed monitoring away from the public eye, but interventions involving a change, or proposed change, in the membership of the board seem routinely to have blown out into highly publicized events. Another observation which flows from this is that it is clear that there were far fewer institutional interventions in Australia, compared to the UK, in first half of the 1990s. This is partly because there were twice as many quoted UK companies as there were quoted Australian companies. That factor does not, however, go anywhere near explaining the difference. It is submitted that the main factor is that, in the early 1990s, as shown earlier, a substantially smaller proportion of the Australian quoted company sector was susceptible to serious institutional action than was the UK equivalent.[100]

The other types of extraordinary action discussed in relation to UK institutions were (a) the conditional exercise of a rights entitlement; (b) rejection of Super Class 1 transactions; and (c) litigation. As regards (a), there is no statutory right of pre-emption in Australia. There is, however, a requirement that listed companies must not, without prior shareholder approval, make a non-rights issue of shares which, taken together with

---

[98] In perhaps a last-ditch attempt to maintain control, the chairman had warned: 'It may be necessary for institutions to seek instructions from people on whose behalf they manage these investments before committing their vote.' In regard to the accountability of fund managers, see Ch. 9, Sec. B.3.   [99] Recall that he was a large shareholder.
[100] See nn. 73–6 above, and accompanying text.

other shares issued during the previous 12 months, exceeds 10% of the nominal value of those shares on issue at the commencement of the 12-month period.[101] The author's interview study suggests, however, that the phenomenon of institutions procuring management changes via a conditional exercise of their rights has not occurred in Australia. There was, however, a case in 1990 where institutions expressed an unwillingness to participate in a syndicate, to buy a placement of a 31% stake in a company, if there were to be no changes to the company's management and board. The company's chief executive resigned a few days later.[102] Regarding (b), the *ASX Listing Rules* do not contain material-transactions provisions like those in Chapter 10 of the London Stock Exchange's *Listing Rules*. There is simply a rule which (i) requires any sale or disposal of the company's 'main undertaking' to be conditional upon ratification by the general meeting; and (ii) gives the ASX discretion to require the ratification of 'a change in activities' by a company.[103] It is submitted that these provisions should be replaced with a set of material-transactions provisions along the lines of the London Stock Exchange model.[104] As regards (c), none of the institutions covered in the Australian interview study had ever taken legal action in their capacity as an equity shareholder against the directors or management of a portfolio company. Some had litigated in the capacity of a preference shareholder or unit-holder in a unit trust. The costs rules in Australia are broadly the same as the English rules. The same financial reasons enunciated by UK institutions were given by the Australian interviewees for the lack of litigation on their part.[105]

C. INDIRECT INDUSTRY-WIDE MONITORING

Industry-wide institutional monitoring actions—the devising and promulgating of generally applicable standards of best practice—have become a

---

[101] *ASX Listing Rules*, LR 3E(6).

[102] See 'Tooth Repays its $20m Loan to Howard Smith "Early" ', *Aust. Fin. Rev.*, 20 Nov. 1990, p. 20; 'Howard Smith Clears Way for Placement', *Aust. Fin. Rev.*, 26 Nov. 1990, p. 19. See also the Westpac case discussed above, which is a slight variation.

[103] *ASX Listing Rules*, LR 3S. See also *AIMA Corporate Governance Guidelines*, para. 3.13.

[104] See Ch. 11, Sec. B.1.vii, where such a recommendation is made.

[105] One procedural difference will probably soon exist between the UK and Australia. The Australian government plans to introduce a statutory derivative action provision into the Corporations Law. This would remove the problems of the rule in *Foss* v. *Harbottle* for Australian shareholders (see Ch. 5, at n. 235). It will not, however, remove most of the all-important financial disincentives to shareholder litigation: see I. M. Ramsay, 'Corporate Governance, Shareholder Litigation and the Prospects for a Statutory Derivative Action' (1992) 15 *UNSWLJ* 149, at 162–4.

regular feature of the Australian quoted corporate sector since the formation of the AIMA in late 1990. The indirect industry-wide monitoring performed by the AIMA became especially pronounced after the establishment of its secretariat in May 1993. As shown in Chapter 7, the AIMA has produced and promoted statements of, and guidelines on, best practice in areas such as board structure and composition, disclosure of executive remuneration, executive share-option schemes, employee share schemes, and shareholder approval of major corporate changes. It has also made representations to government departments and the ASX on matters such as regulatory restrictions on voting by institutional shareholders, continuous disclosure, and the importance of the one-share/one-vote rule in the *ASX Listing Rules*. Finally, three of the AIMA's nominees, one of whom was then a member of AIMA's board, were appointed in 1994 to the private-sector 'consultative group' which is overseeing the work of the task force charged with simplifying the Corporations Law.[106]

D. INDIRECT FIRM-LEVEL MONITORING

In Australia as in the UK, firm-level monitoring has been performed on behalf of institutions (i.e. indirectly) by two types of monitor: the institutions' collective-action vehicle (the AIMA), and non-executive directors.

1. AIMA

The AIMA has a Corporate Governance Committee which becomes involved in firm-level monitoring. For instance, as mentioned earlier in the chapter,[107] the AIMA played an important role in the institutional intervention at Coles Myer Ltd. in 1995. The Corporate Governance Committee is, however, involved more commonly in matters which require the approval of shareholders in general meeting—for instance, executive share-option schemes.

The AIMA's original Practice Note on employee share schemes encouraged company managements 'to consult with their institutional shareholders on these schemes prior to their release and voting on by shareholders'.[108] The AIMA has taken a systematic approach to potentially

---

[106] See 'AMP's Hall to Lead Check on Changes to Law', *Aust. Fin. Rev.*, 4 Feb. 1994, p. 11.   [107] See n. 97 above, and accompanying text.

[108] AIMG, *Corporate Governance Practice Note No. 1: Guide to Employee Share Schemes* (1993). This document was replaced by two new guides in 1994: see AIMA, *Executive Share Option Schemes Guidelines* (1994); AIMA and Australian Institute of Company Directors, *Employee Share Schemes* (1994).

controversial executive share-option schemes. Once an AIMA member
has raised concerns about a proposed scheme, the Corporate Governance
Committee considers whether the proposal breaches the AIMA guidelines.
If so, it then issues a memorandum to all AIMA members. This encourages
those members who are shareholders in the company concerned to discuss
the proposals with the company's management. The memorandum does
not, however, give a voting recommendation.[109] The Corporate Governance Committee highlighted several proposed option schemes in the latter
half of 1993 which breached one or more of the guidelines. However, only
in the case of a medium-sized mining company was the proposed scheme
withdrawn before the AGM.[110] Schemes at four large companies were put
to the general meeting despite a degree of institutional opposition in each
case, and were approved (although some institutions voted against and
some abstained in at least one instance).[111]

Another important matter in which the AIMA's Corporate Governance
Committee was involved heavily was the proposal in late 1993 by News
Corporation Ltd. ('News Corp.') to issue 'super-voting' shares. The
proposal was for a one-for-ten bonus issue of shares, each carrying 25
votes, to be made to existing ordinary shareholders. It was proposed
originally that these super-voting shares would be non-transferable (i.e.
they would revert to ordinary shares carrying just one vote each if
transferred) and unlisted. In the face of enormous institutional opposition,
a revised proposal was tabled under which the super-voting shares would
be transferable and listed on the ASX, and the voting rights of the total
block of super-voting shares would be restricted to 40% of the total voting
rights within the company.

News Corp. sought a one-off waiver of Listing Rule 3K(2) of the *ASX
Listing Rules* (the rule which embodies the one-share/one-vote principle).
However, in the ASX discussion paper which was released shortly after the
announcement of News Corp.'s proposal,[112] there was floated the
possibility that LR 3K(2) might be amended or deleted. The AIMA played
a crucial role in co-ordinating and leading the institutional opposition to
News Corp.'s proposal for a one-off waiver of LR 3K(2), and to any
interference with LR 3K(2) itself. It engaged an external expert on
company law, and a firm of media-relations consultants, to assist it in

---

[109] P. J. Griffin, 'Institutional Investors in Australia: A Shareholders' Perspective' (1993).
It is clear that the absence of a recommendation is due largely to the possibility of a technical
breach of the takeover provisions in the Corporations Law: see Ch. 10, at nn. 102–14, and
accompanying text; Ch. 11, Sec. B.1.ix.

[110] See 'Wielding . . .' (n. 84 above).

[111] See ibid.; 'Chanticleer: Incentives: The Options Are Open', *Aust. Fin. Rev.*, 14 July
1993, p. 52; 'Coles Share Plan Meets AIMG Flak', *Aust. Fin. Rev.*, 22 Nov. 1993, p. 22; 'Not
Everyone Happy at Coles', *Aust. Fin. Rev.*, 26 Nov. 1993, p. 32.

[112] ASX, *Differential Voting Rights* (1993).

lobbying the ASX and the government against these proposals. It would appear to have played the key role in drawing the government into the matter, which ultimately led to the ASX abandoning any plans to amend or delete LR 3K(2).[113] News Corp. also withdrew its application for a waiver of LR 3K(2).[114]

2. NON-EXECUTIVE DIRECTORS

i. Board Composition: The Evidence

The average board of large and medium-sized listed Australian companies has for a long time had a majority of non-executive members. A 1983 study found that the average board size for the largest 500 listed companies (measured by market capitalization) was seven directors, with 30% being executive and 70% being non-executive.[115] These proportions were 'about the same' in 1975.[116] The Cooney Committee cited a study which showed that the figures for listed companies in 1988 were: 9.3 directors; 31% executive; 69% non-executive.[117] At 1992, the figures were: 8 directors; 25% executive; 75% non-executive.[118] There is, however, anecdotal evidence that 400–500 of the smallest listed Australian companies have only the minimum three directors required by the Corporations Law,[119] or slightly more, with these being executives, representatives of major shareholders, and consultants.[120] The incidence of *independent* non-executives is, unfortunately, unclear.[121]

ii. 'Traditional' Non-Executives

The comments made in Chapter 5 about the theoretical role of 'traditional' non-executive directors, and most of those made about the practical

---

[113] See 'Managers Urge Inquiry on News Super-Voting Issue', *Aust. Fin. Rev.*, 12 Nov. 1993, p. 27 (AIMA urges the Australian Securities Commission ('ASC') to investigate the legality of News Corp's proposal); 'Appeal to Lavarch on News Super Shares', *Aust. Fin. Rev.*, 23 Nov. 1993, p. 20 (AIMA writes to the federal Attorney-General: 'It is not just, nor even mainly, a matter for the ASX to decide these issues. . . . [T]he Attorney-General and the ASC should become fully involved . . .'); 'Govt Steps into Super Share Row', *Aust. Fin. Rev.*, 24 Nov. 1993, p. 1 (the Attorney-General writes to the ASX warning that he would disallow (under CL, s. 774(5)) any change to LR 3K(2) unless the ASX delays any action and allows a three-month period of consultation); 'ASX Officially Kills Off Super-Shares Idea', *Aust. Fin. Rev.*, 23 Feb. 1994, p. 22 (ASX abandons possibility of any alteration of LR 3K(2), in line with the draft report of the Attorney-General's expert panel appointed to examine the matter).

[114] See 'Murdoch Yields on Super Shares', *Aust. Fin. Rev.*, 9 Dec. 1993, p. 1.

[115] Cited in J. F. Corkery, *Directors Powers and Duties* (1987) 3.   [116] Ibid.

[117] Australian Senate Standing Committee on Legal and Constitutional Affairs, *Company Directors' Duties* (1989) 117.

[118] Korn/Ferry International, *Boards of Directors in Australia: Twelfth Study* (1993) 3.

[119] See CL, s. 221(1).

[120] See 'Chanticleer: Boards Must Learn to Shape Up or Starve', *Aust. Fin. Rev.*, 9 Aug. 1994, p. 48.   [121] See Ch. 7, at n. 31, and accompanying text.

shortfalls with such directors, apply equally to the Australian scene. In regard to the first shortfall mentioned in Chapter 5, it would seem that many Australian non-executives are also too 'close' to the managers that they are supposed to monitor. There is some evidence that many non-executives in smaller listed companies are affiliated rather than independent.[122] In addition, non-executives (whether independent or affiliated) commonly owe their positions to the chairman or chief executive.[123] Finally, as in the UK, many Australian non-executives are themselves senior executives of other listed companies. As regards the second impediment to effective monitoring by non-executive directors—executive dominance on the board—this would seem to be less of a concern in Australia than in the UK. Non-executive directors normally outnumber executive directors on the boards of listed Australian companies.[124] Most listed Australian companies also have a non-executive chairman,[125] although it is apparently quite common for the chairman to be a former chief executive of the company.[126] The third, fourth, fifth, and sixth barriers to effective monitoring, described in Chapter 5, affect the non-executives of Australian companies as much as they do those of UK companies.

There is a dearth of information in Australia about the incidence of the ultimate monitoring action of non-executive directors—procurement of a change in senior-management personnel. One thing that is clear, however, is that non-executive directors played an assisting role in at least two of the reported institutional interventions to change an under-performing or otherwise unacceptable management team.[127] In addition, the author's interview study confirmed that it is not uncommon for an institution, or group of institutions, that is very concerned about the performance of a company's senior management, to contact and have discussions with a

---

[122] See n. 120 above, and accompanying text.

[123] A survey in 1993 of the 100 largest listed Australian companies found that only 17% had a board nomination committee: AIMG, ASX, and Business Council of Australia, *Survey on Structure and Operation of Board Remuneration and Nomination Committees* (1993).

[124] See Sec. D.2.i, above.

[125] A 1992 survey found that 84% of a sample of listed and unlisted Australian companies had a non-executive chairman: Korn/Ferry (n. 118 above).

[126] 'Chanticleer: Boards Must . . .' (n. 120 above).

[127] See the description of the cases of Bennett & Fisher Ltd., and Goodman Fielder Ltd. (Dec. 1993 episode), under Sec.B.3.ii, above. See also 'WMC Director Disciplined', *Fin. Times*, 1 Sept. 1993, p. 24; 'Editorial: Morgan Must Go From WMC', *Aust. Fin. Rev.*, 21 Jan. 1994, p. 24 (board of a listed Australian mining company disciplined the company's managing director, barred his participation in the company's executive share scheme for two years, and appointed an executive committee to give him advice between board meetings, after it was revealed that the company's exploration teams had trespassed on the leases of another company and withheld vital information when negotiating to buy those leases).

senior non-executive director (normally the chairman, if he or she is a non-executive) if dialogue with the senior management itself has failed to rectify the problem. However, 12 of the 13 interviewees said that their institution did not maintain any dialogue with the non-executive directors of portfolio companies in 'normal' (as opposed to 'problem') circumstances. The lone exception said:

> I make a point of trying to meet with people who are independent directors, to form my own opinions of them. And I keep quite a close liaison with the head-hunters who are involved in appointing independent directors, so I know what's happening in that area . . . as well (so I know how the selection process works). . . . I know most of the independent directors through one mechanism or another.[128]

Three final points should be borne in mind. First, section 227(12) of the Corporations Law prohibits the removal of a director of an Australian public company by 'any resolution, request or notice of the directors or any of them notwithstanding anything in the articles or any agreement'. Given that it is now recognized widely that an important function of the board is to monitor—and thus, by implication, to make any necessary changes to the composition of—the executive management (which includes executive *directors*), this provision is inappropriate.[129] There is in the final chapter a recommendation for the repeal of section 227(12), and for the introduction of an ASX listing requirement that the articles of association of listed companies must empower 75% of the board to dismiss any of its number.[130] In practice, of course, informal pressure may be brought to bear so as to procure the resignation of an unsatisfactory executive director.[131]

The second point to bear in mind is that Australian institutions have twice in the 1990s taken action which has led to the resignation of *non-executive* directors from boards of under-performing companies.[132] Thus, although there are, as mentioned earlier, several barriers or disincentives to the performance of an effective monitoring role by 'traditional' non-executive directors, the threat of removal by discontented institutional shareholders must now serve to some extent as a countervailing incentive to diligent monitoring.

---

[128] Another two interviewees saw merit in there being regular dialogue between institutions and non-executives. Three interviewees mentioned (as did several of the UK interviewees) that they thought that routine dialogue with non-executives separate from the executive directors would undermine the unitary board.

[129] But cf. Corkery (n. 115 above), at 23: 'Such a rule is sensible: directors should be removed only by those to whom they owe their duties.'

[130] See Ch. 11, Sec. B.2.ii.

[131] See Ch. 4, at n. 89, and accompanying text.

[132] See the description of the cases of Westpac Banking Corporation, and Goodman Fielder Ltd. (Aug. 1994 episode), under Sec. B.3.ii, above.

Thirdly, the *AIMA Corporate Governance Guidelines* recommend that 'the non-executive directors should meet on their own at least once annually to review the performance of the board, the company and management and to discuss any other items raised by any of them'.[133] This is a sensible recommendation because such meetings would help to institutionalize the monitoring role of non-executive directors, and enable a frank assessment of the performance of management and the company.

iii. 'Institutional' Non-Executives

As defined in Chapter 5, 'institutional' non-executives are those directors who owe their presence on the board, to a greater or lesser extent, to a large institutional shareholder or group of institutions. They may be either fund managers or persons selected by fund managers.

Regarding the first category of 'institutional' non-executive (i.e. fund managers), it is in Australia (as in the UK) extremely rare for a fund manager or other full-time executive of an institution to serve as a non-executive director of an unrelated *listed* company, whether or not the institution has a holding in that company.[134] The author was aware of only two cases as at mid-1993. First, two executive directors of Lend Lease Corporation Ltd. were on the board of Westpac Banking Corporation. Lend Lease, which owns one of Australia's major life assurers (MLC Life), had an 11.5% stake in Westpac at that time, but it was a 'corporate' holding rather than a portfolio investment.[135] Secondly, Mr Peter Griffin, vice-chairman of Rothschild Australia Asset Management Ltd. (and then chairman of the AIMA), was on the board of Just Jeans Holdings Ltd., a speciality clothing retailer the founding family of which held a 59% stake. It is unknown whether Rothschild had a holding in Just Jeans; it certainly did not have a disclosable (5%+) holding. As in the UK, it is very common for the venture-capital arms of Australian institutions to place their executives onto the boards of *unquoted* companies to which venture or development finance has been provided.

None of the fund managers interviewed by the author was favourable about fund managers acting as non-executive directors of listed companies. Their reasons were remarkably similar to those given by the participants in the UK interview study—which are set out in Chapter 5.[136]

---

[133] *AIMA Corporate Governance Guidelines*, para. 3.7.

[134] However, in Australia as in the UK, there is a reasonably large number of non-executive directors of insurance companies and investment companies, and of the parent banking companies of several bank-owned fund managers, who also serve as non-executives on the boards of companies in which those institutions have holdings.

[135] AMP, which had a 14.95% holding in Westpac at mid-1993 (also a corporate holding; not a portfolio investment), was also represented on Westpac's board—but by two of its own non-executive directors, rather than by executives.

[136] AIST (n. 36 above), at 147–50, reports very similar findings.

As regards the second category of 'institutional' non-executive (i.e. persons selected by fund managers), eight of the interviewees said that their institution was either commonly or occasionally involved in the selection process for portfolio companies' non-executive directors. Five interviewees said that their institution was never or virtually never consulted by companies on this matter.[137] As in the UK, the most common form of involvement was the giving of an opinion on a candidate identified by the company's board. Less commonly, an institution would suggest names of persons it considered suitable. Finally, as shown earlier, institutions have drafted new non-executives onto the boards of problem companies in the course of institutional interventions.[138]

E. CONCLUSION

The monitoring actions carried out by Australian institutions are similar to those of their UK counterparts. In the key area of intervention to change an under-performing management team, however, there was a very wide differential between the level of activity in Australia and the UK, in the first half of the 1990s. This reflects the fact that many listed Australian companies (about 40–50% of the sector) were effectively immune from serious institutional intervention, as at late 1993, by reason of their having a very large non-institutional shareholder which had effective control over the composition of the board. In contrast, in late 1993, about 85–90% of quoted UK companies lacked such a shareholder; their share registers were dominated by institutional shareholders.

---

[137] Cf. AIST, ibid., at 151.

[138] See the cases of Bennett & Fisher Ltd., and Goodman Fielder Ltd., discussed under Sec. B.3.ii, above.

PART IV

*Institutional Involvement in Corporate
Governance: The Potential*

9

The Desirability of Increased Institutional Monitoring

Having analysed the history and current state of institutional monitoring in the UK and Australia, the remainder of the book looks to the future. This chapter seeks to identify the possible benefits and drawbacks from an increased level of institutional monitoring. It concludes that the likely advantages of greater involvement by institutional investors in corporate governance outweigh any disadvantages. Chapter 10 looks at the likelihood of there being an increased level of institutional monitoring in the absence of legal reforms directed at achieving that end. It concludes that there is unlikely to be any significant increase in institutional monitoring as a result of mere exhortation. Given the findings of Chapters 9 and 10, there are recommendations in Chapter 11 for certain (modest) legislative changes and changes to the stock-exchange listing requirements which are designed to induce closer institutional involvement in corporate governance.

An important qualification to the following discussion is that it relates primarily to those quoted companies which lack a non-institutional shareholder with a controlling stake. As shown earlier, as at late 1993, between 40–50% of listed Australian companies had such a shareholder, whilst only about 10–15% of quoted UK companies had one.[1] In 'controlled companies', mechanisms other than institutional monitoring and the market for corporate control operate to ensure that the interests of any professional managers do not diverge excessively from those of the controlling shareholder.[2] Nevertheless, institutional monitoring (together with related-party rules)[3] has an important role to play in controlled companies in ensuring that, in turn, the interests of minority shareholders are not ignored by the controlling shareholder.[4]

---

[1] See Ch. 8, at nn. 73–6, and accompanying text.
[2] See M. L. Lawriwsky, 'Some Tests of the Influence of Control Type on the Market for Corporate Control in Australia' (1984) 32 *J Indust. Econ.* 277, at 279.
[3] See *Listing Rules*, ch. 11; CL, Pt. 3.2A; *ASX Listing Rules*, LR 3J(3).
[4] The possibilities for abuse of minority shareholders by controlling corporate shareholders are illustrated well by the Independent Resources litigation: see *Re Spargos Mining NL* (1990) 3 ACSR 1; *Re Enterprise Gold Mines NL* (1991) 3 ACSR 531; (1992) 6 ACSR 539 (*sub nom. Jenkins* v. *Enterprise Gold Mines NL*). In regard to inter-investor conflicts in

A. POSSIBLE BENEFITS FROM GREATER MONITORING

There would appear to be two possible advantages of greater institutional monitoring. First, it might produce a reduction in agency costs. Secondly, it might lead to a greater focus by corporate management on the long term.[5] If so, closer institutional monitoring would benefit both poorly managed companies and well-managed companies.

1. REDUCTION IN AGENCY COSTS

It was shown in the first chapter that there is some divergence between the interests of managers and shareholders in those companies where there is a separation of the functions of management and risk bearing.[6] There are costs ('agency costs') which flow from this divergence of interests. Total agency costs comprise (a) expenses associated with monitoring activities by and on behalf of the shareholders to limit the non-wealth-maximizing activities of managers;[7] (b) bonding expenditures incurred by the managers to guarantee that they will act in the shareholders' interests; and (c) the residual reduction in the shareholders' maximum possible wealth.[8] At first glance, it appears that the only way in which closer institutional monitoring (which involves expenditure of type (a)) could reduce total agency costs would be if there were a resultant reduction in (c) which more than offset the cost of the increased institutional monitoring. As shown in the next paragraph, it is quite plausible that the expense of closer institutional monitoring *would* lead to a concomitantly larger reduction in the loss of shareholder wealth from managerial shirking and self-dealing. However, there is some evidence that different monitoring devices are, to an extent, substitutes for one another, and in particular that institutional intervention to replace under-performing managements is a substitute for those hostile takeovers which involve well-managed firms acquiring poorly managed firms.[9] Therefore, even if the cost of the increased institutional monitoring

Australia, see I. M. Ramsay and M. Blair, 'Ownership Concentration, Institutional Investment and Corporate Governance: An Empirical Investigation of 100 Australian Companies' (1993) *Melb. ULR* 153, at 173–6.

[5] See P. R. Marsh, *Short-Termism on Trial* (1990) 85–7.

[6] See Ch. 1, Sec. C; E. F. Fama and M. C. Jensen, 'Separation of Ownership and Control' (1983) 26 *J Law & Econ.* 301.

[7] These expenses include not only the direct costs incurred by the shareholders in carrying out their monitoring actions, but also indirect costs such as expenditure by the company on disclosure, audit, investor relations, payments to non-executive directors, etc.

[8] M. C. Jensen and W. H. Meckling, 'Theory of the Firm: Managerial Behavior, Agency Costs and Ownership Structure (1976) 3 *J Fin. Econ.* 305, at 308.

[9] See Ch. 5, at nn. 213–14, and accompanying text. See also Ch. 1, at nn. 62–5 (description of UK empirical study finding that the market for corporate control is a market in contending

were greater than the resultant reduction in (c), the closer monitoring could still be cost efficient if its introduction also resulted in a reduction in the costs associated with alternative monitoring devices.[10]

It was mentioned in Chapter 1 that supporters of the nexus-of-contracts model of the company believe that a separation of management and residual-risk bearing is not merely inevitable in large quoted companies but also economically efficient.[11] Put simply, contractarians argue that the divergence between the interests of managers and shareholders is minimized largely by market forces, and that regulatory action to reduce the remaining divergence is unjustifiable because this would lead to greater costs than benefits.[12] Contractarians believe that the market for corporate control (the threat of hostile takeover) serves to realign significantly the interests of managers and shareholders. However, it was shown in Chapter 1 that there are several major shortcomings with the market for corporate control, and with other market forces, as regards the efficacy of their role in disciplining inefficient managements.[13] Added to those is the fact that 'the hostile bidder, as an external monitor, is unlikely to be the first to detect or respond to managerial inefficiency. Generally, there should be an earlier tripwire—namely, internal monitoring within the firm.'[14] It was also shown in Chapter 1 that the non-market devices for aligning the interests of managers with those of shareholders similarly suffer some sizeable defects.[15] There is good reason to believe, therefore, that there is considerable scope for bolstering institutional monitoring so as to reduce cost-effectively the residual loss referred to in (c), above. In summary, in the words of Eisenberg:

> It is sometimes said that arguments for mandatory [legal] rules [to monitor corporate managements] reflect the Nirvana Fallacy, which consists of believing that just because markets are not perfect, mandatory rules would be better. It is

prospective strategies for firms rather than a mechanism for correcting past poor performance of firms; most hostile bids have little or nothing to do with disciplining inefficient managements).

[10] That is, because of substitutability, an increase in institutional monitoring would not necessarily involve an increase in (a), or an increase in (a) that was larger than the accompanying reduction in (c). The *net* increase (if any) in (a) may well be less than the reduction in (c). [11] See Ch. 1, Sec. E.

[12] That is, the increase in (a) would exceed any resulting decrease in (c).

[13] See Ch. 1, at nn. 61–73, and accompanying text.

[14] J. C. Coffee, 'Regulating the Market for Corporate Control: A Critical Assessment of the Tender Offer's Role in Corporate Governance' (1984) 84 *Colum. L Rev.* 1145, at 1202. The present author's UK interview study provided empirical support for this point: quite a few interviewees mentioned that they tried frequently (and often successfully) to 'engineer a takeover bid' for a problem company: see Ch. 5, at nn. 215–16, and accompanying text. In such an instance, the institution concerned would appear to have detected managerial inefficiency (from its meetings with and monitoring of the company's senior management) before any potential external bidder(s).

[15] See Ch. 1, at nn. 74–8, and accompanying text.

of course true that just because markets are imperfect does not mean that mandatory rules would be better. However, the converse proposition is also true: just because mandatory rules are imperfect does not mean that markets would be better. . . . The brute facts are that most markets are not perfect and most mandatory rules are [im]perfect; that even imperfect markets and legal rules may have positive effects; and that the question in any given case is to determine which of these imperfect mechanisms is better, or, if possible, to determine how these two imperfect mechanisms can be shaped to reinforce each other.[16]

2. OPPORTUNITY FOR STABLE, LONG-TERM MANAGEMENT FOCUS

Some commentators have argued that a closer relationship between institutional shareholders and company managements would facilitate the adoption by the latter of a longer-term approach to the strategy of their companies.[17] As Table 9.1 shows, there has been a relatively lower level of long-term investment in the UK and the US, compared with Japan and Germany, over a considerable period. There has also been a lower level of growth in GDP per capita in the UK and the US, compared with Japan and Germany.

As Marsh says, two inferences are drawn commonly from figures such as those in Table 9.1.[18] First, that there has been insufficient long-term investment in the UK and the US, which has caused relatively lower rates of growth in national wealth (compared to Japan and Germany). Secondly, that the underlying cause of the different levels of long-term investment is the myopia of the UK and US financial markets: it is said that the bank-based financial systems of Japan and Germany facilitate the undertaking of long-term investment projects whilst the market-based financial systems of the UK and the US have forced company managements to adopt a short-term approach.[19] Both inferences are, however, open to question. As regards the first, it is possible that the higher growth rates in Japan and

---

[16] M. A. Eisenberg, 'The Structure of Corporation Law' (1989) 89 *Colum. L Rev.* 1461, at 1524-5.

[17] This theme underlies several of the chapters in J. C. Coffee, R. J. Gilson, and L. Lowenstein (eds.), *Relational Investing* (1996) (forthcoming), and several of the essays in National Association of Pension Funds, *Creative Tension?* (1990).

[18] Marsh (n. 5 above), at 5.

[19] On the differences between the financial systems and systems of corporate governance in the UK/US and Germany/Japan, see Ch. 10, Sec. B.1.i. Short-termism has not been as big an issue in Australia as in the UK and the US (which is not surprising given the lower level of institutional share ownership in Australia). For instance, the terms of reference of the Parliamentary Joint Committee on Corporations and Securities, inquiring into the role of institutional shareholders in Australia, did not embrace any notion of short-termism: see the Committee's *Issues Paper: Inquiry into the Role and Activities of Institutional Investors in Australia* (1994) vii. The issue has surfaced, though: see e.g. Industry Commission, *Availability of Capital* (1991) 164-6.

Table 9.1 Comparative rates of growth and long-term investment

Country	Annual % growth in real GDP per capita			Capital formation (% of GDP)[a]	R&D spending financed by industry (% of GDP)[b]		
	1960–79	1980–9	1960–89	1960–89	1967	1979	1990
Japan	6.5	3.5	5.5	25	0.90	1.35	2.36
W. Germany	3.3	1.7	2.8	16	1.07	1.65	2.12
USA	2.3	2.1	2.2	14	1.15	1.23	1.52
UK	2.2	1.9	2.1	14	1.34	1.17*	1.41

* Figure for 1978.

[a] Gross fixed capital formation, excluding expenditure on residential construction.

[b] The R&D outlay of the top 200 companies worldwide (measured by R&D spending) in 1993 averaged 4.85% of their sales. There were 13 UK companies in the top 200, and their R&D spending averaged 2.29% of sales; figures for some other countries were: US: 81 companies; 4.36%; France: 17 companies; 4.80%; Japan: 49 companies; 5.90%; Germany: 11 companies; 6.80%; author's calculations from information in Company Reporting Ltd., *The 1994 UK R&D Scoreboard* (1994) 62–9. (There were no Australian companies amongst the top 200 R&D spenders in 1993.) See also D. Sawers, 'Blind Faith in R&D', *Fin. Times*, 2 Sept. 1992, p. 12.

Sources: P. R. Marsh, *Short-Termism on Trial* (1990) 4; House of Commons Trade and Industry Committee, *Second Report: Competitiveness of UK Manufacturing Industry* (1994) 46.

Germany are attributable (at least in part) to factors other than the level of investment, and that these comparatively higher rates of growth have presented Japanese and German companies with a greater number of profitable investment opportunities than their UK and US counterparts (which has led to the relatively higher levels of investment in Japan and Germany).[20] In regard to the second inference, there are many differences between the UK/US and Germany/Japan, of which dissimilar financial systems is just one. It is possible that historical, macroeconomic, and microeconomic factors—in particular the latter—have resulted in a comparatively lower level of profitable investment opportunities in the UK and the US, and that this has been the main cause of the relatively lower level of long-term investment in the UK and the US.[21]

Nevertheless, there *is* some evidence suggesting a *direct* link between the

---

[20] That is, causality may have run in the direction opposite to that presumed by the short-termism theorists: see Marsh (n. 5 above), at 5; N. G. Mankiw, 'Comment on C P Mayer, "New Issues in Corporate Finance" ' (1988) 32 *Euro. Econ. Rev.* 1183, at 1185–6; but cf. C. P. Mayer, 'The Assessment: Financial Systems and Corporate Investment' (1987) 3 (4) *Ox. Rev. Econ. Pol.* i, at xi–xii; C. P. Mayer, 'Financial Systems, Corporate Finance, and Economic Development' in R. G. Hubbard (ed.), *Asymmetric Information, Corporate Finance and Investment* (1990) 307, at 317–18.

[21] See Marsh, ibid., at 71–9, for an exposition of this view.

type of financial system and the level of long-term investment (although that possible link is not in the form of short-termism in share prices).[22] There is also evidence of an *indirect* causal connection between the workings of the UK and US market-based financial systems and the relatively lower levels of investment in those countries. Specifically, although the weight of evidence suggests that share prices do not systematically favour the short term, company managements may have acted in a short-termist fashion in the mistaken belief that there *is* a short-term bias in share prices (hereafter 'managerial short-termism through misconception'). In the light of this, and presuming for the moment that institutional shareholders and share prices are not short-termist, it seems reasonable to believe that a closer relationship between institutional shareholders and company managements would—by reducing the possibility of managerial short-termism through misconception—facilitate a greater focus by corporate management upon long-term wealth creation. However, the importance of the stated presumption necessitates a closer examination of the alleged short-termism of institutional shareholders and share prices. If it is concluded that direct (as opposed to merely indirect) short-termism exists, that may be a reason for not enhancing institutional involvement in corporate governance (because to do so might lead to even greater short-term pressure on corporate management). The examination of the short-termism story composes the first subsection of the next section (which deals with eight possible drawbacks of a closer involvement by institutions in corporate governance in the UK and Australia).

B. POSSIBLE PROBLEMS WITH GREATER MONITORING

1. SHORT-TERMISM

The claim that institutional shareholders are short-termist is in one sense difficult to refute, because it is not clear what it is that one is meant to refute: there is no general theory suggesting how institutions are short-termist.[23] Proponents of the short-termism story usually refer to one or more of the following five 'features' of the UK and US financial systems:

---

[22] See nn. 91–142 below, and accompanying text.

[23] In 1987, the CBI City/Industry Task Force (which comprised representatives of corporate management and institutional shareholders, amongst others) concluded that the relatively low level of long-term investment by UK companies 'does not arise primarily from City pressures. It arises mainly from underlying economic and political factors': *Report: Investing for Britain's Future* (1987) 10. Despite that bipartisan rejection of the short-termism story, there has still been a fairly widely held perception amongst company executives that institutions are short-termist: see 'City Working for "Short-Term Gains at Expense of Industry" ', *Fin. Times*, 4 Nov. 1988, p. 24 (one year after the report of the City/Industry Task Force, a CBI survey found that 64% of company managements thought that institutional shareholders were not making a long-term and strategic evaluation of their companies); 3i plc,

(a) the preoccupation of investment analysts and fund managers with current earnings; (b) the distorting effect of the threat of hostile takeover, which institutions have exacerbated; (c) the high level of turnover of shareholdings by institutions; (d) the shortness of the periods within which the performance of external investment managers of pension funds is measured; and (e) the comparatively high dividend pay-out ratio of UK and US quoted companies compared to their Japanese and German counterparts. It is demonstrated below that, in regard to each of 'features' (a)–(d), the empirical evidence contradicts either (i) the existence of the feature itself; or (ii) the suggestion that the feature demonstrates short-termism on the part of institutions and/or in share prices. However, in the case of some and perhaps all of those four features/seeming features of the UK and US financial systems, it appears that *indirectly* they have been a *partial* cause of companies failing to undertake the level of long-term investment undertaken by Japanese and German firms: this is the matter of 'managerial short-termism through misconception' mentioned earlier. Feature (e) is the exception. This feature does definitely exist. In addition, and importantly, it is arguable (and the author argues) that there is a form of short-termism which is inherent in the UK and US 'outsider' systems of corporate ownership and governance[24] (hereafter 'inherent short-termism'), and that feature (e) is a symptom of this inherent short-termism. It is contended below that inherent short-termism has nothing to

Plc UK: The Role of the Finance Director: Part 3—Corporate Governance (1992) 22 (of a large sample of finance directors from the top 750 quoted UK companies, 47.4% 'agreed', 43.7% 'partly agreed', and only 7.9% 'disagreed' that 'bias towards short-term results' was a valid criticism of the UK's system of corporate governance). The House of Commons Trade and Industry Committee concluded in 1994 that there was short-termism in UK manufacturing companies, and that this was 'the result of groups of people responding to a system which requires—indeed insists upon—short-termist behaviour': *Second Report: Competitiveness of UK Manufacturing Industry* (1994) para. 192. The view of the Labour Party in 1994 was that 'Britain's companies are now dominated by short-term shareholders, in the form of financial institutions [which have a] lack of commitment to the long-term futures of the companies in which they hold shares': *Winning for Britain* (1994) 1. The Government was, however, somewhat non-committal: 'The policy of . . . maintaining cash distributions . . . may reinforce a pressure on management to show good returns in the short term, even though this may be at the expense of long term growth. . . . [P]ressure for high dividends is not of itself evidence of a malfunction in the market. . . . The key issue is whether capital is best allocated by being left in the hands of companies or by being returned to shareholders.': *Competitiveness: Helping Business to Win* (1994) paras. 9.9–9.10. In the light of the continued perception of short-termism, in mid-1994 the DTI helped establish a committee composed mostly of fund managers and finance directors to 'suggest practical ways in which the relationship between UK industry and institutional shareholders [could] be improved as a stimulus for long term investment and development': City/Industry Working Group ('Myners Committee'), *Developing a Winning Partnership* (1995) 2.

[24] On the difference between 'outsider' and 'insider' systems of corporate ownership and governance, see J. R. Franks and C. P. Mayer, 'Corporate Control: A Synthesis of the International Evidence' in Coffee, Gilson, and Lowenstein (n. 17 above). See also Ch. 1, Sec. A; Ch. 10, Sec. B.1.i.

do with share prices, the rate of turnover of shares, the time-scale within which the performance of fund managers is measured, or institutional shareholders *per se*. Rather, it is a result of the fact that the ultimate controllers (i.e. equity shareholders) of large and medium-sized UK and US companies are generally arm's-length investors whereas the ultimate controllers of large and medium-sized German and Japanese companies are normally tied closely ('committed') to the company. There would be inherent short-termism in the UK quoted company sector even if individuals rather than institutions dominated the share registers; it is the arm's-length relationship that is the determinative factor. In the light of this, it is concluded that it would not be detrimental (and would possibly be beneficial) to take measures aimed at encouraging a closer relationship between institutional investors and company managements.

'Feature' (a). Many industrialists have complained that brokers' analysts and fund managers are obsessed with current earnings.[25] The implication would appear to be that, because institutions account for such a large proportion of the share register of most quoted UK companies, this preoccupation with companies' short-term prospects means that there is a systematic short-term bias in share prices: more weight (than is justified by the cost of capital) is given to short-term cash flows than long-term cash flows.[26]

The bulk of the evidence points, however, to there being no such bias in share prices.[27] Only two studies have found a short-term bias in the share prices of quoted UK companies. The first found that investors placed between 5–7.5 times more weight on current dividends than on future capital gain.[28] The methodology of, and the data used in, that study have been criticized severely, and some believe that its results are flawed.[29] The second study (conducted by Miles), of 477 quoted non-financial companies over the period 1980–9, found:

---

[25] See e.g. A. D. Cosh, A. Hughes, A. Singh, et al., *Takeovers and Short-Termism in the UK* (1990) 16.   [26] See Marsh (n. 5 above), at 9.

[27] Ibid., at 16–20; J. J. McConnell and C. J. Muscarella, 'Corporate Capital Expenditure Decisions and the Market Value of the Firm' (1985) 14 *J Fin. Econ.* 399 (US study showing that, for industrial companies, on average share prices increase (decrease) in response to announcements of increases (decreases) in planned capital expenditure); S. H. Chan, J. D. Martin, and J. W. Kensinger, 'Corporate Research and Development Expenditures and Share Value' (1990) *J Fin. Econ.* 255 (US study finding that, on average, share-price responses to announcements of increased R&D spending are significantly positive, even for firms that simultaneously experience an earnings decline); B. D. Baysinger, R. D. Kosnik, and T. A. Turk, 'Effects of Board and Ownership Structure on Corporate R&D Strategy' (1991) 34 *Acad. Mgt. J* 205 (US study showing a positive relationship between the level of institutional share ownership and the amount spent by the company on R&D).

[28] S. J. Nickell and S. B. Wadhwani, *Myopia, the 'Dividend Puzzle', and Share Prices* (1987).

[29] See 'Keynes Followers Rally Behind Industrialists', *Fin. Times*, 3 Mar. 1987, p. 8; 'Letters to the Editor: Stock Market Efficiency', *Fin. Times*, 16 Mar. 1987, p. 23.

[P]rojects with only a six month time horizon need, on average, to be 5% more profitable than is optimal if companies which undertake them are not to suffer a decline in stock market value; projects with five years to maturity, however, need to be around 40% more profitable than is optimal. . . . [C]ash flows accruing more than five years in the future are discounted at twice the rate of shorter term flows.[30]

However, Miles concedes that his results could be attributed to mis-measurement of risk premiums, and that a 'substantial' range of assumptions need to be made in order to reject the null hypothesis of no short-termism in share prices.[31]

Ignoring for the moment the possibility that the behaviour of analysts and fund managers may have led to managerial short-termism through misconception, the next question is whether the evidence shows that analysts and fund managers are actually preoccupied with short-term results. (As an aside, there are two main types of analyst: those employed by stockbrokers ('sell-side analysts'), and those employed by fund-management firms[32] ('buy-side analysts').) There are at least three factors indicating that this is not the case. First, although brokers' analysts typically forecast profits and dividends for at most three years (the current year and the following two years),[33] this need not imply that brokers' analysts are taking too short-term a view.[34] In any event, analysts (or fund manager/analysts) employed by fund-management firms forecast over much longer periods. The Head of UK Institutional Investment at J. P. Morgan Investment Management Ltd. told the Trade and Industry Committee that his firm's analysts 'make long-term forecasts of companies . . . going out eight to ten years'.[35] Secondly, a comparison of the methods used by UK and German investment analysts (both sell-side and buy-side) found a remarkable similarity between the importance attached by them to various financial objectives of quoted companies.[36] The authors of the

---

[30] D. Miles, 'Testing for Short-Termism in the UK Stock Market' (1993) 103 *Econ. J* 1379, at 1394.

[31] Ibid. In spite of this, the Trade and Industry Committee, citing only Miles' study, proceeded on the basis that 'share prices apparently do not fully reflect long-term value' (n. 23 above), para. 189.

[32] Further, in some UK fund-management firms there are separate analysts and fund managers, in some firms the fund managers are also analysts, and in other firms the fund managers rely upon brokers' analysts for research material: see Ch. 5, at nn. 126–8, 143, and accompanying text.

[33] House of Commons Trade and Industry Committee, *Second Report: Competitiveness of UK Manufacturing Industry; Vol. II, Memoranda of Evidence* (1994) 270.

[34] See Marsh (n. 5 above), at 11–15.

[35] House of Commons Trade and Industry Committee, *Minutes of Evidence: Competitiveness of UK Manufacturing Industry* (1993) qu. 1257.

[36] See R. Pike, J. Meerjanssen, and L. Chadwick, 'The Appraisal of Ordinary Shares by Investment Analysts in the UK and Germany' (1993) 23 *Acc. & Bus. Research* 489.

study observed that the findings did 'not . . . support the view that British analysts take a shorter-term view than German analysts. It is the German sample which placed slightly greater weight upon short-term profitability . . .'.[37] The participating analysts were also asked to state the relative importance, for the purpose of evaluating a company's share price, of a change in 18 different pieces of non-financial information. New information about product development and about R&D were ranked the second- and third-most-important changes, respectively, by German analysts (behind new information about product quality). UK analysts ranked changes in product development and R&D as the fourth- and fifth-most-important changes, respectively (behind changes in top management, product quality, and the company's reputation).[38] Thus, whilst the quintessentially long-term matters of product development and R&D are of great importance to German securities analysts in assessing share values, they are also of considerable importance to their UK counterparts. The third factor confuting the argument that analysts and fund managers are obsessed with short-term earnings is that in 1992 the Institutional Shareholders' Committee produced a document setting out specific pieces of information regarding R&D which would be useful to institutional shareholders.[39] On top of that, *all* of the fund managers interviewed in the author's UK and Australian interview studies said that long-term strategy and R&D were matters which they typically discussed with company managements at their regular one-to-one meetings. And the institutions' evidence to the Trade and Industry Committee indicates that there is a general level of satisfaction about the amount of information provided by the companies.[40]

In summary, it is submitted that the weight of evidence suggests that 'feature' (a) of the UK and US financial systems is non-existent. However, 'claims of share price short-termism do not have to be true to be believed, and managers who subscribe to the popular myths might still be deterred from investing.'[41] That is, this may well be a prime example of managerial short-termism through misconception.

---

[37] See Pike, Meerjanssen, and Chadwick, at 495–6.   [38] Ibid., at 496–7.

[39] ISC, *Suggested Disclosure of Research and Development Expenditure* (1992). The background of that document is discussed in Ch. 4, Sec. A.1.xi.

[40] See Trade and Industry Committee (n. 33 above), at 1, 3, 15–16; (n. 35 above), at 266, 274, 278, 284, 292, 302, 304–5, 309. This suggests that things have improved since 1987, when a CBI survey of chief executives found that information on long-term plans and proposals was provided on a regular basis to major institutional shareholders and analysts by only 20% of respondents' firms in the case of expenditure on R&D, by only 6% in the case of spending on training, by 29% in the case of spending on other long-term development plans, and by 50% in the case of details of new products: CBI City/Industry Task Force (n. 23 above), at 34.

[41] Marsh (n. 5 above), at 25.

'Feature' (b). If some industrialists claim that they have been forced, by the threat of hostile takeover, to cut long-term investment in order to maximize current earnings, then accepting that that is the case does not imply (as suggested by some company managers) that institutional shareholders are partly to blame or that they have exacerbated the problem. First, it is now fairly well known that some of the largest UK institutional investors have a predisposition to support the incumbent management in a hostile-bid situation, where that management is in good standing.[42] This is borne out by the fact that almost half of the contested bids for quoted UK companies during 1984–9 failed.[43] Secondly, the charge that *the institutions'* desire for steady growth in earnings and dividends has created an atmosphere where company managements feel obliged to grow their firms through acquisition is not convincing. The present author does in fact find considerable merit in the argument that the threat of hostile takeover has effectively 'forced' some quoted firms to grow by acquisition in order to sustain an acceptable level of growth in earnings and dividends.[44] However, it is submitted that it is the UK and US 'outsider' systems of corporate ownership that have engendered a (comparatively) very high level of hostile takeovers. That is, the primary cause of the relatively high level of hostile takeovers is the arm's-length relationship between shareholders and their companies.[45] Whether those shareholders are institutions or individuals is irrelevant. Indeed, in 1969, when individuals owned 47.4%, and institutions owned only 34.2%, of

---

[42] See e.g. Trade and Industry Committee (n. 35 above), at 266, 306; House of Commons Trade and Industry Committee, *Minutes of Evidence: Takeovers and Mergers* (1991) qu. 936; R. E. Artus, 'Tension to Continue' in NAPF (n. 17 above), 12, at 13; P. D. Jackson, 'Management of UK Equity Portfolios' (1987) 27 *Bank Eng. Q Bull.* 253, at 258–9.

[43] See A. Paul, 'Corporate Governance in the Context of Takeovers of UK Public Companies' in D. D. Prentice and P. R. J. Holland (eds.), *Contemporary Issues in Corporate Governance* (1993) 135, at 141. The picture was similar for the years ended 31 Mar. 1992 (34 hostile bids; 17 unsuccessful), 1993 (25 hostile bids; 9 unsuccessful), and 1994 (17 hostile bids; 8 unsuccessful): Panel on Takeovers and Mergers, *Report on the Year Ended 31 March 1992* (1992) 15; *Report on the Year Ended 31 March 1993* (1993) 15; *Report on the year Ended 31 March 1994* (1994) 15.

[44] A comparison of matched samples of large quoted and unquoted UK firms over the period 1980–7 found that the quoted firms spent considerably more than the unquoted firms on takeovers as a proportion of capital expenditure: see C. P. Mayer and I. Alexander, *Stock Markets and Corporate Performance: A Comparison of Publicly Listed and Private Companies* (1995). Interestingly, however, five participants in the UK interview study said (unprompted) that their institutions had on numerous occasions urged company managements to slow down or stop their companies' growth by acquisition, and to concentrate on digesting the acquisitions already made. It is also plausible that many unquoted firms were taken public precisely because their owners sought a greater ability to grow by acquisition, which is provided by a stock-market listing.

[45] See nn. 91–142 below, and accompanying text.

quoted UK equities (see Table 2.1), there were about 100 hostile takeover bids for UK public companies.[46]

Thus, whilst the threat of hostile takeover may have served to distort managements' investment decisions (and indeed this book accepts that claim),[47] that does not imply short-termism on the part of the institutions. There is one qualification to this conclusion. Chapter 4 reveals that the UK institutions' policies on non-voting shares, pre-emption rights, and own-share purchase have all served—intentionally or otherwise—to limit the pre-bid takeover defences potentially available to quoted UK companies.[48] The latest evidence suggests, however, that pre-bid takeover devices have not systematically deterred takeovers in the US. Comment and Schwert examined data for the period 1975–91, covering all firms listed on the New York Stock Exchange or the American Stock Exchange, and found no evidence that State anti-takeover statutes deterred takeovers, and only very weak evidence that poison pills deterred takeovers.[49] They concluded that the demise of the market for corporate control in the US in the early 1990s was probably due to the 1990 recession and credit squeeze, rather than the widespread coverage of anti-takeover measures.[50] A study of 344 US companies by Bhagat and Jefferis found little evidence that the adoption of three different types of anti-takeover device had any deterrent effect during the mid-1980s.[51] It is, therefore, questionable whether the institutional policies which have limited (whether intentionally or otherwise) the availability to quoted UK companies of pre-bid defences have had a significant effect on the market for corporate control in Britain.

'*Feature*' *(c)*. Concerns have been expressed that there has been a high

---

[46] They were hostile in the sense that they were opposed at least initially: see The Panel on Take-overs and Mergers, *Report on the Year Ended 31st March 1969* (1969) 9. Further, hostile bids have been common in the US (e.g. there were 40 hostile bids for listed US companies in 1986: M. C. Jensen, 'Takeovers: Their Causes and Consequences' (1988) 2 *J Econ. Pers.* 21), but as recently as 1984 individuals owned 58% (and institutions owned only 27%) of the equities of listed US companies: see S. D. Prowse, 'The Structure of Corporate Ownership in Japan' (1992) 47 *J Fin.* 1121, at 1123.

[47] See nn. 91–142 below, and accompanying text.

[48] See Ch. 4, at n. 41. See also Ch. 4, Secs. A.1.i, A.1.ii, A.1.v.

[49] See R. Comment and G. W. Schwert, 'Poison or Placebo? Evidence on the Deterrence and Wealth Effects of Modern Antitakeover Measures' (1995) 39 *J Fin. Econ.* 3. The authors found that takeover premiums were higher when target firms were protected by anti-takeover measures. Although 'higher prices surely deter buyers [and therefore] this result is consistent with deterrence, [the study] fail[ed] to detect such deterrence': ibid., at 6. Thus, '[a]ntitakeover measures increase the bargaining position of target firms, but they do not prevent many transactions': ibid., at 3.   [50] Ibid., at 38.

[51] See S. Bhagat and R. H. Jefferis, *Is Defensive Activity Effective?* (1993); cf. J. Pound, 'The Effects of Antitakeover Amendments on Takeover Activity: Some Direct Evidence' (1987) 30 *J Law & Econ.* 353 (comparison of two groups of 100 companies; only one group adopted anti-takeover measures during the 1970s; 38% of the 'unprotected' companies were taken over in period to 1984, compared to only 28% of 'protected' companies).

level of turnover of shareholdings by UK institutions, and that this is an indication of short-termism.[52] Marsh demonstrates that turnover is not bad *per se*, that the rise in institutional share ownership has not led to any increase in volatility in share prices, and that differing time horizons between investors and companies is not necessarily bad or good.[53] One possibly detrimental aspect of a high level of turnover is the difficulty that this would entail for the establishment of close links between fund managers and the senior management of their portfolio companies. The crucial question is, therefore, whether the level of turnover of institutions' UK shareholdings has been high.

The turnover rate for UK equity holdings of each of the four types of UK traditional institution increased significantly from the mid-1960s until the mid-1970s, and thereafter increased more slowly until 1988.[54] Table 9.2 shows the average holding periods which can be inferred from the statistics on turnover levels. These holding periods are calculated as the reciprocal of the turnover rate ($\times$ 100), and as such are only a very rough estimate of the actual average holding periods. They are in fact underestimates of the true averages. The principal reason for this is that, amongst the larger institutions especially, it is rare for complete holdings to be traded: the larger fund managers tend to sell a relatively small proportion of a holding when the share price is considered to be high (i.e. 'top slice'), and buy back a similar amount of shares when the price is considered to be low (i.e. 'top up'); a core holding is generally retained for a considerable number of years.[55]

There is some evidence supporting the proposition that the holding

---

[52] See e.g. Innovation Advisory Board, *Innovation: City Attitudes and Practices* (1990) 13, 16.   [53] Marsh (n. 5 above), at 35–8.

[54] See the sources cited at the foot of Table 9.2. Not surprisingly, there was a similar increase in turnover on the London Stock Exchange generally. This was a feature of all major stock markets worldwide. During the 1980s both the Japanese and German stock exchanges exhibited higher rates of turnover than London: Marsh, ibid., at 39–40.

[55] See Lord Alexander of Weedon, 'Corporate Governance—The Role of the Banks' in Prentice and Holland (n. 43 above), 97, at 103. In addition, turnover levels include a significant amount of non-discretionary turnover that would have to be incurred by even a totally passive fund (e.g. reinvestment of dividends, acquisition proceeds, the sale of rights, etc.): Marsh, ibid., at 110–11. The practice of 'stock lending' is another reason why the implied average holding periods understate the true position. Stock lending is the practice of lending out securities at interest under an agreement by which ownership is transferred to the borrower, who provides collateral and pledges to deliver to the lender equivalent securities when the loan matures. It enables market-makers to meet their delivery obligations to purchasers despite being short of the required stock: Pension Law Review Committee, *Report* (1993) para. 4.9.11. Pension funds and insurance companies are the main lenders of quoted UK equities. Stock lending accounted for 9% of total turnover of the shares of the top 100 listed UK companies during 1993–4: J. L. Monk, *The Dynamics of Institutional Share Ownership in Major Quoted UK Companies* (1994). Much of the turnover in the statistical tables does not, therefore, involve the institutions disposing of entire stakes in companies.

Table 9.2 UK institutions' average holding period for quoted UK equities, 1963–88

Type of institution	Implied average period of holding quoted UK equities (years)					
	1963–7	*1968–72*	*1973–7*	*1981–3*	*1984–6*	*1988*
Insurance companies*	25.6	16.1	9.0	8.6	6.1	5.7
Pension funds	23.3	9.8	6.1	6.9	5.4	4.1
Investment trusts	9.6	6.9	4.6	3.3	2.7	2.9
Unit trusts	9.8	3.3	2.2	2.2	1.9	1.9

* Long-term funds only.

Sources: For 1963–77: Committee to Review the Functioning of Financial Institutions, *Report* (1980) 554; for 1981–6: author's calculations from information in P. D. Jackson, 'Management of UK Equity Portfolios' (1987) 27 *Bank Eng. Q. Bull.* 253, at 256; for 1988: E. V. Morgan and A. D. Morgan, *The Stock Market and Mergers in the United Kingdom* (1990) 12.

periods set out in Table 9.2 are underestimates. First, a 1993 study of the share registers of the largest 250 or so listed UK companies found that, for many of the 50 largest UK-based fund managers, the standard deviation of their holdings in those companies was very low. In the case of index-tracking fund managers, a very low standard deviation is to be expected; but the study also revealed that most of the holdings of many ostensibly 'active' managers were actually very close to index weight.[56] This suggests that many UK-based fund managers are either indexers or 'closet indexers', which maintain a core (index-weight or near index-weight) holding for many years. Secondly, the results of a 12-month study during 1993–4 of the share registers of 10 large listed UK companies suggested that the average holding period for institutional shareholders was eight years and four months. Significantly, of the 45 insurance companies and pension funds covered, only one divested itself of an entire holding during the 12-month period; and only three of the 45 unit trusts and investment trusts in the study did so.[57] Thirdly, the results of a study of the share registers of nine large listed UK companies over the period 1989–94 suggested that the average holding period of those companies' top five registered institutional shareholders was in excess of 15 years.[58] Finally, research by the author revealed that at least 32 of the constituent companies of the FT-SE 100 index at the end of 1991 had at least one

[56] Reported in 'Tracking the Behaviour of Stock Pickers', *Fin. Times*, 6 Dec. 1993, p. 16.
[57] See Monk (n. 55 above).
[58] See M. Gaved, *Ownership and Influence* (1995) 29–30.

notifiable (3%+) institutional interest-holder which was also a large interest-holder at 1976 and/or 1957. For instance, the Prudential had a holding in The General Electric Company plc of 7.03% in 1991, of 6.51% in 1976, and of 4.80% in 1957.[59] The core of this holding was definitely maintained throughout the entire 34 years covered by the study. It is reasonable to presume that in most of the other cases a core holding was likewise kept throughout the entire period of 1957–91 or 1976–91.[60]

In summary, although turnover on the London Stock Exchange increased substantially from the 1960s until the 1980s, this was mirrored on other exchanges worldwide. The traditional institutions' average holding periods for quoted UK equities have fallen since the 1960s, but those of the largest categories of traditional institution (pension funds and insurance companies) were not short at 1988 even going by the underestimates in Table 9.2. Miscellaneous pieces of evidence suggest that most of the major fund-management firms also maintain many core holdings for numerous years. The concern that a high level of turnover affects adversely the development of relationships and communication between fund managers and corporate managers would thus appear to be groundless.

'Feature' (d). A frequently cited indicator of institutional short-termism is that external investment managers of pension funds have their performance measured quarterly. This is in fact a misconstruction: whilst the performance of pension funds' *asset portfolios* is, for good reasons,[61] typically measured on a quarterly basis, the performance of their *investment managers* is normally measured over a period of five years (and only very rarely over a period of less than three years).[62] The evidence does not, in any case, show a high rate of turnover of fund managers. The CBI's Working Party on Pension Fund Investment Management found in 1987 that 45% of externally managed pension funds had not changed their investment managers in the previous five years (and 85% of internally managed funds had not done so).[63] And a 1994 study found that the average external fund manager lasted for 7.25 years with each pension-

---

[59] See App. L, Table L.1.   [60] See App. L, at n. 5.

[61] '[T]he rate at which the assets of [the] fund have grown or declined . . . could impact on decisions about discretionary benefits, contribution rates, and so on': Marsh (n. 5 above), at 33.

[62] Ibid., at 32–3; CBI, *Pension Fund Investment Management* (1987) 28–9. In 1995, the AIMA proposed the introduction of a standard three-year measurement period for the performance of Australia-based fund managers: see 'Agreed Standard Needed to Judge Returns on Funds', *Aust. Fin. Rev.*, 13 Mar. 1995, p. 28. To illustrate the unlikeliness of an asset-management consultant recommending the replacement of a fund manager due to just one quarter (or even one year) of poor performance, it is useful to consider the converse: how likely is it that a consultant would advise trustees to hire a particular fund manager based on merely one quarter (or one year) of good performance?

[63] CBI, ibid., at 56.

fund client.[64] This 'feature' of the UK financial system seems, therefore, to be a myth. But that does not discount the possibility that this seeming feature may have led to managerial short-termism through misconception. Even that, though, would be a strange outcome since it is company managers—in their capacity as trustees of their firms' pension funds—who hire and fire investment managers.

'Feature' (e). Figure 9.1 shows that the dividend pay-out ratio of UK companies has indeed been much higher than that of German and Japanese firms since the mid-1980s. The issue is whether this feature demonstrates short-termism on the part of the institutions.

As the Trade and Industry Committee pointed out, there are two criticisms in regard to the dividends paid by quoted UK companies: first, that the ratio of dividends to profits (i.e. the dividend pay-out ratio) is too high; and, secondly, that dividends are downwardly inflexible.[65] The suggestion is that a regime of high and downwardly inflexible dividends affects adversely the level of long-term investment undertaken by UK firms. This is said to be the case especially in periods of recession or economic downturn, when the latter component of the regime ensures

Figure 9.1 Dividends as proportion of net earnings of non-financial companies, 1982–93

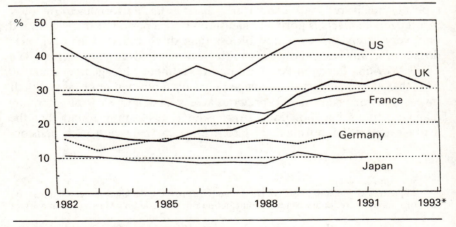

* Figure for first three quarters of 1993.

Source: House of Commons Trade and Industry Committee, *Second Report: Competitiveness of UK Manufacturing Industry* (1994) 71.

[64] Reported in 'Survey: Pension Fund Investment: "Beauty Parade" Blues', *Fin. Times*, 27 Apr. 1994, p. V.
[65] Trade and Industry Committee (n. 23 above), para. 160.

that, in the face of falling profits, companies are unable to maintain investment levels unless external financing is increased.

As regards the first criticism, there is conflicting empirical evidence. A comparison by Mayer and Alexander of the financing of 77 large listed German non-financial companies with that of 73 large listed UK non-financial companies, over the period 1982–8, found that the two groups of firms had a similar investment ratio: about 75%.[66] The UK companies were able to maintain the same level of physical investment relative to profit as the German companies, despite the fact that the dividend pay-out ratio averaged 31% for the UK firms, as opposed to only 13% for the German firms. The UK firms therefore obtained a greater proportion of their investment funds from external sources: the main sources were medium- and long-term bank loans, and trade credit.[67] Mayer and Alexander also examined the financing of a group of small quoted UK electronics firms, over 1982–8. These firms had a very high dividend pay-out ratio over the seven years: an average of 41%. However, they also had a very high investment ratio: an average of 128%. A substantial amount of the external finance for that investment was in the form of new equity issues.[68] Shareholders therefore supported rights issues to provide funds for investment, as well as taking a large slice of the annual profits as dividends. The evidence in regard to the large and the small listed companies does not support the view that the comparatively high dividend pay-out ratio of UK firms is detrimental to investment spending. The period covered in this study did not, however, include a recession—and the second criticized feature of UK dividends (their downward inflexibility) is of most significance during economic downturns.

Further, as mentioned earlier, the evidence regarding the first criticism

---

[66] C. P. Mayer and I. Alexander, 'Banks and Securities Markets: Corporate Financing in Germany and the United Kingdom' (1990) 4 *J Jap. & Inter. Econ.* 450, at 461–2. The 'investment ratio' is defined as the ratio of investment to zero-distribution profits (and is thus a measure of the financing requirements of firms).

[67] Ibid., at 458. On a gross basis, the UK companies raised a sizeable proportion (14%) of their finance from new equity issues, but on a net basis (i.e. after taking account of shares purchased in the acquisition of other companies) the UK firms were purchasers rather than raisers of equity. This suggests that large listed UK companies do have reasonably easy access to finance from rights issues, but that rights issues tend to be used to finance takeovers of other companies rather than to finance physical investment. A possible explanation is that managements generally perceive that relatively higher returns will accrue from acquisitions as opposed to internal investment projects. This in turn justifies the use of what appears to be a comparatively expensive form of finance. (After allowing for best estimates of risk aversion, the cost of equity capital would appear to be too high relative to the cost of debt: this is part of the 'equity premium puzzle', which is summarized in C. P. Mayer, 'Stock-Markets, Financial Institutions, and Corporate Performance' in N. H. Dimsdale and M. Prevezer (eds.), *Capital Markets and Corporate Governance* (1994) 179, at 180, 184–6.)

[68] New equity issues represented 35% of total finance on a gross basis, and 60% on a net basis: ibid., at 464.

is conflicting. Studies by Mayer of the financing of physical investment across the entire non-financial corporate sectors of the UK, the US, Germany, Japan, and other countries, over the period 1970–85, found that there was a comparatively greater reliance upon retained earnings and lesser reliance upon external sources of finance in the UK and the US, compared to Japan and Germany.[69] It is arguable that there is significance in the relatively small role played by outside finance in the UK and US sectors.[70] Namely, the relatively low level of capital formation in the UK and the US (see Table 9.1) is attributable (at least partly) to the lack of use of outside funding by firms, the use of which has been discouraged by a shortage of *committed and flexible* long-term external finance.[71] Mayer provides empirical evidence in support of the direction of causation.[72] Some support for this view is provided by the finding of Mayer and Alexander that medium-sized German firms relied very little on new equity issues (in marked contrast to the small listed UK electronics companies mentioned earlier), but did rely upon bank finance, a very high proportion of which was long-term.[73] A substantial proportion of bank lending to German firms is long-term, whilst a majority of UK bank lending is short-term.[74] Summarizing these findings, Mayer states that '[t]he key difference between the German and the UK financial systems comes as firms develop from being small, entrepreneurial [entities] to more mature entities. In the UK, they typically seek a stock market quotation; in Germany, they [remain unquoted for much longer and] are funded by their banks.'[75] One interpretation is that developing UK companies go public much earlier than their German counterparts because they do not have the

---

[69] See C. P. Mayer, 'New Issues in Corporate Finance' (1988) 32 *Euro. Econ. Rev.* 1167; Mayer (1987, 1990) (n. 20 above).

[70] In contrast to the Modigliani/Miller theory: see F. Modigliani and M. H. Miller, 'The Cost of Capital, Corporation Finance and the Theory of Investment' (1958) 48 *Am. Econ. Rev.* 261.

[71] See Mayer (n. 69 above), at 1180–1; cf. Mankiw (n. 20 above). The argument is not (or not necessarily) that there are 'gaps' in the capital market (i.e. that banks and financial institutions are short of funds to lend/supply to borrowers): 'Most studies of the UK financial system report that banks would be all too willing to lend more if only prospective borrowers would come forth. . . . However, a basic implication of an interrelationship between finance and investment is that a clear distinction between financial and corporate performance cannot be drawn. If borrowers cannot raise finance on sufficiently attractive terms, *which include control over future uncontracted outcomes* as well as more explicit measures, such as the interest rate, then there will be inadequate demand for investment funds': Mayer (1987) (n. 20 above), at viii. (Emphasis added.)

[72] See Mayer (1987, 1990) (n. 20 above) (firms in fast-growth sectors relied even more than the average firm upon retained earnings as opposed to external financing).

[73] Mayer and Alexander (n. 66 above), at 465–6.

[74] Ibid., at 466.

[75] C. P. Mayer, *The Functioning of the UK Financial System: What's Wrong with London?* (1991).

option of growing through long-term 'committed' bank finance. Whether or not most UK firms obtain a stock-market quotation voluntarily,[76] it is argued below that, once quoted and widely held, UK companies operate within an ownership and governance structure that embodies an inherent short-termism.

In regard to the second criticism, some participants in the dividend debate have an exaggerated perception of the extent of the downward inflexibility of dividends in the UK quoted company sector. Marsh conducted a study of nearly 6,000 dividend announcements made by listed UK companies over the period January 1989 to April 1992.[77] In the first three months of the study, dividend increases accounted for over 80% of announcements, whilst reductions and omissions accounted for only about 3%. Thereafter (as the UK economy went into recession), dividend increases showed a steady proportionate decline throughout the sample period (to about 25% of announcements by the first quarter of 1992). Importantly, in each quarter from the last quarter of 1990 until the end of the study period, dividend cuts and omissions accounted for between roughly 15–25% of announcements.[78] These figures are consistent with the general policy of UK institutions, which is that dividends should not be cut if there is (what the company management judges to be) a *temporary* fall in profits.[79]

Nevertheless, contrasted with dividends of unquoted UK companies[80] and quoted German companies,[81] dividends of quoted UK companies are inflexible downwards. During the UK recession of the early 1990s, industrially financed R&D spending fell by 10% in real terms, and investment spending as a whole also fell considerably in real terms.[82]

---

[76] On this point, see Mayer and Alexander (n. 66 above); Mayer, ibid.; and n. 44 above. For a comparison of the evolution of ownership and control following stock-market floatation in the UK and Germany, respectively, see: M. J. Brennan and J. R. Franks, *Underpricing, Ownership and Control in Initial Public Offerings of Equity Securities in the UK* (1995); M. G. J. Goergen, *The Evolution of Ownership and Control in German IPOs* (1995).

[77] P. R. Marsh, *Dividend Announcements and Stock Price Performance* (1992).

[78] A study of companies from the lowest-performing quintile of listed UK companies (measured by share-price performance) in 1985 found that 25% of the companies omitted their dividend and a further 16% reduced it. The dividend was held constant in 29% of cases, and was increased in the remaining 30% of cases: see J. R. Franks and C. P. Mayer, 'Hostile Takeovers in the UK and the Correction of Managerial Failure' (1996) 40 *J Fin. Econ.* (forthcoming).

[79] Whilst this is the basic position, there are many interpretations: see 'A Corporate Conundrum', *Fin. Times*, 26 Jan. 1991, p. 8; Trade and Industry Committee (n. 35 above), qus. 1135, 1218–20, 1223, 1283–5, 1332 (indeed, M&G is not as inflexible as many appear to believe: see qus. 1051, 1073–80, 1101). See also the discussion of institutional involvement in the matter of 'enhanced scrip dividends', in Ch. 4, Sec. A.1.iii.

[80] Mayer and Alexander (n. 44 above), at Table 13, found that, in one sample of paired unquoted and quoted UK firms, the average number of dividend cuts ran at a 5:1 ratio (unquoted:quoted) over 1980–87.   [81] See Mayer (n. 67 above), at 184.

[82] See Trade and Industry Committee (n. 23 above), paras. 117, 166, 167.

Whereas some UK firms are able to reduce their dividends so as to maintain, or more likely minimize the reduction in, their investment spending, German firms that underwent restructurings during the 1980s were found to have 'invariably maintained *and sometimes increased* their expenditures on R&D and employee training'.[83] The retort that UK companies can raise money through rights issues and bank finance to maintain investment when a fall in profits (and relatively inflexible dividends) leaves less (or no) retained earnings for investment[84] is not persuasive. The results of a recent study covering 626 quoted UK manufacturing companies, over the period 1971–86, suggest that the investment spending of a significant fraction of large UK companies is likely to be affected by the availability of internal finance, reflecting some constraint on the ability of those firms to raise external finance for investment.[85] External finance does not appear to be a perfect substitute for internal finance.[86]

Dividends arguably play two roles in the UK and US outsider systems of corporate ownership and governance which are performed by other mechanisms in the Japanese and German insider systems. First, it is arguable that relatively high dividends have a role to play in reducing the divergence between the interests of shareholders and managers in the widely held quoted companies of the UK and the US.[87] This is unnecessary in Germany and Japan where banks and large corporate or family shareholders are in a closer relationship with corporate managements and can monitor them from the 'inside'.[88] Secondly, the downward inflexibility of dividends probably reflects their use as a 'signalling' device—to convey information to outside investors about the firm's future earnings.[89] A central ground rule of the dividend policies of UK quoted companies is that only a drop in current earnings that is expected to persist for some time (one to five years, depending on the company) is likely to elicit a dividend reduction.[90] The closer relationship between company managements and

---

[83] Mayer (n. 75 above). (Emphasis added.) The philosophy of the German managers concerned was that 'their past policies [had] failed; they need[ed] to develop new markets; and therefore they need[ed] to invest more in R&D and training': ibid.

[84] See e.g. Marsh (n. 5 above), at 27.

[85] See S. R. Bond and C. Meghir, 'Financial Constraints and Company Investment' (1994) 15(2) *Fiscal Stud.* 1. [86] See also n. 71 above.

[87] See e.g. F. H. Easterbrook, 'Two Agency-Cost Explanations of Dividends' (1984) 74 *Am. Econ. Rev.* 650; M. C. Jensen, 'Agency Costs of Free Cash Flow, Corporate Finance, and Takeovers' (1986) 76 *Am. Econ. Rev.—Papers & Proc.* 323.

[88] See further Ch. 10, Sec. B.1.i.

[89] See J. S. S. Edwards, 'Recent Developments in the Theory of Corporate Finance' (1987) 3 (4) *Ox. Rev. Econ. Pol.* 1, at 9–11; Marsh (n. 77 above).

[90] See Marsh, ibid. (citing J. S. S. Edwards and C. P. Mayer, *An Investigation into the Dividend and New Equity Practices of Firms: Evidence from Survey Information* (1986)).

investors in insider systems means that the flexibility of dividends is not subject to this restriction.

It is submitted that the above-described nature of dividends in the UK quoted company sector is a symptom of a form of short-termism inherent in the UK and US outsider systems of corporate ownership and governance. Inherent short-termism has nothing to do with share prices, the rate of turnover of shares, the time-scale within which the performance of fund managers is measured, *or* institutional shareholders *per se*. Rather, it is a result of the fact that the ultimate controllers (i.e. equity shareholders) of large and medium-sized UK and US companies are generally arm's-length investors whereas the ultimate controllers of large and medium-sized German and Japanese companies are normally tied closely ('committed') to the company. Significantly, there would be inherent short-termism in the UK quoted company sector even if individuals rather than institutions dominated the share registers; it is the arm's-length relationship that is the determinative factor.

What does this inherent short-termism comprise? It is probably not best described as a positive pressure on company managements to maximize short-term earnings to the detriment of long-term investment. Rather, it is probably best thought of in the negative sense of a lack of incentives for managements, and of underlying structures to enable managements, to look to the long term. Essentially, the implicit contracts associated with the Japanese and German corporate sectors,[91] which are crucial in providing a basis for long-term committed relationships between investors, managers, employees, suppliers, and customers, simply do not arise in the UK and US quoted corporate sectors.[92] The domination of the share registers of UK and US quoted companies by arm's-length investors, as opposed to the committed or 'stable' shareholders which have controlling stakes in German and Japanese quoted companies (as described below), provides the explanation:

> In general, the more liquid the market for the transfer of [control], the less credible will be any commitments that the shareholders enter into that rest on non-contractual means of implementation. The reason is that liquidity, or an

---

[91] See e.g. W. C. Kester, 'Industrial Groups as Systems of Contractual Governance' (1992) 8 (3) *Ox. Rev. Econ. Pol.* 24, at 27: '[I]mplicit, relational contract[s] [are] founded on enduring trust relationships and reinforced by largely non-legalistic mechanisms structured to encourage voluntary compliance with informal agreements'; see also R. J. Gilson and M. J. Roe, 'Understanding the Japanese Keiretsu: Overlaps Between Corporate Governance and Industrial Organization' (1993) 102 *Yale LJ* 871.

[92] See T. Jenkinson and C. P. Mayer, 'The Assessment: Corporate Governance and Corporate Control' (1992) 8 (3) *Ox. Rev. Econ. Pol.* 1, at 8.

active market for [corporate control], makes it very easy for shareholders to 'escape' from implicit or non-contractible agreements.[93]

Franks and Mayer enunciate the full implications:

> *[E]x ante* incentives to invest [for the long-term] are affected by risks of *ex post* expropriation. The possibility that managers and employees may be denied the benefits of their firm-specific investments by changes in ownership may discourage them from engaging in these investments in the first place. For example, employees may be unwilling to incur the costs of firm-specific training in the absence of assurance that benefits will accrue to them. If formal *and informal* contractual arrangements between employees, employers and their owners are inadequate, there will be insufficient investment by firms and their employees and too much emphasis on investments of a general rather than a firm-specific nature. Investment in long-term training may, therefore, be discouraged. Likewise, investment in R&D and other long-term projects that reward managers on the basis of performance may require long-term [express] contracts to provide adequate incentives.[94]

Hostile takeovers (and the more-or-less constant threat of hostile takeover faced by company managements) are a natural consequence of the outsider ownership structure of UK and US quoted companies.[95] They are, on the other hand, very rare in Germany and Japan,[96] where a controlling equity stake is typically in the hands of one committed shareholder (in the case of German companies),[97] or a group of 'stable shareholders' (in the case of

---

[93] P. Sheard, 'Interlocking Shareholdings and Corporate Governance' in M. Aoki and R. P. Dore (eds.), *The Japanese Firm: The Sources of Competitive Strength* (1994) 310, at 323; see also Gilson and Roe (n. 91 above).

[94] J. R. Franks and C. P. Mayer, 'Capital Markets and Corporate Control: A Study of France, Germany and the UK' (1990) 10 *Econ. Pol.* 189, at 214 (emphasis added); see also Mayer (n. 69 above), at 1180–3; O. Hart and J. Moore, 'A Theory of Debt Based on the Inalienability of Human Capital' (1994) 109 *Q J Econ.* 841; Gilson and Roe, ibid., at 887: 'In the Berle-Means corporation, equity has governance rights because the holder of the residual profits interest has the best incentive to reduce agency costs. . . . In contrast, in our Japanese model, a big slice of equity serves not just to encourage monitoring through ownership of the residual profits interest, but also to encourage relation-specific investment by reducing opportunism as well.'

[95] In the UK, there were 18 hostile bids in 1984; 30 in 1985; 44 in 1986; 28 in 1987; 28 in 1988; and 26 in 1989: Paul (n. 43 above). As demonstrated at n. 46 above, and accompanying text, the hostile-bid mechanism is unaffected by whether the arm's-length shareholders are mainly institutions or mainly individuals.

[96] There were only four hostile bids in Germany between 1945–93, but three of these occurred between 1989–91: J. R. Franks and C. P. Mayer, 'German Capital Markets, Corporate Control and the Obstacles to Hostile Takeovers: Lessons from Three Case Studies' in Coffee, Gilson, and Lowenstein (n. 17 above); similarly, 'the [hostile] takeover . . . mechanism hardly operates in Japan': Sheard (n. 93 above), at 310.

[97] In 1990, 146 (i.e. 85.4%) of 171 of the largest quoted German industrial companies had at least one equity shareholder with a stake of 25% or more. The main categories of large stakeholder were other (mostly German) companies (17 stakes of 25–50%; 37 stakes above 50%) and family groups (11 stakes of 25–50%; 28 stakes above 50%): Franks and Mayer,

Japanese companies).[98] The fundamental distinction is thus between the type of ultimate controller: arm's-length investors or committed shareholder(s).[99]

There are three observations about, and three qualifications to, the above propositions. The first observation concerns the proposition that the fundamental difference between the outsider and insider systems of corporate governance relates to the nature of the shareholders who or which are in the position of ultimate control. Jenkinson and Mayer, and Franks and Mayer, argue that, in addition to the ownership structure of companies, there is a second central component to international differences in the incidence of hostile takeovers: the legal form of companies.[100] They point to the fact that every German public company (*Aktiengesellschaft*), and every German private company (*Gesellschaft mit beschränkter Haftung*) with 500 or more employees, must have a supervisory board (*Aufsichtsrat*) with employee as well as shareholder representation. The supervisory board appoints and monitors the managing board (*Vorstand*). For companies with 2,000 or less employees, the employee representatives make up one-third of the supervisory board; for those with more than 2,000 employees, half of the supervisory board consists of employee representatives. Jenkinson and Mayer note that the shareholder representatives on supervisory boards are commonly representatives of other companies,[101] and continue:

ibid. Where there is no such large stakeholder, voting-right restrictions are common. These normally restrict the votes that can be cast by any one shareholder to a specified proportion (say 5% or 10%) of the total votes, regardless of the size of the actual shareholding. However, since quoted companies lacking a 25%+ shareholder are rare, companies with voting-right restrictions are relatively rare: only 19 of the 171 companies referred to above had them (17 of those companies lacked a 25%+ shareholder): Franks and Mayer, ibid. Controlling equity stakes are also the major barrier to hostile takeovers in the other major EU countries (other than Holland): see Department of Trade and Industry, *Barriers to Takeovers in the European Community* (1989) 22 (hence the study's conclusion that 'achieving a technical "openness" to contested bids may be of little practical impact . . . unless the underlying patterns of shareholders come to change').

[98] Japanese 'stable shareholding arrangements' (*antei kabunushi kosaku*) involve reciprocal shareholdings between transaction partners (banks, insurance companies, suppliers, customers, and trading companies) and affiliated firms. The individual shareholdings are typically about 1% for non-financial firms and 2–5% for financial institutions. Taken together, shares held in this way usually constitute a majority of the firm's issued shares. Stable shareholders agree implicitly not to sell their shares to third parties unsympathetic to the incumbent management: see Sheard (n. 93 above).

[99] Of course, banks also play a crucial role in the systems of corporate governance in Germany and Japan: see further Ch. 10, Sec. B.1.i.

[100] See Jenkinson and Mayer (n. 92 above), at 5–7; Franks and Mayer (n. 24 above).

[101] Note that not all shareholder representatives represent an equity holder. A 1979 study of the supervisory boards of German public companies with more than 2,000 employees found that, on a typical supervisory board, German non-banking companies provided about 40% of the shareholder representatives, but almost half of those companies did not have an equity

Boards with representatives from other companies rather than individual members may provide not only a greater degree of continuity but more significantly a greater assurance of good governance. The representative of a prominent German firm has his firm's reputation at stake; an individual has his or her own reputation at stake—individuals come and go but German firms go on for ever.[102]

They then suggest that hostile takeovers in the UK and the US 'are the product of dispersed shareholdings *and comparatively ineffective boards*'.[103] The implication is that a more effective board structure and composition would result in fewer hostile takeovers in the UK. This is inconsistent with the finding (of a recent study of UK hostile bids, discussed in Chapter 1) that the market for corporate control is a market in contending prospective strategies for firms rather than a mechanism for correcting past poor performance of firms.[104] Although changes to the legal requirements for board structure and board representation may see a reduction in those hostile bids which involve a well-managed firm bidding for a poorly managed firm, such changes are, it is submitted, very unlikely to have any effect upon the bulk of hostile bids—which have more to do with the strategy of the bidder than the performance of the target. Further support for this view is found in the fact that Japanese boards are single tier, with no employee representation either required or observed in practice, and hostile takeovers are virtually non-existent in Japan. In summary, the one cardinal factor affecting the likelihood of hostile takeovers is the nature of the shareholders who or which are in the position of ultimate control: are they arm's-length investors or committed share-holders?

This leads to the second observation, which concerns the reason(s) why the (ultimate) controlling shareholders in most German and Japanese quoted companies are committed shareholders whilst those in most UK and US quoted companies are arm's-length investors. Mayer suggests that, not only the active market for corporate control, but also 'the UK system of dispersed ownership . . . has emerged as a response to inadequate internal mechanisms of control. [The UK is] now locked into a system that *requires dispersed ownership* and markets for corporate control *because of*

stake in the company: see J. S. S. Edwards and K. Fischer, *Banks, Finance and Investment in Germany* (1994) 211. (A significant proportion may of course have been suppliers and customers of the company.)

[102] Jenkinson and Mayer (n. 92 above), at 8.

[103] Ibid. (Emphasis added.) The same argument is made in C. P. Mayer, *Ownership* (1993).

[104] See Ch. 1, at nn. 62–5, and accompanying text. See also T. Jenkinson and C. P. Mayer, *Takeover Defence Strategies* (1991) 33 (finding a relationship between hostile bids and the corporate strategy of the bidder).

poorly performing mechanisms for changing control within firms.'[105] The present author argues, however, that there is little or no causal connection between the legal rules regulating, or the effectiveness of, the board structure of quoted UK companies and the fact that the ultimate controllers of such companies are arm's-length investors. But it has also been argued that the UK regulatory structure in a broader sense has been a cause of the arm's-length relationship between shareholders and company managements in the UK:

> Regulation may go a long way towards explaining patterns of ownership and control changes in different countries. In the UK, stock exchange and takeover codes have discouraged direct investor involvement in corporate control, for example, by limiting share stakes that can be accumulated without requiring full takeover bids to be made. . . . The Stock Exchange has discouraged the use of discriminatory voting rights. . . . Insider trading laws discourage privileged access to information. . . . The rationale behind these rules and regulations is the promotion of securities markets. Equal access to information and protection of small investors from exploitation by dominant shareholders are regarded as central to that process.[106]

It is not presently disputed that these regulations are designed to maintain the 'integrity' of the liquid securities market. However, it is doubted that they explain the present situation in the UK where the ultimate controllers are normally arm's-length investors. There are two reasons for this view.

First, it appears that arm's-length investors have been a feature of many large English companies ever since the birth of the joint-stock company in 1553.[107] The stock market assumed extra importance when Britain went through the Industrial Revolution:

> [Britain's] industrialisation took place as a result of the myriad activities of small family-controlled enterprises which financed their operations from the wealth of their controlling families and with the support of local country banks. The big London banks . . . took no active part in funding the manufacturers, and those enterprises which sought to expand had to raise new capital through the sale of their shares in the stock exchange.[108]

Similarly, Allen states that in 'the second half of the nineteenth century the stock market played an important role in the financing of industry in the

---

[105] Mayer (n. 103 above). (Emphasis added.)
[106] Franks and Mayer (n. 94 above), at 209–10. For a somewhat similar thesis in regard to the US, see M. J. Roe, 'A Political Theory of American Corporate Finance' (1991) 91 *Colum. L Rev.* 10; cf. J. C. Coffee, 'Liquidity Versus Control: The Institutional Investor as Corporate Monitor' (1991) 91 *Colum. L Rev.* 1277, at 1313–17 (evidence that the relative passivity of US institutional shareholders is not attributable mainly to regulatory restrictions on monitoring).
[107] See W. R. Scott, *The Constitution and Finance of English, Scottish and Irish Joint Stock Companies to 1712*, vol. I (1912) 45; A. B. Du Bois, *The English Business Company After the Bubble Act 1720–1800* (1938) 27, 289.
[108] J. Scott, *Capitalist Property and Financial Power* (1986) 2.

UK. . . . [R]oughly one-quarter of capital formation was raised through the London Stock Exchange in 1853; by 1913 this had grown to one-third.'[109] This external equity finance was raised from *rentiers* and other wealthy individuals,[110] who were investors rather than committed business partners. It seems that banks simply were not needed to supply large amounts of debt and equity finance to UK firms during the mid-to-late nineteenth century.[111] There certainly was no regulatory restriction on them owning equity.[112] Thus, arm's-length investors, and a liquid stock market, have a long history in the UK. On the other hand, insider dealing was not outlawed in the UK until 1980,[113] the *Takeover Code* (with its 30% mandatory-bid rule) goes back only to 1959,[114] and the opposition to non-voting shares by the Stock Exchange (and institutional investors) dates back only to the 1950s. The dominant position of arm's-length investors predates those regulations.

Secondly, a comparison of overseas jurisdictions suggests no causal connection between regulations and the type of controlling shareholders (arm's length or committed). In Japan, the stable shareholders each have only a relatively small holding,[115] and banks are in fact precluded from holding more than 5% of the equity of any domestic company. In the light of this, it is clear that it would be possible for committed (rather than arm's-length) shareholders to control quoted UK companies even with the

[109] F. Allen, 'Stock Markets and Resource Allocation', in C. P. Mayer and X. Vives (eds.), *Capital Markets and Financial Intermediation* (1993) 81.

[110] '[A] broad cross-section of the well-to-do': E. R. Schneider-Lenné, 'Corporate Control in Germany' (1992) 8 (3) *Ox. Rev. Econ. Pol.* 11, at 18.

[111] In contrast, when German industrialization began, 'a deficiency of savings coupled with the lack of a developed [stock market meant that] banks had to assume an active role both by granting credit and injecting equity capital': Schneider-Lenné, ibid. See also R. B. H. Hauswald, *On the Origins of Universal Banking: An Analysis of the German Banking Sector 1848 to 1910* (1995). In Japan, 'economic development occurred under the aegis of wealthy families which used the massive banks and trading companies which they owned to build up large manufacturing enterprises and to exercise control over their operations. This control . . . could be reinforced by the establishment of shareholding relations among the enterprises, but at no stage was the stock exchange *per se* an important element in the process.': Scott (n. 108 above), at 4.

[112] However, from World War II until the late 1970s, the Bank of England discouraged banks from holding equity, by not counting any equity holdings as part of a bank's required regulatory capital: see B. S. Black and J. C. Coffee, 'Hail Britannia? Institutional Investor Behavior Under Limited Regulation' (1994) 92 *Mich. L Rev.* 1997, at 2066. Nevertheless, before, during, and after this period banks owned an insignificant amount of the quoted UK equity market. See Ch. 2, Table 2.1, for holdings between 1963–94.

[113] See Companies Act 1980, ss. 68–73; see now Criminal Justice Act 1993, Pt. V.

[114] The forerunner of the *Takeover Code* was a document published by the Issuing Houses Association, *Notes for the Amalgamation of British Businesses* (1959). Partial bids were originally banned altogether, but are now possible with the Panel's consent (although they are discouraged): *Takeover Code*, Rule 36.1.   [115] See n. 98 above.

mandatory-bid rule in place.[116] On the same point, there is no mandatory-bid rule in the US, but its absence has not led to German-style committed shareholders with stakes of 25% or more. As regards the prohibition on insider dealing, the committed shareholders of German and Japanese companies do not actively trade their holdings. Any would-be committed shareholders of UK companies would therefore have nothing to fear from insider-dealing legislation if they proposed (as by definition they would) not to actively trade their holdings.[117] Finally, it was shown in Chapter 8 that about half of all quoted Australian companies have a controlling non-institutional shareholder.[118] This situation exists despite the fact that the Australian companies legislation contains a mandatory-bid rule with a 20% threshold,[119] and provisions outlawing insider trading.[120]

The last comment leads to the third observation about inherent short-termism. The discussion so far has related to the UK. There is, however, every reason to believe that inherent short-termism affects those 50% or so of quoted Australian companies which are widely held, and lack a controlling shareholder. Hostile takeovers are prevalent in Australia,[121] because the share registers of non-controlled companies are dominated by institutional and individual shareholders[122] (who have an arm's-length relationship with the company managements). The controlled companies, on the other hand, do not face the threat of hostile takeover. Nevertheless, it is insightful to contrast the family-controlled with the company-controlled listed companies. The management, employees, suppliers, and customers of the latter seem to have a fairly stable control environment

---

[116] Note, however, that typically some Japanese stable shareholders are suppliers and customers of the company concerned (see ibid.). Stable shareholders of this type may fall foul of the anti-trust provisions of the Fair Trading Act 1973. The committed corporate shareholders of quoted German companies are, however, only rarely trading partners: see Mayer (n. 103 above). Regard would also have to be had to the *Takeover Code*, Rule 9, under which persons 'acting in concert' and holding between 30–50% of the voting rights must make a full bid if they acquire (in a 12-month period) additional shares carrying more than 1% of the votes.

[117] In addition, insider dealing became an offence in Germany in Aug. 1994 under the Financial Markets Promotion Act (*Finanzmarktförderungsgesetz*) (implementing Directive 89/592/EC). Prior to then, many banks and companies followed a voluntary code of conduct outlawing insider dealing: 'Survey: German Banking and Finance: A Tightening of the Rules', *Fin. Times*, 31 May 1994, p. II.

[118] See Ch. 8, at nn. 73–6, and accompanying text.

[119] CL, ch. 6. Certain limited types of partial bids are, however, allowed: CL, s. 635(b).

[120] CL, Part 7.11, Div. 2A.

[121] There were 70 hostile bids in 1988; 30 in 1989; 12 in 1990; and 22 in 1991: I. M. Ramsay, 'Corporate Governance, Shareholder Litigation and the Prospects for a Statutory Derivative Action' (1992) 15 *UNSWLJ* 149, at 154.

[122] This is discernible easily from the aggregate figures in Table 2.2, when it is borne in mind that the holdings of 'other companies' and 'overseas' are mostly large stakes in controlled companies.

within which to build relationships. However, it is probable that the controlling shareholders of many family-controlled listed companies are gradually ceding more and more control to outside investors (mainly institutions), due to a relative[123] lack of long-term bank finance.[124] The non-shareholder stakeholders in these firms may not, therefore, act on the assumption that these companies will be in a stable state of ownership over the long term.

The first qualification to the proposition about inherent short-termism relates to the comparison of matched samples of large quoted and unquoted UK firms carried out by Mayer and Alexander.[125] The study found, first, that the quoted companies grew more rapidly, displayed higher labour productivity, raised more medium- and long-term debt finance, were more profitable, and were more concentrated in high-technology industries. However, secondly, the quoted companies also had a higher dividend pay-out ratio, reduced their dividends much less freely, and spent substantially more on takeovers in relation to physical investment. The first group of findings indicates that the quoted firms were run considerably more efficiently than the unquoted firms. This supports the hypothesis that the 'discipline' of the stock market reduces agency costs. However, one finding from the first group, and all three findings from the second group, appear to be empirical support for the proposition that there is inherent short-termism in the UK quoted company sector. The finding that unquoted firms raised considerably less medium- and long-term bank finance is consistent with the argument that unquoted UK firms which require a large injection of external finance must turn to the stock market rather than to banks.[126] The second group of findings is consistent with the arguments that (a) the disciplinary effect of the market for corporate control causes many companies to grow by acquisition rather than organically, in order to sustain an adequate level of dividend growth;[127] and (b) quoted UK firms are more likely than unquoted UK firms (and German or Japanese firms) to cut investment rather than dividends in periods of economic downturn.

The second qualification regarding inherent short-termism is that, although the UK and US outsider systems seem to be at a competitive disadvantage (due to inherent short-termism) in co-operative activities that

---

[123] Compared to Germany and Japan.

[124] There seems to be little information as to the ratio of short-term to medium- and long-term bank lending in Australia. However, the indications are that a majority of bank lending to business is short-term: see Industry Commission (n. 19 above), at 96–8, 131; see also nn. 73–6 above, and accompanying text.

[125] See Mayer and Alexander (n. 44 above).

[126] See text accompanying nn. 73–76 above.

[127] See nn. 44–46 above, and accompanying text.

involve several different stakeholders (for example product development, and specialized products which require skilled labour forces),[128] they appear to have a competitive advantage in speculative ventures, such as oil exploration, pharmaceuticals, and biotechnology.[129] The latter clearly involve large amounts of investment spending but, crucially, it is investment which has a high resale value outside the firm, whereas investment in firm-specific assets such as employee training and pure research has a low resale value outside the firm.[130] The UK and US outsider systems also seem to have a competitive advantage in industries subject to rapid changes in the competitive environment.[131]

The third qualification concerns the durability of the German and Japanese insider systems of corporate ownership and governance. One commentator has suggested that '[t]he rise of an international capital market may spell the end for financial monitors in internal capital markets'.[132] It is true that there have been some changes, including a reduction in the dependence of German and Japanese firms upon bank finance, a reduction in the equity holdings of German banks, and a reduction in the number of supervisory-board seats held by German banks.[133] In 1993, Daimler-Benz took the unprecedented step of listing on the New York Stock Exchange (although there was no rush by other German firms to follow suit).[134] However, there are good reasons for believing that substantial changes to the insider systems are unlikely: (a) although the equity holdings of German banks have been falling, it is non-financial corporations and families that account for the bulk of the 25%-or-larger stakes in quoted German firms;[135] (b) activism by overseas

---

[128] See Mayer (n. 67 above), at 191.

[129] See Franks and Mayer (n. 24 above); Allen (n. 109 above), at 102: 'In industries where there is little consensus on how the firms should be managed, an allocation of resources through a stock market [rather than banks] is desirable.' See also H. Hax, 'Debt and Investment Policy in German Firms: The Issue of Capital Shortage' (1990) 146 *J Inst. & Theor. Econ.* 106.

[130] See Franks and Mayer (n. 94 above), at 194.

[131] See R. J. Gilson, 'Corporate Governance and Economic Efficiency' in M. Isaksson and R. Skog (eds.), *Aspects of Corporate Governance* (1994) 131.

[132] Coffee (n. 106 above), at 1302.

[133] See C. F. Sabel, J. R. Griffin, and R. E. Deeg, 'Making Money Talk: Towards a New Debtor-Creditor Relation in German Banking' in Coffee, Gilson, and Lowenstein (n. 17 above); J. Esser, 'Bank Power in West Germany Revised' (1990) 13 *West Eur. Pol.* 17; 'Cracks Around the Edges', *Fin. Times*, 27 Feb. 1995, p. 11.

[134] See 'Daimler-Benz Gears Up for a Drive on the Freeway', *Fin. Times*, 29 Apr. 1993, p. 18. It had the modest aim of increasing the percentage of its shares owned by US investors from 6.5% to 10%, but only achieved 8%: 'Daimler Considers Anglo–US Policy on Dividends', *Fin. Times*, 8 July 1994, p. 19.

[135] See n. 97 above.

institutions and small German shareholders has occurred recently,[136] but will achieve little structural change so long as the large family and inter-corporate stakes exist; (c) the EC takeover directive seems to be irreconcilably stalled,[137] and in any event its adoption would have little effect upon the structure of shareholding in the German quoted sector;[138] and (d) the evidence suggests that the Japanese system has not altered much in recent years.[139]

In summary, there *is* a form of short-termism inherent in the UK quoted corporate sector, but it is not of a type which might be worsened if steps were taken aimed at enhancing institutional monitoring. Indeed, a closer relationship between institutions and corporate managements may well be beneficial in this respect. Any benefit would probably only be marginal, however, because, so long as the hostile takeover (and the threat of hostile takeover) remains a centre-piece of the UK and US systems of corporate governance, there will be a lack of incentives for managements, and of underlying structures to enable managements, to look to the long term.[140] The market for corporate control will remain at the centre of the UK and US systems whilst share registers are dominated by arm's-length investors.

---

[136] See e.g. 'Investors Seek More European Rights', *Fin. Times*, 15 July 1992, p. 27; 'Assault on Corporate Germany's Defences', *Fin. Times*, 22 Dec. 1992, p. 17; 'Demand for Shareholder Equality at Siemens', *Fin. Times*, 11 Mar. 1993, p. 32.

[137] See M. Andenas, 'The Future of EC Company Law Harmonisation' (1994) 15 *Co. Law.* 121.   [138] See nn. 113–20 above, and accompanying text.

[139] See J. Corbett, 'An Overview of the Japanese Financial System' in Dimsdale and Prevezer (n. 67 above), at 306.

[140] Note that this view should not be interpreted as implicitly endorsing proposals such as the one set out in M. Lipton and S. A. Rosenblum, 'A New System of Corporate Governance: The Quinquennial Election of Directors' (1991) 58 *U Chic. L Rev*. 187. Under the Lipton and Rosenblum proposal, the board of directors would be elected for a five-year term. Further, between the five-yearly elections: (a) no hostile takeovers would be possible (the board's consent would be required for any takeover, and for any acquisition of more than 10% of the equity); and (b) shareholders would not be able to remove directors except for illegal conduct. Whilst item (a) would address the short-termism problem, item (b) would leave the directors effectively unaccountable for five years. Of course, members of the managing board of a German public company are normally appointed for the statutory maximum term of five years, and can be dismissed before the expiry of that term by the supervisory board only for an 'important reason' (*Aktiengesetz*, s. 84(3)) (important reasons include a serious neglect of duty; inability to conduct business in an orderly manner; or the withdrawal of confidence by the shareholders' general meeting): Edwards and Fischer (n. 101 above), at 191. However, in practice, 'members of the board of managing directors who no longer have the confidence of the supervisory board may well resign of their own accord': Schneider-Lenné (n. 110 above), at 17. If shareholders of UK quoted companies were disenfranchised in the manner suggested by Lipton and Rosenblum, it is to be doubted that non-executive directors would be in a position effectively to monitor the executive directors: see Ch. 5, Sec. D.2.ii.(c) (evidence from author's UK interview study suggesting that non-executives only very rarely act against under-performing or unacceptable executive directors without prompting and support from institutional shareholders). The implicit threat of being voted out of office by the shareholders (see CA 1985, s. 303) would appear to have been crucial in non-executive-led boardroom coups.

It has been suggested that there are historical reasons for the dominance of arm's-length, rather than committed, shareholders in the UK quoted corporate sector. It is submitted that there is very little, by way of regulatory change, that can be done so as to replace the UK's arm's-length investors with committed shareholders.[141] The final chapter contains some modest proposals which may bring institutional shareholders into a closer relationship with company managements, but none of these would alter the essentially arm's-length character of the existing relationship. These proposals may, however, reduce 'managerial short-termism through misconception'.[142]

2. DETRIMENT TO INTERESTS OF OTHER STAKEHOLDERS

Vagts notes that 'those who feel that what is wrong with the corporation is that it does not adequately take into account the interests of . . . groups [other than shareholders] will not applaud any move that gives the shareholders more effective influence'.[143] Although a reference to US companies,[144] this issue is, for two reasons, of particular relevance to the UK and Australia.

First, as mentioned in the opening chapter, (a) in the UK and Australia, directors and senior executives owe their fiduciary and other duties to the company as a legal entity; but (b) under the general law the 'interests of the company' means, whilst the company is solvent, the interests of the

---

[141] The only potential committed shareholders are (a) other quoted companies; (b) banks; and (c) the institutions. Regarding (a) and (b), there seems to be little or no desire amongst UK industrial companies or banks to take large equity stakes (or even small Japanese-style interlocking stakes) in quoted firms. A relaxation of rules governing insider dealing, takeovers, and differential-voting shares would, it is argued, have little effect here: see nn. 113–120 above, and accompanying text. As for the institutions, seemingly the only way to force them into the role of committed shareholders would be to require them to hold 20%+ stakes (for such a proposal, see Coffee (n. 106 above), at 1355–7), and to place severe restrictions on the disposal of such stakes. This is too radical (and hence too improbable politically) for serious consideration.

[142] It is recognized that other factors have impacted adversely upon the level of long-term investment in the UK and the US: see n. 21 above, and accompanying text; Marsh (n. 5 above), at 52–79. Note, however, that the comparatively poor level of vocational training in the UK is cited often as a supply-side factor affecting the level of investment (see e.g. Marsh, ibid., at 76). The arguments made at nn. 91–4 above, and accompanying text, indicate, on the other hand, that the willingness of employees to undertake, and of employers to provide for, such training is constrained by the inherent short-termism in the UK quoted corporate sector.

[143] D. F. Vagts, 'Reforming the "Modern" Corporation: Perspectives from the German' (1966) 80 *Harv. L Rev.* 23, at 49.

[144] The comment would have less relevance in many US states now, since the passing of the 'constituency statutes', which empower directors to have regard also to the interests of non-shareholder constituencies (typically employees, suppliers, customers, creditors, and the local community): see L. Herzel and R. W. Shepro, *Bidders and Targets* (1990) 62–4.

shareholders, present and future, as a group.[145] Legislation has altered the position slightly in the UK: directors of UK companies have, since 1980, been required when performing their functions to have regard also to the interests of the company's employees.[146] However, the company law of Australia (definitely) and the UK (probably) places greater emphasis upon the interests of shareholders than does German company law. Under German law, there is an 'implicit' obligation on the managing board to abide by the '*Gemeinwohlklausel*': a requirement that the company be directed 'in accordance with the requirements of the enterprise and its working force and the common welfare of the people and the empire'.[147] In practice, however, the significant difference between Germany on the one hand and the UK and Australia on the other hand does not lie in the area of directors' duties.

Germany has a system of co-determination (*Mitbestimmung*), a main component of which is the compulsory representation of employees on the supervisory boards of all public companies, and all private companies having 500 or more employees.[148] Employee-directors are virtually unknown in the UK,[149] the US,[150] and Australia, where it has been argued that

---

[145] See Ch. 1, at nn. 24–30, and accompanying text.   [146] CA 1985, s. 309.

[147] See G. Teubner, 'Corporate Fiduciary Duties and Their Beneficiaries' in K. J. Hopt and G. Teubner (eds.), *Corporate Governance and Directors' Liabilities* (1985) 149, at 154; Vagts (n. 143 above), at 40–8. Note that this was a provision of the 1937 German company-law statute, but it was not re-enacted in the 1965 statute. However, it is considered to be 'implicit' in the company law of Germany: Teubner, ibid. The duties of directors in Germany are, as in the UK and Australia, owed to 'the company': K. J. Hopt, 'Directors' Duties to Shareholders, Employees, and Other Creditors: A View from the Continent' in E. McKendrick (ed.), *Commercial Aspects of Trusts and Fiduciary Obligations* (1992) 115, at 116, 119–20.   [148] See the text following n. 100 above.

[149] The Bullock Committee recommended employee representation on boards: see Committee of Inquiry on Industrial Democracy, *Report* (1977). Its report was criticized vigorously by the CBI and industry generally, and a change of government effectively ended any hopes for the implementation of its recommendations. The proposed Fifth EC Directive on harmonization of company law (1983 OJ (C 240) 2) requires either (a) board representation for employees—on the supervisory board under a two-tier structure, or on the single-tier board; or (b) the establishment of another means of employee participation (one option being an employee representative body which would receive a copy of all board materials). The CBI and the Conservative government have been completely opposed to the co-determination aspects of the proposed Fifth Directive, and the only hope of it being acceptable to a British government is if the Labour Party were to come to power. Even in this case, however, the former express support for employee-directors has been replaced by the somewhat equivocal statement that 'it is essential that non-executive directors are not regarded as representing solely the interests of shareholders. . . . We believe that in the appointment of non-executive directors companies should recognise that there are other stakeholders in the future of the company than shareholders': Labour Party, *Winning for Britain* (1994) 11.

[150] There have been some exceptions in the US: see 'The Unions Step on Board', *Fin. Times*, 27 Oct. 1993, p. 14 (US steel companies appointing employee representatives to their boards).

[t]he board is mainly a general purpose control instrument designed to safeguard the investments of those who have taken an equity position in the firm. Other constituencies may sometimes be invited onto the board for the limited purpose of sharing information in a timely and credible manner. To assign other and larger purposes to the board risks impairing its quality and yields doubtful benefits.[151]

The implication of this argument is that the interests of non-shareholder constituencies can be factored into the corporate decision-making process[152] by means other than board representation. Whether this occurs adequately in practice is unclear,[153] and beyond the scope of this book.

It is submitted on three grounds that facilitating greater (institutional) shareholder monitoring need not affect detrimentally the interests of other stakeholders. First, as pointed out by Davies, '[t]he institutions invest, typically, not the funds of speculators or the incomes of *rentiers*, but the earnings of workers, albeit the better-off workers, who aim to save against loss of income in old age. Insurance companies and pension funds represent a form of employee interest in the enterprise, although not . . . the whole of the employee interest . . .'.[154] With the recent moves towards better accountability in UK and Australian pension and superannuation funds,[155] this argument assumes greater weight. Secondly, institutional monitoring is not incompatible with employee (or even supplier, customer, or creditor) representation at board (i.e. non-executive director) level.[156] Thirdly, the interests of other stakeholders such as creditors, suppliers, customers, and the community can be, and are, protected by non-company law measures.[157]

3. Accountability of the Monitors: Finance Capitalism

The concern here is essentially the age-old one of 'who shall guard the guardian?' This is an unavoidable problem, and exists in every system of corporate governance. In order to 'avoid the charge of illegitimacy in their

---

[151] O. E. Williamson, 'Corporate Governance' (1984) 93 *Yale LJ* 1197 (using the framework of transaction-cost economics).

[152] Terminology from D. D. Prentice, 'Some Aspects of the Corporate Governance Debate' in Prentice and Holland (n. 43 above), 25, at 26.

[153] Interestingly, despite Britain's opt-out from the Social Chapter of the Maastricht Treaty, many large UK companies will be required to form works councils for their workers on the continent, after the implementation of the draft Directive on information and consultation in transnational companies: 1983 OJ (C 217) 3.

[154] P. L. Davies, 'Institutional Investors in the United Kingdom' in Prentice and Holland (n. 43 above), 69, at 80.   [155] See Sec. B.3.i, below.

[156] There is insufficient space here to discuss how that change to board make-up could be brought about, or indeed whether it would be a positive development.

[157] See D. D. Prentice, 'The Theory of the Firm: Minority Shareholder Oppression: Sections 459-461 of the Companies Act 1985' (1988) 8 *Ox. J Legal Stud.* 55, at 64-5.

interaction with their portfolio firms',[158] it is important for there to be a practical chain of accountability running from the fund manager to the trustees or board of the institution, and then to the contributors/unit-holders/shareholders of the institution. Two mechanisms may establish this chain of accountability: fiduciary duties; and 'the decision-making structure and processes'[159] of the institution. Due to the cost-related difficulties of litigation (and hence the difficulties associated with enforcement of fiduciary duties) in the UK and Australia,[160] attention is focused upon the latter.

i. Pension and Superannuation Funds

Trustees[161] of a pension or superannuation fund are in a fiduciary relationship with the beneficiaries of the trust, and must act in the best interests of the beneficiaries. There is some disagreement, but the better view is that any investment manager employed by the trustees of a pension fund also owes fiduciary duties to the beneficiaries (in addition to the contractual and fiduciary duties it owes to the trustees).[162]

In terms of the decision-making structure for pension and superannuation funds, there are two levels to be considered: the fund manager: trustees level, and the trustees: beneficiaries level. What does proper accountability necessitate at the first level? Where, as in the usual case, an external fund manager is employed, proper accountability necessitates a contractual term (in either the fund-management agreement or a collateral letter) requiring the fund manager to (a) notify the trustees of any serious intervention at, or proposed controversial vote at a general meeting of, a portfolio company; and (b) act in accordance with any directions given by the trustees in relation to any such matter. The UK and Australian interview studies revealed that most fund managers do inform their clients about any proposed intervention at a portfolio company, but there is rarely any formal requirement for them to do so.[163] This is an area that should be

---

[158] R. M. Buxbaum, 'Institutional Owners and Corporate Managers: A Comparative Perspective' (1991) 57 *Brook. L Rev.* 1, at 52.   [159] Buxbaum, ibid., at 46.

[160] See, however, 'Pension Members Win Costs Ruling', *Fin. Times*, 30 July 1994, p. 7 (Court of Appeal upholding a pre-emptive costs order granted to beneficiaries suing pension-fund trustees for breach of duty); 'Qantas Superannuation Fund Sues Legal & General', *Aust. Fin. Rev.*, 6 Sept. 1995, p. 21 (superannuation-fund trustees bringing a negligence action against an external fund manager in respect of losses incurred on six fixed-interest transactions).   [161] Or the directors of the trustee company, where there is one.

[162] See Australian Law Reform Commission, and Companies and Securities Advisory Committee, *Discussion Paper: Collective Investment Schemes: Superannuation* (1992) para. 5.27; *Report: Collective Investments: Superannuation* (1992) para. 8.38; 'Survey: Pension Fund Investment: Focus on Investors' Behaviour', *Fin. Times*, 6 May 1993, sec. III, p. VII (citing J. Quarrell of Nabarro Nathanson, solicitors).

[163] See Ch. 5, at nn. 82–4, and accompanying text; Ch. 8, at nn. 47–8, and accompanying text.

covered by a formal agreement.[164] It should be noted that the *AIMA Corporate Governance Guidelines* contain a recommendation that fund managers should report to clients *after* a controversial exercise of voting rights or a behind-the-scenes resolution of 'material corporate governance issues'.[165] However, proper accountability necessitates *prior* notification, so that the trustees may—if they deem it appropriate—influence the course of action taken by the fund manager.[166]

The second level of the decision-making structure for pension and superannuation funds concerns the structural accountability of the trustees to the beneficiaries, in particular the members.[167] The Pensions Act 1995 introduced for the first time in the UK a requirement for representation of members amongst the trustees of UK occupational pension schemes.[168] Nevertheless, at early 1993, 65% of large UK occupational schemes had member-nominated trustees,[169] and in about a quarter of large schemes the member-nominated trustees made up at least 50% of the trustee body.[170] From 1987–93, Australian occupational superannuation schemes with 200 or more members were effectively required to have an equal number of member-nominated and employer-nominated trustees, and those with less than 200 members were effectively required to have at least one member-nominated trustee.[171] Since mid-1995, all Australian schemes, regardless of size, have been required to have equal representation.[172] It is submitted that these legislative initiatives in the UK and Australia have legitimated the role in corporate governance of the trustees of pension and superannuation funds.

---

[164] See Ch. 11, Sec. B.1.viii, for a recommendation along these lines.

[165] *AIMA Corporate Governance Guidelines*, para. 2.4.

[166] This recommendation is reinforced by the 'British Gas affair' of 1995: see Ch. 4, at nn. 114–18, and accompanying text. After the vast majority of fund managers supported the company management on two shareholder resolutions which criticized the company's policy on executive remuneration, a trustee of a large pension fund said: 'We should have had this discussion [with our external fund manager] ahead of the British Gas meeting but now we need to look at the implications for the future': 'Big Investors Threaten to Revolt on Pay', *Guardian*, 26 June 1995, p. 14.

[167] The reference to 'members' is to members who are not also senior managers of the sponsoring company. Note that the sponsoring employer of a UK occupational scheme can also be a beneficiary: see R. L. Nobles, 'The Exercise of Trustees' Discretion Under a Pension Scheme' [1992] *JBL* 261.

[168] Pensions Act 1995, ss. 16–21 (schemes must have at least two (or one, in the case of schemes with less than 100 members) member-nominated trustees, and member-nominated trustees must compose at least one-third of the total number of trustees, unless the members agree under a statutory consultation procedure to different arrangements proposed by the sponsoring employer).

[169] NAPF, *Annual Survey of Occupational Pension Schemes* (1993) 30.

[170] 'The Survey: Occupational Schemes—Challenging Times', *Pensions Mgt.*, Apr. 1993, p. 33, at 38.

[171] Occupational Superannuation Standards Act 1987 (Cth.), regs. 13(1) and 15(1).

[172] Superannuation Industry (Supervision) Act 1993 (Cth.), Pt. 9.

It should be noted that, especially in the US, some believe that the legitimation of pension funds as institutional shareholders requires 'pass-through voting' (i.e. a mechanism for the body of members to determine how to vote each shareholding). There were suggestions in mid-1995 that the British Labour Party was considering pushing for an amendment to the (then) Pensions Bill, under which trustees would be required to consult with scheme beneficiaries before voting on a particular resolution at a general meeting of a portfolio company, if more than 5% of beneficiaries were in favour of such consultation.[173] This process would, however, be unwieldy and unnecessary (given the advent of member-nominated trustees), and likely to increase agency costs.[174]

ii. Insurance Companies

The directors of an insurance company owe fiduciary duties to the company, but not to the members of the company.[175] The 'interests of the company' means, however, the interests of the members, present and future, as a group.[176] At this point it is necessary to distinguish between two main types of insurance company: mutual companies and share-capital companies.[177] Mutuals are 'owned' by their policyholders; the policy-holders (or certain of the policyholders) are the members of the company. Share-capital insurance companies have (as their name suggests) share-holders, who are the members of the company; the policyholders of share-capital companies are not members. The directors of mutual companies are therefore required to act in the best interests of the body of policyholders, whilst the directors of share-capital companies are required to act in the best interests of the body of shareholders.[178] In each case, the assets which comprise the insurance funds belong to the insurance company. The policyholders have no collective rights of ownership in respect of the assets underlying their contracts of insurance; they are creditors of the company.[179]

In terms of accountability through the decision-making structure, the

---

[173] See 'Spar Showdown is No Surrender', *Guardian*, 24 June 1995, p. 38.

[174] See F. H. Easterbrook and D. R. Fischel, 'Voting in Corporate Law' (1983) 26 *J Law & Econ.* 395, at 426; Buxbaum (n. 158 above), at 47–9.

[175] *Percival* v. *Wright* [1902] 2 Ch. 421. But see Life Insurance Act 1945 (Cth.), s. 38(8), discussed in R. B. Sharpe and C. A. Manolios, *Wickens: The Law of Life Insurance in Australia* (6th edn., 1990) paras. 20.400–20.450.

[176] See Ch. 1, at nn. 26–30, and accompanying text.

[177] In Australia there is a third type: companies limited by shares and guarantee. Both the policyholders and the shareholders of such companies are members.

[178] But see Life Insurance Act 1945 (Cth.), s. 38(8); and Sharpe and Manolios (n. 175 above).

[179] Linklaters & Paines, *Unit Trusts: The Law and Practice* (1989) paras. A2.0310, A2.0420.

two points made above about the identity of the members and the ownership of fund assets are important. As regards share-capital companies, it is the shareholders rather than the policyholders who are the ultimate controllers. Several large UK insurance companies are listed companies, with institutional shareholders dominating their share registers. Many other share-capital companies are wholly owned subsidiaries of other companies: some of which are listed domestic companies, and some of which are overseas companies. In any event, the board (which employs the investment managers)[180] of a share-capital insurer, is elected by the company's shareholders, and the company is thereby a legitimated institutional shareholder—despite no involvement by the policyholders.[181] In the case of a mutual insurer, the board is elected by the policyholders and the insurer is by that means legitimated as an institutional investor.[182]

iii. Unit Trusts, Investment Trusts, and Investment Companies

Both the trustee and the manager of a unit trust stand in a fiduciary relationship with the unit-holders.[183] Investment trusts and investment companies (closed-end funds) are companies limited by shares, and those of present interest are listed on the London Stock Exchange or the ASX. The directors of an investment trust or investment company owe fiduciary duties to the company, but the 'interests of the company' means the interests of the shareholders, present and future, as a group.

For two reasons stated by Buxbaum, the corporate-governance activities of managers of unit trusts, and of managers and directors of investment trusts and investment companies, are legitimated adequately without the need for any involvement by the unit- holders/shareholders in the decision-making structure.[184] First, since the concern is with vehicles whose units/ shares are listed on a stock exchange, or whose unit-holders are entitled to

---

[180] Recall that most insurance funds are managed in-house: see Ch. 3, Sec. B.2.i; Ch. 6, Sec. A.1.i.

[181] Listed UK insurance companies should, additionally, comply with the *Cadbury Code* and *Listing Rules*, para. 12.43(j); and listed Australian insurers should comply with *ASX Listing Rules*, LR 3C(3)(j).

[182] But note that, given that the usual rule in mutuals is one-person, one-vote (i.e. votes do not increase with the number or size of policies held), 'paradoxically, such enterprises may come closest to the situation of the "managerial" enterprises conceptualised by Berle and Means': Scott (n. 108 above), at 52.

[183] See P. D. Finn, *Fiduciary Obligations* (1977) 12.

[184] See Buxbaum (n. 158 above), at 47. But, nevertheless, the shareholders of an investment trust or investment company would usually have the power under the articles to elect the directors. See also *Australian Fixed Trusts Pty. Ltd.* v. *Clyde Industries Ltd.* (1959) 59 SR (NSW) 33 (proposed alteration to articles of listed Australian company to disenfranchise shareholders who were trustees of unit trusts, unless they obtained a direction as to how to vote from a majority of unit-holders; held not bona fide for the benefit of the company as a whole).

have their units redeemed at a price related to the net value of the property to which the units relate,[185] there is the monitoring effect of the price for the units/shares. The second legitimating factor is the existence of (very wide) market choice for investment vehicles of varying investment philosophies.[186]

In summary, the corporate-governance activities undertaken by or on behalf of the various types of institution are legitimate, in the sense that there is a proper degree of accountability to the underlying investors.

4. INSIDER DEALING

Some argue that there is an irreconcilable conflict between moves designed to achieve a closer relationship between the management and major institutional shareholders of a company, and the insider-dealing legislation.[187] This view is too simplistic. In both the UK and Australia, most regular one-to-one meetings (and indeed many presentations to groups of institutions and brokers' analysts) are held soon after an announcement of results. A primary reason for this is to minimize the possibility of undisclosed price-sensitive information being released at these selective meetings. Further, Chapter 5 revealed that the UK practice of 'pre-marketing' very often involves the imparting of undisclosed price-sensitive information.[188] Institutions insist on being warned in advance if a company management wishes to make them an insider; this is also a requirement of the *Listing Rules*.[189] Most institutions are unwilling to be made insiders (and put in a position of being unable to trade) for more than six or seven days, but some institutions prefer a maximum insider period of just two days. The constituent members of an institutional coalition intervening to change an under-performing management team would have an informal agreement not to trade in the company's shares during the course of the intervention. This can sometimes take those institutions 'off-market' for many weeks.

If institutions were to move to the stage where their fund managers sat as non-executive directors on the boards of portfolio companies,[190] Chinese

---

[185] See Financial Services Act 1986 (UK), s. 78(6); CL, s. 1069(1)(d).

[186] It is clear that the first factor is inapplicable to occupational pension schemes and insurance funds. The second does not apply to occupational pension schemes, although it does apply to personal pension schemes, and also to insurance funds.

[187] See Criminal Justice Act 1993 (UK), Pt. V; CL, Pt. 7.11, Div. 2A; R. B. Jack, *How Level a Playing Field Does Company Law Provide?* (1991) 17–22.

[188] See Ch. 5, at n. 180, and accompanying text.

[189] *Listing Rules*, para. 9.3. See also London Stock Exchange, *Guidance on the Dissemination of Price Sensitive Information* (1995) para. 30; *AIMA Corporate Governance Guidelines*, para. 2.1.　　　　　　　　　　　　　　　[190] See Ch. 11, Sec. B.2.iii.

Walls could be employed so as to partition the individuals concerned from the trading fund managers for the companies concerned. Finally, it would be foolish to suggest that no insider dealing occurs in the fund-management industry. In all likelihood, though, it is very limited and does not involve very large trades, given (a) that fund managers are investing the funds of others, and therefore stand to gain relatively little from a successful insider trade whilst facing a large downside risk;[191] and (b) the sophistication of the stock exchanges' detection programmes for possible insider trades.[192] The insider dealing that occurs would not justify restrictions upon institutional contacts with company managements.

5. DISCLOSURE OF CONFIDENTIAL, PROPRIETARY INFORMATION

There may be a concern that closer involvement by institutions would leave companies at risk of having commercially sensitive information revealed to their competitors (since most large institutions have a holding in many of the firms in any one industry).[193] There is evidence that company managements can be loath to reveal proprietary information to fund managers for just this reason.[194] There is also evidence that 'cross-fertilisation is an important part of investment management . . . testing whether what [one company has said] makes sense by bouncing the idea off [a competitor]'.[195] However, no realistic measure for facilitating a closer involvement by institutions in corporate governance could compel or effectively compel company managements to reveal such information against their better judgement.

6. CONFLICTS OF INTEREST

The main issue here is the perceived problem that 'institutional dog does not eat institutional dog'.[196] That is, there is said to be a conflict of interest which causes institutional investors to monitor their portfolio companies in a systematically selective way: namely, by avoiding interference with quoted companies which happen also to be institutional investors.[197] There

---

[191] See B. S. Black, 'Agents Watching Agents: The Promise of Institutional Investor Voice' (1992) 39 *UCLA L Rev.* 811, at 868.

[192] See 'A Click of the Mouse is all it Takes to Track the Share Raiders', *Fin. Times*, 3 Oct. 1994, p. 11. Detection and successful prosecution are, of course, two entirely different matters.   [193] See Marsh (n. 5 above), at 27–8, 99.

[194] See Ch. 5, at n. 146, and accompanying text.

[195] Trade and Industry Committee (n. 35 above), qu. 1267.

[196] 'The Limits to Institutional Power', *Fin. Times*, 22 May 1990, p. 20.

[197] The example cited in the article, ibid., is the alleged failure in the 1970s of insurance companies, which held shares in the listed insurer, Commercial Union, to take any action despite 'widespread scepticism about [Commercial Union's] management'.

are, however, two reasons for believing that in practice there is little reason for concern. First, there have been instances where institutions have intervened in the affairs of other institutions.[198] Secondly, there are not many *widely held*, quoted UK institutions, and very few widely held, quoted Australian institutions. At mid-1994, of about 2,500 quoted UK companies, there were only half-a-dozen quoted UK life insurers, and a similar number of quoted UK composite insurers.[199] The handful of quoted merchant banks which had fund-management subsidiaries were mostly controlled, rather than widely held, companies. And the several quoted fund-management firms were also predominantly controlled companies.[200] Of course, some of the High Street banks had fund-management subsidiaries, but it would be overstating this concern to suggest that institutions would be loath to interfere in the management of an under-performing bank on the grounds that the bank itself owned a large institutional investor.[201]

A different conflict-of-interest problem is discussed in the next chapter: the effect that potential conflicts of interest may have on the willingness of certain institutions to engage in detailed monitoring of any or some companies.[202] It should be borne in mind that those conflicts not only restrict the amount of institutional monitoring, but also detract from the integrity of the institutions as a monitoring body. Despite that, it would be a gross overreaction to restrict the involvement of those institutions which *are* prepared to conduct monitoring, on the grounds of other institutions' conflict-induced passivity.

7. Excessive or Inappropriate Interference

Another possible drawback from promoting closer institutional involvement in corporate governance is that institutions may intervene excessively, in an inappropriate manner, or in inappropriate circumstances.[203] The root

---

[198] See 'Punter's Progress', *Econ.*, 7 Sept. 1991, p. 112: 'A sumptuous package of share options for [executives of a listed fund-management company] had conditions attached to it after fellow fund managers protested'); 'M&G Faces Criticism of Executive Option Scheme', *Fin. Times*, 22 Jan. 1994, p. 22.

[199] In addition, Eagle Star and Allied Dunbar were then subsidiaries of the listed conglomerate, BAT Industries plc, whilst Scottish Mutual was owned by the listed bank, Abbey National plc.

[200] Investment trusts and listed investment companies are disregarded as they are not operational companies.

[201] Indeed, the institutional involvement in the early departure of the chairman/chief executive of Barclays plc in 1992 (see 'British Banks Face Turmoil', *Sunday Times*, 26 Apr. 1992, sec. 3, p. 1), and in ensuring that the successor split the roles of chairman and chief executive (see 'Called to Account for Past Practices', *Fin. Times*, 8 Mar. 1993, p. 18), suggests just the opposite.   [202] See Ch. 10, Secs. B.1.vi, B.2.i.

[203] See J. Plender, *That's the Way the Money Goes* (1982) 70–4; H. M. Morgan, 'Dealing with Institutional Shareholders: A Corporate Perspective' (1993).

concern seems to be that fund managers simply are not qualified to monitor the performance of company managers. It is true that most UK and Australian financial analysts and fund managers have little or no industrial experience. However, there are four reasons why this does not imply that fund managers are inappropriate monitors of corporate managers. First, '[fund] managers can assess whether manager A is running steel company X as well as his [or her] industry peers . . . without being able to run a steel company themselves'.[204] Secondly, interventions to change the management of a company have occurred in the past only where there has been consensus amongst a group of the largest institutional shareholders that a change must be made. Such consensus has been achieved only in circumstances where it has been abundantly clear, by any measure, that there has been a case of managerial failure. Thirdly, serious interventions in the affairs of portfolio companies have involved *senior* fund managers, who have had many years of experience and interacted with dozens (probably hundreds) of company managements over their careers. Although there are many inexperienced fund managers, it is not they who decide whether or not an intervention is to take place. Fourthly, in relation to the power of shareholders to vote upon proposed large transactions,[205] it is arguable that 'the skills involved in formulating a decision to merge with Corporation B . . . are similar to the skills involved in formulating a decision to invest in Corporation B, and are quite different from the skills needed to formulate an advertising campaign, conduct employee relations, or make steel'.[206]

Nevertheless, there is bound occasionally to be an intervention or other form of detailed institutional monitoring which appears later to have been inappropriate. For instance, several commentators argued that the institutional intervention which resulted in the departure of a co-founder of Saatchi & Saatchi plc in late 1994 was short-sighted having regard to the substantial degree of client loyalty to the individual concerned.[207] Also, Australian institutions were criticized strongly in 1995 for allegedly pressurizing the management of Pacific Dunlop Ltd. into selling its food assets.[208] This criticism was particularly telling given that the chief

---

[204] B. S. Black, 'Agents Watching Agents: The Promise of Institutional Investor Voice' (1992) 39 *UCLA L Rev.* 811, at 851.

[205] See Ch. 5, Sec. B.3.vii.(b); Ch. 8, at nn. 103–4, and accompanying text.

[206] M. A. Eisenberg, *The Structure of the Corporation: A Legal Analysis* (1976) 15. Note that this statement was made in the context of closely held corporations, but it applies equally to large firms (see at 58).

[207] See 'Saatchi Doesn't Work', *Fin. Times*, 14 Jan. 1995, p. 6.

[208] See 'Who Turned the Screws to Put PacDun in a Spin?', *Age*, 21 Apr. 1995, p. 21; 'Resentment Over PacDun Grows', *Aust. Fin. Rev.*, 7 Aug. 1995, p. 17; but cf. 'Funds Reject Blame in PacDun Sell-Off', *Aust. Fin. Rev.*, 8 Aug. 1995, p. 20.

executive of Nestlé Australia Ltd. (the Australian arm of the multinational food group, which bought a large portion of the assets) said later that he believed 'that Pacific Dunlop were moving the business along in a very satisfactory way and . . . from a Nestle point of view, it would not have been bothering us if we saw a [Nestlé] business developing the way they were developing it. Fortunately, we're not under quite as much pressure.'[209] Instances such as these are a cause for some concern. However, for the reasons stated in the previous paragraph, detailed institutional monitoring probably has been, and is likely in future to be, undertaken in appropriate circumstances in a large majority of cases.

A secondary concern within the excessive-or-inappropriate-interference category relates to fund managers who are 'political entrepreneurs'. Political entrepreneurs are those 'who, for their own career reasons, find it in their private interest to work to provide collective benefits to relevant groups'.[210] This concept has surfaced in the US literature, and has been used to explain the relatively activist role played in corporate governance in the early 1990s by public pension funds led by high-profile figures.[211] The concern is more that such entrepreneurs may engage in inappropriate monitoring[212] than that they may engage in over-monitoring. These concerns are probably more valid in the US, where public pension schemes commonly have no member-nominated trustees, or only a small number of member-nominated trustees.[213] Public-sector, or quasi-public-sector, pension and superannuation schemes in the UK and Australia were, on the other hand, amongst the earliest to introduce member-nominated trustees.[214] Secondly, there have traditionally been very few internal managers of public-sector pension and superannuation schemes amongst the largest fund managers in the UK and Australia.[215] The potential

---

[209] 'Resentment Over . . .', ibid.

[210] E. B. Rock, 'The Logic and (Uncertain) Significance of Institutional Shareholder Activism' (1991) 79 *Georgetown LJ* 445, at 465, n. 62 (citing R. Hardin, *Collective Action* (1982)). See further Ch. 10, Sec. B.3.

[211] See Rock, ibid., at 460, 465, 479–81; R. Romano, 'Public Pension Fund Activism in Corporate Governance Reconsidered' (1993) 93 *Colum. L Rev.* 796, at 822.

[212] '[T]heir incentives [may] drive them to champion the kinds of activities that garner political benefits but do not benefit the corporation': Rock, ibid., at 481.

[213] See Romano (n. 211 above), at 823.

[214] At 1993, 16 out of 18 large UK public-sector/quasi-public-sector schemes had member-nominated trustees: NAPF (n. 169 above). Local-authority schemes in the UK are an exception: they are not constituted under a trust deed, but under the Superannuation Act 1972, and they do not have trustees as such. They typically have a 'panel' including the council treasurer/finance director, the leader of the council or the chairperson of the council's finance committee, the scheme actuary, a representative of the external fund manager (the investments of most local-authority schemes are externally managed), and an external property adviser.

[215] See Table 3.2 (only one wholly public-sector operation (CIN) amongst top 50 managers of UK equities at 31 Dec. 1991; PosTel was partly a public-sector operation: it was owned

dangers with political entrepreneurs would not, therefore, seem to be a practical concern in either the UK or Australia.[216]

8. DETRIMENT TO PRIVATE SHAREHOLDERS

There has been some concern expressed from time to time in both the UK[217] and Australia[218] that a closer involvement by institutional share-holders in corporate governance could be detrimental to the interests of small shareholders. It can be said immediately that in most respects the interests of institutional and small non-institutional shareholders will coincide. However, concerns which have been expressed have centred on (a) inequality of access to senior management (and hence to information); and (b) differing aversions to risk.

Regarding (a), one point is that small shareholders would have little or no access to senior management even if there were no institutional shareholders. A second response is that, in terms of laws governing insider dealing and stock-exchange regulations governing the release of new information, private shareholders in quoted UK and Australian companies are in a superior position to those in German and Japanese quoted companies. Thirdly, small shareholders are able to free-ride on the monitoring efforts of institutional shareholders. As regards (b), the conflict of interest lies in the fact that small shareholders, holding less diversified portfolios than institutions, are generally more risk averse. The first response is, as pointed out by Rock, that, although the conflict is real, there is unlikely to be any significant practical problem because where they 'agree on future prospects, the institution and the [small] shareholder have an incentive to trade, ameliorating any conflict'.[219] Secondly, any argument for protecting undiversified shareholders rests on the assumption that they are 'commercially incompetent and thus [unaware of] the ease with which full diversification could be achieved by investing in [unit trusts

jointly by the Post Office (government-owned) and British Telecommunications plc (then a partly privatized listed company); note also the special case of BRPTC: see Ch. 3, at n. 6); Table 6.2 (only four wholly public-sector operations amongst top 30 managers of Australian equities at 31 Dec. 1993: State Superannuation Investment & Management Corp.; Queensland Investment Corp.: Commonwealth Funds Management; Suncorp Insurance).

[216] Perhaps the nearest thing in the UK to this phenomenon was the highly public campaign by the chief executive of PosTel Investment Management Ltd. (known now as Hermes) against lengthy, rolling contracts of service for senior executives (although there was fairly wide support amongst other institutions on the issue, if not the methods used, in this case): see Ch. 4, at nn. 127–9, and accompanying text; Ch. 5, at nn. 3–4, and accompanying text.

[217] See e.g. 'Letters: Cadbury Must Not Lead to Creation of "Two-Tier" Shareholders', *Fin. Times*, 11 Dec. 1992, p. 21.

[218] See e.g. 'No Sharing Between Rivals', *Aust. Fin. Rev.*, 28 Jan. 1994, p. 21.

[219] Rock (n. 210 above), at 468.

or investment trusts]'.[220] There is, however, good reason to believe that many private shareholders are actually risk preferrers, who intentionally do not seek the benefits of diversification.[221]

In sum, the conflict between institutional and private shareholders is not of great concern, especially when weighed against the potential benefits of closer institutional involvement in corporate governance—upon which small shareholders can free-ride.

C. CONCLUSION

This chapter has argued that closer institutional monitoring would lead to a net reduction in agency costs. It has also found no support for the theory that the institutions behave in a short-term manner. On the other hand, it has been contended that there is a form of short-termism which is inherent in the outsider systems of corporate ownership and governance of the UK and the US, and to a lesser extent Australia. If anything, closer institutional involvement in corporate governance should mitigate, rather than compound, this problem—for which there is no panacea. Several other possible problems with closer monitoring have been assessed, and found to lack weight. The conclusion is thus that the likely advantages of greater monitoring outweigh any disadvantages.

---

[220] J. C. Coffee, 'Shareholders Versus Managers: The Strain in the Corporate Web' (1986) 85 *Mich. L Rev.* 1, at 68. [221] Ibid.

10

The Potential for Increased Institutional Monitoring, Without Legal Reform

Given the finding in Chapter 9 that closer institutional monitoring is desirable, this chapter addresses the question of whether there is likely to be any increase in the level of monitoring without specific legal reforms. This is an important matter because several commentators, especially in the UK, have found that greater institutional monitoring would be a good thing *but* have relied upon mere exhortation as a way of achieving that end.[1] The main aim of this chapter is to show that there is an array of disincentives to the performance of detailed firm-level monitoring by institutions—external fund managers in particular. The fact that this sort of monitoring does occur (as detailed in Chapters 5 and 8) shows that these disincentives are sometimes surmountable. However, it is concluded that, in the absence of positive regulatory changes, it is probable that there will be no significant increase on current levels in the UK, and only a small increase on current levels in Australia.

A. DIRECT AND INDIRECT INDUSTRY-WIDE MONITORING

Before addressing the important area of firm-level monitoring, a brief mention should be made about industry-wide monitoring. It would appear that, in the light of the focus given to board structure and composition by the Cadbury Committee in the UK and the Bosch Committee and the AIMA in Australia, there is only limited scope for further industry-wide action by institutions and their trade associations in that area. On the other

---

[1] See e.g. A. Sykes, 'Proposals for a Reformed System of Corporate Governance to Achieve Internationally Competitive Long-Term Performance' in N. H. Dimsdale and M. Prevezer (eds.), *Capital Markets and Corporate Governance* (1994) 111, at 126 (recommendation for institutional non-executive directors and a 'radical compact' between institutional shareholders and company managements, but 'no need for legislation to force the new system to come to pass').

hand, in areas such as disclosure of executive remuneration, and disclosure generally, there is considerable room for more industry-wide monitoring.[2]

B. DIRECT FIRM-LEVEL MONITORING

This section deals with the disincentives to, and incentives for, the performance of *detailed* firm-level monitoring by fund managers. Several of the disincentives and incentives relate specifically to institutional interventions to change management, but some relate to detailed monitoring in a broader sense: encompassing vigorous, continual examination of the performance of the management of *all* portfolio companies.

1. STRUCTURAL DISINCENTIVES TO DETAILED MONITORING

The disincentives discussed under this subsection are characterized as 'structural' disincentives. The reason for this is that they all flow from either the structure of the system of corporate ownership and governance, the structure and workings of the fund-management industry, or the structure of the institutions themselves. Most of the 11 disincentives discussed below fall within one of the following three broad groupings. First, the 'outsider' system of corporate ownership and governance in the UK quoted sector (and in the widely held half of the Australian quoted sector[3]) (a) entails the real option of sale rather than costly monitoring, and thus perpetuates the collective-action problem (associated with monitoring) even where the largest few shareholders hold a significant proportion of the equity; and (b) means that fund managers have very limited personnel available to perform the monitoring function. Secondly, there are divergences between the interests of the various parties composing an institutional shareholder (for example the fund manager, trustees, and members of a pension fund), which means that the optimal amount of monitoring from the point of view of the ultimate beneficiaries is normally greater than the amount of monitoring that is actually

---

[2] See also 'Institutions Agree to Share Information on Governance', *Fin. Times*, 7 Sept. 1994, p. 28 (agreement between institutional-investor trade associations in several countries, including the UK and Australia, to exchange information on local 'best practice' in matters of corporate governance).

[3] It was shown in Ch. 8, at nn. 73–6, and accompanying text, that about half of all quoted Australian companies have a controlling non-institutional shareholder. References in the remainder of this section to 'widely held Australian companies' are to those quoted Australian companies which do not have a controlling non-institutional shareholder. Institutional monitoring in 'controlled' companies serves a purpose different from that in widely held companies: see Ch. 9, at nn. 2–4, and accompanying text.

performed. Thirdly, the highly competitive nature of the fund-management business, and of the insurance, unit-trust, and investment-trust sectors, means that co-operation between different institutions is not easy.

i. The Structure of Corporate Ownership and Governance: Institutions as Arm's-Length Investors

It was demonstrated in the previous chapter that there is a fundamental difference between the type of shareholder or shareholders which have ultimate control over quoted German and Japanese companies, and the type of shareholders which ultimately control most quoted UK companies (and about half of all quoted Australian companies). The ultimate controllers of German and Japanese firms are 'committed' shareholders, whilst the ultimate controllers of UK companies and widely held Australian companies are 'arm's-length' shareholders.[4] This has a major ramification: when there are serious problems with the management of a UK company or a widely held Australian company, the first instinct of many institutional shareholders is to try to extricate themselves from the situation by selling the shares. The dominant shareholders of German and Japanese companies, on the other hand, have a default strategy of staying put whilst a restructuring is conducted. In Japan, this often involves the 'main bank'.[5] In Germany, it occasionally involves the 'house bank' (but not as often as in Japan),[6] sometimes involves the supervisory board, and sometimes involves no external intervention at all.[7] It is of some significance that the main/house bank typically has an equity holding in the company as well as a lender-borrower relationship with it.[8] In Coffee's

---

[4] See Ch. 9, at text following n. 90; and at nn. 95–9, 107–12, and accompanying text.

[5] See P. Sheard, 'The Main Bank System and Corporate Monitoring and Control in Japan' (1989) 11 *J Econ. Bahav. & Org.* 399, at 407–9.

[6] See J. S. S. Edwards and K. Fischer, *Banks, Finance and Investment in Germany* (1994) 156–77.

[7] See C. P. Mayer, *The Functioning of the UK Financial System: What's Wrong with London?* (1991) 14–15 (discussing an analysis by Franks and Mayer of 14 major restructurings of poorly performing German companies over the 1980s, which found that a majority of restructurings did not involve any outside intervention at all; only in cases of clear financial failure did the supervisory board intervene; usually the management board itself initiated the changes).

[8] Of more significance in Japan is that 'the relationship which goes by the name of debt . . . appears to have many of the features of an equity relationship': J. Corbett, 'International Perspectives on Financing: Evidence from Japan' (1987) 3 (4) *Ox. Rev. Econ. Pol.* 30, at 54. Since most shares in German companies are in bearer form, and are typically deposited for safe-keeping with banks, and since a corollary of deposit is the voting of the shares, the large German banks have an enormous amount of potential voting power: see Edwards and Fischer (n. 6 above), at 111–15, 198–210; J. Köndgen, 'Duties of Banks in Voting Their Clients' Stock' in T. Baums, R. M. Buxbaum, and K. J. Hopt (eds.), *Institutional Investors and Corporate Governance* (1994) 531.

terminology, the German and Japanese banks, and other committed shareholders, have traded liquidity for control.[9]

One caveat to the above concerns the monitoring of the management of Japanese and German firms whilst performance is satisfactory, or at least not clearly inadequate. Some commentators believe that Japanese main banks, and German banks and supervisory boards, play an active role in routinely monitoring the management of firms. Kallfass, for example, states:

> Through the exercise of voting rights the big banks greatly influence hirings and firings in West German corporations' [non-]executive bodies, the supervisory boards; as well as on managing boards. They have a voice in all fundamental business decisions. This is evident not only from the high proportion of bank representatives on supervisory boards, but also from the frequent namings of bank managers as chairs of corporate supervisory boards.[10]

However, the latest evidence supports strongly the view that, in normal states, the managers of Japanese and German firms have substantial discretion and leeway:

> In the normal course of events . . . the [Japanese] main bank exercises explicit control neither in the selection of management nor in corporate policy making. Well-run companies that incur little or no debt from banks appear to be virtually free from banks' intervention, and their managements enjoy the highest degree of autonomy. . . . [Banks] remain as silent business partners in good profit states. Their power becomes visible only in bad states.[11]

It must be emphasized that, despite the problems associated with selling a large stake (resulting from the depressing effect upon the share price if it is not done with great caution), the UK and Australian interview studies

[9] J. C. Coffee, 'Liquidity Versus Control: The Institutional Investor as Corporate Monitor' (1991) 91 *Colum. L Rev.* 1277.

[10] H. H. Kallfass, 'The American Corporation and the Institutional Investor: Are There Lessons from Abroad?' [1988] *Colum. Bus. L Rev.* 775, at 783.

[11] M. Aoki, 'Toward an Economic Model of the Japanese Firm' (1990) 28 *J Econ. Lit.* 1, at 14–15. However, Aoki argues that something akin to the Anglo-American market for corporate control (but minus the inherent short-termism which accompanies the UK/US version) operates to keep Japanese managements on their toes: 'Because 'internal' management naturally abhors 'external' interference by the main bank, and bank control is a humiliating blow to the failed manager, management aspires to pursue high profits': ibid., at 15–16. *Keiretsu* firms may monitor each other in normal states: see E. Berglöf and E. Perotti, 'The Governance Structure of the Japanese Financial Keiretsu' (1994) 36 *J Fin. Econ.* 259. As for non-*keiretsu* firms, see S. D. Prowse, 'The Structure of Corporate Ownership in Japan' (1992) 47 *J Fin.* 1121. In regard to Germany, see Edwards and Fischer (n. 6 above), at 196–227; J. R. Franks and C. P. Mayer, 'Corporate Control: A Synthesis of the International Evidence' in J. C. Coffee, R. J. Gilson, and L. Lowenstein (eds.), *Relational Investing* (1996) (forthcoming); T. Baums, 'Takeovers Versus Institutions in Corporate Governance in Germany' in D. D. Prentice and P. R. J. Holland (eds.), *Contemporary Issues in Corporate Governance* (1993) 151, at 165–73.

revealed that sale is still very much a major option for most institutions when serious problems emerge at a portfolio company. One fund manager from a large UK insurer explained how a sale in these circumstances would not necessarily involve a large discount:

> Poor managerial performance occasionally surfaces like a crevasse, down which one falls. More often, however, one has what I would perhaps describe as a 'creeping effect' of poor managerial performance, which is a long sliding slope. And depending on quite where you are on that slope when you realise that it is poor management, and the dimensions of the slope, can influence the judgment that you take in that situation. In this . . . situation it is generally speaking more appropriate to sell your shares to somebody who sees the hill going up rather than down.

The nature of the outsider system of corporate ownership and governance means that, although the benefits from exit decrease as concentration of shareholding increases, exit will always be a reasonably attractive option. The outsider system seems, therefore, to have perpetuated the collective-action problem (associated with monitoring) during the period when increased institutional share ownership was increasing substantially the concentration of shareholding in the UK and Australia.[12]

Another effect of the outsider system, where institutions have the option of sale in the market or to a hostile bidder, is that even large institutions have only a fairly small number of fund managers and analysts available to perform detailed monitoring, and those persons each have only a short time that they can spend on any one company.[13]

ii. Collective-Action and Free-Rider Problems

Once a company has more than one shareholder, the 'collective-action' problem surfaces. The monitoring of management is a collective good: any positive effects from monitoring are enjoyed by *all* shareholders regardless of whether or not they have participated in, or contributed to, the monitoring.[14] For this reason, a shareholder behaving in an economically rational way will undertake monitoring only in limited circumstances. At the most basic level, it seems that a shareholder will provide the collective good of monitoring if the costs to that shareholder are outweighed by the

---

[12] In regard to the collective-action problem, see Sec. B.1.ii, below.

[13] See A. Blair, 'A Coalition Versus a Dictator', *Fin. Times*, 27 May 1992, p. 13 (a typical UK fund manager runs a portfolio of between 50–150 stocks and, as well as examining up to 100 new stocks per year for possible investment, has commitments such as reports to investors, marketing presentations, and internal meetings). On numbers of qualified staff in large institutions, see E. V. Morgan and A. D. Morgan, *Investment Managers and Takeovers: Information and Attitudes* (1990) 16–17.

[14] See R. C. Clark, *Corporate Law* (1986) 389–400.

benefits it receives from the monitoring.[15] However, as Rock points out,[16] in the context of companies, the basic theory of collective action needs to be adjusted for the possibility of alternative courses of action: simply holding the shares (and free-riding on the monitoring efforts, if any, of others); selling the shares; or acquiring the company in a takeover or (of more relevance in the present context)[17] engineering a takeover bid for the company. The crucial condition for the provision of monitoring is, as it happens, that the shareholder in question must stand to gain more from monitoring than from any alternative course of action.[18] If this condition is satisfied then, in contrast to the basic theory of collective action, it is rational for a shareholder to perform monitoring *even if* the gains derived by that shareholder are exceeded by the cost of the monitoring. Also, and importantly, if a shareholder stands to gain more from an alternative course of action than from monitoring, then it is *not* in the shareholder's economic interests to perform any monitoring *even if* the shareholder would enjoy a net gain from monitoring.[19] The latter scenario can lead to a classic prisoners' dilemma, where (a) shareholders would gain collectively if each contributed to monitoring, but (b) it is in the interests of each shareholder not to contribute, so (c) no monitoring occurs and all shareholders are worse off than if they had all contributed.[20]

Of importance for present purposes is the fact that greater concentration of shareholding makes monitoring more rational for large shareholders for two reasons. First, it increases the benefits which flow from, and lowers the costs of, monitoring. Secondly, it decreases the benefits from alternative courses of action: free-riding becomes less likely, and selling out becomes comparatively less attractive compared to monitoring.[21] The increase in institutional share ownership in the UK and Australia from the 1960s until the 1990s led to greater concentration in shareholding. Why, then, are

---

[15] See M. Olson, *The Logic of Collective Action: Public Goods and the Theory of Groups* (2nd edn., 1971) 23–4.

[16] E. B. Rock, 'The Logic and (Uncertain) Significance of Institutional Shareholder Activism' (1991) 79 *Georgetown LJ* 445, at 455. See also A. Hirschman, *Exit, Voice, and Loyalty: Responses to Decline in Firms, Organizations, and States* (1970).

[17] See Ch. 5, at n. 216, and accompanying text.   [18] Rock (n. 16 above).

[19] Ibid., at 455–6.   [20] Ibid., at 456–7.

[21] See Rock, ibid., at 460–3, for a full explanation. It seems that the third alternative—engineering a takeover bid—is not affected by an increase in concentration of shareholding. What is clear, however, is that it becomes more rational for institutions to undertake detailed monitoring as takeovers decline in frequency: ibid., at 463; see also Ch. 5, at n. 214, and accompanying text: evidence suggesting that institutional interventions are substitutes for takeovers (specifically, for those takeovers which involve poorly performing firms being taken over by good performers: see Ch. 1, at nn. 62–5, and accompanying text). In regard to the option of selling the shares, the outsider system of corporate ownership and governance ensures that this is rarely ruled out completely, regardless of the size of the institution's stake: see Sec. B.1.i, above.

most large fund managers still more likely to sell than intervene when serious managerial problems arise?[22] It was suggested in the previous subsection that the nature of the outsider system of corporate ownership and governance means that, although the benefits from exit decrease as concentration of shareholding increases, exit will always be a reasonably attractive option. There are, however, other explanatory factors.

The discussion to this point has been based on the assumption that the ultimate beneficial owners (for example the beneficiaries of pension and superannuation schemes, and the unit-holders in unit trusts) of the institutions' equity holdings are the persons who decide whether or not to partake in monitoring.[23] In practice, of course, this decision is taken in most cases by the fund manager (external or in-house), and in some cases by the trustees (in the case of a pension or superannuation scheme) or the board (in the case of an insurance company or investment-trust company).

Just as the divergence between the interests of shareholders and managers of a company gives rise to agency costs, agency costs also arise from divergences between the interests of (a) an external fund manager and its clients (for example the trustees of pension and superannuation schemes, and charities; investment-trust companies; private clients); (b) the manager and unit-holders of a unit trust; and (c) *some* of the trustees (namely the sponsor's representatives) and the body of members of a pension or superannuation scheme.[24] The agency problem in (c) is being diminished by the recent moves towards compulsory member-trustees in UK and Australian pension and superannuation schemes.[25] Problems (a) and (b) are, however, much more difficult to reduce to any great extent. The significance of the divergences detailed in (a) and (b) has been described as follows: 'Because of this divergence between the interests of [fund] managers and the interests of their principals, one cannot assume that because improving corporate governance may increase the value of the managed portfolios, improving corporate governance will be in the interests of the [fund] managers.'[26]

As demonstrated in the next subsection, monitoring that increases the value of a company is a collective good for external fund managers.[27] On the other hand, the next four subsections show that only rarely will it be in the interests of individual fund managers to provide that collective good. The divergence between the interests of external fund managers and their clients means that the factors influencing whether it would be rational for a

---

[22] See Ch. 5, at n. 215, and accompanying text.
[23] See Rock (n. 16 above), at 464.
[24] See Rock, ibid., at 469–76; Coffee (n. 9 above), at 1283–4; J. C. Coffee, 'The SEC and the Institutional Investor: A Half-Time Report' (1994) 15 *Cardozo L Rev.* 837, at 843–6, 862–9.   [25] See Ch. 9, Sec. B.3.i.   [26] Rock (n. 16 above), at 473.
[27] At this point the author's analysis departs from that of Rock: see n. 33 below, and accompanying text.

particular fund manager to engage in monitoring are different from those which would determine the rationality of monitoring if that decision were in the hands of that fund manager's clients. As a result, less monitoring is performed by external fund managers than is optimal from the point of view of their clients.

iii. Fund-Manager Performance Measurement

In the UK, the US, and Australia, the performance of a fund-management firm is measured *relatively* rather than *absolutely*. The performance of external managers of pension funds, and the performance of unit trusts, is assessed mostly in comparison to that of other pension-fund managers and other (equivalent) unit trusts, respectively, and less frequently in comparison to stock indices.[28] Therefore, in the (not so extreme) case[29] where the holdings of each external fund manager with a stake in company X are index-weight, or near index-weight,[30] Rock says that monitoring 'that benefits all will benefit none'.[31] This is correct in regard to benefit in the form of winning new clients through better relative performance. However, it disregards another benefit that a fund manager derives from an increase in the value of a portfolio company: the great majority of UK, US, and Australian fund managers charge their clients an *ad valorem* fee— a (decreasing) percentage of the value of funds managed. Therefore, any monitoring which increases the value of the funds under management also leads to an increase in the fund manager's fee. This is discussed further in the next subsection. For the moment it is enough to say that, where every external fund manager has an index-weight or near index-weight holding, even though it may be irrational for any one fund manager to provide the collective good (monitoring),[32] the fund managers as a group would be

---

[28] See Confederation of British Industry ('CBI'), *Pension Fund Investment Management* (1987) 63 (of a large sample of (*inter alia*) externally managed UK pension funds, at mid-1987, the performance of 93% was compared regularly with 'external performance data'—mostly league tables produced by CAPS and WM (actuarial performance-measurement companies); 45% also or instead used stock indices as a benchmark).

[29] See Ch.9, at n. 56, and accompanying text.

[30] A fund manager's 'market' or 'index' weighting in quoted UK equities, for example, is calculated as the market value of its total quoted UK equities under management divided by the market value of all quoted UK equities. The index weightings for the largest managers of UK equities at 31 Dec. 1991, and Australian equities at 31 Dec. 1993, are set out in Tables 3.2 and 6.2, respectively. A holding larger than index-weight is an 'overweight' holding; a holding smaller than index-weight is an 'underweight' holding.

[31] Rock (n. 16 above), at 473–4. See also A. F. Conard, 'Beyond Managerialism: Investor Capitalism?' (1988) 22 *U Mich. J L Ref.* 117, at 147: 'The portfolio manager has little to gain from enhancements of enterprise returns that are shared by all its competitors, but has something to lose by spending money on supervision . . .'

[32] It might, in fact, be rational for a large fund manager to perform some monitoring: this would be so if the expected increase in its fee exceeded the total costs (direct and indirect) involved in the monitoring, and if the expected net gain from monitoring exceeded the expected gain from alternative courses of action. See further Sec. B.1.iv, below.

better off if the good were provided. It is at this point that the writer's analysis departs from that of Rock, who suspects that *not* monitoring is normally the collective good as far as external fund managers are concerned.[33] This is because Rock does not take into consideration the increase in fee that flows from an increase in the value of a portfolio company.

Once one relaxes the assumption that all external fund managers have an index-weight holding in company X, it becomes clear that some fund managers (namely, those with an overweight holding) have a greater incentive than others (namely, those with either an index-weight or an underweight holding) to engage in monitoring. Even though monitoring conducted by an overweighted fund manager would also benefit the performance of index-weighted and underweighted competitors, it would benefit the performance of the overweighted fund manager to a greater degree.[34] By the same token, an underweighted fund manager would probably never have an incentive to expend resources on monitoring. Any increase in its fee would be overridden by the cost in terms of having improved the performance of those competitors which had index-weight or overweight holdings even more than it improved its own performance— and possibly for no cost to those competitors! That UK-based fund managers do not participate in interventions when they have underweight holdings has been confirmed in (separate) interviews conducted by Coffee[35] and the present author. The way in which the performance of external fund managers is measured is thus part of the reason why less monitoring is performed by fund managers than is optimal from the point of view of their clients.[36]

---

[33] See Rock (n. 16 above), at 474 (n. 92), 476.

[34] In theory, and disregarding for the moment the gain from an increased fee, only the fund manager which is *more* overweight in the company than any of its competitors (including those which also have overweight holdings) has the incentive to monitor. Compare Table 3.2 (showing the proportion of the UK equity market held by major fund managers) with Table 5.6 (showing the average collective holding of the top 1, top 2, top 3, top 4, top 5, and top 6 institutional interest-holders in sample listed UK companies): it seems very likely that, in the early 1990s, each of the top six institutional interest-holders in any particular listed UK company would have had an overweight holding.

[35] Reported in B. S. Black and J. C. Coffee, 'Hail Britannia? Institutional Investor Behavior Under Limited Regulation' (1994) 92 *Mich. L Rev.* 1997, at 2063–4. See also P. D. Jackson, 'Management of UK Equity Portfolios' (1987) 27 *Bank Eng. Q Bull.* 253, at 257.

[36] External fund managers are major players in both the UK and Australia. Five of the 10 largest managers of quoted UK equities at 31 Dec. 1991, and of quoted Australian equities at 31 Dec. 1993, were firms which managed predominantly or solely external funds: see Tables 3.2 and 6.2. At early 1993, 62% of the assets of directly invested UK pension schemes were managed externally (see Ch. 3, at nn. 28–9, and accompanying text); at mid-1993, 64% of the assets of directly invested Australian superannuation schemes were managed externally (see Ch. 6, at n. 11, and accompanying text).

In-house pension-fund managers should not be affected by this consideration, because they are not competing for clients. However, the performance of most in-house investment managers used by UK pension funds is measured using league tables.[37] An in-house management team that consistently under-performs the industry's average manager may well be replaced by one or more external fund manager(s).[38] An in-house manager with an underweight holding or even an index-weight holding may not, therefore, wish to take part in an intervention which, if successful, would improve the performance of other fund managers proportionally more than the performance of its own fund. This raises the question of whether other fund managers which have solely or predominantly internal funds under management—particularly the fund-management arms of insurance companies—are influenced by whether they are overweighted, underweighted, or market-weighted, when it comes to deciding whether or not to participate in an intervention. Certainly, from the point of view of the policyholders, an insurance company's fund managers should not take this matter into consideration.[39] But the executives of the insurance company want to win new policyholders, and there are many insurance companies in competition for potential new policyholders.[40] If an underweighted insurer (with, say, a 1% holding) plays a major part in a successful intervention, which improves the performance of its life fund for its existing policyholders, it might also be making a rod for its own back when the performance tables for with-profits funds are next published. A rival insurer with an overweight holding (say 6%) would, whether or not it also took part in the intervention, have achieved a gross return relatively greater (500% greater, in this example) than that of the underweighted insurer. Nevertheless, it may be significant that, of the four UK fund managers interviewed by the author who were engaged full-time (or almost full time) on matters of corporate governance and problem companies, two were senior executives of fund-management arms of large insurers, and one was a senior officer of an in-house pension-fund manager.[41]

---

[37] See CBI (n. 28 above) (the performance of 79% of internally managed funds, at mid-1987, was compared regularly with 'external performance data').

[38] There was a shift towards external managers during the 1980s and early 1990s: see Ch. 3, at n. 27, and accompanying text.

[39] There is every possibility, of course, that an insurer with an underweight holding would conclude that the likely financial benefit to its life funds from free-riding would exceed the likely benefit from contributing to the monitoring action. That would be a perfectly legitimate judgement from the point of view of the policyholders.

[40] In addition, the fund-management arms of some insurers manage a considerable amount of external funds: see Ch. 3, at n. 32, and accompanying text.

[41] See Ch. 5, at n. 185, and accompanying text.

iv. Financial Constraints

Any form of monitoring involves costs for the fund manager(s) concerned.[42] An intervention obviously entails greater costs than less vigorous actions. Before discussing the actual outlays involved in an intervention, it is important to note that there are other substantial costs involved. Some which are termed 'private costs' are discussed in Subsection B.1.(6), below. Another one is the opportunity cost of the time spent by senior fund managers in organizing and conducting the intervention. As mentioned in Chapter 9, it is only senior fund managers who are involved in detailed monitoring actions.[43] When tied up in an intervention at one portfolio company, a senior fund manager loses the chance to market the firm to potential clients, and to consolidate relationships with existing clients.[44] A fund manager interviewed by the author said that, in one major intervention, he had spent a total of 48 hours in meetings, not including travelling time.

There are numerous outlays involved in an intervention. Legal fees are commonly a major expense, as it is usual for the advice of solicitors to be obtained. It is also common for a merchant bank to be engaged to find a new management team. Sometimes the members of a potential new management team will require that they be indemnified by the intervening institutions as a condition of accepting their positions. (This is especially the case where the company is in very poor financial shape, as is often the case here.) If the matter gets to the stage of an extraordinary general meeting, there is the expense of an explanatory circular to all shareholders—a right which the intervening institutions would invariably wish to utilize.[45] If the intervening institutions send out their circular themselves, they must bear the cost of that. They are entitled to have the company circulate it for them.[46] In the latter case, the intervening institutions would have to pay (up front)[47] the company's expenses, but these can be

---

[42] See Rock (n. 16 above), at 460–1, who notes that some types of cost are smaller the higher the level of concentration of shareholding, whilst other types of cost remain constant.

[43] See Ch. 9, Sec. B.7.

[44] See Black and Coffee (n. 35 above), at 2059.

[45] See CA 1985, s. 376(1)(b); CL, s. 252(1)(e). Note that the company must bear the cost of actually convening the meeting requisitioned by the intervening institutions: CA 1985, s. 368(1); CL, s. 246(1). The notice convening the meeting would probably state only in brief terms the requisitionists' proposals (see CA 1985, s. 368(5); Table A, art. 38; Table A (Aust.), reg. 41(1)), and therefore the circular is important as a means of explaining the case for replacing the director(s). If the directors fail to convene a meeting after having been requisitioned to do so, the requisitioning institutions can convene one (CA 1985, s. 368(4); CL, s. 246(3)), and the company must reimburse the requisitionists out of remuneration or fees payable to the defaulting directors: CA 1985, s. 368(6); CL, s. 246(6).

[46] CA 1985, s. 376(1)(b); CL, s. 252(1)(e).

[47] CA 1985, s. 377(1)(b); CL, s. 252(5)(b).

reimbursed if the general meeting so resolves[48] (which it probably would do if the institutions had the numbers to implement successfully their other resolutions at the meeting).

In one UK intervention, the solicitors' bill came to £60,000,[49] and another intervention described by an interviewee had expenses of £20,000. In each case, two institutions were forced to share those expenses—it is difficult for the proactive member(s) of an institutional coalition to persuade the supporting institutions (who are business competitors) to contribute to the outlays. Most external fund managers do not even bother to ask their pension-fund trustee clients for a contribution towards such expenses, due to the highly competitive nature of the pension-fund management business.[50] But, as Black and Coffee point out, if an external 'pension fund manager does not seek reimbursement from its clients for expenses, then the expected benefit [from the intervention] must be huge to justify the manager incurring any expense'.[51]

Black and Coffee give the example of an external fund manager with a 1% stake in a company capitalized at £1,000 million. As this stake is worth £10 million, a proposed intervention thought likely to increase the company's share price by 10% would yield the fund manager's clients a £1 million gain.[52] It would clearly be in the interests of the fund manager's clients for the fund manager to contribute £30,000 towards the cost of an intervention (assuming total costs of £60,000 and only two institutions footing the bill).[53] It was mentioned earlier that UK fund managers charge their clients an *ad valorem* fee. For standard discretionary balanced management for pension funds, the average fees in 1994 were 49.6 basis points (i.e. 0.496 of 1%) for the first £10–50 million of funds under management; 30.7 basis points for funds between £50–100 million; 23 basis points for funds between £100–200 million; and 19.8 basis points for funds above £200 million.[54] Even taking the fee for the smallest portfolios (49.6

---

[48] CA 1985, s. 376(1); CL, s. 252(1).

[49] 'When the Time Comes for Shareholders to Stand Up and be Counted', *Fin. Times*, 6 Apr. 1992, p. 12.   [50] See Black and Coffee (n. 35 above), at 2058.

[51] Ibid., at 2057.

[52] It should be noted, however, that actuarial valuations of pension funds are based more on current income and expected future income from investments held, than on the market value of the investments.

[53] See Black and Coffee (n. 35 above), at 2057. It must be borne in mind, however, that the anticipated gain from monitoring must exceed the anticipated gain from other options: see n. 18 above, and accompanying text.

[54] 'The Research Feature: The Price of Clean Living', *Pensions Mgt.*, Nov. 1994, p. 61, at 65. The fees are higher for unit trusts—mostly between 100–150 basis points annually, as well as a one-off initial charge of between 300–600 basis points. The funds under management of most major external fund managers operating in the UK are, however, composed largely of pension-fund moneys rather than the higher-yielding unit-trust moneys: see Ch. 3, at n. 30 (second-last column of table).

basis points) the expected £1 million increase in the value of the shareholding in the above example would yield the fund manager an increase in remuneration of only £4,960. Clearly, the expected increase in share price from an intervention in a small or medium-sized quoted company (which is where most interventions have occurred) must be very large to vindicate an *external* fund manager becoming an expense-sharing member of an institutional coalition. And, of course, it would be rational for an external fund manager to perform some monitoring only if (a) the expected increase in its fee exceeded the total costs (direct and indirect) incurred by it in the monitoring, *and* (b) the expected net gain from monitoring exceeded the expected gain from alternative courses of action.[55]

Coffee proposes incentive compensation for external fund managers as a partial cure of the agency problem just described.[56] He was, however, told in his interviews with UK fund managers that the introduction of worthwhile incentive compensation is commercially infeasible in the UK due to client distrust of high fees and the highly competitive market for fund management.[57] Indeed, as at early 1993, the investment-management contracts of only 6% of UK pension funds made provision for performance-related compensation.[58]

Managers of internal funds, such as fund-management arms of insurance companies and in-house pension-fund managers, do not have the disincentive just described. For them, the relevant consideration for present purposes is whether the sums add up from the point of view of their fund(s). On the other hand, they do not seem to be entirely free from the agency problem set out in the previous subsection.[59]

v. Increased Level of Indexed Investing

The gradual trend towards passive fund-management techniques, whereby index-weight stakes are held in a wide spread of companies, can be expected to exacerbate the problems referred to in the previous two subsections. In the first instance, an indexer will not, by definition, have any significantly overweight holdings, and thus (especially if an external manager) will always face the disincentive of improving the relative performance of overweighted rivals if it considers intervening at a portfolio company. Secondly, the fees charged for managing funds passively are, naturally, much lower than for discretionary management. The average

---

[55] See n. 18 above, and accompanying text.
[56] See Coffee (n. 9 above), at 1362–6.
[57] See Black and Coffee (n. 35 above), at 2058.
[58] 'The Cost of Performance Related Fees', *Pensions Mgt.*, Mar. 1993, p. 35.
[59] See nn. 37–41 above, and accompanying text.

fees charged in 1994 for managing a segregated fund, tracking the FT-A All Share index, were just 12 basis points (for a £10 million fund), 10 basis points (for a £75 million fund), and 5.5 basis points (for a £200 million fund).[60] These fees are so low that a fund manager would virtually never recoup the expense of organizing and implementing an intervention.

Consistent with these predictions, two Australian fund managers interviewed by the author, whose firms used indexing and quantitative management techniques, said that their institutions did not even have the usual meetings[61] with the senior management of portfolio companies, on the ground that they would hold the stock regardless of what the management had to say. It would be a waste of money for them to expend resources on monitoring of any sort, let alone an intervention. In contrast, two UK interviewees said that their institutions did engage in monitoring despite the fact that they indexed most of their holdings. As *in-house* pension-fund managers, they did not have the same interest in cost-minimizing as *external* indexers; their interest was in the benefit to their funds that would flow from any increase in the value of portfolio companies, resulting from their monitoring.

vi. Structural Conflicts of Interest

Several US works have analysed in detail the conflicts of interest which serve to dissuade various types of institution from becoming involved actively in corporate governance.[62] The evidence indicates that many UK and Australian institutions face similar conflicts, although, overall, conflicts of interest would seem not to have been as large a deterrent to activism as in the US. This is possibly explicable by the fact that most institutional interventions, and other detailed monitoring actions, occur 'behind closed doors' in the UK and Australia, whereas institutional activism in the US has mostly been very public. Since some conflicts of interest are 'reputational', there is less at stake in monitoring in private compared to monitoring in the public arena.

Most large UK and Australian fund-management firms are affiliated with firms that provide services (besides fund management) to quoted companies. These firms may incur 'private costs'[63] from being involved in an intervention or other form of detailed monitoring action, especially if the detailed monitoring takes place at a company with which other relationships exist. If a fund manager intervenes at company X, company X might take business away from another arm of the fund manager's firm

---

[60] 'The Research Feature . . .' (n. 54 above), at 67.
[61] See Ch. 5, Sec. B.2.ii; Ch. 8, Sec. B.2.
[62] See e.g. B. S. Black, 'Shareholder Passivity Reexamined' (1990) 89 *Mich. L Rev.* 520, at 595–607.   [63] See Rock (n. 16 above), at 460.

(for example commercial banking, corporate advisory, stockbroking, or commercial insurance), or it may take business away from the fund manager itself where the fund manager manages assets for company X's pension/superannuation scheme. However, business may also be lost by both a fund-management firm and its affiliates even where they have no relationship (other than the fund manager's shareholding) with the company subject to the intervention. Such a loss of business could occur as a result of the fund manager gaining a 'bad' reputation amongst corporate managements—that is, the reputation of being an 'interventionist'. Corporate managements may switch business to more 'loyal' financial firms.[64] The fund manager may also find that the managements of other portfolio companies start to 'clam up'. Thus, one insider has said that UK fund managers that are affiliated with merchant banks 'like to keep their profile [on corporate-governance matters] below the level of the floor'.[65]

Despite these possibilities, it is clear that the fund-management subsidiaries of merchant-banking companies ('financial conglomerates') have been involved in many interventions in the UK. When an illiquid stake of, say, 12% or 18% is held, the possible private costs (and other costs) of intervening may be outweighed by the potential benefits from installing a new management. In addition, there has been at least one well-publicized case where the fund-management arm of a financial conglomerate, holding a 13.5% stake in a company to which the fund manager's affiliate merchant bank was the key adviser, sold out to a hostile bidder despite the obvious resultant loss of business for its affiliate.[66]

The AIMA has directly addressed this issue. The *AIMA Corporate Governance Guidelines* recommend that AIMA members should have a written policy on the exercising of voting rights.[67] The *Guidelines* continue:

> Each investment manager's proxy voting policy and procedures should include a statement recognising that the investment manager must only vote in the client's interest, and that it is the investment manager's duty to put any other client relationship or interest to one side when deciding how to vote on behalf of

---

[64] Another possibility came to light in the Coles Myer intervention: see Ch. 8, at nn. 95–9, and accompanying text. Allegations were made that a senior trade-union official, who was said to be a friend of the impugned chairman of Coles Myer, had intimated to one of the intervening institutions that, unless that institution stopped intervening, it risked having union superannuation funds withdrawn from its management. The allegations were denied strenuously: see 'Questions Raised on Coles, Kelty and AMP', *Aust.*, 18 Oct. 1995, p. 1.

[65] 'Corporate Assassins', *Sunday Tel.*, 17 Oct. 1993, City & Bus. sec., p. 5. The merchant banks' trade associations refused to join the Institutional Shareholders' Committee in 1973, on the basis that to do so would conflict with their members' role as corporate advisers: see Ch. 3, at n. 66, and accompanying text.

[66] See 'Invergordon Loses Independence', *Fin. Times*, 22 Oct. 1993, p. 21; see also 'MAM Cuts Business with Parent Warburg Over Lasmo', *Fin. Times*, 13 Aug. 1994, p. 24.

[67] *AIMA Corporate Governance Guidelines*, para. 2.3.

clients. It is recommended that the investment manager have in place a procedure for dealing with conflicts of interest . . . It is recommended that wherever a client delegates responsibility for exercising proxy votes, the investment manager should report back to the client when votes are cast (including abstentions) on investments owned by the client. . . . [T]he report should include a positive statement that the investment manager has complied with its obligation to exercise voting rights in the client's interests only. If an investment manager is unable to make this statement without qualification, the report should include an explanation.[68]

Company executives in the US, acting in their capacity as pension-scheme trustees, have applied pressure to the external fund managers of their companies' pension funds to take a pro-management approach to the voting of shares.[69] It is unclear whether the (management-appointed) trustees of UK and Australian pension funds have taken such action. In any case, the recent move towards compulsory member-trustees is a positive step towards removing this potential conflict of interest.

vii. Qualificational Constraints

The disincentives discussed to this point, which relate to the problems of collective action and agency, represent a fairly formidable set of obstacles to serious intervention by managers of external funds, and a sizeable set of obstacles for managers of internal funds. Even assuming that those barriers do not suppress the desire to monitor of *all* of a company's major institutional shareholders, there are other barriers that serve to discourage the performance of, and diminish the probability of success of, any detailed monitoring either contemplated or initiated by the otherwise-undeterred institution(s).

One such disincentive is that, whilst fund managers are probably adequately qualified to monitor the performance of company managers,[70] many may lack the skills necessary to run a campaign to replace an under-performing management team. In the words of one fund manager with experience in this area, '[f]und managers are listeners, not persuaders'.[71]

viii. Informational Constraints

Following on from the previous factor, there is the problem that, even if the intervenor (or prospective intervenor) has 'a flair for presentation' (to assist in winning over other uncommitted institutions), it would be 'difficult to match the management's arguments because [the intervenor would be] working only on the basis of the information' provided by the management.[72] As conceded by one of the participants in the UK interview study,

---

[68] Ibid, at paras. 2.3, 2.4.
[70] See Ch. 9, Sec. B.7.
[72] Ibid.

[69] See Rock (n. 16 above), at 469–70 (n. 80).
[71] Blair (n. 13 above).

institutions 'operate from a position, really, of very limited knowledge'. The reason why this factor appears under the head of 'structural disincentives' is because part of the reason for its existence lies in the fact that UK and Australian institutions typically have information solely from their equity holdings. They do not benefit (as do German and Japanese banks) from other relationships besides that of an equity holder. Even where a fund-management firm is affiliated with a commercial bank which lends to the company in question, or with an investment bank which provides financial-advisory or broking services to the company, any useful information possessed by the other divisions or subsidiaries would be (or should be) inaccessible due to Chinese Walls.

ix. Lack of Homogeneity Amongst Institutional Viewpoints

A UK fund manager interviewed by the author said that he believed that institutional interventions happened too late in the day. He continued: 'We pick up things *very* early. In a number of cases we've picked up things very early that are going wrong, but profits are going up; dividends are going up; everybody loves them; the shares are sky high. . . . It's very difficult to influence, or go and see, other shareholders when everything appears fine but you've picked things up.' Another UK fund manager said: 'The problem you've got is that institutions . . . consist of people with widely differing views on an interpretation of markets and events. And, to get them to agree is—I wouldn't say futile—but it is very, very difficult.'

In the case of institutional interventions to change under-performing managements, this lack of homogeneity in views can play a destabilizing role at two stages. First, as implied by the first of the quotations above, it can delay or prevent the formation of an institutional coalition. Secondly, where a coalition is up and running, it can either (a) defeat altogether the goals of the coalition—this has occurred where non-coalition institutions have sided with the impugned management;[73] or (b) lead to a more moderate outcome than that sought initially.[74] Looking at the first case in more detail, UK fund managers interviewed by the author commented that the ideal coalition would have two or three members, that four is the maximum for a workable group, and that these institutions should, ideally, represent at least 20–30% of the equity. An analysis of Table 5.6 in Chapter 5 shows that these conditions were unlikely to be met in the top 100 listed UK companies in 1993. It is also apparent from the figures in

---

[73] For an Australian example, see Ch. 8, at nn. 88–9, and accompanying text.

[74] See e.g. 'When Men in Grey Suits Choose to Apply Savage Pressure', *Fin. Times*, 20 Dec. 1990, p. 21 (a coalition, which initially supported unanimously a prospective new management team, succeeded in removing the impugned directors, but then divided over whether to support the new team or an alternative offered by the company's non-executive directors; the latter prevailed).

Table 5.6 that, as at 1993, if any of the three largest institutional interest-holders in a small or medium-sized listed UK company did not wish to join a coalition, an ideal coalition (as described above) probably could not have been formed.[75]

Differing institutional views affect not only attempted oustings of under-performing managements. The UK practice of pre-marketing of large transactions, rights issues, etc. was described in Chapter 5. It was noted that most pre-marketed proposals elicit a diversity of views—some favourable, some unfavourable (to varying degrees), and some indifferent—and that some proposals are, therefore, carried into effect in spite of the strong opposition of a major shareholder.[76]

In conclusion, it is only when something is blatantly wrong that there will be sufficient like-minded institutions for a successful intervention to be possible. However, it seems likely that, from a comparative perspective, this is not a weakness in the UK and Australian systems. Interventions in Germany and Japan rarely occur until a late stage of under-performance.[77]

x. Logistical and Practical Constraints

The UK interview study revealed that there are logistical problems which add to the expected cost of a planned intervention. In combination with other factors, they could deter some possible actions from taking place. They certainly hinder those interventions which do occur. Getting a group of just three or four institutions together for meetings at a mutually convenient time, at short notice, is difficult. This is the case even in the City of London, which is tailor-made for interventions because most of the large English institutions are based there. This is one of the reasons why coalitions larger than four members become unwieldy. It is difficult for the Scottish institutions to play an active role in a coalition because of the distance factor. This is also a problem in Australia, where it would not be uncommon to find that half of the potential members of an institutional coalition are located in Sydney and the other half are located in Melbourne. Another practical difficulty for a minority of institutions is a requirement to obtain the prior blessing of all or many clients before voting or taking other action in relation to controversial matters.[78]

xi. Presence of a Non-Institutional Controlling Shareholder

This factor appears under 'structural disincentives' because, as revealed in

---

[75] Recall that it was not possible to obtain an equivalent institutional-shareholder profile for listed Australian companies: see Ch. 8, at n. 78, and accompanying text; App. K.

[76] See Ch. 5, at nn. 177–8, and accompanying text.

[77] See n. 11 above, and accompanying text.

[78] See Ch. 5, at n. 79–84, and accompanying text; Ch. 8, at nn. 46–8, and accompanying text.

Chapter 8, about half of all quoted Australian companies have a non-institutional shareholder with an effectively controlling stake. Thus, the disincentive to institutional intervention which this entails flows from the structure of the corporate sector.

Where a non-institutional shareholder has a stake of such a size that a successful institutional intervention is not possible, the institutional shareholders in the company would be aware of this and would adopt an even more arm's-length approach to the investment than in the case of their investments in widely held firms. If there is a 30%+ (non-institutional) shareholder, and it is prepared to suffer bad management, then disaffected institutions will in most cases be better off by taking an alternative course of action to monitoring.[79]

2. OTHER FACTORS WHICH INHIBIT DETAILED MONITORING

The following are some further factors which serve as disincentives to detailed monitoring. These factors are not related to the structure of the system of corporate ownership and governance, the structure and workings of the fund-management industry, or the structure of the institutions themselves.

i. Non-Structural Conflicts of Interest

Conflicts of interest which arise out of the organizational structure of the institutions are not the only conflicts which deter monitoring. There are also *non-structural* conflicts, which deter certain institutions from conducting monitoring in certain areas. For instance, one UK fund-management firm would be unlikely to join other institutions in pushing for the enfranchisement of non-voting shares at portfolio companies because its listed parent company has non-voting shares. A second example is that some listed UK merchant-banking companies, which have large fund-management subsidiaries, have a tradition of scanty disclosure in their accounts[80]—in an age when institutions are increasingly urging their portfolio companies to disclose more information. A third example is that a listed UK insurance company, which did not comply with the *Cadbury Code* in four respects in 1994, reportedly failed to provide in its 1994 annual report a 'material reason for non-compliance' as required by

---

[79] Note, however, that one of the successful interventions in the UK in the early 1990s was in a company whose founder held 23% of the equity: see Ch. 5, at n. 206; cf. Ch. 8, at nn. 88–9, and accompanying text (director with a 33% stake in an Australian company fought off an institutional challenge—but not before purchasing a further 3% of the equity in the market). [80] See e.g. 'Lex: Schroders', *Fin. Times*, 4 Sept. 1993, p. 22.

[81] See 'Top UK Companies "Fail to Meet Code of Practice" ', *Fin. Times*, 23 Jan. 1995, p. 18.

paragraph 12.43(j) of the *Listing Rules*.[81] In a fourth instance, one listed UK fund manager recently implemented an executive share-option scheme which did not comply with the ABI and NAPF guidelines on performance criteria.[82] Finally, the executive directors of several listed UK insurers had three-year rolling service contracts as at 1993–4, which explained the reluctance of the ABI Investment Committee to join the call for rolling contracts to be shortened or changed to fixed-term contracts.[83]

ii. Fear of Political Repercussions

There is no doubt that, during the 1960s and 1970s, the UK institutions (in particular, the large insurers) were extremely wary about the extent of their potential power over corporate managements being seized upon as an excuse for nationalization or other major regulatory intervention.[84] There were still some concerns in the early 1980s,[85] but the 1992 interview study of Coffee suggested that fear of political retaliation was not then a significant deterrent to intervention.[86] It is possible that a change of government could alter the perception of fund managers on this matter.[87]

As regards Australia, there has been an instance of political retaliation against institutional power. A provision was introduced into the companies legislation in 1961 which required that unit-trust deeds contain a covenant barring the manager and the trustee from voting on the election of directors in portfolio companies, without the consent of a majority of unit-holders.[88] The Minister for Justice, speaking on the Bill, said: '[T]he restrictions imposed by the Bill arise out of the necessity to impose some curb on the enormous power capable of being exercised, not by the interest holders themselves but by the managers of the [unit trust] who actually

---

[82] See 'M&G Faces Criticism of Executive Option Scheme', *Fin. Times*, 22 Jan. 1994, p. 22.

[83] See 'Directors Cool to Plea on Contracts', *Fin. Times*, 14 June 1993, p. 8; 'Insurers Join Outcry Against Large Pay-Offs', *Fin. Times*, 20 Aug. 1994, p. 7. Note that one of these insurers, Prudential, announced in late 1994 that it was to reduce the length of its executives' service contracts: see 'Prudential Set to Reduce Directors' Service Contracts', *Fin. Times*, 11 Nov. 1994, p. 19.

[84] See A. Sampson, *The Anatomy of Britain* (1962) 409; K. Midgley, *Companies and Their Shareholders—The Uneasy Relationship* (1975) 77 (setting out a passage from the chairman's statement from the Prudential's 1970 annual report: '[W]e have in the past . . . had cause to be apprehensive about political reaction to any strong display of influence over companies in which we have holdings').

[85] See J. H. Farrar and M. Russell, 'The Impact of Institutional Investment on Company Law' (1984) 5 *Co. Law.* 107, at 109.

[86] See Black and Coffee (n. 35 above), at 2066–8.

[87] See P. L. Davies and G. P. Stapledon, 'Comment on B. S. Black and J. C. Coffee, "Hail Britannia? Institutional Investor Behavior Under Limited Regulation" ' in Coffee, Gilson, and Lowenstein (n. 11 above).

[88] See now CL, s. 1069(1)(k). This provision still exists, and a recommendation for its repeal is made in Ch. 11, Sec. B.1.iii; see also Ch. 8, at nn. 50–4, and accompanying text.

may have little financial interest in a particular trust.'[89] None of the participants in the author's Australian interview study mentioned fear of political repercussions as a disincentive to detailed monitoring. It should be noted that a Parliamentary inquiry into the role of institutional share-holders in Australia was conducted during 1993–5. The inquiry was, however, concerned more about a lack of, rather than too much, institutional involvement in corporate governance.[90]

iii. Legal Constraints

UK institutional shareholders are subject to significantly less legal constraints than their US counterparts.[91] None of the interviewees in the UK interview project cited legal constraints as a major deterrent to their intervening at a problem company. The situation for Australian institutions falls somewhere between the restrictive US situation and the UK situation. Several of the Australia-based fund managers interviewed by the author said that legal constraints served as a significant deterrent to their engaging in collective action at a portfolio company. The main provisions affecting UK and Australian institutions are detailed below.

Both countries have insider-trading legislation.[92] It does not matter if an institution comes into possession of insider information during the course of monitoring, so long as it does not trade on it, encourage or procure another party to trade in the shares, or communicate the information to others.[93] But does the insider-trading legislation cause institutions to conduct significantly less monitoring than they would conduct in its absence? First, the legislation is not a barrier to routine meetings with company managements.[94] Secondly, it is difficult to see how the legislation could stymie interventions, because institutions only initiate or join coalitions when they have decided that they do not want to sell their shares at the prevailing price. Thirdly, in relation to pre-marketing of proposed large transactions, although most of the UK institutions covered in the interview project were happy to be made insiders for a few days,[95] it might

---

[89] The passage is set out in D. Harding, 'Do Institutional Investors in Australia Have a Fiduciary Responsibility to Vote?' (1994).

[90] See Parliamentary Joint Committee on Corporations and Securities, *Background Paper: Institutional Investor Inquiry* (1993) 4.

[91] See Black (n. 62 above), at 530–60, for a thorough analysis of the US situation.

[92] See Criminal Justice Act 1993 (UK), Pt. V; CL, Pt. 7.11, Div. 2A.

[93] This is a generalization of the UK and Australian provisions, which are very technical—with considerable importance attaching to the words and phrases used.

[94] Indeed, five months after the introduction of new insider-dealing legislation in the UK, which was widely perceived as stricter than the earlier legislation, a survey of listed companies found that 86% of respondents were having one-to-one meetings with major institutional shareholders the 'same as before', 11% 'less often', and only 3% 'not at all': Focus Communications, *Criminal Justice Act 1993: Its Impact Upon Financial Communications* (1994) 10.

[95] See Ch. 5, at n. 180, and accompanying text; *Listing Rules*, para. 9.3.

be argued that without the prohibition on insider trading they would be able to become involved at an earlier stage. However, it is likely that, even in the absence of the legislation, a company's management would divulge undisclosed price-sensitive information to an institutional shareholder only if the institution first gave an undertaking not to trade in the shares until the information became public. The desire for freedom to trade would ensure the same relatively short period during which the institution would be happy to be an insider. Finally, inability to trade the shares is cited commonly as a reason why institutions do not want 'institutional' non-executive directors. A Chinese Wall could, however, be utilized to enable the institution to trade the shares of a company at which one of its fund managers or a nominee was a non-executive director.[96] In addition, there are several other reasons usually given by institutions when explaining their antipathy to the concept of institutional non-executives.[97] These other factors would remain as strong disincentives to institutional non-executives even if there were no insider-trading legislation.

It is possible in each country for an institution to be held liable for wrongful or insolvent trading at a portfolio company, if the institution is a party in accordance with whose directions or instructions the directors of the company are accustomed to act (i.e. a 'shadow director').[98] In addition, in Australia, if it is a shadow director, an institution is subject to all of the provisions of the Corporations Law to which any director is subject.[99] Importantly, there are numerous directors' duties codified in the Australian legislation,[100] and these would be applicable. Despite the fact that this is a rather harsh eventuality, most of the UK fund managers interviewed by Coffee denied that this possibility entered their thinking when intervening at, or otherwise monitoring the management of, a portfolio company. Whether an institution *is* a party in accordance with whose instructions the board is accustomed to act must be determined from the point of view of the board.[101] However, probably the last thing that a board, which was the subject of an institutional intervention, would do would be to act in accordance with the instructions of the institutions (if any were given, which is most unlikely). It is not surprising then that, as Coffee's interviews indicated, this potential legal problem is not considered to be of practical importance by UK institutions.

---

[96] See CL, s. 1002M; also s. 1002J (exception for underwriters).
[97] See Ch. 5, at nn. 348–9, and accompanying text; Ch. 8, at n. 136, and accompanying text.
[98] Insolvency Act 1986 (UK), ss. 214(7), 251; CL, ss. 588G, 60(1)(b).
[99] This is because a 'shadow director' is included within the basic definition of a director: CL, s. 60(1). [100] CL, s. 232.
[101] D. D. Prentice, 'Directors, Creditors, and Shareholders' in E. McKendrick (ed.), *Commercial Aspects of Trusts and Fiduciary Obligations* (1992) 73, at 81 (n. 39).

Australia has a statutory system for regulating takeovers and, as Hill points out, the provisions 'are more than capable of catching conduct not strictly associated with a takeover bid at all'.[102] Section 615 of the Corporations Law prohibits an acquisition of shares in a company if it would result in (a) any person presently 'entitled' to less than 20% of the voting shares in the company becoming entitled to more than 20% of the voting shares; or (b) any person already entitled to between 20–90% of the voting shares becoming entitled to a greater percentage of the voting shares.[103] Part 6.7 of the Corporations Law[104] contains a regime under which any person who becomes a 'substantial shareholder', or whose substantial shareholding changes by a certain amount, or who ceases to be a substantial shareholder, must notify the company and the ASX of certain prescribed particulars. A person has a substantial shareholding for the purposes of Part 6.7 if the person is 'entitled' to 5% or more of the voting shares.[105] The crucial concept in section 615 and Part 6.7 is, therefore, 'entitlement' to shares. The shares to which a person is entitled include not only shares in which that person has a 'relevant interest',[106] but also shares in which an 'associate' has a relevant interest.[107] An associate includes a person *in concert* with whom the primary person is acting or proposes to act;[108] and a person with whom the primary person has, or proposes to enter into, an *agreement, arrangement, or understanding* (formal or informal, written or oral, legally enforceable or otherwise) for the purpose of controlling or influencing the composition of the company's board or the conduct of the company's affairs.[109]

A handful of institutions which form a loose coalition in order to replace an under-performing management team or board would almost certainly be 'associates'. Even co-operation between a group of institutions in relation to a non-control issue (for example a proposed, excessively generous, executive share-option scheme) may constitute the institutions associates of each other. A breach of Part 6.7 and possibly also section 615 could result. Section 615 is, for two reasons, less likely to be breached than Part 6.7. First, the threshold for Part 6.7 is 5% of the voting shares whereas the threshold for section 615 is 20% of the voting shares. Secondly, section 615 has the extra requirement that there must be an 'acquisition' of

---

[102] J. Hill, 'Institutional Investors and Corporate Governance in Australia' in Baums, Buxbaum, and Hopt (n. 8 above), 583, at 606.
[103] CL, Ch. 6 specifies numerous exceptions to this prohibition: e.g. for acquisitions under takeover schemes and takeover announcements, and for creeping acquisitions.
[104] Pt. 6.7 applies to all listed companies and to any unlisted companies specified by the Minister: CL, s. 707(1).   [105] CL, s. 708(1).
[106] A person has a 'relevant interest' in a share if the person has power to vote in respect of, or to dispose of, the share: CL, s. 31.   [107] CL, s. 609(1).
[108] CL, s. 15(1)(a).   [109] CL, s. 12(1)(e).

shares.[110] Nevertheless, in the case of most large Australia-based institutions, the total shareholding in a particular company consists of many—possibly dozens of—separate holdings for particular funds and/or clients. The acquisition element of section 615 could therefore be satisfied almost unintentionally. For example, by an 'index' purchase of shares for a unit trust which tracks an ASX index of which the particular company is a constituent.

It might be argued that the foregoing is largely academic, and that in practice there is little likelihood of institutions ever suffering any consequences as a result of a 'technical' breach of section 615 or Part 6.7. Any such argument would, for two reasons, be misconceived. First, several interviewees in the Australian interview project said that the potential application of these provisions served as a significant deterrent to their engaging in collective action at a portfolio company. Secondly, the overseas experience suggests that there is cause for concern. In the US, where there are provisions similar to those in Part 6.7 of the Corporations Law, lawyers who advise corporate managements provided the following advice in a public forum: '[I]f several institutional investors communicate with each other with respect to an election of registrant directors or an alternative slate of nominees, registrants should consider asserting the application of Schedule 13D [i.e. the equivalent of Corporations Law, Part 6.7].'[111] It is reasonable to expect that equivalent advice would be given by advisers to an Australian corporate management which was subject to an institutional intervention. A significant weapon in this context could be section 1324 of the Corporations Law. Under this provision, the Australian Securities Commission or any person whose interests have been, are, or would be affected by a contravention of the Corporations Law has standing to apply to the court for an injunction or damages. The impugned directors could bring an application under section 1324 in the name of the company,[112] alleging a breach of Part 6.7 and/or section 615. There is also the prospect of criminal prosecution. Any person who breaches the prohibition in section 615 or one of the notification provisions in Part 6.7 is guilty of a criminal offence, and is subject to a fine of up to A$2,500 (or A$12,500 if the person is a body corporate), or imprisonment for 6 months, or both.[113]

---

[110] CL, ss. 615, 51, 64; Hill (n. 102 above), at 607.

[111] Cited in B. S. Black, 'Next Steps in Proxy Reform' (1992) 18 *J Corp. Law* 1, at 51–2.

[112] There can be little doubt that the company would be 'a person whose interests have been . . . affected' by the contravention.

[113] CL, ss. 1311, 1312; Sch. 3. There are potentially further consequences. Although an acquisition of shares is not invalid because of a contravention of s. 615(1) (see CL, s. 615(6)), in this situation the ASC, the company, a member of the company, or the person from whom the shares were acquired, may apply to the court for an order. The court may make such order or orders as it thinks just, including orders restraining the exercise of voting rights, directing

The potential for collective action by institutions to contravene section 615 and/or Part 6.7 of the Corporations Law does not sit comfortably with a model of corporate governance in which monitoring by institutional shareholders plays an important role. Therefore, in the final chapter a recommendation is made for legislative reform in this area.[114]

There are several other legal and regulatory restrictions which may affect institutional investors. First, the Reserve Bank of Australia discourages banks from holding equity in non-financial companies.[115] Secondly, an Australian investment company (a closed-end fund) is barred from holding more than 5% of the issued ordinary shares of any company.[116] Thirdly, the London Stock Exchange requires that investment trusts, investment companies, and unit trusts wishing to list on the Exchange must be passive investors, and must not control or seek to control, or be actively involved in the management of, their portfolio companies.[117] Fourthly, the minimum notice period for extraordinary general meetings is just 14 days.[118]

3. FACTORS WHICH PRECIPITATE DETAILED MONITORING

The UK interview study revealed four main factors which serve to increase an institution's propensity to intervene to change an under-performing management: (a) unattractiveness of alternative strategies; (b) an over-weight holding in the company; (c) fundamental soundness of the underlying business; and (d) deliberate misrepresentations by the management. Observation of the reported interventions suggests a further factor: (e) entrepreneurs.

In relation to (a), it is fairly obvious why an institution, when it considers itself 'locked in' (essentially, unable to dispose of its shareholding at a sensible price), and can see no prospect of—or cannot engineer—a takeover, should be more inclined to intervene than at other times. Factor (b) is discussed in Section B.1.(3), above. Three of the four UK interviewees who mentioned factor (c) worked for firms which managed predominantly *external* funds. This indicates that the fund manager

---

the disposal of the shares, or vesting the shares in the ASC: CL, ss. 737, 613(1); cf. s. 743. A person who contravenes one of the notification provisions in Pt. 6.7 is liable to pay, to any person who suffers loss or damage as a result of the contravention, damages in respect of that loss or damage, unless it is proved that the contravention was due to inadvertence or mistake (not being ignorance of, or a mistake concerning, a matter of law: CL, s. 610): CL, s. 716(1).

[114] See Ch. 11, Sec. B.1.ix. See also the recent proposals of the Corporations Law Simplification Task Force, in *Takeovers: Proposal for Simplification* (1996), which (if implemented) would remove the problem detailed in the text.

[115] Reserve Bank of Australia, *Prudential Statement No. G1* (1990).

[116] CL, s. 401(2).   [117] *Listing Rules*, para. 21.2(c).

[118] CA 1985, s. 369(1); CL, s. 247(2). See further Ch. 11, Sec. B.1.iv.

believes that, with better management, the company's share price would improve to such an extent that the costs of the intervention would be more than offset by the anticipated increase in the fund manager's fees (which are based on the value of funds under management).[119] Regarding (d), three of the UK interviewees mentioned that they had initiated, or taken part in, an institutional intervention where they believed that they had been 'lied to' by the impugned management. In one case, the institution had been buying more and more shares in the company—right up until it issued a profits warning—because of the very positive sentiments being expressed at its meetings with the management. Obviously, as in other areas of life, considerations other than purely financial ones may carry weight in this sort of situation.

As regards (e), there is no evidence of US-style *political* entrepreneurs[120] operating on a significant scale in either the UK or Australia.[121] There is, on the other hand, evidence that an entrepreneur of another type contributed to some institutional interventions in the UK. Fidelity Investments International, the UK arm of the large US-based mutual-fund manager, Fidelity Investments, appears to have taken a deliberately high-profile approach to corporate governance in the early 1990s. Despite its relatively small size (it was not amongst the largest 50 managers of quoted UK equities at the end of 1991), it employed a full-time Corporate Finance Director to deal with 'problem companies' in its portfolio. This seems to be an example of an external fund manager believing that it can derive 'private benefits [for example an increase in investors into its unit trusts] from being perceived as an active shareholder advocate'.[122] Ironically, however, Fidelity parted company with this fellow in 1992 because 'his actions had received too much adverse publicity'.[123]

4. CONCLUSIONS

There are numerous disincentives to institutional activism in both the UK and Australia, which affect particularly the managers of external funds. It would be only in rare circumstances that an external fund manager would stand to gain more from an intervention than from an alternative course of action. In the absence of positive regulatory changes, it is probable that

---

[119] See nn. 51–5 above, and accompanying text.
[120] Political entrepreneurs are described in Ch. 9, at nn. 210–11, and accompanying text.
[121] See Ch. 9, at nn. 215–16, and accompanying text.
[122] Rock (n. 16 above), at 460.
[123] 'Tough Tactics Behind the Unit Trusts', *Fin. Times*, 5 Aug. 1992, p. 15. He later cautioned, in a brief guide to conducting institutional interventions: 'How does your marketing director feel about your efforts? [Improving] corporate governance may be a good thing, but it tends to draw clients' attention to your bad investments': Blair (n. 13 above).

there will be no significant increase on the current level of detailed firm-level monitoring in the UK, and only a small increase on the current level in Australia. The explanation for the expected small increase in Australia is that institutional share ownership, and with that the concentration of shareholding, is likely to increase in the next few years in Australia.[124]

C. INDIRECT FIRM-LEVEL MONITORING

1. COLLECTIVE-ACTION VEHICLES

There is nothing to suggest that the level of firm-level monitoring performed by the various trade associations will increase significantly in the next few years. It is clear that the institutions, in both the UK and Australia, see their associations' role in this area as being one of support for, and facilitation of, action by the institutional shareholders which have holdings in the company concerned. The great majority do not support a role such as that which some hoped the Institutional Shareholders' Committee might play when it was first formed, and when it was reconstituted.[125]

2. NON-EXECUTIVE DIRECTORS

The *Cadbury Code* (in the UK) and the *AIMA Corporate Governance Guidelines* (in Australia) will probably result in an increase in the proportion of non-affiliated (or 'independent') non-executive directors on boards over the next few years. On the other hand, it is likely to remain extremely rare for fund managers to serve as non-executive directors, and very rare for institutions to place nominees (other than fund managers) onto company boards, in the absence of regulations requiring shareholder-constituted appointment committees.[126] It should be noted, however, that there have been some important, if only gradual, improvements in the dependence of non-executive directors upon shareholder choice. These are discussed in earlier chapters.[127] It is considered likely that there will be a continued gradual improvement in this area even without any regulatory change.

---

[124] See Ch. 2, Sec. B.
[125] See Ch. 5, at nn. 257–8, 265–70, and accompanying text.
[126] See further Ch. 11, Sec. B.2.iii.
[127] See Ch. 5, at nn. 333–40, and accompanying text; Ch. 8, at n. 132, and accompanying text.

11

Conclusion and Suggested Reforms

A. CONCLUSION

In the aftermath of the takeovers boom which occurred in the UK and the US during the mid-to-late 1980s, and the scandals concerning Australian entrepreneurial companies of that period, many commentators in all three countries called for a greater involvement by institutional shareholders in corporate governance. This book has explored the topic of institutional monitoring of corporate managements in the UK and Australia. The aim of the book has been twofold: to present a picture of the extent and nature of institutional monitoring in the UK and Australia, and to analyse the possibilities for institutional monitoring in the future in each country.

Any study of institutional-shareholder involvement in corporate governance in the UK must take account of the fact that the systems of corporate ownership and governance in the UK and the US are fundamentally different from those in most other major 'western' economies. The UK and US corporate sectors are characterized by a relatively large number of quoted companies, a liquid capital market where ownership and control rights are traded frequently, and few inter-corporate equity holdings.[1] The corporate sectors of Germany and Japan are, in contrast, characterized by a relatively small number of quoted companies, an illiquid capital market where ownership and control rights are traded infrequently, and many inter-corporate shareholdings. The UK and US systems of corporate ownership and governance are 'outsider' systems, whilst the German and Japanese systems are 'insider' systems.[2] The characteristics of the Australian corporate sector are a hybrid of those of the corporate sectors just mentioned. Not only is the quoted corporate sector not as significant a part of the economy in Australia as it is in Britain, but inter-corporate shareholdings and 'founding-family' shareholdings of 30% or more of the issued capital (which are in effect controlling shareholdings) are prevalent in the Australian quoted corporate sector although scarce in the UK equivalent. A large proportion of the Australian quoted corporate sector is, therefore, virtually immune to hostile takeover *and* to intervention by institutional shareholders.

---

[1] See J. R. Franks and C. P. Mayer, 'Corporate Control: A Synthesis of the International Evidence' in J. C. Coffee, R. J. Gilson, and L. Lowenstein (eds.), *Relational Investing* (1996) (forthcoming).
[2] Ibid.

Although the book has paid particular attention to the role of the institutions as monitors of managerial performance at the individual-firm level, Chapters 4 and 7 demonstrated that the institutions have had considerable involvement in procedural and general issues. UK institutions have, both directly and indirectly (through their trade associations), played a significant role in shaping the regulatory framework within which quoted UK companies operate.[3] They have exerted an influence over matters ranging from the pre-emption right to board structure and composition, executive remuneration, and disclosure of financial information. Australian institutions have, in recent years, taken steps in the same direction. The procedural and general issues upon which the institutions have focused their attention invariably possess some or all of the same important features: (a) they are reasonably uncomplicated; (b) they exist in, or have the potential to arise at, a large number of companies; and (c) they can be addressed relatively easily and inexpensively across a wide range of companies.

Company-specific matters, on the other hand, possess none of those characteristics. The most important company-specific matter with which the institutions have been concerned is seriously sub-optimal performance by senior management. The opening chapter showed that institutional monitoring of managerial performance fits within a broad tapestry of devices and market forces which operate to reduce the divergence between the interests of managers and shareholders in non-controlled quoted companies. There are weaknesses in each element of that monitoring environment. The market for corporate control, in particular, was demonstrated to have serious shortcomings as a monitoring force. The weaknesses in the other components of the monitoring environment raised the question early in the book of whether steps could usefully be taken to facilitate a greater level of monitoring by institutional shareholders.

Chapters 5 and 8 were devoted mainly to an examination of the nature and extent of firm-level monitoring by institutions—individually and collectively, and through trade associations and non-executive directors. Firm-level monitoring in the UK was found to consist of (a) routine one-to-one meetings with company managements; (b) a high level of voting on controversial or momentous issues, but a fairly low level on routine matters (partly due to the practical difficulties faced by some managers of external funds); (c) a systematic and proactive approach to 'problem companies' and corporate-governance concerns by only a (significant) minority of the major fund managers (mostly managers of internal funds); (d) infrequent

---

[3] Terminology from D. D. Prentice, 'Some Aspects of the Corporate Governance Debate' in D. D. Prentice and P. R. J. Holland (eds.), *Contemporary Issues in Corporate Governance* (1993) 25, at 38.

interventions to change the management of problem companies,[4] confined to (i) cases where a management had been 'completely discredited' (most often through the company's disastrous financial performance; sometimes combined with a strong suspicion of deliberately misleading or improper conduct by the impugned management); and (ii) small and medium-sized quoted companies (partly due to the inability to form a coalition of three or four institutions with 25–30% of the votes in a top 100 company);[5] (e) virtually no use of litigation; and (f) liaison between institutions and non-executive directors only in problem situations (but with signs in the late 1980s to early 1990s of a slightly greater level of contact in non-problem situations).

Firm-level monitoring in Australia was found to possess features (a), (b), (e), and (f). In regard to (c), there was probably only one Australian institution which devoted the level of resources to corporate governance that was devoted by a handful of the major UK institutions, at 1993. In the key area of intervention to change an under-performing management team, there was a very wide differential between the level of activity in Australia and the UK. This reflects the fact that, as at late 1993, many listed Australian companies (accounting for about 40–50% of the quoted sector) were effectively immune from serious institutional intervention, by reason of their having a very large non-institutional shareholder which had effective control over the composition of the board. In contrast, as at late 1993, about 85–90% of quoted UK companies lacked such a shareholder; their share registers were dominated by institutional shareholders.

The level of serious institutional intervention has thus been fairly low in the UK, and very low in Australia. It was estimated in Chapter 5 that there were about 18 interventions per year in the UK during 1990–3, but less in the preceding five-year period. Although 18 interventions per year certainly is not a low level of intervention compared to the level in Australia and the US, it must be borne in mind that at the end of 1990 there were about 2,370 quoted UK companies (i.e. listed and USM-quoted). That means that some 99.24% of quoted UK companies were (each year) untouched by serious institutional intervention during the early 1990s. Whilst it is undoubtedly true that the great majority of quoted UK companies are managed well, it is hard to believe that only seven-tenths of one per cent suffer from very poor management. The fairly low level

---

[4] The comparative prevalence of which in the early 1990s gives weight to the theory that they are a substitute for those hostile takeovers which involve the acquisition of poorly managed firms by efficiently managed firms.

[5] The statistics produced in Study B illustrate why this is so. In general, the smaller the (quoted) company, the greater is the concentration of shareholding amongst the largest five or six institutions: see Table 5.6.

of intervention suggests that, despite a lack of substantial regulatory barriers to intervention by institutions, there are other barriers to detailed monitoring. That matter was addressed in Chapter 10. Prior to that, however, attention was turned to the issue of the pros and cons of detailed institutional involvement in corporate governance.

Chapter 9 found no support for the theory that the institutions behave in a short-term manner. On the other hand, it was contended that there *is* a form of short-termism inherent in the UK quoted corporate sector. 'Inherent short-termism' results from the fact that the ultimate controllers of the great majority of quoted UK companies are essentially arm's-length investors, whereas the controlling shareholders of most quoted German and Japanese companies are 'committed shareholders'. Inherent short-termism would exist whether the share registers of quoted UK companies were dominated by institutions or individual shareholders. It was argued that there are historical reasons for the dominance of arm's-length, rather than committed, shareholders in the UK quoted sector; and that there is very little, by way of regulatory change, that could be done so as to replace the UK's arm's-length investors with committed shareholders. On a positive note, inherent short-termism is not likely to be made worse if steps were to be taken aimed at enhancing institutional monitoring. A closer relationship between institutions and corporate managements may in fact be beneficial in this respect. Any benefit would probably only be marginal, however, because, so long as the hostile takeover (and the threat of hostile takeover) remains a centre-piece of the UK system of corporate governance, there will be a lack of incentives for managements, and of underlying structures to enable managements, to look to the long term.

Chapter 10 found that the fundamental reason for interventions being confined to the very worst cases of sub-optimal performance is that in most instances of under-performance there are only weak incentives for, but strong disincentives to, intervention through an institutional coalition.[6] The largest disincentives affect external fund managers more than managers of internal funds. There are agency costs associated with the relationship between external fund managers and their clients, and these result in a lower level of detailed monitoring being performed by the fund managers than is optimal from the point of view of their clients. This begs the question of what could be done to increase the incentives for, and decrease the disincentives to, intervention. Coffee proposes one measure which might well adjust the incentives in the way mentioned. His

---

[6] Interestingly, it seems likely that, from a comparative perspective, intervention at a late stage of under-performance is not a weakness in the UK and Australian systems. Interventions in Germany and Japan rarely occur until a crisis situation: see Ch. 10, at n. 11, and accompanying text.

suggestion is that the ability of institutions to diversify be restricted.[7] Since the holding of a significantly overweight stake is one of the few factors precipitating intervention by an institution,[8] any regulation which forced fund managers to hold much larger stakes in fewer companies would probably lead to more use of 'voice' (including intervention) and less use of 'exit'.[9] However, restricted diversification would almost certainly be extremely unattractive, politically, and is therefore considered an unrealistic option for reform.[10] Coffee also proposes incentive compensation for external fund managers, as a measure towards aligning the interests of such fund managers with those of their clients.[11] He was, however, told in his interviews with UK fund managers that the introduction of worthwhile incentive compensation is infeasible commercially in the UK due to client distrust of high fees and the highly competitive market for fund management.[12] It would appear, therefore, that there is no realistic reform that could be made to reduce the economic disincentives to detailed monitoring. Accordingly, the reforms recommended below are fairly modest. Most are directed at removing regulatory obstacles so as to assist monitoring by those institutions which do have incentives to take action. One exception is a recommendation directed at removing a substantial legal disincentive to collective action by Australia-based institutions. Another exception relates to the material-transactions provisions.

It might be argued that, because in practice proposed Super Class 1

---

[7] See J. C. Coffee, 'Liquidity Versus Control: The Institutional Investor as Corporate Monitor' (1991) 91 *Colum. L Rev.* 1277, at 1355–7.

[8] See Ch. 10, Sec. B.1.iii.

[9] See A. Hirschman, *Exit, Voice, and Loyalty: Responses to Decline in Firms, Organizations, and States* (1970).

[10] At present, diversification is effectively a legal *requirement* for trustees in the UK, and for trustees of superannuation schemes in Australia. The Trustee Investments Act 1961 (UK), s. 6(1), requires trustees to have regard to 'the need for diversification of investments . . . insofar as it is appropriate to the circumstances of the trust'. (See also Pensions Act 1995 (UK), s. 36(2).) Under the Superannuation Industry (Supervision) Act 1993 (Cth.), s. 52, a superannuation trust deed is required to contain a covenant by the trustees to give effect to an investment strategy that has regard to, *inter alia*, 'the composition of the [scheme's] investments as a whole including the extent to which the investments are diverse or involve the [scheme] in being exposed to risks from inadequate diversification'.

[11] See Coffee (n. 7 above), at 1362–6.

[12] See B. S. Black and J. C. Coffee, 'Hail Britannia? Institutional Investor Behavior Under Limited Regulation' (1994) 92 *Mich. L Rev.* 1997, at 2058. The disincentive resulting from the structural conflicts of interest which affect many fund managers (see Ch. 10, Sec. B.1.vi) would be overcome partially by confidential voting: see E. B. Rock, 'The Logic and (Uncertain) Significance of Institutional Shareholder Activism' (1991) 79 *Georgetown LJ* 445, at 489–90. (One Australian interviewee favoured the introduction of confidential voting.) However, since many interventions do not reach the stage of an EGM, the problem would largely remain so far as interventions were concerned. There are also difficulties associated with confidential voting: see Rock, ibid., at 490.

transactions and reverse takeovers[13] are almost never voted down,[14] the material-transactions provisions serve only to add to net agency costs. To so argue would, however, overlook the important effect of the provisions at an earlier stage. A proposed large transaction very rarely gets to the stage of a shareholder vote at a general meeting if the bulk of the company's main institutional shareholders are opposed to it. In such cases, things do not normally even reach the stage of a meeting being convened, because the proposal (at least in the opposed form) would be abandoned at the pre-marketing stage. This illustrates the importance of the material-transactions provisions in the *Listing Rules*: pre-marketing occurs much more frequently for transactions which require general-meeting approval than for those which do not.[15] Indeed, the provisions probably have an effect even further back: in all likelihood, managements propose only those deals for which they are confident that there will be institutional-shareholder support. Some would-be 'empire-building' deals have doubt-less been abandoned before any discussions were held with institutions, or possibly after a preliminary 'sounding out' exercise was done on a hypothetical basis. It is recommended below that the threshold for Super Class 1 transactions should be reduced, and that material-transactions provisions should be introduced into the listing rules of the ASX.

B. RECOMMENDED REFORMS

As discussed in Chapter 9, the two main possible advantages of greater institutional monitoring are that it might produce a reduction in agency costs, and lead to a greater focus by corporate management on the long-term.[16] The reforms that are suggested in the remainder of this chapter are directed primarily at the first of those aims. Although better communication and liaison between companies' managements and major institutional shareholders should help to reduce the problem of 'managerial short-termism through misconception',[17] there seems to be little in the way of realistic regulation that could alter significantly the existing, essentially arm's-length, relationship between company managements and institutions.[18] However, the tightening of the rules governing shareholder approval of large transactions would necessitate a greater amount of pre-marketing. As well as affording large shareholders the opportunity to,

---

[13] See *Listing Rules*, ch. 10.

[14] The last-minute withdrawal of a proposal by British Land plc in 1989 (see Ch. 5, at nn. 229–31, and accompanying text) is the only recent case of a 'defeat' of a proposed Super Class 1 transaction.   [15] See Ch. 5, at n. 176, and accompanying text.

[16] See Ch. 9, Sec. A; P. R. Marsh, *Short-Termism on Trial* (1990) 85–7.

[17] See Ch. 9, Secs. A.2, B.1.   [18] See nn. 7–12 above, and accompanying text.

for example, forestall 'empire-building' transactions, the additional pre-marketing with large shareholders may have some minor benefits in terms of less managerial short-termism through misconception.

Two general points should be noted in regard to the reforms which are outlined below. First, several of the proposals include suggested changes to the listing requirements of the London Stock Exchange and the ASX. In years to come, the *Listing Rules* and the *ASX Listing Rules* may prove to be a less effective regulatory vehicle than is currently the case. The reason for this cautionary note is that it seems likely that in future UK companies will have the opportunity of listing on a UK exchange other than the London Stock Exchange, and Australian companies will have the opportunity of listing on an Australian exchange other than the ASX.[19] The second general point to note is that the arguments underlying several of the reforms suggested below are presented in earlier chapters, and are not repeated below—although references are provided to the appropriate passages in the earlier chapters.

1. REFORMS AFFECTING DIRECT MONITORING

i. Compulsory Voting?

It was argued in Chapter 5 that it is not a part of the fiduciary duties of the trustees of pension and superannuation schemes to exercise their voting rights on all occasions.[20] Nevertheless, a case can be made for the introduction of a requirement that institutions vote their shares on all occasions 'as a useful discipline to monitoring'.[21] Indeed, there were calls from the Labour Party and from a minority of the House of Commons Employment Committee, in 1995, for voting to be made compulsory for the trustees (or fund managers) of UK pension funds.[22]

Helpfully, there is an analogue by which to judge the likely outcome of a compulsory-voting requirement in the UK and Australia. Since the mid-1980s, the US Department of Labor has required that the voting rights

---

[19] See 'SIB Recognises Tradepoint: Stock Exchange', *Fin. Times*, 8 June 1995, p. 13; 'New Trading System Set for Launch', *Aust. Fin. Rev.*, 21 Sept. 1995, p. 22. Another point to note is that in 1995 the London Stock Exchange demonstrated an aversion to having its *Listing Rules* used to promote standards of best practice developed by bodies other than the Exchange: see London Stock Exchange, *Proposed Changes to the Listing Rules: Amendment 5* (1995).   [20] See Ch. 5, Sec. B.1.ii.

[21] P. L. Davies, 'Institutional Investors in the United Kingdom' in Prentice and Holland (n. 3 above), 69, at 92.

[22] See 'Labour Pushes Pension Funds to Fight Gravy Train', *Guardian*, 16 Jan. 1995, p. 13; House of Commons Employment Committee, *Third Report: The Remuneration of Directors and Chief Executives of Privatised Utilities* (1995) lxiii (cf. the non-prescriptive statement of the majority of the Committee: 'institutional shareholders . . . ought, as a matter of course, to exercise their voting rights': para. 98).

attached to the equity investments of each US non-public pension plan be voted 'on issues that may affect the value of the plan's investment'.[23] The Department of Labor has taken the view that voting rights are an asset of a pension plan, and therefore must be exercised 'solely in the interests of . . . and for the exclusive purpose of providing benefits to participants and beneficiaries'.[24] Where, as in the usual case, the pension-plan trustees have delegated the investment-management task to one or more external fund manager(s), the regulations state that the obligation to vote rests with the external fund manager(s) unless the trustees have expressly retained the voting right. Further, where voting is the responsibility of the external fund manager(s), the trustees are obliged to 'periodically monitor [the] decisions made and actions taken by the investment manager with regard to proxy voting decisions'.[25] Therefore, as Coffee says, there is both a duty to vote (which usually falls on the external investment manager), and a duty to monitor voting (which falls on the trustees, and which is effectively a duty of care imposed upon the trustees to supervise the voting performance of the investment manager).[26]

The US experience would not instil confidence into proponents of a compulsory-voting rule. There is evidence that some external fund managers have created formalized procedures and voting guidelines that are basically window-dressing.[27] Further, there is little legal incentive for fund managers to take their voting responsibilities seriously, because the Department of Labor has inadequate resources to take widespread legal actions,[28] and fund beneficiaries have not brought any actions for breach of

---

[23] 'DOL Issues New Guidelines on Proxy Voting, Active Investing', *IRRC Corp. Gov. Bull.*, July/Aug. 1994, p. 1, at 5 (citing Department of Labor, *Interpretive Bulletin 94–2*). The determination of which issues may affect the value of the shares is left to the party with voting authority, whether that be the trustees or the external investment manager(s): ibid. This voting requirement was initially contained in informal guidelines, based around the 'Avon letter', but in mid-1994 the guidelines were consolidated into regulations: ibid.

[24] Coffee (n. 7 above), at 1353.

[25] 'DOL Issues . . .' (n. 23 above), at 5 (citing Department of Labor, *Interpretive Bulletin 94–2*).   [26] Coffee (n. 7 above), at 1354.

[27] Ibid., at 1353 (see also at 1341, n. 244).

[28] The Department of Labor has not examined proxy voting activities as part of its normal audits of ERISA funds, and had no plans to do so as at mid-1994: 'DOL Issues . . .' (n. 23 above), at 7. The Department conducted only two enforcement efforts in the seven years to 1994. In 1988 it queried 120 investment managers on how they voted on controversial voting issues at 23 companies; and in 1993 it questioned 75 bank nominee companies as to their performance in passing proxy forms on to the voting party. In early 1995, it announced that it would shortly carry out its third initiative—an examination of the conduct of those responsible for voting, with a focus on the process adopted in deciding how to vote (on a limited number of issues at 1994 general meetings, including 'incentive stock option plans in companies that had poor performance; the elimination of existing shareholder rights and protections; shareholder proposals to adopt confidential voting; and election of [directors]'): 'DOL Launches New Investigation of Proxy Voting by Pension Funds', *IRRC Corp. Gov. Bull.*, Jan./Mar. 1995, p. 1.

fiduciary duty based on failure to vote, or failure to vote in an informed or proper manner.[29] Thus, even with the substantially greater incentives to litigate existing in the US, compared to the UK and Australia, and a reasonably well-resourced regulator, the US experience with compulsory voting has not been terribly positive.

If a compulsory-voting requirement were introduced in either the UK or Australia, the regulator could be expected to have less resources than the US regulator to enforce the rule, and pension-scheme members would have far fewer incentives than their US counterparts to take legal action against a fund manager or their trustees.[30] Even if members of pension schemes (for instance) had the incentives to litigate, it would often be extremely difficult to establish the necessary causative link between the lack of voting (or lack of informed voting) and the losses incurred by the trust funds on the shareholding in question. Finally, and most importantly, in the face of these very weak legal incentives to take a voting requirement seriously, it is to be expected that many external fund managers would—given the structural disincentives to detailed monitoring which they face[31]—rationally adopt only the sort of window-dressing approach evident in the US.[32] For these reasons, it is concluded that a compulsory-voting requirement would not be a worthwhile reform.

In mid-1995, the British Labour Party was considering whether its policy on City matters should include a requirement that fund managers must, after each general meeting, disclose publicly how they voted.[33] Such a requirement would be inappropriate, for two reasons. First, fund managers should be accountable to their clients, not to all other shareholders in the company concerned or some wider audience. In the case of a pension or superannuation fund, there would be adequate accountability at the level of fund manager: trustees if there were adopted a reform like that suggested in Section B.1.viii, below. The advent of compulsory member-nominated trustees has ensured adequate accountability at the level of trustees: beneficiaries. Secondly, the obtaining by a fund manager of an 'activist' reputation carries with it the potential for a loss of business (both in the fund-management area and in affiliated businesses).[34] Less, rather than more, detailed monitoring is likely to result from any regulation which

---

[29] See Rock (n. 12 above), at 476–8; A. F. Conard, 'Beyond Managerialism: Investor Capitalism?' (1988) 22 *U Mich. J Law Ref.* 117, at 151–2.

[30] But see Ch. 9, n. 160.   [31] See Ch. 10, Sec. B.1.

[32] Coffee's suggestion (n. 7 above, at 1354–5) of 'unbundling' the price charged for voting from that charged for investment management would, it is submitted, have no significant effect in the UK or Australia, where fee-minimization is of great importance to the trustees of pension and superannuation schemes.

[33] See 'Labour Attacks Investor "Secrecy" ', *Fin. Times*, 5 June 1995, p. 16.

[34] See Ch. 10, Sec. B.1.vi.

exposes to a wide audience the way in which fund managers have exercised their voting rights.

Despite the negative nature of the foregoing, there is room for some optimism in this area. One of the UK fund managers interviewed by the author mentioned that his institution, which is part of a large financial conglomerate, is required not only to vote by some of its local-authority clients, but also to follow 'strict guidelines on how to exercise voting rights—namely, according to the recommendations of PIRC'.[35] Where the trustees of an externally managed pension or superannuation fund consider that a systematic and informed use of voting rights is in the interests of their beneficiaries, they can take similar action to overcome the agency problem associated with the exercise of voting rights by external fund managers.[36]

There are some regulatory obstacles in the path of voting by fund managers. Although the removal of these barriers (as recommended in the next three subsections) would not alter the fundamental disincentives to a systematic, informed use of voting rights by managers of external funds, it would facilitate voting by those fund managers which do wish to vote, or are required by their clients to vote. This would be a positive step, albeit one with relatively minor impact.

ii. Clarification of Trustee Acts on Delegation of the Right to Vote

The powers of delegation in the Trustee Acts in Australia[37] are too narrow.[38] Although a properly drafted trust deed will solve the problem for an individual superannuation scheme, it is, as the Goode Committee said, 'unsatisfactory for the law to be so unresponsive to the needs of modern fund management that it requires supplementation by scheme rules as a matter of course'.[39] The concerns expressed in Australia about the power of trustees to delegate the voting right should be addressed by an amendment to the Trustee Acts to allow decision-making powers to be delegated.[40]

iii. Repeal of Corporations Law, Section 1069(1)(k)

The impact of section 1069(1)(k) of the Corporations Law upon the power to vote of managers of Australian unit trusts is described in Chapter 8.[41]

---

[35] On the voting-information service provided by PIRC, see Ch. 5, Sec. B.1.v.

[36] Recall that a voting-information service commenced operation in Australia in 1994: see Ch. 8, Sec. B.1.iv.

[37] See e.g. Trustee Act 1958 (Vic.), s. 28; Trustee Act 1925 (NSW), s. 53.

[38] See Ch. 8, at nn. 37–43, and accompanying text.

[39] Pension Law Review Committee ('Goode Committee'), *Report* (1993) para. 4.9.25.

[40] Pensions Act 1995 (UK), s. 34, is a useful precedent.

[41] See Ch. 8, at nn. 50–4, and accompanying text.

This provision serves no useful purpose given that there is no account-ability problem associated with the involvement of unit-trust managers in corporate governance.[42] It should be repealed.[43]

iv. Increase in Minimum Notice Period for General Meetings

The minimum notice period for extraordinary general meetings ('EGMs') in the UK and Australia is 14 days; for the annual general meeting ('AGM') it is 21 days in the UK and 14 days in Australia.[44] As discussed in Chapters 5 and 8, the 14-day minimum notice period can be too short when one considers the fact that (a) under most companies' articles, proxy forms must reach the company at least 48 hours before the meeting,[45] and (b) some fund managers have to consult with, or obtain the blessing of, many external clients before voting.[46] Increasing the period would have costs as well as benefits: some corporate deals require a speedy progression. However, an increase in the period to 21 days (for EGMs in the UK, and for the AGM and EGMs in Australia) should help to alleviate the practical difficulties faced by some fund managers, without reducing unduly the ability of management to take advantage of opportunities which require quick implementation.

v. Requirement that all Directors be Subject to Triennial Re-Election

The 'insulation' of executive directors from the need periodically to retire and seek re-election sits uneasily with the concept of accountability to the shareholders.[47] There should be introduced into the listing rules of the London Stock Exchange and the ASX a requirement that the articles of association of listed companies must require *all* directors to be subject to retirement and re-election by rotation at least every three years.

vi. Reduction in Threshold for 'Super Class 1 Transactions'

Morgan and Morgan point out that in 1990 any of the top 20 listed UK companies (measured by market capitalization) could have bid for any

---

[42] See Ch. 9, Sec. B.3.iii.

[43] Note that its repeal has also been recommended by the ASC: see Parliamentary Joint Committee on Corporations and Securities, *Issues Paper: Inquiry into the Role and Activities of Institutional Investors in Australia* (1994) para. 4.26. (The Joint Committee was 'inclined to agree' with the ASC's recommendation: ibid., at para. 4.27.)

[44] CA 1985, s. 369(1); CL, s. 247(2); cf. *Exposure Draft—Second Corporate Law Simplification Bill* 1995 (Cth).

[45] Table A, art. 62(a); Table A (Aust.), reg. 55; see also CA 1985, s. 372(5); CL, s. 248(1)(c).

[46] See Ch. 5, at nn. 75–6, and accompanying text; Ch. 8, at nn. 44–6, and accompanying text.

[47] See Ch. 4, Sec. A.1.xv; Table A, art. 84; Table A (Aust.), reg. 79(2); *ASX Listing Rules*, LR 3L(1).

quoted UK company outside of the top 100 companies without creating a
Super Class 1 transaction (that is, without the need for shareholder
approval).[48] Further, there were more than 1,300 listed and USM
companies that could have been acquired by any of the top 500 companies
without creating a Super Class 1 transaction. The present author's analysis
of the largest 100 companies at mid-September 1993 revealed that any of
the top 20 companies could have taken over the 81st ranked company (and
any below that of course) without shareholder approval. It is clear that
very substantial deals can be effected without the need for shareholder
approval. However, any alteration to the 25% threshold for Super Class 1
transactions must take into account the expense involved in the requisite
general meeting and related disclosures. It is going too far, therefore, to
suggest, as Wright does, that all bids for listed companies (of whatever
size) should require prior consent by the bidder's shareholders.[49] On the
other hand, it seems reasonable to reduce the threshold to at least 20%,
and possibly 15% (the threshold for Class 1 transactions). A proposed
alteration of the threshold to 15% would be unlikely to win widespread
support, so the realistic proposal seems to be a reduction to 20%.

vii. Introduction of Material-Transactions Provisions into ASX Listing Rules

The *ASX Listing Rules* do not contain material-transactions provisions like
those in chapter 10 of the London Stock Exchange's *Listing Rules*.[50] There
is simply a rule which requires any sale or disposal of the company's 'main
undertaking' to be conditional upon ratification by the general meeting,
and gives to the ASX discretion to require the ratification of 'a change in
activities' by a company.[51] These provisions should be replaced with a set
of material-transactions provisions along the lines of the London Stock
Exchange model. The threshold for shareholder approval should be 20%,
as recommended in the previous subsection.

viii. Enhanced Accountability of the Institutions

It was concluded in Chapter 9 that, with one exception, UK and Australian
institutions and their fund managers are sufficiently accountable for their
involvement in corporate governance. The exception concerns external
fund managers of pension and superannuation schemes.[52] Here, proper
accountability necessitates a contractual term (in either the fund-

---

[48] E. V. Morgan and A. D. Morgan, *The Stock Market and Mergers in the United Kingdom*
(1990) 54.

[49] S. Wright, *Two Cheers for the Institutions* (1994) 61–2.

[50] But see House of Representatives Standing Committee on Legal and Constitutional
Affairs, *Corporate Practices and the Rights of Shareholders* (1991) paras. 4.6.1–4.6.12.

[51] *ASX Listing Rules*, LR 3S. See also *AIMA Corporate Governance Guidelines*, para.
3.13.   [52] See Ch. 9, at nn. 163–6, and accompanying text.

management agreement or a collateral letter) requiring the fund manager to (a) notify the trustees of any serious intervention at, or proposed controversial vote at a general meeting of, a portfolio company; and (b) act in accordance with any directions given by the trustees in relation to any such matter. A requirement of this nature should be inserted into the Pensions Act 1995 (UK) and the Superannuation Industry (Supervision) Act 1993 (Cth.).

ix. Limiting the 'Associate' Concept in the Corporations Law

It was pointed out in Chapter 10 that the potential for collective action by institutions to contravene section 615 and/or Part 6.7 of the Corporations Law does not sit comfortably with a model of corporate governance in which monitoring by institutional shareholders plays an important role.[53] There is a strong case for an amendment to the Corporations Law to ensure that these provisions do not 'catch' institutional shareholders engaging in collective action on matters of corporate governance. A possible reform would be the addition of a 'specified exclusion' to those already specified in section 16(1) of the Corporations Law. Section 16(1) states: 'A person is not an associate of another person by virtue of section 12 or subsection 15(1) . . . merely because of one or more of the following: . . .' By this mechanism, section 16(1) ensures that certain persons are not deemed to be associates. This is crucial in limiting the 'entitlement' of those persons to voting shares in the company concerned.[54]

2. REFORMS AFFECTING INDIRECT MONITORING

i. Board Composition and Structure

The Cadbury Committee in the UK, and the Bosch Committee and the AIMA in Australia, have dealt reasonably thoroughly with the issues of board structure and composition. There are, however, some areas which could be improved. First, given that executive domination (by numbers) of the board is an impediment to effective monitoring by non-executives,[55] Cadbury Mark II ought to give serious consideration to the recommendation of the AIMA that the board of every listed company should comprise a majority of independent non-executive directors.[56] Secondly, as

---

[53] See Ch. 10, at nn. 102–14, and accompanying text.
[54] See Ch. 10, at nn. 106–9, and accompanying text. Note, however, that this reform would not be necessary if the recent proposals of the Corporations Law Simplification Task Force were to be implemented: see *Takeovers: Proposal for Simplification* (1996).
[55] See Ch. 5, at nn. 313–14.
[56] See *AIMA Corporate Governance Guidelines*, para. 3.2 See also the proposed Fifth EC Directive on harmonization of company law: 1983 OJ (C 240) 2, art. 21a (a majority of directors on a one-tier board would have to be non-executives).

discussed at length in Chapter 4, proper accountability within the one-tier board system requires that the chairman should be an independent *part-time* director.[57] The growing UK practice of having an executive chairman and a separate chief executive, ironically hastened by the Cadbury Committee's preference for a separation of the roles of chairman and chief executive, should be addressed by Cadbury Mark II. Finally, in the light of the negative findings (in Section B.2.iii, below) about shareholder committees for the selection of non-executive directors, it is important that board nomination committees—preferably composed entirely of non-executive directors—should be a requirement for quoted companies. The Cadbury Committee merely expressed its support for such committees.[58]

It is recognized that even with the 'best' structures, things can go wrong, and that there have been many successful companies where, for instance, the roles of chairman and chief executive have been combined. However, 'best-practice' board composition and structure should not affect detrimentally the ability of the executive management to drive the company forward,[59] but should—despite the shortcomings with 'traditional' non-executive directors[60]—increase the chances of corrective action being taken if management's performance becomes unsatisfactory.[61]

ii. Grant of Director-Dismissal Power to Boards

Neither the Companies Act 1985 (UK) nor the Table A articles confers on the board a power of dismissal in relation to one of its number. What is more, section 227(12) of the Australian Corporations Law prohibits the removal of a director of a public company by 'any resolution, request or notice of the directors or any of them notwithstanding anything in the articles or any agreement'. Given that it is now recognized widely that an important function of the board is to monitor—and thus, by implication, to make any necessary changes to the composition of—the executive management (which includes executive *directors*),[62] this provision is inappropriate. Section 227(12) should be repealed. Further, there should be introduced into the listing rules of the London Stock Exchange and the ASX a requirement that the articles of association of listed companies must empower 75% of co-directors to dismiss a director.

---

[57] See Ch. 4, at nn. 104–13, and accompanying text.

[58] *Cadbury Report*, paras. 4.15, 4.30.

[59] Cf., however, J. A. Brickley, J. L. Coles, and G. Jarrell, *Corporate Leadership Structure: On the Separation of the Positions of CEO and Chairman of the Board* (1995).

[60] See Ch. 5, Sec. D.2.ii.(b).

[61] There are signs of improvement in the dependence of traditional non-executives upon shareholder choice: see Ch. 5, at nn. 333–40, and accompanying text; Ch. 8, at n. 132, and accompanying text.

[62] See Ch. 1, Sec. B; Ch. 5, Sec. D.2.ii.(a).

iii. 'Institutional' Non-Executive Directors?

The Cadbury Committee made numerous recommendations regarding board structure and composition but it did not explore adequately, in regard to non-executive directors, 'the basic issue of motivation'.[63] Admittedly, it did address and take steps to resolve some aspects of the motivation problem: 'affiliated' non-executives;[64] lack of impartiality in the selection process;[65] and loss of ability to take a detached viewpoint.[66] However, there is strength in the argument that 'independence from management can be provided in practice only by making the non-executives dependent on a powerful group capable of counter-balancing the incumbent management'.[67] In the case of quoted UK companies, and non-controlled quoted Australian companies, the 'powerful group' would naturally seem to be the institutional shareholders. Indeed, in recent years there have been at least a couple of proposals for mechanisms under which institutions could appoint representatives to company boards. The best-known proposal is that of Gilson and Kraakman, who argue that US institutions (especially indexed investors) could elect professional non-executive directors to a minority of positions on the boards of quoted companies.[68] Sykes has proposed a more formal mechanism, under which institutions would be required to establish secretariats to support the 3–5 'shareholder directors' who would be appointed to each of the top 100 listed UK companies under a 'compact' between the institutions and the executive directors of those companies.[69]

Unfortunately, acceptance of the view that true independence from management requires dependence on institutional shareholders does not imply that the introduction of some form of institutional-shareholder

---

[63] Wright (n. 49 above), at 52–3.

[64] *Cadbury Code*, para. 2.2 (majority of non-executives should be independent of management and free from any relationship with the company which could interfere with the exercise of independent judgement).

[65] *Cadbury Code*, para. 2.4; *Cadbury Report*, paras. 4.15, 4.30 (non-executives should be selected via a formal process; it is good practice for a nomination committee to carry out that process).

[66] *Cadbury Code*, para. 2.3 (non-executives should be appointed for specified terms; reappointment should not be automatic).

[67] P. L. Davies and G. P. Stapledon, 'Corporate Governance in the United Kingdom' in M. Isaksson and R. Skog (eds.), *Aspects of Corporate Governance* (1994) 55, at 80.

[68] See R. J. Gilson and R. Kraakman, 'Reinventing the Outside Director: An Agenda for Institutional Investors' (1991) 43 *Stan. L Rev.* 863.

[69] See A. Sykes, 'Proposals for a Reformed System of Corporate Governance to Achieve Internationally Competitive Long-Term Performance' in N. H. Dimsdale and M. Prevezer (eds.), *Capital Markets and Corporate Governance* (1994) 111. There have also been calls for some form of 'shareholder panel' to nominate and monitor the auditors: see e.g. D. Hatherly, 'The Future of Audit: The Case for the Shareholder Panel' (1994); Auditing Practices Board, *The Future Development of Auditing* (1992) 11.

committee (formal or informal) to select and monitor some or all of the non-executive directors would make those non-executives any more dependent on shareholder choice than are today's non-executive directors. One must ask whether the institutions would have any strong incentive to monitor such 'institutional non-executives', or rather whether the incentive would be any greater than it is presently with regard to 'traditional non-executives'. There is nothing to suggest that the implementation of a structure—however well designed—under which institutions rather than existing board members would choose (some or all) new non-executive directors would realize the optimal situation where non-executive directors would be uninhibited in (a) taking a forceful approach whenever they disagreed strongly with a management proposal; and (b) pushing for a change in top management if they believed that the incumbent(s) had failed to achieve the required standard of performance. The reason is that the strong economic disincentives to detailed institutional monitoring, which are discussed in Chapter 10, would not go away if a system for appointment of institutional directors were introduced:

> The problem is not with what Professors Gilson and Kraakman say, but with what they leave out. Their solution works to align the interests of principal and agent only at the directorial level, not at the institutional level. At the institutional level, there is considerable reason to believe that [external fund] managers would remain rationally apathetic about [institutional] directors . . .[70]

And, as stated earlier, there appears to be no realistic reform that could be made to enhance the incentives for, or to decrease the economic disincentives to, a higher level of detailed monitoring.[71]

Support for this pessimistic view can be found in the fact that institutions commonly have their executives serving as non-executive directors on the boards of unquoted companies to which they have provided 'venture' or 'development' capital.[72] Apart from the lack of a liquid market for the shares, there are two crucial factors differentiating these unquoted companies from quoted companies—on whose boards the institutions are

---

[70] Coffee (n. 7 above), at 1361; see also Rock (n. 12 above), at 474–5. This is not to say that no institutions would become actively involved in monitoring the proposed new breed of non-executives. Some would, but they would be the same institutions (viz., some of the (largest) fund-management operations with predominantly internal funds under management) which currently have the incentive to do just that. External fund managers would commonly find it rational not to engage in monitoring of institutional non-executives.

[71] See nn. 7–12 above, and accompanying text. Ironically, Gilson and Kraakman hint unwittingly at the weakness in their proposal for professional directors. They state that their agenda does not require regulatory reform: '[i]nstitutional investors must merely decide to act': n. 68 above, at 905. They then note that they cannot think of a reason why US institutions have not already begun to implement a scheme similar to their proposal: ibid.

[72] See Ch. 5, Sec. D.2.iii.(a).

loath to be represented. First, since an unquoted company is not held widely by the fund-management community, an institution can spend resources on monitoring the management without the unattractive prospect of benefiting its business rivals.[73] Secondly, because the *ad valorem* fee charged to clients for managing money invested in a venture-capital fund is much higher than the fee charged for managing a 'normal' equity fund, the fund manager stands to gain far more from any increase in the value of the companies in the venture-capital portfolio.[74]

In summary, therefore, although the Cadbury Committee can be criticized for failing to address the issue of the dependence of non-executive directors upon shareholder choice,[75] the existence of powerful economic disincentives to systematic, detailed institutional monitoring probably means that there is nothing realistic that the Committee could have recommended which might have effectively transformed non-executive directors into powerful 'truly independent' monitors of management performance.[76]

---

[73] See Ch. 10, Sec. B.1.iii.

[74] See Ch. 10, Sec. B.1.iv.

[75] Cf. *Cadbury Report*, paras. 6.2, 6.3.

[76] As a final point, there have been some important, but only gradual, improvements in the dependence of non-executive directors upon shareholder choice: see Ch. 5, at nn. 333–40, and accompanying text; Ch. 8, at n. 132, and accompanying text. It is considered likely that there will be a continued gradual improvement in this area.

PART V
Appendices

Appendix A

Participants in UK Interview Study

Fund-management arms of financial conglomerates:

Mercury Asset Management plc
Barclays de Zoete Wedd Investment Management Ltd.
Phillips & Drew Fund Management Ltd.
Robert Fleming Asset Management Ltd.
Schroder Investment Management Ltd.
Gartmore Investment Management plc
Framlington Group plc

Insurers or fund-management arms of insurance companies:

Prudential Portfolio Managers Ltd.
The Standard Life Assurance Company
Norwich Union Investment Management Ltd.
Scottish Amicable Investment Managers Ltd.
The Equitable Life Assurance Society

'Independent' fund managers:

M&G Investment Management Ltd.
Baillie Gifford & Co.
Fidelity Investments International

In-house pension-fund managers:

PosTel Investment Management Ltd.
CIN Management Ltd.

Any comments made by the interviewees, which are quoted or referred to in the text, are not attributed to a named source because of undertakings of confidentiality provided by the author. The author thanks the interviewees for their participation in the study, and also thanks Mr Peter Brierley, Senior Manager, Financial Markets and Institutions Division, Bank of England, for his invaluable assistance in arranging the interviews.

Appendix B

Questions Asked in UK Interview Study

1. Pre-Emption Rights/Non-Voting Shares

1.1 What is the primary motivation behind the institutional stance on pre-emption rights? Is it the protection of percentage stakes in portfolio companies for the purpose of maintaining one's existing 'leverage' as against company managements? Or is it protection from the financial detriment (through a fall in the share price) and the transfer of value that would flow from a large discounted issue being made to outsiders?

1.2 What is the primary motivation behind the institutional stance on non-voting shares? Is it preservation of the shareholders' position of ultimate control? Or is it the fact that the market rates enfranchised shares more highly (for reasons such as greater liquidity, etc.) than it does non- or restricted-voting shares?

2. 'Super Class 1 Transactions'/Other Large Deals

2.1 Is your institution in favour of a reduction in the threshold level for 'Super Class 1 Transactions' requiring shareholder consent under the Stock Exchange Listing Rules (the threshold level currently being 25%)?

2.2 Is it common for company managements to consult with, and/or obtain the prior blessing of, your institution in relation to proposed large transactions (such as acquisitions, etc.) that do not legally require shareholder approval?

2.3 It is accepted almost universally that it would be inappropriate (and in most cases impossible) for institutional shareholders to become involved in the day-to-day management of portfolio companies. However, do you agree with the following proposition?

> Through (i) their ability to decline, unless certain changes are made to the company's management, to take up their entitlements to a rights issue (for example Granada and Asda in 1991); (ii) their ability to vote down a proposed 'Super Class 1 Transaction' (for example British Land in 1989); and (iii) (subject to the answer to 2.2) their ability to veto proposed transactions on which management seeks their informal blessing; institutions are able to—and regularly do—exert an influence upon the broad strategic development of portfolio companies.

3. REGULAR MEETINGS WITH MANAGEMENT

3.1 Does your institution meet regularly with the senior management of companies in which you have a holding/a large holding?

(The next three questions are relevant only if 3.1 was answered 'yes'.)

3.2 Are those meetings normally on a one-to-one basis in your offices? (i.e. As opposed to 'institutional road-shows' and analysts' briefings involving numerous institutions and/or brokers' analysts?)

3.3 At those meetings, how many persons are commonly present representing (a) the company; and (b) your institution? And how senior are the representatives of (a) the company (for example CEO; finance director; etc.); and (b) your institution?

3.4 What sort of matters are discussed at these meetings?

4. VOTING

4.1 Does your institution exercise its voting rights/proxies on a regular or systematic basis?

4.2 (This question applies only to those institutions that have external funds under management.) Do all or most clients (especially pension fund trustees) delegate the exercise of their voting rights to your institution?

5. DISPUTES WITH MANAGEMENT/ SHAREHOLDER CONFERENCES/ INSTITUTIONAL COALITIONS

5.1 Can you give an estimate of the average number of 'extraordinary actions' undertaken by your institution annually? The phrase 'extraordinary actions' encompasses collectively: (i) approaches made by your institution (alone) to company managements, regarding specific concerns; (ii) shareholder conferences which your institution either convened or attended, for the purpose of discussing specific concerns about a specific company (but which did not reach the stage of a 'shareholder coalition'); (iii) approaches made by your institution (either alone or with the backing of other institutions) to companies' non-executive director(s) and/ or companies' corporate advisers, for the purpose of discussing specific concerns about the companies' managements (and which did not reach the stage of a shareholder coalition); (iv) institutional-shareholder coalitions which your institution either led or joined, for the purpose of producing specific changes at specific companies (usually changes in management/board composition); and (v) case committees of either the ABI or the NAPF which your institution joined.

5.2 (This question applies only to those institutions that manage many segregated funds (for example for external pension schemes).) Are there any major practical difficulties/complexities if your institution decides to communicate with a company's management with a view to persuading that company to alter its strategy/board composition/etc.? The possible complexities envisaged are those relating to the fact that your institution's total 'stake' in the company is really a collection of several separate holdings, many of which are in any case managed for outside entities. In particular, does your institution have to communicate continuously with the trustees of pension-fund clients, so as to 'keep them posted' or obtain permission to take certain actions?

6. NON-EXECUTIVE DIRECTORS

6.1 Given that a recent survey (PRO NED, *Research into the Role of the Non-Executive Director* (1992)) found that only 3% of institutional-shareholder respondents believed that today's non-executive directors are 'very effective', what are the perceived shortcomings with non-executives and how are they to be overcome?

6.2 Does your institution ever seek direct representation upon the board of a company in which you have a large stake (through the appointment of one of your own executives, or a nominee, as a non-executive director)?

6.3 Does your institution become involved in the selection process for new non-executive directors at portfolio companies? If not, why not?

6.4 How closely does your institution liaise with the non-executives of companies in which you have a holding—both in 'good times' and when a company's performance is unsatisfactory?

7. LITIGATION

Has your institution ever considered utilizing the legal process (either alone or with other institutional shareholders) where (i) you were extremely dissatisfied with the management of a portfolio company; and (ii) the problem was potentially the subject of litigation? (For instance, at a company where your institution had an overweight holding.) If not, is the lack of a contingency-fee system (coupled with the English 'loser pays all' costs system) a major factor?

Appendix C
Participants in Australian Interview Study

Fund-management arms of financial conglomerates:

Bankers Trust Australia Ltd.
County NatWest Australia Investment Management Ltd.
Lend Lease Corporate Services
Westpac Investment Management Pty. Ltd.
Rothschild Australia Asset Management Ltd.
Potter Warburg Asset Management Ltd.
Macquarie Bank Ltd.
ANZ Funds Management

Fund-management arms of insurance companies:

AMP Investments Australia Ltd.
National Mutual Funds Management
Prudential Portfolio Managers Australia Ltd.
GIO Investment Services Ltd.

Government-owned investment manager of public-sector superannuation funds:

State Superannuation Investment & Management Corporation

Any comments made by the interviewees, which are quoted or referred to in the text, are not attributed to a named source because of undertakings of confidentiality provided by the author. The author thanks the interviewees for their participation in the study, and also thanks Mr Ian Matheson, Executive Director, Australian Investment Managers' Association, and his assistant, Melissa Wheeler, for their invaluable assistance in arranging the interviews.

Appendix D

Questions Asked in Australian Interview Study

1. NATURE AND SIZE OF HOLDINGS

1.1 Is most of the total market value of your institution's holdings of listed Australian equities accounted for by your holdings of 'Top 50' or 'Top 100' listed Australian companies (measured by market capitalization)?

1.2 Does your institution have many large holdings in listed Australian companies (i.e. large in relation to the particular company's issued capital)? (For instance, holdings of 3% and above, or 5% and above?)

2. REGULAR MEETINGS WITH SENIOR MANAGEMENT OF PORTFOLIO COMPANIES

2.1 Does your institution meet regularly (say every 12 months, or every two years) with the senior management of companies in which you have a holding/a large holding?

(The next three questions are relevant only if 2.1 was answered 'yes'.)

2.2 Are those meetings normally on a one-to-one basis in your offices? (i.e. As opposed to 'institutional road-shows' and analysts' briefings involving numerous institutions and/or brokers' analysts?)

2.3 At those meetings, how many persons are commonly present representing (a) the company; and (b) your institution? And how senior are the representatives of (a) the company (for example CEO; finance director; etc.); and (b) your institution?

2.4 What sort of matters are discussed at these meetings?

2.5 In the UK, it is reasonably common for listed companies to 'pre-market' their major institutional shareholders before finalizing major deals, even where shareholder approval is not required under the Listing Rules. Is it common for Australian companies to consult with, and/or obtain the prior blessing of, their major institutional shareholders in relation to proposed large transactions that do not legally require shareholder approval?

3. Voting

3.1 (This question applies only to those institutions that have external funds under management.) Do all or most of your institution's clients (especially super-annuation fund trustees) delegate the exercise of their voting rights to your institution in the fund-management agreement?

3.2 Does your institution exercise its voting rights/proxies on a regular or systematic basis?

4. Disputes with Management/Shareholder Conferences/ Institutional Coalitions

4.1 The recent episode at Goodman Fielder Ltd., when the company's chief executive was forced to resign amid alleged pressure from some of the company's large institutional shareholders, was reminiscent of several recent CEO departures from listed UK companies. In a series of interviews with UK fund managers, I managed to get a rough impression of the prevalence of the behind-the-scenes actions taken by UK institutions at problem companies. The term that I gave to the range of behind-the-scenes measures was 'extraordinary actions'. The 'extra-ordinary actions' in which a particular institution might have been involved would include, collectively: (i) approaches made by the institution (alone) to a portfolio company's management, regarding specific concerns; (ii) shareholder conferences which the institution either convened or attended, for the purpose of discussing specific concerns about a specific company (but which did not reach the stage of a 'shareholder coalition'); (iii) approaches made by the institution (either alone or with the backing of other institutions) to a company's non-executive director(s) and/or a company's corporate advisers, for the purpose of discussing specific concerns about the company's senior management (and which did not reach the stage of a shareholder coalition); (iv) institutional shareholder coalitions which the institution either led or joined, for the purpose of producing specific changes at a specific company (usually changes in board/senior management composition); (v) the convening of, and, if necessary, the exercise of voting rights at, an extraordinary general meeting calling for the removal of a director or directors and/ or the election of new directors. Could you give an estimate of the average number of 'extraordinary actions' (concerning Australian companies) in which your institution has participated, annually over the past few years?

4.2 On a handful of occasions over the past few years, some major UK institutions have managed to bring about the removal of an ailing company's CEO (and sometimes other executive directors) by informing the company's corporate advisers that they would only support a rights issue if changes were made to the company's management. Has this sort of persuasion been employed by your institution in relation to under-performing Australian companies?

4.3 (This question applies to those institutions which manage many segregated funds (for example for external occupational superannuation schemes), for most of which there would be a holding in a particular company (company X).) Are there any major practical difficulties/complexities for your institution if you decide to communicate with company X's board or senior management with a view to persuading company X to alter its strategy/board composition/etc.? The possible complexities envisaged are those relating to the fact that your institution's total 'stake' in company X is really a collection of several separate holdings, many of which are in any case managed for outside entities. In particular, do you have to communicate continuously with the trustees of client superannuation funds, so as to 'keep them posted' or obtain permission to take certain actions?

5. Employee Share Schemes/Non-Voting Shares

5.1 I have a copy of the AIMG Corporate Governance Practice Note No. 1 ('Guide to Employee Share Schemes'), issued in June 1993. Did your institution— either alone or with other institutional shareholders—ever make submissions to portfolio companies on the matter of their executive share schemes, prior to the release of the AIMG Practice Note No. 1?

5.2 The News Corporation Ltd. super-voting shares matter of late-1993 provided a glimpse of the potential persuasiveness of Australian institutional shareholders' views. Is the undesirability of restricted- and non-voting (and indeed super-voting) shares a matter which your institution has raised with other companies in the past?

6. Non-Executive Directors

6.1 A recent UK survey found that only 3% of institutional-shareholder respondents believed that non-executive directors of UK companies are 'very effective'. Do you think that (a) the majority, or (b) a substantial proportion of the non-executive directors of listed Australian companies are not 'very effective'? If so, what are their shortcomings and how are they to be overcome?

6.2 Does your institution ever seek direct representation upon the board of a company in which you have a large stake (through the appointment of one of your own executives, or a nominee, as a non-executive director)?

6.3 Does your institution ever become involved in the selection process for non-executive directors at companies in which you have a large holding? (For instance, by suggesting a few names when asked by the company; or by giving your opinion on a person suggested by the company.)

6.4 How closely does your institution liaise with the non-executives of companies in which you have a holding—both in 'good times' and when a company's performance is unsatisfactory?

7. Litigation

7.1 Has your institution ever considered utilizing the legal process (either alone or with other institutional shareholders) where (i) you were extremely dissatisfied with the management of a portfolio company; and (ii) the problem was potentially the subject of litigation? (For instance, at a company where your institution had an overweight holding.) If not, is the lack of a contingency-fee system (coupled with the Australian/English 'loser pays all' costs system) a major factor?

Appendix E

Abbreviations in Chapters 3 and 5

Abu Dhabi	*Abu Dhabi Investment Authority*
Allied Dun.	*Allied Dunbar Asset Management plc*
AMP	*AMP Asset Management plc*
Baillie	*Baillie Gifford & Co.*
Baring	*Baring Asset Management Ltd.*
Britannic	*Britannic Assurance plc*
Brit. Air.	*British Airways Pension Investment Management Ltd.*
Brit. Gas	*British Gas Pension Funds Management Ltd.*
BZWIM	*Barclays de Zoete Wedd Investment Management Ltd.*
CIN	*CIN Management Ltd.*
Cler. Med.	*Clerical Medical Investment Group*
Conf. Life	*Confederation Life Insurance Company*
Co-op.	*Co-operative Insurance Society Ltd.*
County	*County NatWest Invetment Management Ltd.*
Edinburgh	*Edinburgh Fund Managers plc*
Equit. Life	*The Equitable Life Assurance Society*
Fleming	*Robert Fleming Asset Management Ltd.*
Framling.	*Framlington Group plc*
Friends'	*Friends' Provident Life Office*
Gartmore	*Gartmore Investment Management plc*
GRE	*GRE Asset Management Ltd.*
Henderson	*Henderson Administration Group plc*
Hill Sam.	*Hill Samuel Investment Management Group Ltd.*
J. Capel	*James Capel Fund Managers Ltd.*
L&G	*Legal & General Investment Management Ltd.*
Lloyds	*Lloyds Investment Managers Ltd.*
MAM	*Mercury Asset Management plc*
M&G	*M&G Investment Management Ltd.*
Morg. Gren.	*Morgan Grenfell Asset Management Ltd.*
Norwich	*Norwich Union Investment Management Ltd.*
PDFM	*Phillips & Drew Fund Management Ltd.*
PosTel	*PosTel Investment Management Ltd.*
PPM	*Prudential Portfolio Managers Ltd.*
Prov. Mut.	*Provident Mutual Life Assurance Association*
Royal Ins.	*Royal Insurance Asset Management Ltd.*
Schroder	*Schroder Investment Management Ltd.*
Scot. Amic.	*Scottish Amicable Investment Managers Ltd.*
Scot. Mut.	*Scottish Mutual Assurance plc*
Scot. Wid.	*Scottish Widows Investment Management Ltd.*
Stan. Life	*The Standard Life Assurance Company*

Sun All.	*Sun Alliance Investment Management Ltd.*
Sun Life	*Sun Life Investment Management Services Ltd.*
3i	*3i Group plc*
FC	*fund-management arm of financial conglomerate*
Indep.	*independent fund manager*
Ins.	*fund-management arm of insurance company*
O/S	*overseas-based institution*
Pens.	*in-house investment manager of pension funds(s)*
†	*3i, the venture- and development-capital firm, was owned by seven UK commercial banks, and the Bank of England, at the time of Study B*

Appendix F

Sources for Table 3.2

In addition to the sources cited at the foot of Table 3.2, the following persons provided information which assisted in the compilation of Table 3.2. The author thanks them for their assistance.

A. K. Lyle, Allied Dunbar Asset Management plc, London

N. Burgoyne, Fund Manager, AMP Asset Management plc, London

J. W. Martin, Head of Investments, BP Pension Fund, London

A. M. K. Jourdier, Investment Manager, Britannic Assurance plc, Birmingham

M. A. Catell, Administration Manager, British Aerospace Pension Funds Investment Management Ltd., London

J. Rosser, Secretary and Pension Manager, British Airways Pensions, Hounslow, Middlesex

F. E. Curtiss, Assistant Company Secretary, British Rail Pension Trustee Company Ltd., London

R. Johnson, Systems Co-ordinator, The Canada Life Assurance Company, Potters Bar, Hertfordshire

S. T. Meldrum, Investment Director, Cannon Lincoln plc, London

A. P. Watson, Marketing Statistician, Capital International Ltd., London

P. Foster, Commercial Union Asset Management Ltd., London

J. Franks, Investment Department, Co-operative Insurance Society Ltd., Manchester

T. J. R. Mitson, Secretary, Courtaulds Pensions Investment Trustees Ltd., London

P. Clarke, Deputy General Manager, The Daiwa Bank Ltd., London

S. Kelly, Unit Manager (Technical Enquiries), The Equitable Life Assurance Society, Aylesbury, Buckinghamshire

P. Smith, Managing Director, Equity & Law Investment Managers Ltd., London

W. B. Matthews, Finance Director, ESN Pension Management Group Ltd., London

I. Seymour, Investment Accounts Controller, Friends' Provident Life Office, London

I. H. Graubert, Senior Portfolio Manager, GRE Asset Management Ltd., London

G. K. Allen, Investment Director, ICI Investment Management Ltd., London

J. Bean, Secretary to Managing Director, Kemper Investment Management Company Ltd., London

A. Begg, Chief Investment Officer, Kleinwort Benson Investment Management Ltd., London

A. Flook, Investment Marketing, Laurentian Fund Management Ltd., Barnwood, Gloucester

R. W. Ammon, Senior Fund Manager, London and Manchester (Portfolio Management) Ltd., Exeter

Lucas Pension Fund, Solihull, West Midlands

G. R. Logan, Head of Investments, MGM Assurance, London

J. Scott, Marketing Analyst, Morgan Stanley International, London

J. R. Bishop, Investment Manager, National Mutual Life Assurance Society, Hitchin, Hertfordshire

A. Ross Goobey, Chief Executive, PosTel Investment Management Ltd., London

P. Roantree, Prolific Asset Management Ltd., London

J. M. Longstaff, Investment Liaison Manager, Royal Insurance Asset Management Ltd., London

J. Jenkins, Marketing Department, The Scottish Life Assurance Company, Edinburgh

R. O. Bogle, Director, Albert E. Sharp & Co., Birmingham

C. Price, Investment Services Manager, Shell International Petroleum Company Ltd., London

M. D. Clements, Research Manager, Sun Alliance Investment Management Ltd., London

H. White, Senior Asset Manager (UK Equities), Ulster Bank Investment Managers Ltd., Dublin, Ireland

P. G. Moon, Chief Investment Officer, Universities Superannuation Scheme Ltd., London

Annual reports of the following pension schemes were a further source of information for Table 3.2.

British Coal Staff Superannuation Scheme
Mineworkers' Pension Scheme
British Gas Staff Pension Scheme
British Gas Corporation Pension Scheme
British Steel Pension Scheme

Appendix G

Abbreviations in Chapters 6 and 8

AMP	*AMP Investments Australia Ltd.*
BT	*Bankers Trust Australia Ltd.*
Capital	*Capital Group Inc. (USA)*
CBA	*CBA Financial Services*
County	*County NatWest Australia Investment Management Ltd.*
FAI	*FAI Insurances Ltd.*
Indosuez	*Banque Indosuez (France)*
J. P. Morg.	*J. P. Morgan Investment Management Australia Ltd.*
Lend Lse.	*Lend Lease Corporate Services Ltd.*
NMFM	*National Mutual Funds Management*
NRMA	*NRMA Investment Pty. Ltd.*
Pott. War.	*Potter Warburg Asset Management Ltd.*
PPMA	*Prudential Portfolio Managers Australia Ltd.*
QIC	*Queensland Investment Corporation*
Rothschd.	*Rothschild Australia Asset Management Ltd.*
SSIMC	*State Superannuation Investment and Management Corporation*
Suncorp	*Suncorp Insurance Investments*
Tyndall	*Tyndall Australia Ltd.*
FC	*fund-management arm of financial conglomerate*
Ins.	*fund-management arm of insurance company*
O/S	*overseas-based institution*
Pub.	*government-owned investment manager of public-sector super-annuation funds and other public-sector funds*

Appendix H

Sources for Table 6.2

In addition to the sources cited at the foot of Table 6.2, the following persons provided information which assisted in the compilation of Table 6.2. The author thanks them for their assistance.

C. Morris, Advance Asset Management Ltd., Sydney

R. J. Patterson, Managing Director, Argo Investments Ltd., Adelaide

B. J. Tiernan, Company Secretary, Australian Foundation Investment Company Ltd., Melbourne

P. Redshaw, International Investment Manager (Superannuation), BHP Superannuation Funds, Melbourne

A. P. Watson, Marketing Associate, Capital International Ltd., London, UK

S. J. Paynter, Manager (Financial Planning), CBA Financial Services, Sydney

N. B. Page, Chief Investment Manager, Commonwealth Funds Management Ltd., Canberra

Equitilink Ltd., Sydney

B. R. J. Bateman, Managing Director, Fidelity Investment Services Ltd., Tonbridge, UK

W. R. Ebsworth, Managing Director, Fidelity Investments Management (HK) Ltd., Hong Kong

R. H. Giles, Investment Manager, ICIANZ Pension Fund Securities Pty. Ltd., Melbourne

B. J. Riordan, Managing Director, Legal & General Investment Management Ltd., Sydney

W. A. H. Webster, Investment Director, Lend Lease Corporate Services Ltd., Sydney

P. Bedbrook, Director & General Manager, Mercantile Mutual Investment Management Ltd., Sydney

S. Chan, Senior Manager (Administration), NRMA Investments Pty Ltd., Sydney

J. Diasinos, Company Secretary, Permanent Trustee Company Ltd., Sydney

A. Arkell, Manager (Compliance), Queensland Investment Corporation, Brisbane

J. Fazio, Investment Manager, State Superannuation Board of Victoria, Melbourne

M. Anderson, General Manager Investments, Transport Accident Commission, Melbourne

Appendix I
Details of Study B

There is a lack of publicly available information as to the proportion of the issued ordinary share capital of individual quoted UK companies which was, as at the early 1990s, *controlled* by the fund managers with the 6–10 largest stakes in those companies. For present purposes, 'control' of a share rests with the party which has power to control the exercise of the right to vote attached to the share. As noted in Chapter 5, by the early 1990s it was very common for UK fund managers to control the voting right attached to their clients' equity investments.[1] One way of determining the identity of the persons/bodies having control over the largest chunks of the equity of a particular company is to ascertain the identity of the persons/bodies having the largest 'interests' in its issued ordinary share capital, within the meaning of the Companies Act 1985. Section 208(2) of the Companies Act 1985 states that '[a] reference to an interest in shares is to be read as including an interest of any kind whatsoever in the shares'. Section 208(4) deems a person to have an interest in shares if, 'not being the registered holder, [the person] is entitled to exercise any right conferred by the holding of the shares or is entitled to control the exercise of any such right'. Fund managers to whom the voting right has been delegated clearly have an interest in the relevant shares.

Table 3.2 might be thought useful not only for the market-wide information which it contains, but also as a means of ascertaining firm-level information. If an institution *indexes* all or nearly all of its UK equity portfolios, knowledge of the fact that its total UK equities under management are worth x% of the value of the UK equity market means that it can be assumed to control roughly x% of the issued ordinary share capital in ABC plc. There is an immediate problem, however: active stock selection rather than passive index-matching has for many years been the primary management method used by a significant majority of UK-based fund managers.[2] It is thus impossible to derive estimates of the interests of most institutions in any one company simply from total 'market' data. The researcher requires company-specific information.

This information could, in the case of certain companies (mainly medium-sized

---

[1] See Ch. 5, at n. 74, and accompanying text. The usual situation was that the fund manager had discretion to vote as it saw fit, subject to any express instructions from the client.

[2] A survey in 1992 of 679 pension schemes, most of which were directly invested, found that only 15% of schemes had at least some of their assets managed passively—i.e. indexed, formally or informally: NAPF, *Annual Survey of Occupational Pension Schemes* (1992) Table 119. Of the large UK-based fund managers, only PosTel, BZWIM, NatWest Investment Management, and Legal & General Investment Management had several billions of pounds worth of UK equities under management on an indexed basis in 1994. Note, however, that many supposed 'active' fund managers were actually little different from indexers, as at 1993: 'Tracking the Behaviour of Stock Pickers', *Fin. Times*, 6 Dec. 1993, p. 16.

and smaller listed companies, where it is reasonably common for there to be six or more institutions each with a stake of at least 3%), until late 1993 be garnered from the notifiable interests set out in companies' annual reports.[3] The usefulness of that source has, however, declined enormously due to an adjustment made in 1993 to the disclosure threshold applying to fund managers. Since September 1993, fund managers have had to notify interests of 10% or more in each class of a company's issued ordinary share capital.[4] The prior threshold for fund-management firms which had the power to vote their clients' shares[5] was the standard 3%.[6]

Obtaining a list of each (sample) company's largest 10 or 20 *registered* shareholders might at first glance be considered worthwhile. It is reasonably easy (though not necessarily inexpensive) to obtain a list of the 20 largest registered shareholders of listed UK companies.[7] Unfortunately, however, such information is not very helpful for current purposes. This is because a large proportion of UK equities under the management of UK-based fund managers has for many years been registered in the names of nominee companies.[8] It is true that a list of the 20 largest registered shareholdings would normally give some indication of the insurance companies with large interests in a company's issued share capital— because the equities purchased by insurance companies with their policyholders' funds are normally registered in the insurers' own names. Even so, there would be an understatement of the actual interest of any insurer that also managed significant amounts of external funds,[9] because shares purchased for external segregated clients would not be registered in the particular insurer's name (they

---

[3] See CA 1985, Pt. VI; *Listing Rules*, para. 12.43(l) (see also para. 12.43(k)). The legislation refers to 'relevant share capital', which is defined as 'the company's issued share capital of a class carrying rights to vote in all circumstances at general meetings of the company': s. 198(2). References in the text to 'issued ordinary share capital' should be construed in this way.

[4] See CA 1985, s. 199(2), (2A)(a) and (b); Disclosure of Interests in Shares (Amendment) Regulations 1993 (SI 1993/1819) (which implemented Directive 88/627/EEC).

[5] Under the former set of provisions, a fund manager was able to disregard, for the purposes of the 3% test, those shares (a) of which it was not the registered holder, *and* (b) in respect of which its only interest was a power over their disposal (i.e. in respect of which it did not have the power to vote): Public Companies (Disclosure of Interests in Shares) (Investment Management Exclusion) Regulations 1988 (SI 1988/706).

[6] However, as mentioned in the text, it is only in medium-sized and smaller listed UK companies that it is reasonably common for there to be six or more institutions each with a stake of at least 3%. Therefore, in the case of large companies (e.g. the FT-SE 100 index companies), the notifiable interests set out in annual reports were not an adequate information source, for present purposes, even when the disclosure threshold for fund managers was still 3%.

[7] Firms such as ICC Information Group Ltd. (located in Cardiff, near Companies House) can provide almost instantly a fairly recent list of (e.g.) each registered holder of 0.25% or more of a company's issued ordinary share capital. The practices described in this paragraph are those which were most common as at 1992–5.

[8] Around one-third of all listed UK ordinary shares were held through nominees at 1992: Central Statistical Office, *Economic Trends* (No. 466, 1992) 91.

[9] e.g. assets of external UK pension funds managed as segregated portfolios accounted for 20% of the total funds under management of Prudential Portfolio Managers Ltd., at 31 Dec. 1991: Hymans Robertson, *Pension Fund Investment Manager Survey: Manager Analysis* (1992).

would be registered either in the names of nominee companies or in the clients' names). But it is when consideration is given to fund managers which manage predominantly external funds that lists of largest registered shareholders really lose much of their usefulness. This is because the typical UK-based fund manager registers the equity holdings of each external segregated client in the name of a nominee company. Most major UK fund-management firms use in-house nominee companies for custodian purposes.[10] Medium-sized and smaller fund managers tend to use nominee companies operated by independent custodians. Most UK custodians (whether operated by a fund-management firm or independent) use a 'designated nominee system' under which each client's holding is registered in a unique name[11] (and some even have a separate nominee company for each client). All or most of the registered holdings in ABC plc which are managed by fund manager X might be outside of the top 20 registered shareholdings in ABC plc, but the aggregate holding may give fund manager X a significant stake in the company.[12] The major shortcoming of a list of largest registered shareholdings is thus clear: it cannot normally provide a reliable picture of the bodies which *control* the few largest chunks of a company's issued ordinary share capital.

Research conducted by the sociologist, John Scott, assisted the present author in determining how to uncover the largest institutional interest-holders in each of a number of UK companies.[13] Scott had a team of researchers analyse the share registers of 140 companies at Companies House in Cardiff. All registered shareholdings above a certain cut-off level were recorded, so as to obtain a list of the 60–100 largest registered shareholders in each company. In some cases all holdings in specified family names were also recorded. From this large and time-consuming exercise, Scott was able to compile lists (for 1976) of what he described as the 20 largest 'vote-holders' in each company—which is similar to, but not

---

[10] The collapse in 1995 of Barings Bank, the fund-management arm of which used an in-house custodian, led to calls for an end to this practice or at least for its regulation: see 'Back to the Drawing Board', *Pensions Mgt.*, Apr. 1995, p. 100. Limited regulation was proposed in Aug. 1995: see 'Watchdogs Propose New Rules for Custody of Investors' Assets', *Fin. Times*, 1 Aug. 1995, p. 16.

[11] e.g. at Sept. 1993, Phillips & Drew Fund Management Ltd. had a stake in a UK company which was actually 12 separate registered holdings. Three of those 12 holdings were registered in the names Phildrew Nominees Limited a/c CC, Phildrew Nominees Limited a/c RRP, and Phildrew Nominees Limited a/c GAL—for its clients, the trustees of Central Regional Council Superannuation Fund, Rolls Royce Pension Fund, and Gallaher Pension Fund, respectively: information gleaned by the author from a company's 'section 212 register' (see CA 1985, ss. 212–19).

[12] Admittedly, some UK fund managers, including the giant Mercury Asset Management plc, register the vast bulk of the equity holdings of their external segregated clients in the name of just one *internal* nominee company, without the use of numeric, alphabetic, or alphanumeric designations for separate accounts. (Such fund managers are, however, required by the rules of the Investment Management Regulatory Organisation to maintain *internal* records showing how much of each holding is held for each client.) The registered holding of that nominee company (which can be identified as owned by the custodian division of the fund-management firm) thus gives a reasonable guide as to the size of that fund manager's interest in the company. There may, however, still be substantial extra holdings which clients have required to be registered in other names.

[13] See J. Scott, *Capitalist Property and Financial Power* (1986) 39–45, 94–107.

exactly the same as, the 20 largest interest-holders. (For reasons given below, the statistics produced by Scott's study could not, unfortunately, be used in the present work as a comparative study.)

The present author did not have sufficient resources to conduct a task similar to that of Scott. Fortunately, though, there was actually no need to do so. This is because, some years after Scott's research was carried out, a practice (which by 1993 had become very widespread) began whereby companies themselves regularly obtain information about the holdings of their largest interest-holders. This research is usually carried out by the company's stockbroker.[14] The broker gleans from the share register every registered holding above a threshold level (which in some cases is as low as 10,000 shares, but is usually either 20,000, 25,000, or 30,000 shares).[15] Both commercially published registers showing the beneficial share-holders and controlling fund managers behind nominee companies, and other databases, are then employed to sort the collected registered holdings into 'interest' groupings.[16] What was required of the author was, therefore, to construct a suitable sample of companies and then to obtain from the sample companies this (highly confidential) information about their largest interest-holders.

The sampling frame for Study B comprised the 695 companies which made up the FT-A All Share index (excluding investment trusts) at September 1993. A sample of 69 companies (roughly 10% of the mentioned index) was selected, in such a way that small, medium-sized, and large companies were represented in proportion to the number of such companies in the index.[17] That is, a stratified-sampling procedure was used, so as to produce a sample with 10 large companies, 25 medium-sized companies, and 34 small companies.[18] Letters were sent to the

---

[14] There are also at least two independent firms providing this service.

[15] It is common for registered holdings of 10,000 and above (in the case of medium-sized and small listed companies) and of 30,000 and above (in the case of large listed companies) to account for over 90% of the issued ordinary share capital.

[16] In some instances, the companies themselves supplement and/or confirm this information by regularly serving notices under CA 1985, s. 212, upon their largest nominee shareholders. Section 212 empowers a public company to require a person whom the company knows or reasonably believes to have, or to have had, an interest in its shares, to provide details about that interest.

[17] The selection process was as follows. The 695 index companies were ranked in descending order by their market capitalization as at the end of trading on 10 Sept. 1993. A random number between one and 10 was chosen, and the first company selected was the one which had the corresponding rank in the list. The next 68 companies were chosen by marking every tenth company on the list. The sampling procedure was, therefore, systematic rather than random. The sample drawn was nevertheless equivalent to a random sample because there was no periodicity in the list. An undertaking of confidentiality given to all companies approached precludes the identification of those that made up the sample. It is for this reason that the exact numbering sequence used for the sample cannot be disclosed (as the sample companies could be identified from that information).

[18] These companies were representative of the largest 100, the middle 250, and the smallest 345 companies in the FT-A All Share index (excluding investment trusts) as at 10 Sept. 1993. They were not exactly representative of the three component indices of the FT-A All Share index (i.e. the FT-SE 100, the FT-SE Mid 250, and the FT-SE SmallCap indices) at that date,

sample companies, asking them to provide a list of the bodies/persons having the 10 largest 'interests'[19] in their issued ordinary share capital,[20] and the size (expressed as a percentage figure) of those interests.[21]

Study B sought some similar information to that in Study A, but three important differences should be noted. First, Study A concerned companies with market capitalizations (at the end of 1991) ranging from £769 million to £25,624 million— i.e. all large companies, but with the top few being enormous. In contrast, Study B included companies ranging from the very small (the smallest was capitalized at mid-September 1993 at under £20 million) through to enormously large (the largest was capitalized at an amount above £12,000 million and below £15,000 million at

because the membership of those indices was set at the end of June 1993 and over the ensuing 2½ months some FT-SE Mid 250 companies had become larger than some FT-SE 100 companies, whilst some FT-SE SmallCap companies had become larger than some FT-SE Mid 250 companies. The indices are revised quarterly to take account of such changes.

[19] Within the meaning of CA 1985, s. 208.

[20] All but one of the sample companies had just one class of ordinary shares, with each ordinary share carrying the right to one vote on a poll. One sample company had two classes of ordinary shares, with differential voting rights. This company provided details of the 10 largest vote-holders, when holdings of both 'A' and 'B' shares were taken into consideration. This information was used in the study because, even though it did not give an accurate picture of the 10 largest interest-holders in either class of the issued ordinary capital, it actually represented precisely the information with which Study B was concerned.

[21] Forty-seven responses were received as a result of the initial 69 letters sent out. Of those, 18 either stated that the company would not participate in the study or provided irrelevant or insufficient information. This left 29 usable responses. Those companies that had supplied irrelevant information (which was invariably a list of the 10 largest registered shareholders with the beneficial owners identified) or insufficient information (which was a list of something less than 10 of the largest interest-holders) were followed up, which resulted in six extra usable replies. Additional letters were then sent out to the two companies below and the two companies above the 34 remaining non-respondents/non-participants, as they appeared on the list of 695 companies in the sampling frame. From here on, where more than one usable reply was received in respect of a particular 'region' on the list, the first response received was used and the other response(s) was disregarded. The required information for a handful of the very small sample companies (viz. those which had at least 10 interest-holders with notifiable interests of 3% or more) was obtained from Extel cards and the *Hambro Company Guide* (Nov. Quarter, 1993). With some further follow-up work, the full sample of 69 companies was then achieved.

The reasons given by companies which declined to participate were, in order of frequency: (a) that the information was confidential to the company; (b) that the company did not wish to disclose such information without the shareholders' consent; and (c) that the company did not respond to any such research surveys. There would not appear to have been any scope for non-response bias related to the subject of the study. Recall, however, that there were also some companies which responded with irrelevant or insufficient information. Some of those that provided simply a list of their 10 largest registered shareholders indicated that, due to the presence on the share register of a substantial controlling shareholder, they did not bother to engage their broker or a research firm to conduct an analysis of the interests held by institutions and other 'external' shareholders. This initially gave rise to a fear of bias in the sense that companies with a large family shareholding (or some other sort of controlling shareholder) might be under-represented because they did not have the information at their disposal to be able to provide a satisfactory response. This anxiety was deemed groundless after an examination was made of all of the usable responses and the 'irrelevant/insufficient information' unusable responses, which revealed that there was in each group a similar proportion of 'controlled companies' to 'widely held companies'.

the date of the study.[22] Secondly, Study A covered all of the top 100 companies, whilst the participants in Study B comprised a sample (69 companies) of a very large group of companies: the FT-A All Share index, excluding investment trusts (695 companies). Thirdly, the studies did not seek to address identical objectives. Study A was concerned with obtaining information about the equity holdings of a few well-known UK institutions, rather than with examining the 'institutional-shareholder profile' of the sample companies. The second objective could not be met using Study A data, because not every company in Study A had institutions with notifiable interests in its equity, and even those that did have such institutional interest-holders did not have the same number of institutional interest-holders. However, Study B was devised precisely for the purpose of addressing that second objective. Within the confines of the 10 largest interest-holders, the information gathered in Study B allows an examination of the relative position of the dominant institutions in large, medium-sized, and small companies. Study B was also concerned with the first objective.

Study B was by no means the first piece of research into the shareholding structure of listed UK companies. As mentioned earlier, Scott carried out some fairly similar research for the year 1976.[23] Sargant Florence conducted large-scale studies as at 1936 and 1951,[24] and Leech and Leahy carried out a study involving 470 companies for 1983–5.[25] Smaller studies were conducted by Cosh and Hughes for 1981,[26] and by Farrar for 1984.[27] None of those studies is, unfortunately, directly comparable with Study B.

Florence looked merely at the largest registered shareholdings, and did not seek to identify the beneficial holders behind, or the bodies controlling the votes attached to, nominee holdings. As Scott states:

> His assumption was that nominees tended to hold for large numbers of individuals and, therefore, did not constitute cohesive voting blocks. . . . This assumption may well have been correct for 1936 [but later research showed] that many nominees in the post-war period have been custodians for substantial shareholders, and it must be recognised that Florence's analysis of the 1951 data may be considerably flawed by his focus on registered holdings.[28]

Florence's studies were also confined to industrial companies; financial companies were excluded from his samples. Scott confined his detailed analysis of the 20 largest 'vote-holders' to those 140 companies (out of the 250 in his study) which

---

[22] The exact capitalizations are not given for the parameter companies in Study B for the reason set out in n. 17 above.

[23] See n. 13 above, and accompanying text.

[24] P. Sargant Florence, *Ownership, Control and Success of Large Companies* (1961).

[25] D. Leech and J. Leahy, 'Ownership Structure, Control Type Classifications and the Performance of Large British Companies' (1991) 101 *Econ. J* 1418.

[26] A. D. Cosh and A. Hughes, 'The Anatomy of Corporate Control: Directors, Shareholders and Executive Remuneration in Giant US and UK Corporations' (1987) 11 *Camb. J Econ.* 285.

[27] J. H. Farrar, 'Ownership and Control of Listed Public Companies: Revising or Rejecting the Concept of Control' in B. G. Pettet (ed.), *Company Law in Change* (1987) 39, at 48–51.   [28] Scott (n. 13 above), at 37.

were unable to be classified on annual-report data as under some form of majority or minority control.[29] Further, Scott published lists of top 20 vote-holders for only 100 companies,[30] leaving 150 companies for which there is no such data.[31] This means that there are, in Scott's published lists, no companies like J. Sainsbury, Whitbread, and Pilkington Brothers—essentially, no companies which had a family or other shareholder with a 10% or greater stake.[32] Scott's study does, however, provide an important comparative source of data in Chapter 9.[33] The other studies mentioned do not provide sufficient relevant data for any sort of comparison.[34]

[29] Ibid., at 39–40.

[30] These lists are in J. Scott, *The Controlling Constellations* (1984).

[31] Admittedly, 59 of those 150 companies were either government-owned corporations, mutuals, or wholly owned companies. However, that still leaves 91 companies, the vast majority of which were listed companies, for which there is no relevant published data.

[32] This is not a criticism of Scott's work; it is merely an explanation of why a detailed comparison is not possible. As Scott's central aim was the identification of different modes of control, rather than a detailed study of institutional shareholding, there was no need for him to engage in a study of the top 20 vote-holders of those companies which could by other means be classified as under majority or minority control.

[33] See Ch. 9, Sec. B.1; and App. L.

[34] But cf. Cosh and Hughes (n. 26 above), at 300–1 (and Table 12): in a sample of 27 large listed industrial companies (all top 100) in 1981, the median company had seven shareholdings of 1% or more held by institutions, amounting to 10.9% of the issued ordinary share capital.

Appendix J
Details of Study C

The sampling frame used was the top 100 listed UK companies (measured by market capitalization) at 31 December 1971, 1981, and 1991. All of the top 100 companies were covered for 1991 (these were the FT-SE 100 constituents).[1] The information for 1991 was derived entirely from annual reports. Seventy-two of the top 100 companies were covered for each of 1971 and 1981. The details for those years were derived from annual reports (for financial years ending between 1 July 1971 and 30 June 1972, and between 1 July 1981 and 30 June 1982), augmented heavily by information supplied by company secretaries and investor-relations personnel,[2] for which the author is extremely grateful. The 72 companies covered for 1971 and 1981 were not selected randomly—they were simply the only ones for which it was possible to obtain the relevant details.

Although the sampling frame used was the top 100 companies at 31 December 1971, 1981, and 1991, the information collected for the 1971 and 1981 sample companies relates to the composition of their boards at the date of their annual reports (which spanned a period of approximately 12 months in each case). This is because it would have been extremely difficult, given the passage of time, to obtain the relevant information as at exactly 31 December 1971 and 31 December 1981. On the other hand, the information for the 1991 companies relates to the composition of their boards at exactly 31 December 1991. There are two reasons for this: (a) it was relatively easy to determine the composition of each company's board at that one date from information about the directorate, and changes therein, contained in the companies' 1991 and 1992 annual reports;[3] and (b) the 1991 study began as a wider study of interlocking directorships amongst the top 100 companies: a study which required information at a uniform date.

In relation to that part of Study C which concerned the roles of chairman and

---

[1] The FT-SE 100 constituents covered in Study C were not actually the largest 100 UK companies by market capitalization at 31 Dec. 1991. This is because the membership of the index was set at the end of Sept. 1991, and over the ensuing three months some FT-SE Mid 250 companies had become larger than some FT-SE 100 companies. The indices are revised quarterly to take account of such changes.

[2] It was unusual for directors to be identified as executive or non-executive in annual reports in 1971 and 1981. There has been a requirement since 1987 that non-executive directors of listed companies be identified, and described with 'a short biographical note', in the annual report and accounts: see now *Listing Rules*, para. 12.43(i).

[3] CA 1985, s. 234(2) requires the directors' report to 'state the names of the persons who, at any time during the financial year, were directors of the company'. The chairman's statement also commonly contains details of changes in the directorate over the previous 12 months.

chief executive,[4] it was necessary to rely greatly upon information from company secretaries and investor-relations personnel for the years 1971 and 1981. For 1991, however, the author relied upon information in the annual reports. Regarding 1991, in the great majority of cases it was easy to establish whether or not the chairman was a full-time director. Where there was a combined chairman/chief executive, for instance, it was straightforward. However, two companies, each of which had a separate chairman and chief executive, described their chairmen, somewhat strangely, as non-executive directors. A closer examination of the report and accounts revealed that in each case the chairman was the highest-paid director for both 1990 and 1991, participated in the executive share-option scheme, and received bonus remuneration as well as base salary. In these two instances, discretion was exercised in classifying the chairmen as executives rather than non-executives.

[4] See Ch. 4, Sec. A.1.xvi.

Appendix K

Details of the Australian Study

The author attempted to conduct a study in Australia equivalent to Study B, described in Chapter 5 and Appendix I. Letters were sent to a sample of All Ordinaries Index companies, asking them to provide a list of the bodies/persons having the 10 largest 'entitlements'[1] to their issued ordinary share capital, and the percentage size of those entitlements. The responses from the sample companies revealed, however, that such information could not be obtained in this manner. The responses made it apparent that, as at 1993, and in contrast to the situation in the UK, almost no listed Australian companies engaged their stockbrokers to analyse their share registers and extract this kind of information. In fact, it would appear that, as at 1993, only a minority of listed Australian companies used the statutory power to obtain information about the holders of relevant interests in their shares.[2] Most of the sample companies supplied simply a list of their disclosed 'substantial shareholders',[3] and a list of their 20 largest registered shareholders.[4]

In order to identify the bodies/persons having the 10 largest 'entitlements', it would be necessary to (a) conduct a study like that conducted by Scott in the UK;[5] and (b) supplement the information derived thereby with information obtained by companies under the statutory power to obtain information about the holders of relevant interests in their shares.[6] Step (b) would be necessary because of two practices. First, as at mid-1995, Australian fund-management firms tended to use a

[1] CL, s. 609 states that the shares to which a person is 'entitled' include shares in which the person, certain of the person's associates, and certain others, have a 'relevant interest'. 'Relevant interest' is defined in CL, Pt. 1.2, Div. 5. CL, s. 31 states that a person who has power to vote in respect of, or to dispose of, a share has a relevant interest in the share. (CL, s. 30(2) states that '[p]ower to vote in respect of a share is power to exercise, or to control the exercise of, the right to vote attached to the share'; s. 30(3) states that 'power to dispose of a share includes . . . power to exercise control over the disposal of the share'.) Fund managers would therefore invariably have a relevant interest in Australian equity investments under management.

[2] See CL, Pt. 6.8; Corporations Regulations, Sch. 2, forms 607–10.

[3] Under CL, s. 708, a substantial shareholder is one who is 'entitled' to not less than 5% of any class of a company's voting shares. On the meaning of 'entitlement', see n. 1 above. A substantial shareholder is required to notify the company and the ASX of its interests and certain changes therein: ss. 709–14. The company is required to keep a register of its substantial shareholders (CL, s. 715), and to list them in its annual report: *ASX Listing Rules*, LR 3C(3)(e)(i).

[4] The latter is required to be disclosed in the annual report of all listed companies (or in a statement lodged with the ASX at the time of lodgement of the annual report): *ASX Listing Rules*, LR 3C(3)(e)(v).

[5] See J. Scott, *Capitalist Property and Financial Power* (1986) 39–45, 94–107; Scott's study is described in App. I, at n. 13, and accompanying text.

[6] See CL, Pt. 6.8; Corporations Regulations, Sch. 2, forms 607–10.

small number of *independent* custodian companies—owned by major banks and trustee companies—to hold the equity investments of external clients whose funds were managed on a segregated basis. (In contrast, the major UK fund-management firms and their external segregated clients mostly used in-house nominee companies for custodian purposes.) Secondly, these independent custodians tended to register the equity investments of their many clients in just one name, and then use internal registers to record the number of shares held for each different client (known as a 'pooled nominee system'). (In contrast, most UK custodians used a 'designated nominee system' under which each client's holding was registered in a unique name.) Where, as in Australia, a pooled nominee system rather than a designated nominee system is in widespread use, recourse to a register of nominee companies and the fund managers and beneficial owners 'behind' them clearly would not assist in the identification of the fund managers which control the largest few stakes in particular companies. Step (b)—involving recourse to information obtained by companies under Part 6.8 of the Corporations Law—would, however, assist in this respect. Prior to December 1995, companies were required to keep a register of the information received under Part 6.8, and members of the public were entitled to inspect and obtain a copy of these registers. The removal of the requirement for companies to maintain a register of Part 6.8 information has made the researcher's task more difficult. Another practical problem for the researcher is, of course, that companies are under no obligation to utilize Part 6.8 to obtain this information about persons having relevant interests in their shares.

The Australian Study involved an examination by the author of 'substantial shareholder' information[8] for 234 of the 276 companies which composed the All Ordinaries Index at 31 August 1993. Forty-two of the 276 All Ordinaries Index constituents were excluded from the Australian Study. These were 10 overseas-based companies and 32 entities which were property trusts or companies involved merely in equity investment. The All Ordinaries Index generally consists of the largest companies (measured by market capitalization) listed on the ASX, the monthly trading in whose shares meets a minimum turnover threshold. The 234 companies which were included in the Australian Study were thus approximately the 234 largest Australia-based *operational* companies listed on the ASX at 31 August 1993.

The Australian Study ignored all substantial shareholders which were custodians—whether bank-nominee companies or trustee companies. The reason for this is as follows. Custodian companies may (under their contractual agreements with clients or otherwise under equitable principles) exercise voting rights or dispose of shares only on the explicit instructions of their clients, and they are therefore irrelevant for present purposes. However, under section 12(1) of the Corporations Law, a nominee company's clients who have power to vote or sell, or to direct the nominee company how to vote or sell, the shares which the nominee company holds for them are 'associates' of the nominee company. And, unless a nominee company has obtained a certificate from the Australian Securities Commission ('ASC') under Corporations Law, section 609(3), declaring it to be an

---

[7] See CL former, s. 724; First Corporate Law Simplification Act 1995 (Cth.), Sch. 6, s. 55.
[8] See n. 3 above.

'approved nominee body corporate', it is deemed by section 609(1)(b) to be entitled to all of the shares in which its associates have relevant interests. Although several of Australia's large custodian companies have obtained a certificate under section 609(3), some have not applied for one due to the harshness of the conditions imposed by the ASC,[9] and the latter therefore appear commonly as substantial shareholders.

There have been a number of studies of the 20 largest registered shareholders of listed Australian companies.[10] Whilst these have provided useful information as to the increasing level of institutional shareholding at the level of the market,[11] they have a significant shortcoming for present purposes: a list of largest registered shareholdings cannot normally provide a reliable picture of the bodies which *control* the few largest chunks of a company's issued ordinary share capital.[12]

---

[9] See Butterworths, *Australian Corporations Law—Principles and Practice* (1991) para. 6.2.0030.

[10] See I. M. Ramsay and M. Blair, 'Ownership Concentration, Institutional Investment and Corporate Governance: An Empirical Investigation of 100 Australian Companies' (1993) 19 *Melb. ULR* 153, and the studies cited therein at 165–6.

[11] See e.g. G. J. Crough, *Financial Institutions and the Ownership of Australian Corporations* (1981) 3–4.

[12] See App. I, at nn. 7–12, and accompanying text. The difficulties for the researcher associated with the fact that, in many companies, several of the largest registered shareholders are nominee companies were recognized by Ramsay and Blair (n. 10 above), at 169, 185.

Appendix L

Long-Term Institutional Shareholdings

At least 32[1] of the constituent companies of the FT-SE 100 index at the end of 1991 had at least one notifiable (3%+) institutional interest-holder which was also a large interest-holder at 1976 and/or 1957.[2] These 32 companies and the details of the interest-holders are set out in Table L.1.[3] An important qualification is that it is not certain in every case that the institution maintained a sizeable holding for the entire period between 1957–76 and/or 1976–91 and/or 1957–91. In some cases (for example Prudential's holdings in The General Electric Company plc, and Marks & Spencer plc) it is, however, known that a large core holding was maintained.[4] It is considered likely that in a majority of the other cases a core holding was similarly held throughout the relevant period.[5]

---

[1] The number could be greater, because the companies listed in Clayton and Osborn (n. 2 below) include only 14 of the FT-SE 100 constituents from 31 Dec. 1991, and those listed in Scott (n. 2 below) include only 37 of the FT-SE 100 constituents from 31 Dec. 1991.

[2] The information for 1991 is from Study A, described in Ch. 5, Sec. B.3.i; the information for 1976 is from J. Scott, *The Controlling Constellations: A Directory of 100 Large Companies* (1984); and the information for 1957 is from G. Clayton and W. T. Osborn, *Insurance Company Investment: Principles and Policy* (1965) 117.

[3] Note that the names of the companies and the institutions are as at 31 Dec. 1991. Some of the companies, and some of the institutions, had different names at 1957 and/or 1976.

[4] In regard to the GEC holding, see House of Commons Trade and Industry Committee, *Minutes of Evidence: Competitiveness of UK Manufacturing Industry* (1993) qu. 1288.

[5] Indirect support for this view can be found in the evidence given to the Trade and Industry Committee, ibid. The (in-house) investment manager for the Coats Viyella Pension Funds said that his funds' shareholdings were held on average for 'the best part of 20 years': ibid., at qu. 1254. The (in-house) investment manager for the ICI and Zeneca pension funds estimated his funds' average holding period at seven to 10 years: ibid., at qu. 1255. The group managing director of M&G Group plc told the committee that 'many' of M&G's shareholdings were held for 20 or 30 years: ibid., at qu. 1085. This is of particular significance since M&G specializes in managing unit-trust funds, and many unit trusts are 'income funds' which have a fairly high turnover of their equity investments.

(See Table L.1 on page 334).

Appendix L

Table L.1 Long-term institutional shareholdings

Company	Institution	Interest in issued ordinary share capital		
		1957	*1976*	*1991*
The BOC Group plc	PPM	6.10%	4.19%	3.60%
Blue Circle Industries plc	PPM	1.80%	?	3.00%
Courtaulds plc	PPM	1.80%	1.80%	3.90%
	Fleming	?	0.56%	4.00%
The General Electric Company plc	PPM	4.80%	6.51%	7.03%
Imperial Chemical Industries plc	PPM	1.80%	3.36%	3.65%
Marks & Spencer plc	PPM	6.10%	6.18%	6.30%
Reckitt & Coleman plc	PPM	1.30%	2.22%	4.40%
Reed International plc	PPM	2.40%	4.08%	6.01%
	CIN	?	2.07%	3.01%
Unilever plc	PPM	3.80%	?	6.00%
Barclays plc	PPM	?	1.70%	4.02%
Bass plc	PPM	?	4.39%	5.00%
The Boots Company plc	PPM	?	3.18%	4.00%
BET plc	PPM	?	1.66%	6.41%
	BZWIM	?	0.84%	3.46%
BTR plc	MAM	?	0.76%	5.50%
	PPM	?	3.93%	4.40%
Cadbury Schweppes plc	Fleming	?	0.59%	3.86%
Commercial Union plc	BZWIM	?	0.59%	3.08%
Fisons plc	PPM	?	3.36%	5.07%
General Accident plc	Schroder	?	0.50%	3.29%
	PPM	?	0.51%	3.21%
Glaxo Holdings plc	PPM	?	2.77%	4.09%
Grand Metropolitan plc	Norwich	?	1.91%	4.99%
	PPM	?	2.57%	3.95%
Guardian Royal Exchange plc	PPM	?	1.83%	3.20%
Hanson plc	PPM	?	7.21%	3.60%
Lloyds Bank plc	PPM	?	2.45%	3.30%
National Westminster Bank plc	MAM	?	0.80%	5.18%
Northern Foods plc	PPM	?	2.22%	3.29%
The Peninsular & Oriental Steam Navigation	Schroder	?	0.52%	4.93%
Company	PPM	?	2.58%	4.43%
RMC Group plc	Schroder	?	1.54%	3.91%
	PPM	?	4.53%	3.68%

Table L.1 Long-term institutional shareholdings (*continued*)

Company	Institution	Interest in issued ordinary share capital		
		1957	*1976*	*1991*
The RTZ Corporation plc	PPM	?	3.20%	4.41%
	Fleming	?	0.46%	3.08%
Scottish & Newcastle plc	PPM	?	1.58%	4.50%
	Norwich	?	0.67%	3.00%
Sears plc	PPM	?	2.69%	3.99%
	Schroder	?	1.16%	3.03%
The 'Shell' Transport & Trading Company plc	PPM	?	3.09%	4.19%
Tate & Lyle plc	PPM	?	4.12%	4.04%
	BZWIM	?	1.23%	3.65%

Note: abbreviations: see App. E.

Sources: Author's Study A; J. Scott, *The Controlling Constellations: A Directory of 100 Large Companies* (1984); G. Clayton and W. T. Osborn, *Insurance Company Investment: Principles and Policy* (1965) 117.

Bibliography

Accounting Standards Board, *Statement: Operating and Financial Review* (Accountancy Books, Milton Keynes, 1993).

Aghion, P., and Bolton, P., 'The Financial Structure of the Firm and the Problem of Control' (1989) 33 *European Economic Review* 286.

Alchian, A. A., and Demsetz, H., 'Production, Information Costs, and Economic Organization' (1972) 62 *American Economic Review* 777.

Alcock A., 'Insider Dealing—How Did We Get Here?' (1994) 15 *Company Lawyer* 67.

Alexander, Lord, 'Corporate Governance—The Role of the Banks' in D. D. Prentice and P. R. J. Holland (eds.), *Contemporary Issues in Corporate Governance* (Clarendon Press, Oxford, 1993) 97.

Allen, F., 'Stock Markets and Resource Allocation' in C. P. Mayer and X. Vives (eds.), *Capital Markets and Financial Intermediation* (Cambridge University Press, Cambridge, 1993) 81.

American Law Institute, *Principles of Corporate Governance: Analysis and Recommendations* (Proposed final draft, American Law Institute, Philadelphia, 1992).

Andenas, M., 'The Future of EC Company Law Harmonisation' (1994) 15 *Company Lawyer* 121.

Annual Report and Accounts of Budgens plc (Budgens plc, London, 1991).

Aoki, M., 'Toward an Economic Model of the Japanese Firm' (1990) 28 *Journal of Economic Literature* 1.

Arthur Andersen, *Audit Committees in the 1990s: Results of the 1992 Arthur Andersen Survey of Audit Committees* (Arthur Andersen, Sydney, 1993).

Artus, R. E., 'Tension to Continue' in National Association of Pension Funds, *Creative Tension?* (National Association of Pension Funds, London, 1990) 12.

Association of British Insurers, *Share Option and Profit Sharing Incentive Schemes: Guidelines to Requirements of Insurance Offices as Investors* (Association of British Insurers, London, 1987) (as amended).

—— *The Role and Duties of Directors—A Discussion Paper* (Association of British Insurers, London, 1990).

—— *Long Term Remuneration for Senior Executives* (Association of British Insurers, London, 1994).

Association of British Insurers, and National Association of Pension Funds Ltd., *Share Scheme Guidance* (Association of British Insurers and National Association of Pension Funds, London, 1993).

Association of Corporate Treasurers, *The Treasurer's Handbook* (Association of Corporate Treasurers, London, 1994).

Association of Superannuation Funds of Australia Ltd., *Corporate Governance Survey* (Association of Superannuation Funds of Australia Ltd., Sydney, 1994).

Auditing Practices Board, *The Future Development of Auditing* (Auditing Practices Board, London, 1992).

Australian Bureau of Statistics, *Assets of Superannuation Funds and Approved Deposit Funds, September Quarter* (Catalogue No. 5656) (Australian Bureau of Statistics, Canberra, 1993).

—— *Managed Funds: Australia, September Quarter* (Catalogue No. 5655) (Australian Bureau of Statistics, Canberra, 1993).

Australian Institute of Superannuation Trustees, *Corporate Governance in Australia: The Attitudes and Practices of Funds Managers* (A Research Report by Mirador Pty. Ltd.) (Australian Institute of Superannuation Trustees, Melbourne, 1994).

Australian Investment Managers' Association, *Executive Share Option Schemes Guidelines* (Australian Investment Managers' Association, Sydney, 1994).

—— *Corporate Governance: A Guide for Investment Managers and a Statement of Recommended Corporate Practice* (Australian Investment Managers' Association, Sydney, 1995).

Australian Investment Managers' Association, and Australian Institute of Company Directors, *Employee Share Schemes* (Australian Investment Managers' Association, Sydney, 1994).

Australian Investment Managers' Association, and Minter Ellison, *Board Committees in Australia* (Australian Investment Managers' Association, Sydney, 1995).

Australian Investment Managers' Group, *Corporate Governance Practice Note No. 1: Guide to Employee Share Schemes* (Australian Investment Managers' Group, Sydney, 1993).

—— *Incidence of Proxy Voting by Major Shareholders: Preliminary Statistics from a Sample of 8 Major Publicly Listed Companies* (Australian Investment Managers' Group, Sydney, 1993).

—— 'Media Release: Call for More Formalised Approach to Board Remuneration and Nomination: New Peak Body Survey', 4 Nov. 1993 (Australian Investment Managers' Group, Sydney, 1993).

—— *Standard Investment Management Agreement and Commentary* (Australian Investment Managers' Group, Sydney, 1993).

—— *December 1993 Half-Year Member Survey* (Australian Investment Managers' Group, Sydney, 1994).

Australian Investment Managers' Group, Australian Stock Exchange, and Business Council of Australia, *Survey on Structure and Operation of Board Remuneration and Nomination Committees* (Australian Investment Managers' Group, Sydney, 1993).

Australian Law Reform Commission, and Companies and Securities Advisory Committee, *Discussion Paper: Collective Investment Schemes: Superannuation* (Australian Law Reform Commission Discussion Paper No. 53) (Australian Government Publishing Service, Canberra, 1992).

—— and —— *Report: Collective Investments: Superannuation* (Australian Law Reform Commission Report No. 59) (Australian Government Publishing Service, Canberra, 1992).

—— and ——*Collective Investments: Other People's Money* (Australian Law Reform Commission Report No. 65) (Australian Government Publishing Service, Canberra, 1993).

Australian Securities Commission, *Policy Statement 23* (Australian Securities Commission, Sydney, 1993).
—— *Policy Statement 55* (Australian Securities Commission, Sydney, 1994).
Australian Stock Exchange Ltd., *Official Listing Rules* (Australian Stock Exchange, Sydney).
—— *All Ordinaries Index Companies Handbook* (Australian Stock Exchange, Sydney, 1990).
—— *Exposure Draft: Proposed Listing Rule Amendments and Other Issues* (Australian Stock Exchange, Sydney, 1992).
—— *All Ordinaries Index Companies Handbook* (Australian Stock Exchange, Sydney, 4th edn., 1993).
—— *Differential Voting Rights: ASX Discussion Paper* (Australian Stock Exchange, Sydney, 1993).
—— *Disclosure of Corporate Governance Practices by Listed Companies: ASX Discussion Paper* (Australian Stock Exchange, Sydney, 1994).
—— 'Media Release', 1 June 1994.
—— *Fact Book 1995* (Australian Stock Exchange, Sydney, 1995).
Axworthy, C. S., 'Corporate Directors—Who Needs Them?' (1988) 51 *Modern Law Review* 273.
Bank of England, 'Press Announcement' (1973) 13 *Bank of England Quarterly Bulletin* 148.
—— 'The Composition of Company Boards in 1982' (1983) 23 *Bank of England Quarterly Bulletin* 66.
—— 'The Boards of Quoted Companies' (1985) 25 *Bank of England Quarterly Bulletin* 233.
—— 'Pre-emption Rights' (1987) 27 *Bank of England Quarterly Bulletin* 545.
Baums, T., 'Takeovers Versus Institutions in Corporate Governance in Germany' in D. D. Prentice and P. R. J. Holland (eds.), *Contemporary Issues in Corporate Governance* (Clarendon Press, Oxford, 1993) 151.
Baysinger, B. D., Kosnik, R. D., and Turk, T. A., 'Effects of Board and Ownership Structure on Corporate R&D Strategy' (1991) 34 *Academy of Management Journal* 205.
BDO Binder Hamlyn, *Non-Executive Directors—Watchdogs or Advisers?* (BDO Binder Hamlyn, London, 1994).
Berglöf, E., and Perotti E., 'The Governance Structure of the Japanese Financial Keiretsu' (1994) 36 *Journal of Financial Economics* 259.
Berle, A. A., 'For Whom Corporate Managers *Are* Trustees: A Note' (1932) 45 *Harvard Law Review* 1365.
Berle, A. A., and Means, G. C., *The Modern Corporation and Private Property* (Harcourt Brace & World, New York, revised edn., 1968).
Bhagat, S., and Jefferis, R. H., *Is Defensive Activity Effective?* (Working Paper) (University of Colorado, Boulder, 1993).
Black, B. S., 'Shareholder Passivity Reexamined' (1990) 89 *Michigan Law Review* 520.
—— 'Agents Watching Agents: The Promise of Institutional Investor Voice' (1992) 39 *UCLA Law Review* 811.
—— 'Next Steps in Proxy Reform' (1992) 18 *Journal of Corporation Law* 1.

Black, B. S., and Coffee, J. C., 'Hail Britannia? Institutional Investor Behavior Under Limited Regulation' (1994) 92 *Michigan Law Review* 1997.

Bond, S. R., and Meghir, C., 'Financial Constraints and Company Investment' (1994) 15(2) *Fiscal Studies* 1.

Bosch, H., ' "Corporate Practices and Conduct": Setting Standards for Corporate Governance in Australia' (1993) 1 *Corporate Governance: An International Review* 196.

Brennan, M. J., and Franks, J. R., *Underpricing, Ownership and Control in Initial Public Offerings of Equity Securities in the UK* (Institute of Finance and Accounting, Working Paper 209–1995) (London Business School, London, 1995).

Brickley, J. A., Coles, J. L., and Jarrell, G., *Corporate Leadership Structure: On the Separation of the Positions of CEO and Chairman of the Board* (Bradley Policy Research Center, William E. Simon Graduate School of Business Administration, Financial Research and Policy Studies Working Paper Series 95–02) (University of Rochester, Rochester, 1995).

Brickley, J. A., and James, C. M., 'The Takeover Market, Corporate Board Composition, and Ownership Structure: The Case of Banking' (1987) 30 *Journal of Law and Economics* 161.

BR Pension Scheme Annual Report and Financial Statements 1992 (Pensions Management, Durham, 1992).

British Rail Pension Trustee Company Ltd., *Corporate Governance: Policy Statement* (British Rail Pension Trustee Company Ltd., London, 1992).

Brudney, V., 'Corporate Governance, Agency Costs, and the Rhetoric of Contract' (1985) 85 *Columbia Law Review* 1403.

Burkart, M., *Overbidding in Takeover Contests* (London School of Economics Financial Markets Group Discussion Paper No. 180) (London School of Economics, London, 1994).

Butterworths, *Australian Corporations Law—Principles and Practice* (Butterworths, Sydney, 1991).

Buxbaum, R. M., 'Institutional Owners and Corporate Managers: A Comparative Perspective' (1991) 57 *Brooklyn Law Review* 1.

Cadbury, Sir Adrian, *The Company Chairman* (Director Books, Cambridge, 1990).

Cannella, A. A., Fraser, D. R., and Lee, D. S., 'Firm Failure and Managerial Labor Markets: Evidence from Texas Banking' (1995) 38 *Journal of Financial Economics* 185.

Carr, Lord, 'The Function of Ownership and the Role of Institutional Shareholders' in K. Midgley (ed.), *Management Accountability and Corporate Governance* (Macmillan, London, 1982) 91.

CBI City/Industry Task Force, *Report: Investing for Britain's Future* (Confederation of British Industry, London, 1987).

CCH, *Australian Superannuation Law and Practice* (CCH, Sydney, 1991).

Central Statistical Office, *Economic Trends* (No. 466) (HMSO, London, 1992).

—— *Economic Trends* (No. 480) (HMSO, London, 1993).

—— *Share Ownership* (HMSO, London, 1995).

Chan, S. H., Martin, J. D., and Kensinger, J. W., 'Corporate Research and

Development Expenditures and Share Value' (1990) 26 *Journal of Financial Economics* 255.

Chandler, A. D., *Strategy and Structure: Chapters in the History of the Industrial Enterprise* (MIT Press, Cambridge Mass, 1962).

Charkham, J. P., *Corporate Governance and the Market for Control of Companies* (Bank of England Panel Paper No. 25) (Bank of England, London, 1989).

—— *Corporate Governance and the Market for Companies: Aspects of the Shareholders' Role* (Bank of England Discussion Paper No. 44) (Bank of England, London, 1989).

—— 'Are Shares Just Commodities?' in National Association of Pension Funds, *Creative Tension?* (National Association of Pension Funds, London, 1990) 34.

Chartered Accountants Joint Ethics Committee, *Rotation of Audit Partners* (Chartered Accountants Joint Ethics Committee, Milton Keynes, 1993).

City Capital Markets Committee, 'Share Repurchase by Quoted Companies' (1988) 28 *Bank of England Quarterly Bulletin* 382.

City/Industry Working Group ('Myners Committee'), *Developing a Winning Partnership* (Department of Trade and Industry, London, 1995).

Clark, R. C., 'The Four Stages of Capitalism: Reflections on Investment Management Treatises' (1981) 94 *Harvard Law Review* 561.

—— *Corporate Law* (Little Brown & Co., Boston, 1986).

Clayton, G., and Osborn, W. T., *Insurance Company Investment: Principles and Policy* (George Allen & Unwin, London, 1965).

Coase, R. H., 'The Nature of the Firm' (1937) 4 *Economica* 386.

Coffee, J. C., 'Regulating the Market for Corporate Control: A Critical Assessment of the Tender Offer's Role in Corporate Governance' (1984) 84 *Columbia Law Review* 1145.

—— 'Shareholders Versus Managers: The Strain in the Corporate Web' (1986) 85 *Michigan Law Review* 1.

—— 'Liquidity Versus Control: The Institutional Investor as Corporate Monitor' (1991) 91 *Columbia Law Review* 1277.

—— 'The SEC and the Institutional Investor: A Half-Time Report' (1994) 15 *Cardozo Law Review* 837.

Coffee, J. C., Gilson, R. J., and Lowenstein, L. (eds.), *Relational Investing* (Oxford University Press, New York, 1996) (forthcoming).

Committee of Inquiry into the Australian Financial System, *Final Report* (Australian Government Publishing Service, Canberra, 1981).

Committee of Inquiry on Industrial Democracy ('Bullock Committee'), *Report* (Cmnd 6706) (HMSO, London, 1977).

Committee on the Financial Aspects of Corporate Governance ('Cadbury Committee'), *Draft Report* (Committee on the Financial Aspects of Corporate Governance, London, 1992).

—— *Code of Best Practice* (Gee & Co., London, 1992).

—— *Report* (Gee & Co., London, 1992).

—— *Compliance with the Code of Best Practice* (Gee Publishing, London, 1995).

Committee on the Working of the Monetary System ('Radcliffe Committee'), *Minutes of Evidence* (24 April 1958) (HMSO, London, 1960).

Committee to Review the Functioning of Financial Institutions ('Wilson Committee'), *Report* (Cmnd. 7937) (HMSO, London, 1980).

Commonwealth Funds Management Ltd., *Annual Report 1992–93* (Commonwealth Funds Management Ltd., Canberra, 1993).

Company Law Committee ('Jenkins Committee'), *Report* (Cmnd. 1749) (HMSO, London, 1962).

Company Reporting Ltd., *The 1994 UK R&D Scoreboard* (Company Reporting Ltd., Edinburgh, 1994).

Competitiveness: Helping Business to Win (Cm. 2563) (HMSO, London, 1994).

Conard, A. F., 'Beyond Managerialism: Investor Capitalism?' (1988) 22 *University of Michigan Journal of Law Reform* 117.

Confederation of British Industry, *Pension Fund Investment Management* (Confederation of British Industry, London, 1987).

—— *Response to the Draft Report of the Committee on the Financial Aspects of Corporate Governance* (Confederation of British Industry, London, 1992).

Conyon, M. J., 'Corporate Governance Changes in UK Companies Between 1988 and 1993' (1994) 2 *Corporate Governance: An International Review* 97.

Conyon, M. J., Gregg, P., and Machin, S., 'Taking Care of Business: Executive Compensation in the UK' (1995) 105 *Economic Journal* 704.

Corbett, J., 'International Perspectives on Financing: Evidence from Japan' (1987) 3 (4) *Oxford Review of Economic Policy* 30.

—— 'An Overview of the Japanese Financial System' in N. H. Dimsdale and M. Prevezer (eds.), *Capital Markets and Corporate Governance* (Clarendon Press, Oxford, 1994) 306.

Corkery, J. F., *Directors Powers and Duties* (Longman Cheshire, Melbourne, 1987).

Cosh, A. D., and Hughes, A., 'The Anatomy of Corporate Control: Directors, Shareholders and Executive Remuneration in Giant US and UK Corporations' (1987) 11 *Cambridge Journal of Economics* 285.

Cosh, A. D., Hughes, A., Lee, K., and Singh, A., 'Institutional Investment, Mergers and the Market for Corporate Control' (1989) 7 *International Journal of Industrial Organisation* 73.

Cosh, A. D., Hughes, A., Singh, A., et al., *Takeovers and Short-Termism in the UK* (Institute for Public Policy Research Industrial Policy Paper No. 3) (Institute for Public Policy Research, London, 1990).

Crough, G. J., *Financial Institutions and the Ownership of Australian Corporations* (Transnational Corporations Research Project, Research Monograph No. 12) (University of Sydney, Sydney, 1981).

Daniels, R. J., and MacIntosh, J., 'Toward a Distinctive Canadian Corporate Law Regime' (1991) 29 *Osgoode Hall Law Journal* 863.

Davies, P. L., 'Institutional Investors: A UK View' (1991) 57 *Brooklyn Law Review* 129.

—— 'The Regulation of Defensive Tactics in the United Kingdom and the United States' in K. J. Hopt and E. Wymeersch (eds.), *European Takeovers—Law and Practice* (Butterworths, London, 1992) 195.

—— 'Institutional Investors in the United Kingdom' in D. D. Prentice and P. R. J.

Holland (eds.), *Contemporary Issues in Corporate Governance* (Clarendon Press, Oxford, 1993) 69.

Davies, P. L., and Stapledon, G. P., 'Corporate Governance in the United Kingdom' in M. Isaksson and R. Skog (eds.), *Aspects of Corporate Governance* (Juristförlaget, Stockholm, 1994) 55.

—— and —— 'Comment on B. S. Black and J. C. Coffee, "Hail Britannia? Institutional Investor Behavior Under Limited Regulation" ' in J. C. Coffee, R. J. Gilson, and L. Lowenstein (eds.), *Relational Investing* (Oxford University Press, New York, 1995) (forthcoming).

Davis, E. P., *International Diversification of Institutional Investors* (Bank of England Discussion Papers, Technical Series, No. 44) (Bank of England, London, 1991).

Defina, A., Harris, T. C., and Ramsay, I. M., 'What is Reasonable Remuneration for Corporate Officers? An Empirical Investigation into the Relationship Between Pay and Performance in the Largest Australian Companies' (1994) 12 *Company and Securities Law Journal* 341.

Demsetz, H., 'The Structure of Ownership and the Theory of the Firm' (1983) *Journal of Law and Economics* 375.

Department of Trade and Industry, *Barriers to Takeovers in the European Community* (A Study by Coopers & Lybrand for the DTI) (Department of Trade and Industry, London, 1989).

—— *Companies in 1989–90* (HMSO, London, 1990).

Dodd, E. M., 'For Whom Are Corporate Managers Trustees?' (1932) 45 *Harvard Law Review* 1145.

Du Bois, A. B., *The English Business Company after the Bubble Act 1720–1800* (The Commonwealth Fund, New York, 1938).

Easterbrook, F. H., 'Two Agency-Cost Explanations of Dividends' (1984) 74 *American Economic Review* 650.

Easterbrook, F. H., and Fischel, D. R., 'Voting in Corporate Law' (1983) 26 *Journal of Law and Economics* 395.

Edwards, J. S. S., 'Recent Developments in the Theory of Corporate Finance' (1987) 3 (4) *Oxford Review of Economic Policy* 1.

Edwards, J. S. S., and Fischer, K., *Banks, Finance and Investment in Germany* (Cambridge University Press, Cambridge, 1994).

Eisenberg, M. A., *The Structure of the Corporation: A Legal Analysis* (Little Brown & Co., Boston, 1976).

—— 'The Structure of Corporation Law' (1989) 89 *Columbia Law Review* 1461.

Esser, J., 'Bank Power in West Germany Revised' (1990) 13 *West European Politics* 17.

Ethical Investment Research Service, *Attitudes to Ethical Investment* (EIRIS, London, 1993).

Extel Financial Ltd., *Survey of Investment Analysts* (Extel Financial, London, 1992).

Fama, E. F., 'Agency Problems and the Theory of the Firm' (1980) 88 *Journal of Political Economy* 288.

Fama, E. F., and Jensen, M. C., 'Separation of Ownership and Control' (1983) 26 *Journal of Law and Economics* 301.

—— and —— 'Agency Problems and Residual Claims' (1983) 26 *Journal of Law and Economics* 327.

Farrar, J. H., 'Ownership and Control of Listed Public Companies: Revising or Rejecting the Concept of Control' in B. G. Pettet (ed.), *Company Law in Change* (Stevens, London, 1987) 39.

—— 'Legal Restraints on Institutional Investor Involvement in Corporate Governance', Unpublished paper prepared for the Australian Investment Managers' Group, 1993.

Farrar, J. H., and Russell, M., 'The Impact of Institutional Investment on Company Law' (1984) 5 *Company Lawyer* 107.

Finch, V., 'Board Performance and Cadbury on Corporate Governance' [1992] *Journal of Business Law* 581.

Finch, V., 'Company Directors: Who Cares About Skill and Care?' (1992) 55 *Modern Law Review* 179.

Finn, P. D., *Fiduciary Obligations* (Law Book Company, Sydney, 1977).

Fischel, D. R., 'The Corporate Governance Movement' (1982) 35 *Vandabilt Law Review* 1259.

Focus Communications, *Criminal Justice Act 1993: Its Impact Upon Financial Communications* (Focus Communications, London, 1994).

Franks, J. R., and Harris, R., 'Shareholder Wealth Effects of UK Take-overs: Implications for Merger Policy' in J. A. Fairburn and J. A. Kay (eds.), *Mergers and Merger Policy* (Oxford University Press, Oxford, 1989) 148.

Franks, J. R., and Mayer, C. P., 'Capital Markets and Corporate Control: A Study of France, Germany and the UK' (1990) 10 *Economic Policy* 189.

—— and —— 'Hostile Takeovers in the UK and the Correction of Managerial Failure' (1996) 40 *Journal of Financial Economics* (forthcoming).

—— and —— 'Corporate Control: A Synthesis of the International Evidence' in J. C. Coffee, R. J. Gilson, and L. Lowenstein (eds.), *Relational Investing* (Oxford University Press, New York, 1996) (forthcoming).

—— and —— 'German Capital Markets, Corporate Control and the Obstacles to Hostile Takeovers: Lessons from Three Case Studies' in J. C. Coffee, R. J. Gilson, and L. Lowenstein (eds.), *Relational Investing* (Oxford University Press, New York, 1996) (forthcoming).

Friedman, M., *Capitalism and Freedom* (University of Chicago Press, Chicago, 1962).

Gaved, M., *Ownership and Influence* (Institute of Management, London School of Economics, London, 1995).

Gilson, R. J., 'Corporate Governance and Economic Efficiency' in M. Isaksson and R. Skog (eds.), *Aspects of Corporate Governance* (Juristflörlaget, Stockholm 1994) 131.

Gilson, R. J., and Kraakman, R., 'Reinventing the Outside Director: An Agenda for Outside Directors' (1991) 43 *Stanford Law Review* 863.

Gilson, R. J., and Roe, M. J., 'Understanding the Japanese Keiretsu: Overlaps Between Corporate Governance and Industrial Organization' (1993) 102 *Yale Law Journal* 871.

Goergen, M. G. J., *The Evolution of Ownership and Control in German IPOs* (Working Paper) (Keble College, Oxford, 1995).

Gower, L. C. B., 'Corporate Control: The Battle for the Berkeley' (1955) 68 *Harvard Law Review* 1176.

—— *Gower's Principles of Modern Company Law* (Sweet & Maxwell, London, 5th edn., 1992).

Griffin, P. J., 'Institutional Investors in Australia: A Shareholders' Perspective', Unpublished paper presented at the Australian Investment Managers' Group and Business Council of Australia conference on 'Corporate Governance and Australian Competitiveness: The Role of Institutional Investors', Sydney, 11 November 1993.

Griffith, G., 'The Role of the General Meeting in the Conduct of Business in the Registered Company' D.Phil. thesis (Oxford, 1971).

Grossman, S. J., and Hart, O. D., 'Corporate Financial Structure and Managerial Incentives' in J. J. McCall (ed.), *The Economics of Information and Uncertainty* (University of Chicago Press, Chicago, 1982) 107.

Grout, J., and Ross, D., *Foreign Exchange Management in Non-Financial Corporations: A Checklist of Major Issues for Institutional Investors* (Association of Corporate Treasurers, London, 1992).

Hambros Bank, *Hambro Company Guide* (November Quarter) (Hemmington Scott, London, 1993).

Hannah, L., *Inventing Retirement: The Development of Occupational Pensions in Britain* (Cambridge University Press, Cambridge, 1986).

Harding, D., 'Do Institutional Investors in Australia Have a Fiduciary Responsibility to Vote?', Unpublished paper presented at the Australian Investment Managers' Association and Institute of Corporate Managers Secretaries and Administrators conference on 'Proxy Voting', Sydney, 7 September 1994.

Hart, O., and Moòre, J., 'A Theory of Debt Based on the Inalienability of Human Capital' (1994) 109 *Quarterly Journal of Economics* 841.

Hatherly, D., 'The Future of Audit: The Case for the Shareholder Panel', Unpublished paper presented at the 17th Annual Congress of the European Accounting Association, Venice, April 1994.

Hauswald, R. B. H., *On the Origins of Universal Banking: An Analysis of the German Banking Sector 1848 to 1910* (Working Paper) (College of Business and Management, University of Maryland, 1995).

Hax, H., 'Debt and Investment Policy in German Firms: The Issue of Capital Shortage' (1990) 146 *Journal of Institutional and Theoretical Economics* 106.

Hayton, D., 'Trustees and the New Financial Services Regime' (1989) 10 *Company Lawyer* 191.

Herzel, L., and Shepro, R. W., *Bidders and Targets* (Basil Blackwell, Oxford, 1990).

Hill, J., 'Institutional Investors and Corporate Governance in Australia' in T. Baums, R. M. Buxbaum, and K. J. Hopt (eds.), *Institutional Investors and Corporate Governance* (Walter de Gruyter, Berlin, 1994) 583.

Hirschman, A. O., *Exit, Voice, and Loyalty: Responses to Decline in Firms, Organizations, and States* (Harvard University Press, Cambridge Mass, 1970).

Hirshleifer, D., and Thakor, A. V., 'Managerial Performance, Boards of Directors and Takeover Bidding' (1994) 1 *Journal of Corporate Finance* 63.

Hopt, K. J., 'Directors' Duties to Shareholders, Employees, and Other Creditors:

A View from the Continent' in E. McKendrick (ed.), *Commercial Aspects of Trusts and Fiduciary Obligations* (Clarendon Press, Oxford, 1992) 115.

House of Commons Employment Committee, *Third Report: The Remuneration of Directors and Chief Executives of Privatised Utilities* (Session 1994–5) (HMSO, London, 1995).

House of Commons Trade and Industry Committee, *Minutes of Evidence: Takeovers and Mergers* (Session 1990–1, HC 226-x, 8 May 1991) (HMSO, London, 1991).

—— *First Report: Takeovers and Mergers* (Session 1991–2) (HMSO, London, 1991).

—— *Minutes of Evidence: Competitiveness of UK Manufacturing Industry* (Session 1993–4, HC 41-i, -ii, 24 November 1993 and 1 December 1993) (HMSO, London, 1993).

—— *Second Report: Competitiveness of UK Manufacturing Industry* (Session 1993–4) (HMSO, London, 1994).

—— *Second Report: Competitiveness of UK Manufacturing Industry; Vol. II, Memoranda of Evidence* (Session 1993–4) (HMSO, London, 1994).

House of Lords Science and Technology Committee, *First Report: Innovation in Manufacturing Industry* (Session 1990–1) (HMSO, London, 1991).

House of Representatives Standing Committee on Legal and Constitutional Affairs ('Lavarch Committee'), *Corporate Practices and the Rights of Shareholders* (Australian Government Publishing Service, Canberra, 1991).

Hubbard, R. G., and Palia, D., 'Executive Pay and Performance: Evidence from the US Banking Industry' (1995) 39 *Journal of Financial Economics* 105.

Hymans Robertson, *Pension Fund Investment Manager Survey: Manager Analysis* (Hymans Robertson, Glasgow, 1992).

Industry Commission, *Availability of Capital* (Report No. 18) (Australian Government Publishing Service, Canberra, 1991).

Inglis-Jones, N., *The Law of Occupational Pension Schemes* (Sweet & Maxwell, London, 1989).

Innovation Advisory Board, *Innovation: City Attitudes and Practices* (Department of Trade and Industry, London, 1990).

—— *Promoting Innovation and Long Termism* (Department of Trade and Industry, London, 1990).

Inquiry into Corporate Takeovers in the United Kingdom: Evidence from the Association of British Insurers (and others) (Hume Occasional Paper No. 18) (David Hume Institute, Edinburgh, 1990).

Institutional Fund Managers' Association, *Voting by Institutional Shareholders* (Institutional Fund Managers' Association, London, 1991).

Institutional Fund Managers' Association, and British Merchant Banking and Securities Houses Association, *Terms and Conditions for Discretionary Fund Management* (Institutional Fund Managers' Association and British Merchant Banking and Securities Houses Association, London, 1991).

Institutional Shareholders' Committee, *Management Buy-Outs* (Institutional Shareholders' Committee, London, 1989).

—— *The Responsibilities of Institutional Shareholders in the UK* (Institutional Shareholders' Committee, London, 1991).

—— *The Role and Duties of Directors—A Statement of Best Practice* (Institutional Shareholders' Committee, London, 1991).

—— *Newsletter No. 1* (Institutional Shareholders' Committee, London, 1992).

—— *Suggested Disclosure of Research and Development Expenditure* (Institutional Shareholders' Committee, London, 1992).

—— *Report on Investigation of Use of Voting Rights by Institutions* (Institutional Shareholders' Committee, London, 1993).

Insurance and Superannuation Commission, *Quarterly Statistical Bulletin* (June edition) (Australian Government Publishing Service, Canberra, 1993).

The International Stock Exchange of the United Kingdom and the Republic of Ireland Ltd., *Quality of Markets Quarterly Review* (Spring) (The International Stock Exchange of the United Kingdom and the Republic of Ireland Ltd., London, 1990).

ISS Australia, *Major Australian Public Companies: Proxy Voting Statistics: September 1994 to March 1995* (Corporate Governance International Pty. Ltd., Sydney, 1995).

Issuing Houses Association, *Notes for the Amalgamation of British Businesses* (Issuing Houses Association, London, 1959).

Jack, R. B., *How Level a Playing Field Does Company Law Provide?* (Hume Occasional Paper No. 30) (David Hume Institute, Edinburgh, 1991).

Jackson, P. D., 'Management of UK Equity Portfolios' (1987) 27 *Bank of England Quarterly Bulletin* 253.

Jenkinson, T., 'Regulating Hostile Takeovers in the EC' [1992] (Spring) *Stock Exchange Quarterly* 13.

Jenkinson, T., and Mayer, C. P., *Takeover Defence Strategies* (Oxford Economic Research Associates, Oxford, 1991).

—— and —— 'The Assessment: Corporate Governance and Corporate Control' (1992) 8 (3) *Oxford Review of Economic Policy* 1.

Jensen, M. C., 'Agency Costs of Free Cash Flow, Corporate Finance, and Takeovers' (1986) 76 *American Economic Review—Papers and Proceedings* 323.

—— 'Takeovers: Their Causes and Consequences' (1988) 2 *Journal of Economic Perspectives* 21.

—— 'The Modern Industrial Revolution, Exit, and the Failure of Internal Control Systems' (1993) 48 *Journal of Finance* 831.

Jensen, M. C., and Meckling, W. H., 'Theory of the Firm: Managerial Behavior, Agency Costs and Ownership Structure' (1976) 3 *Journal of Financial Economics* 305.

Kallfass, H. H., 'The American Corporation and the Institutional Investor: Are There Lessons from Abroad?' [1988] *Columbia Business Law Review* 775.

Kester, W. C., 'Industrial Groups as Systems of Contractual Governance' (1992) 8 (3) *Oxford Review of Economic Policy* 24.

King, M., 'Take-over Activity in the United Kingdom' in J. A. Fairburn and J. A. Kay (eds.), *Mergers and Merger Policy* (Oxford University Press, Oxford, 1989) 99.

Kini, O., Kracaw, W., and Mian, S., 'Corporate Takeovers, Firm Performance, and Board Composition' (1995) 1 *Journal of Corporate Finance* 383.

Knight, J., 'The Role of the Shareholder and the Institutions' in The Corporate

Policy Group, *Control of the Corporation: A Review of the British Company in the 1980s* (The Corporate Policy Group, Oxford, 1980) 11.

Knoeber, C. R., 'Golden Parachutes, Shark Repellents, and Hostile Tender Offers' (1986) 76 *American Economic Review* 155.

Köndgen, J., 'Duties of Banks in Voting Their Clients' Stock' in T. Baums, R. M. Buxbaum, and K. J. Hopt (eds.), *Institutional Investors and Corporate Governance* (Walter de Gruyter, Berlin, 1994) 531.

Korn/Ferry International, *Boards of Directors Study* (Korn/Ferry International, London, 1980).

—— *Boards of Directors Study UK* (Korn/Ferry International, London, 1988).

—— *Boards of Directors Study UK* (Korn/Ferry International, London, 1993).

—— *Boards of Directors in Australia: Twelfth Study* (Korn/Ferry International, Sydney, 1993).

KPMG Peat Marwick, *Survey of Non-Executive Directors* (KPMG Peat Marwick, London, 1994).

The Labour Party, *Winning for Britain* (The Labour Party, London, 1994).

Laing, Sir Hector, 'The Balance of Responsibilities' in National Association of Pension Funds Ltd., *Creative Tension?* (National Association of Pension Funds Ltd., London, 1990) 59.

Lawriwsky, M. L., 'Some Tests of the Influence of Control Type on the Market for Corporate Control in Australia' (1984) 32 *Journal of Industrial Economics* 277.

Leech, D., and Leahy, J., 'Ownership Structure, Control Type Classifications and the Performance of Large British Companies' (1991) 101 *Economic Journal* 1418.

Linaker, L. E., 'The Institutional Investor—Investment from M&G's Viewpoint' in D. D. Prentice and P. R. J. Holland (eds.), *Contemporary Issues in Corporate Governance* (Clarendon Press, Oxford, 1993) 107.

Linklaters & Paines, *Unit Trusts: The Law and Practice* (Longman, London, 1989).

Lipton, M., and Rosenblum, S. A., 'A New System of Corporate Governance: The Quinquennial Election of Directors' (1991) 58 *University of Chicago Law Review* 187.

London Stock Exchange, 'Quality of Markets Review' [1991] (Winter) *Stock Exchange Quarterly* 36.

—— *The Listing Rules* (The International Stock Exchange of the United Kingdom and the Republic of Ireland Ltd., London, 1993).

—— *Guidance on the Dissemination of Price Sensitive Information* (The International Stock Exchange of the United Kingdom and the Republic of Ireland Ltd., London, 1995).

—— *Proposed Changes to the Listing Rules: Amendment 5* (The International Stock Exchange of the United Kingdom and the Republic of Ireland Ltd., London, 1995).

McConnell, J. J., and Muscarella, C. J., 'Corporate Capital Expenditure Decisions and the Market Value of the Firm' (1985) 14 *Journal of Financial Economics* 399.

Mace, M. L., 'Directors: Myth and Reality—Ten Years Later' (1979) 32 *Rutgers Law Review* 293.

Main, B. G. M., 'The Governance of Remuneration for Senior Executives', Unpublished paper presented at the Financial Markets Group and Centre for

Economic Performance conference on 'Structure of Corporate Governance', London School of Economics, 15 June 1995.

Main, B. G. M., and Johnston, J., *The Remuneration Committee as an Instrument of Corporate Governance* (Hume Occasional Paper No. 35) (David Hume Institute, Edinburgh, 1992).

Mallin, C., 'Enhanced Scrip Dividends' [1993] (Autumn) *Stock Exchange Quarterly* 13.

—— *Voting: The Role of Institutional Investors in Corporate Governance* (Research Board of the Institute of Chartered Accountants in England and Wales, London, 1995).

Mandelbaum, A., 'Efficiency and Equity Implications of the Proposed New Zealand Takeovers Code' (1994) 12 *Company and Securities Law Journal* 489.

Mankiw, N. G., 'Comment on C. P. Mayer, "New Issues in Corporate Finance"' (1988) 32 *European Economic Review* 1183.

Manne, H. G., 'Mergers and the Market for Corporate Control' (1965) 73 *Journal of Political Economy* 110.

Marsh, P. R., *Short-Termism on Trial* (Institutional Fund Managers' Association, London, 1990).

—— *Dividend Announcements and Stock Price Performance* (London Business School Working Paper) (London Business School, London, 1992).

Marshman, P., and Davies, P., 'The Role of the Stock Exchange and the Financial Characteristics of Australian Companies' in R. Bruce, B. McKern, I. Pollard, and M. Skully (eds.), *Handbook of Australian Corporate Finance* (Sydney, 4th edn., 1991) 78.

Matheson, A. W., 'The Institutional Investor's Viewpoint' (1993) 1 *Corporate Governance: An International Review* 178.

Mayer, C. P., 'The Assessment: Financial Systems and Corporate Investment' (1987) 3 (4) *Oxford Review of Economic Policy* i.

—— 'New Issues in Corporate Finance' (1988) 32 *European Economic Review* 1167.

—— 'Financial Systems, Corporate Finance, and Economic Development' in R. G. Hubbard (ed.), *Asymmetric Information, Corporate Finance and Investment* (University of Chicago Press, Chicago, 1990) 307.

—— *The Functioning of the UK Financial System: What's Wrong with London?* (Working Paper) (City University Business School, London, 1991).

—— *Ownership: An Inaugural Lecture* (Warwick Economic Research Papers No. 402) (University of Warwick, Warwick, 1993).

—— 'Stock-Markets, Financial Institutions, and Corporate Performance' in N. H. Dimsdale and M. Prevezer (eds.), *Capital Markets and Corporate Governance* (Clarendon Press, Oxford, 1994) 179.

Mayer, C. P., and Alexander, I., 'Banks and Securities Markets: Corporate Financing in Germany and the United Kingdom' (1990) 4 *Journal of the Japanese and International Economies* 450.

—— and —— *Stock Markets and Corporate Performance: A Comparison of Publicly Listed and Private Companies* (Working paper for the Centre for Economic Policy Research 'International Study of the Financing of Industry') (University of Oxford, Oxford, 1995).

Midgley, K., 'How Much Control Do Shareholders Exercise?' (1974) 14 *Lloyds Bank Review* 24.

—— *Companies and Their Shareholders—The Uneasy Relationship* (Institute of Chartered Secretaries and Administrators, London, 1975).

Miles, D., 'Testing for Short-Termism in the UK Stock Market' (1993) 103 *Economic Journal* 1379.

Minns, R., *Pension Funds and British Capitalism* (Heinemann, London, 1980).

Modigliani, F., and Miller, M. H., 'The Cost of Capital, Corporation Finance and the Theory of Investment' (1958) 48 *American Economic Review* 261.

Monk, J. L., *The Dynamics of Institutional Share Ownership in Major Quoted UK Companies* (Investor Relations Society, London, 1994).

Moody, P. E., 'A More Active Role for Institutional Shareholders', *The Banker*, February 1979, p. 49.

Morgan, E. V., and Morgan, A. D., *Investment Managers and Takeovers: Information and Attitudes* (Hume Occasional Paper No. 25) (David Hume Institute, Edinburgh, 1990).

—— and —— *The Stock Market and Mergers in the United Kingdom* (Hume Occasional Paper No. 24) (David Hume Institute, Edinburgh, 1990).

Morgan, H. M., 'Dealing with Institutional Shareholders: A Corporate Perspective', Unpublished paper presented at the Australian Investment Managers' Group and Business Council of Australia conference on 'Corporate Governance and Australian Competitiveness: The Role of Institutional Investors', Sydney, 11 November 1993.

National Association of Pension Funds Ltd., *Creative Tension?* (National Association of Pension Funds Ltd., London, 1990).

—— *Annual Survey of Occupational Pension Schemes* (National Association of Pension Funds Ltd., London, 1990).

—— *Annual Survey of Occupational Pension Schemes* (National Association of Pension Funds Ltd., London, 1991).

—— *Annual Survey of Occupational Pension Schemes* (National Association of Pension Funds Ltd., London, 1992).

—— *Annual Survey of Occupational Pension Schemes* (National Association of Pension Funds Ltd., London, 1993).

—— *Annual Survey of Occupational Pension Schemes* (National Association of Pension Funds Ltd., London, 1994).

—— *Corporate Relations: Reminder on Good Investor Relations* (National Association of Pension Funds Ltd., London, 1994).

—— *Investment Committee Briefing—December 1994: Directors' Service Contracts* (National Association of Pension Funds Ltd., London, 1994).

National Companies and Securities Commission, *Eleventh Annual Report and Financial Statements* (Australian Government Publishing Service, Canberra, 1990).

—— *Release 126* (National Companies and Securities Commission, Melbourne).

Nickell, S. J., and Wadhwani, S. B., *Myopia, the 'Dividend Puzzle', and Share Prices* (London School of Economics, Centre for Labour Economics Discussion Paper No. 272) (London School of Economics, London, 1987).

Nobles, R. L., 'The Exercise of Trustees' Discretion Under a Pension Scheme' [1992] *Journal of Business Law* 261.

Nyman, S., and Silberston, A., 'The Ownership and Control of Industry' (1978) 30 *Oxford Economic Papers* 74.

Olson, M., *The Logic of Collective Action: Public Goods and the Theory of Groups* (Harvard University Press, Cambridge Mass, 2nd edn., 1971).

Paatsch, D., and Smith, G., 'The Regulation of Australian Superannuation: An Industrial Relations Law Perspective' (1992) 5 *Corporate and Business Law Journal* 131.

Panel on Take-overs and Mergers, *Report on the Year Ended 31st March 1969* (Panel on Take-overs and Mergers, London, 1969).

Panel on Take-overs and Mergers, *The City Code on Takeovers and Mergers* (Panel on Takeovers and Mergers, London).

—— *Report on the Year Ended 31 March 1992* (Panel on Takeovers and Mergers, London, 1992).

—— *Report on the Year Ended 31 March 1993* (Panel on Takeovers and Mergers, London, 1993).

—— *Report on the year Ended 31 March 1994* (Panel on Takeovers and Mergers, London, 1994).

Parkinson, J. E., *Corporate Power and Responsibility* (Clarendon Press, Oxford, 1993).

Parliamentary Joint Committee on Corporations and Securities, *Background Paper: Institutional Investor Inquiry* (The Parliament of the Commonwealth of Australia, Canberra, 1993).

—— *Issues Paper: Inquiry into the Role and Activities of Institutional Investors in Australia* (The Parliament of the Commonwealth of Australia, Canberra, 1994).

Paul, A., 'Corporate Governance in the Context of Takeovers of UK Public Companies' in D. D. Prentice and P. R. J. Holland (eds.), *Contemporary Issues in Corporate Governance* (Clarendon Press, Oxford, 1993) 135.

Peacock, A., and Bannock, G., *Corporate Takeovers and the Public Interest* (Report of an Inquiry Conducted for the Joseph Rowntree Foundation by the David Hume Institute) (Aberdeen University Press, Aberdeen, 1991).

Pension Law Review Committee ('Goode Committee'), *Report* (Cm. 2342) (HMSO, London, 1993).

Pensions & Investment Research Consultants Ltd., *Submission to the Committee on the Financial Aspects of Corporate Governance* (Pensions & Investment Research Consultants Ltd., London, 1992).

Pettigrew, A., and McNulty, T., 'Power and Influence in and Around the Boardroom' (1995) 48 *Human Relations* 845.

Phillips & Drew Fund Management Ltd, *Survey of Investment Management Arrangements* (Phillips & Drew Fund Management Ltd, London, 1991).

Pike, R., Meerjanssen, J., and Chadwick, L., 'The Appraisal of Ordinary Shares by Investment Analysts in the UK and Germany' (1993) 23 *Accounting and Business Research* 489.

Plastow, Sir David, 'Corporate Strategy and the Institutional Shareholder' in National Association of Pension Funds Ltd., *Creative Tension?* (National Association of Pension Funds Ltd., London, 1990) 70.

Pound, J., 'The Effects of Antitakeover Amendments on Takeover Activity: Some Direct Evidence' (1987) 30 *Journal of Law and Economics* 353.

Plender, J., *That's the Way the Money Goes* (André Deutsch, London, 1982).

The Pre-emption Group, *Pre-emption Guidelines* (The International Stock Exchange of the United Kingdom and the Republic of Ireland Ltd., London, 1987).

Prentice, D. D., 'The Theory of the Firm: Minority Shareholder Oppression: Sections 459–461 of the Companies Act 1985' (1988) 8 *Oxford Journal of Legal Studies* 55.

—— 'Directors, Creditors, and Shareholders' in E. McKendrick (ed.), *Commercial Aspects of Trusts and Fiduciary Obligations* (Clarendon Press, Oxford, 1992) 73.

—— 'Regulation of Takeover Bids in the United Kingdom' in K. Kreuzer (ed.), *Öffentliche Übernahmeangebote* (Nomos Verlagsgesellschaft, Baden-Baden, 1992) 133.

—— 'Some Aspects of the Corporate Governance Debate' in D. D. Prentice and P. R. J. Holland (eds.), *Contemporary Issues in Corporate Governance* (Clarendon Press, Oxford, 1993) 25.

Price Waterhouse, *Investment Management Survey* (Price Waterhouse, London, 1992).

PRO NED, *Code of Recommended Practice on Non-Executive Directors* (PRO NED, London, 1987).

—— *Research into the Role of the Non-Executive Director: Executive Summary* (PRO NED, London, 1992).

Prowse, S. D., 'The Structure of Corporate Ownership in Japan' (1992) 47 *Journal of Finance* 1121.

Proxy Voting Reform Working Party, *Model Proxy Form: Explanatory Memorandum* (Australian Investment Managers' Association, and Chartered Institute of Company Secretaries in Australia Ltd., Sydney, 1995).

Quarrell, J. J., *The Law of Pension Fund Investment* (Butterworths, London, 1990).

Rabinowitz, L., *Weinberg and Blank on Take-overs and Mergers* (Sweet & Maxwell, London, 5th edn., 1989).

Ramsay, I. M., 'Corporate Governance, Shareholder Litigation and the Prospects for a Statutory Derivative Action' (1992) 15 *University of New South Wales Law Journal* 149.

Ramsay, I. M., and Blair, M., 'Ownership Concentration, Institutional Investment and Corporate Governance: An Empirical Investigation of 100 Australian Companies' (1993) 19 *Melbourne University Law Review* 153.

Reid, M. I., *All-Change in the City* (Macmillan, Basingstoke, 1988).

Reserve Bank of Australia, *Prudential Statement No G1* (Reserve Bank of Australia, Canberra, 1990).

—— *Bulletin* (March edition) (Reserve Bank of Australia, Canberra, 1994).

Rock, E. B., 'The Logic and (Uncertain) Significance of Institutional Shareholder Activism' (1991) 79 *Georgetown Law Journal* 445.

Roe, M. J., 'A Political Theory of American Corporate Finance' (1991) 91 *Columbia Law Review* 10.

Romano, R., 'Public Pension Fund Activism in Corporate Governance Reconsidered' (1993) 93 *Columbia Law Review* 796.

Rydqvist, K., 'Dual-Class Shares: A Review' (1992) 8 (3) *Oxford Review of Economic Policy* 45.

Sabel, C. F., Griffin, J. R., and Deeg, R. E., 'Making Money Talk: Towards a New Debtor-Creditor Relation in German Banking' in J. C. Coffee, R. J. Gilson, and L. Lowenstein (eds.), *Relational Investing* (Oxford University Press, New York, 1996) (forthcoming).

Sampson, A., *The New Anatomy of Britain* (Hodder & Stoughton, London, 1971).

Sargant Florence, P., *Ownership, Control and Success of Large Companies* (Sweet & Maxwell, London, 1961).

—— *The Logic of British and American Industry* (Routledge & Kegan Paul, London, 3rd edn., 1972).

Scharfstein, D., 'The Disciplinary Role of Takeovers' (1988) 55 *Review of Economic Studies* 85.

Schleifer, A., and Summers, L. H., 'Breach of Trust in Hostile Takeovers' in A. J. Auerbach (ed.), *Corporate Takeovers: Causes and Consequences* (University of Chicago Press, Chicago, 1988) 33.

Schneider-Lenné, E. R., 'Corporate Control in Germany' (1992) 8 (3) *Oxford Review of Economic Policy* 11.

Scott, J., *The Controlling Constellations: A Directory of 100 Large Companies* (Working Paper for the Company Analysis Project) (University of Leicester, Leicester, 1984).

Scott, J., *Capitalist Property and Financial Power* (Wheatsheaf, Brighton, 1986).

Scott, K. E., and Kleidon, A. W., 'CEO Performance, Board Types and Board Performance: A First Cut' in T. Baums, R. M. Buxbaum, and K. J. Hopt (eds.), *Institutional Investors and Corporate Governance* (Walter de Gruyter, Berlin, 1994) 181.

Scott, W. R., *The Constitution and Finance of English, Scottish and Irish Joint Stock Companies to 1712* (Cambridge, 1912).

Sealy, L. S., 'The Director as Trustee' [1967] *Cambridge Law Journal* 83.

—— 'The 'Disclosure' Philosophy and Company Law Reform' (1981) 2 *Company Lawyer* 51.

—— *Cases and Materials in Company Law* (Butterworths, London, 5th edn., 1992).

Securities and Investments Board, *Custody Review Discussion Paper* (Securities and Investments Board, London, 1993).

Senate Standing Committee on Legal and Constitutional Affairs ('Cooney Committee'), *Company Directors' Duties: Report on the Social and Fiduciary Duties and Obligations of Company Directors* (Australian Government Publishing Service, Canberra, 1989).

Sharpe, R. B., and Manolios, C. A., *Wickens: The Law of Life Insurance in Australia* (Law Book Company, Sydney, 6th edn., 1990).

Sheard, P., 'The Main Bank System and Corporate Monitoring and Control in Japan' (1989) 11 *Journal of Economic Behavior and Organization* 399.

—— 'Interlocking Shareholdings and Corporate Governance' in M. Aoki and

R. P. Dore (eds.), *The Japanese Firm: The Sources of Competitive Strength* (Oxford University Press, Oxford, 1994) 310.

Shivdasani, A., 'Board Composition, Ownership Structure, and Hostile Takeovers' (1993) 16 *Journal of Accounting and Economics* 167.

Smith, A., *The Wealth of Nations* (Random House, New York, 1937).

Stapledon, G. P., 'The AWA Case: Non-Executive Directors, Auditors, and Corporate Governance Issues in Court' in D. D. Prentice and P. R. J. Holland (eds.), *Contemporary Issues in Corporate Governance* (Clarendon Press, Oxford, 1993) 187.

Stokes, M., 'Company Law and Legal Theory' in W. L. Twining (ed.), *Legal Theory and Common Law* (Basil Blackwell, Oxford, 1986) 155.

Study Group on Directors' Remuneration ('Greenbury Committee'), *Code of Best Practice* (Gee Publishing, London, 1995).

—— *Report* (Gee Publishing, London, 1995).

Sykes, A., 'Proposals for a Reformed System of Corporate Governance to Achieve Internationally Competitive Long-Term Performance' in N. H. Dimsdale and M. Prevezer (eds.), *Capital Markets and Corporate Governance* (Clarendon Press, Oxford, 1994) 111.

Tegner, I. N., 'A View from the Board Room' (1993) 1 *Corporate Governance: An International Review* 191.

Teubner, G., 'Corporate Fiduciary Duties and Their Beneficiaries' in K. J. Hopt and G. Teubner (eds.), *Corporate Governance and Directors' Liabilities* (Walter de Gruyter, Berlin, 1985) 149.

Tombs, Sir Francis, 'The Inter-Relationship Between Institutional Investors, the Company in Which They Invest, and Company Management' in National Association of Pension Funds Ltd., *Creative Tension?* (National Association of Pension Funds Ltd., London, 1990) 79.

Vagts, D. F., 'Reforming the 'Modern' Corporation: Perspectives from the German' (1966) 80 *Harvard Law Review* 23.

Wadhwani, S., and Shah, M., *The Equity-Bond Debate in the UK* (Goldman Sachs International Ltd., London, 1993).

Walker, D. A., 'Some Perspectives for Pension Fund Managers' (1987) 27 *Bank of England Quarterly Bulletin* 247.

Wedderburn, Lord, 'The Legal Development of Corporate Responsibility' in K. J. Hopt and G. Teubner (eds.), *Corporate Governance and Directors' Liabilities* (Walter de Gruyter, Berlin, 1985) 3.

Weisbach, M. S., 'CEO Turnover and the Firm's Investment Decisions' (1995) 37 *Journal of Financial Economics* 159.

Williamson, O. E., 'The Modern Corporation: Origins, Evolution, Attributes' (1981) 19 *Journal of Economic Literature* 1537.

—— 'Corporate Governance' (1984) 93 *Yale Law Journal* 1197.

WM Company, *UK Pension Fund Service Annual Review* (The World Markets Company plc, London, 1990).

Working Group of the Business Council of Australia, et al. ('Bosch Committee'), *Corporate Practices and Conduct* (Information Australia, Melbourne, 1991).

—— *Corporate Practices and Conduct* (Information Australia, Melbourne, 2nd edn., 1993).

Wright, S., *Two Cheers for the Institutions* (Social Market Foundation, London, 1994).

3i plc, *PLC UK: The Role of the Finance Director: Part 3—Corporate Governance* (3i plc, London, 1992).

'Protection in the City: Safeguards for the Small Investor', *The Times*, 17 April 1964.

'Aer Lingus-Kingsley Hotel Deal Strongly Opposed', *Financial Times*, 11 February 1970, p. 30.

'How the Mighty are Falling', *The Times*, 3 July 1970, p. 25.

'A Special Report: Insurance: Institutional Investors Make Their Mark', *The Times*, 8 February 1971, p. V.

'Men and Matters: What They Get for £50', *Financial Times*, 28 April 1971, p. 20.

'£12m.–£20m Thalidomide Offer Likely', *The Times*, 5 January 1973, p. 1.

'Bank Hails BIA Decision to Join City Investors' "Ginger Group" ', *Financial Times*, 17 April 1973, p. 1.

'Outsider for Rank in Board Changes', *Financial Times*, 18 March 1983, p. 22.

'Keynes Followers Rally Behind Industrialists', *Financial Times*, 3 March 1987, p. 8.

'Letters to the Editor: Stock Market Efficiency', *Financial Times*, 16 March 1987, p. 23.

'Institutions Seek Curb on Share Issues', *Financial Times*, 30 April 1987, p. 1.

'City Working for "Short-Term Gains at Expense of Industry" ', *Financial Times*, 4 November 1988, p. 24.

'Pre-emption rights "Still on Agenda" ', *Financial Times*, 4 May 1989, sec. III, p. XIV.

'Chanticleer: Kiwi Hijacking May Spark War With Australia Inc', *Australian Financial Review*, 8 June 1989, p. 104.

'Goodman Fielder Bid for IEL Runs Foul of NCSC', *Australian Financial Review*, 13 June 1989, p. 16.

'Goldberg Leads IEL Buy-Out', *Australian Financial Review*, 4 July 1989, p. 1.

'Opposition to British Land Reconstruction', *Financial Times*, 16 December 1989, p. 8.

'Fleming Votes Against British Land Scheme', *Financial Times*, 20 December 1989, p. 19.

'British Land Scraps Restructuring', *Financial Times*, 21 December 1989, p. 15.

'The Limits to Institutional Power', *Financial Times*, 22 May 1990, p. 20.

'Why the Ideal Board Remains So Elusive', *Financial Times*, 4 July 1990, p. 10.

'Institutional Investors as Interventionists', *Financial Times*, 10 August 1990, p. 10.

'James White Resigns from Bunzl Board', *Financial Times*, 2 November 1990, p. 23.

'Tooth Repays its $20m Loan to Howard Smith "Early" ', *Australian Financial Review*, 20 November 1990, p. 20.

'Goodman Revises Option Scheme', *Australian Financial Review*, 21 November 1990, p. 22.

'AMP Says No to Property Deal with Company Chairman's Wife', *Australian Financial Review*, 23 November 1990, p. 28.

'Howard Smith Clears Way for Placement', *Australian Financial Review*, 26 November 1990, p. 19.

'Institutions Force Resignations of Savage Chairman and Chief Executive', *Financial Times*, 26 November 1990, p. 17.

'Poor Showing from Goodman Comes Under Fire', *Australian Financial Review*, 27 November 1990, p. 16.

'B&F Dissension Over Property Deal Vote', *Australian Financial Review*, 30 November 1990, p. 23.

'When Men in Grey Suits Choose to Apply Savage Pressure', *Financial Times*, 20 December 1990, p. 21.

'A Corporate Conundrum', *Financial Times*, 26 January 1991, p. 8.

'More Dialogue Between Boards and Shareholders is Needed', *The Independent*, 11 February 1991, p. 21.

'Pension Funds Attacked Over Failure to Vote', *Financial Times*, 2 March 1991, p. 7.

'City Forces Sacking of Stoy Hayward', *Financial Times*, 9 April 1991, p. 26.

'Budgens Meets to Set Terms for Fletcher Departure', *Financial Times*, 1 May 1991, p. 21.

'Institutions Launch Bid to Oust Tace Board', *Financial Times*, 4 May 1991, p. 10.

'Granada Loses Chief, Gains Cash', *The Independent*, 11 May 1991, p. 15.

'Sacrifice to Woo the Franchise Gods', *Financial Times*, 11 May 1991, p. 10.

'British Steel Denies Rift as Chief Executive Resigns', *Financial Times*, 21 May 1991, p. 19.

'George Walker Ousted Under Pressure from Banks', *Financial Times*, 31 May 1991, p. 1.

'Squandering the Potential of Annual Meetings', *The Independent*, 10 June 1991, p. 23.

'The Institutions Get Militant', *Financial Times*, 11 June 1991, p. 18.

'Tace Board Quits at Angry EGM', *Financial Times*, 20 June 1991, p. 23.

'Confessions of a Non-Executive', *Financial Times*, 15 July 1991, p. 11.

'Shareholder Revolt Rocks Darrell James', *Australian Financial Review*, 9 August 1991, p. 16.

'Institutions Want Fuller Financial Information', *Financial Times*, 2 September 1991, p. 14.

'Punters' Progress', *The Economist*, 7 September 1991, p. 112.

'Photo Finish for Darrell James', *Australian Financial Review*, 9 September 1991, p. 64.

'Darrell James Coup Blocked', *The Australian*, 14 September 1991, p. 43.

'Darrell James Board on Notice', *Australian Financial Review*, 16 September 1991.

'Tougher at the Top', *Financial Times*, 28 September 1991, p. 7.

'Brown & Jackson Chief Resigns Over Performance', *Financial Times*, 10 October 1991, p. 24.

'Brown & Jackson Appoints New Adviser', *Financial Times*, 23 October 1991, p. 24.

'Shareholders Wage War', *Financial Times*, 6 November 1991, p. 14.

'Bennett Election Balked by Court', *Australian Financial Review*, 2 December 1991, p. 23.

'Trio Clear to Contest B and F Board Poll', *Australian Financial Review*, 9 December 1991, p. 24.

'New Bennett Board Promises Stability', *Australian Financial Review*, 16 December 1991, p. 24.

'Brown & Jackson Board Shuffle', *Financial Times*, 11 February 1992, p. 22.

'When the Time Comes for Shareholders to Stand Up and be Counted', *Financial Times*, 6 April 1992, p. 12.

'Worcester Holders Angry Over £72m German Offer', *Financial Times*, 18 April 1992, p. 8.

'Worcester Shareholders at Odds with Takeover Panel', *Financial Times*, 22 April 1992, p. 22.

'Barclays Chairman to Stand Down', *Financial Times*, 25 April 1992, p. 1.

'British Banks Face Turmoil', *Sunday Times*, 26 April 1992, sec. 3, p. 1.

'Institutions Demand Fair Shares for All', *Financial Times*, 30 April 1992, p. 23.

'Institutions Tackle "Short-Termism" ', *Financial Times*, 30 April 1992, p. 8.

'Political Payments', *Pensions Management*, May 1992, p. 6.

'Knives Are Out in the Boardroom', *Financial Times*, 1 May 1992, p. 11.

'Schofield Will Steer MTM', *Financial Times*, 1 May 1992, p. 20.

'Survey: Pension Fund Investment: Investors Urged to Behave Like Owners', *Financial Times*, 7 May 1992, sec. III, p. VIII.

'Summers Sacked as Bennett's MD', *The Advertiser*, 9 May 1992.

'Sacked Boss Refuses to Go Quietly', *Australian Financial Review*, 11 May 1992, p. 1.

'Institutions Fail to Block Bosch's Bid for Worcester', *Financial Times*, 12 May 1992, p. 22.

'Lack of Voting on Directors Attacked', *Financial Times*, 18 May 1992, p. 11.

'A Coalition Versus a Dictator', *Financial Times*, 27 May 1992, p. 13.

'Ricardo Chief Quits After Pressure from Directors', *Financial Times*, 4 June 1992, p. 30.

'B&F May Sue Summers', *The Advertiser*, 5 June 1992.

'Former Bennett Chief Finally Heeds the Call', *Australian Financial Review*, 5 June 1992, p. 21.

'Inner City Circle Holds the Key to Top Boardrooms', *Sunday Times*, 14 June 1992, sec. 3, p. 8.

'Horton is Ousted as Chairman of British Petroleum', *Financial Times*, 26 June 1992, p. 1.

'In Shops Drops Plans to Bid for Amber Day', *Financial Times*, 2 July 1992, p.24.

'Shareholder Group Calls for Changes to Stock Option Plans', *Financial Times*, 6 July 1992, p. 1.

'The Shape of Things to Come', *Financial Times*, 10 July 1992, p. 15.

'Investors Seek More European Rights', *Financial Times*, 15 July 1992, p. 27.

'Funds "Back Equities Over Gilts" ', *Financial Times*, 29 July 1992, p. 6.

'Tough Tactics Behind the Unit Trusts', *Financial Times*, 5 August 1992, p. 15.

'Institutional Concern Over a Top Banker's Dual Role', *Financial Times*, 6 August 1992, p. 19.

'Blind Faith in R&D', *Financial Times*, 2 September 1992, p. 12.

'Theory of Bond Investment Culture Comes Unstuck', *Financial Times*, 19 September 1992, p. 4.

'How It All Went Horribly Wrong', *Sydney Morning Herald*, 25 September 1992, p. 25.

'Editorial: Time for the Westpac Board to Declare', *Australian Financial Review*, 1 October 1992, p. 17.

' "Still a Long Way to Go" for Westpac', *Australian Financial Review*, 2 October 1992, p. 26.

'Westpac: Neal and Four Directors Go', *Australian Financial Review*, 2 October 1992, p. 1.

'Pru Chief Issues Plea for Greater Treasury Detail', *Financial Times*, 16 October 1992, p. 31.

'Continental Firms Pose Threat to UK Brokers, Study Says', *Financial Times*, 29 October 1992, p. 27.

'Too Many Eggs in One Basket', *Financial Times*, 11 November 1992, p. 20.

'Plysu Managing Director Quits', *Financial Times*, 13 November 1992, p. 31.

'Institutions Turn Against Sugar's Bid for Amstrad', *Financial Times*, 3 December 1992, p. 23.

'Opposition Grows to Sugar's Plans', *Financial Times*, 8 December 1992, p. 18.

'Amstrad Vote Halts Battle', *Financial Times*, 11 December 1992, p. 25.

'Letters: Cadbury Must Not Lead to Creation of "Two-Tier" Shareholders', *Financial Times*, 11 December 1992, p. 21.

'Boardroom Shake-up at Pegasus', *Financial Times*, 16 December 1992, p. 24.

'Assault on Corporate Germany's Defences', *Financial Times*, 22 December 1992, p. 17.

'Bonds May Deliver KO', *Financial Times*, 9 January 1993, sec. II, p. I.

'Lazard To Manage Crown Funds', *Financial Times*, 19 January 1993, p. 21.

'BA Shareholders Concerned at Combined Top Jobs', *Financial Times*, 20 January 1993, p. 21.

'Of Hats and Heads', *Financial Times*, 5 February 1993, p. 10.

'Measuring Up', *Pensions Management*, March 1993, p. 43.

'The Cost of Performance Related Fees', *Pensions Management*, March 1993, p. 35.

'Tate & Lyle Chief Executive Leaves After 11 Months', *Financial Times*, 2 March 1993, p. 19.

'Called to Account for Past Practices', *Financial Times*, 8 March 1993, p. 18.

'Demand for Shareholder Equality at Siemens', *Financial Times*, 11 March 1993, p. 32.

'The Secret of T&N', *Financial Times*, 12 March 1993, p. 13.

' "Two-Tier" Fund Market Identified', *Financial Times*, 12 March 1993, p. 8.

'Glaxo's Bitter Pill', *Sunday Times*, 14 March 1993, sec. 3, p. 3.

'The Survey: Occupational SchemesoChallenging Times', *Pensions Management*, April 1993, p. 33.

'Company Doctor Joins Spring Ram', *Financial Times*, 1 April 1993, p. 23.

'Directors Size Up New Rules', *Financial Times*, 10 April 1993, p. 7.

'Fashion for the Thinly Veiled Rights Offering', *Financial Times*, 19 April 1993, p. 17.

'Institutions Force Management Change at Alexon Group', *Financial Times*, 23 April 1993, p. 19.

'Daimler-Benz Gears Up for a Drive on the Freeway', *Financial Times*, 29 April 1993, p. 18.

'Survey: Pension Fund Investment', *Financial Times*, 6 May 1993, sec. III, p. II.

'Survey: Pension Fund Investment: Focus on Investors' Behaviour', *Financial Times*, 6 May 1993, sec. III, p. VII.

'Gartmore Seeks Insider Dealing Review', *Financial Times*, 7 May 1993, p. 19.

'Letters to the Editor', *Financial Times*, 7 May 1993, p. 16.

'Calls Grow for Action on Insider Dealing', *Financial Times*, 8 May 1993, p. 1.

'Management Changes Sought at Tiphook', *Financial Times*, 8 May 1993, p. 10.

'Treasury Expands Defences to Insider Dealing Charges', *Financial Times*, 8 May 1993, p. 10.

'Crackdown Over Private Briefings for Analysts', *Financial Times*, 15 May 1993, p. 1.

'AIMG Opts for a More Open Role', *Australian Financial Review*, 18 May 1993.

'Price Increase Behind Rise at Thames Water', *Financial Times*, 3 June 1993, p. 24.

'Warburg Gives Up £80m Equity Plan', *Financial Times*, 5 June 1993, p. 26.

'Huge Claim Alleges Fraud by Summers', *The Advertiser*, 6 June 1993.

'Hanson Power Provokes Concern', *Financial Times*, 10 June 1993, p. 21.

'Ifma Attacks Long-Term Contracts for Directors', *Financial Times*, 10 June 1993, p. 9.

'BA Proposes Changes to Boardroom Election Process', *Financial Times*, 12 June 1993, p. 12.

'Directors Cool to Plea on Contracts', *Financial Times*, 14 June 1993, p. 8.

'Hanson Softens on Voting Rights', *Financial Times*, 14 June 1993, p. 18.

'Rule Changes for Open-Ended Funds', *Financial Times*, 17 June 1993, p. 6.

'Booker Meets Postel Concern on Pay-Offs', *Financial Times*, 18 June 1993, p. 17.

'Hanson Backs Down Over Proposed Rule Changes', *Financial Times*, 18 June 1993, p. 17.

'Institutions' Firm Line on Exec Share Plans', *Australian Financial Review*, 18 June 1993, p. 11.

'All the Nasties Cleared from the Books', *Financial Times*, 28 June 1993, p. 18.

'Exchange Will Review Disclosure Guidelines', *Financial Times*, 6 July 1993, p. 20.

'Broad-Brush Approach for a Truer Picture', *Financial Times*, 8 July 1993, p. 12.

'Chairman of Spring Ram Urged to Quit by Shareholder', *Financial Times*, 10 July 1993, p. 24.

'Chanticleer: Incentives: The Options Are Open', *Australian Financial Review*, 14 July 1993, p. 52.

'Pressure Builds on Spring Ram Chief', *Financial Times*, 14 July 1993, p. 20.

'AIMG Moves to Help Restore Our Credibility', *Australian Financial Review*, 15 July 1993, p. 27.

'Boards Face Share Option Pressure', *Financial Times*, 15 July 1993, p. 9.

'Lex: S.G. Warburg', *Financial Times*, 22 July 1993, p. 20.

'Warburg Seeks £91m Via Bond Issue', *Financial Times*, 22 July 1993, p. 22.

'Cash Returns', *Financial Times*, 27 July 1993, p. 17.

'Spring Ram Gives Rooney a Reprieve', *Financial Times*, 28 July 1993, p. 19.

'How to Replace the Board—By Stealth', *Governance*, August 1993, p. 8

'Wielding the Institutional Club', *Australian Financial Review*, 9 August 1993, p. 15.

'WMC Director Disciplined', *Financial Times*, 1 September 1993, p. 24.

'Lex: Schroders', *Financial Times*, 4 September 1993, p. 22.

'Spring Ram in Board Shake-Out', *Financial Times*, 23 September 1993, p. 19.

'Whitbread Gives Equal Rights', *Financial Times*, 7 October 1993, p. 25.

'Doubts Rise Over Enhanced Scrips', *Financial Times*, 13 October 1993, p. 20.

'Corporate Assassins', *Sunday Telegraph*, 17 October 1993, City & Business sec., p. 5.

'Hammerson Share Vote Changes', *Financial Times*, 20 October 1993, p. 22.

'Invergordon Loses Independence', *Financial Times*, 22 October 1993, p. 21.

'The Unions Step on Board', *Financial Times*, 27 October 1993, p. 14.

'Former Electronics Chief Cleared', *Financial Times*, 12 November 1993, p. 8.

'Managers Urge Inquiry on News Super-Voting Issue', *Australian Financial Review*, 2 November 1993, p. 27.

'An Art That Deserves a High Priority', *Financial Times*, 15 November 1993, p. 14.

'Coles Share Plan Meets AIMG Flak', *Australian Financial Review*, 22 November 1993, p. 22.

'Appeal to Lavarch on News Super Shares', *Australian Financial Review*, 23 November 1993, p. 20.

'Govt Steps into Super Share Row', *Australian Financial Review*, 24 November 1993, p. 1.

'Not Everyone Happy at Coles', *Australian Financial Review*, 26 November 1993, p. 32.

'Why No News Would be Bad News for ASX', *Australian Financial Review*, 26 November 1993, p. 28.

'ABM Top 500 Companies', *ABM*, December 1993, p. 64.

'Tracking the Behaviour of Stock Pickers', *Financial Times*, 6 December 1993, p. 16.

'Murdoch Yields on Super Shares', *Australian Financial Review*, 9 December 1993, p. 1.

'Chanticleer: Storm Clouds Gather', *Australian Financial Review*, 14 December 1993, p. 44.

'Bloodbath at Goodman', *Australian Financial Review*, 15 December 1993, p. 1.

'Chanticleer: "Perform or Get the Chop" ', *Australian Financial Review*, 15 December 1993, p. 36.

'Editorial: Morgan Must Go From WMC', *Australian Financial Review*, 21 January 1994, p. 24.

'M&G Faces Criticism of Executive Option Scheme', *Financial Times*, 22 January 1994, p. 22.

'Investors Seek Clear Proxy Law', *Australian Financial Review*, 24 January 1994, p. 19.

'No Sharing Between Rivals', *Australian Financial Review*, 28 January 1994, p. 21.

'AMP's Hall to Lead Check on Changes to Law', *Australian Financial Review*, 4 February 1994, p. 11.

'Chanticleer: Directors Face More Pressure', *Australian Financial Review*, 11 February 1994, p. 64.

'Pioneering MLC has the Formula Right', *Weekend Australian*, 12 February 1994, p. 31.

'Central to Spin Off Diamonds', *Australian Financial Review*, 15 February 1994, p. 20.

'ASX Officially Kills Off Super-Shares Idea', *Australian Financial Review*, 23 February 1994, p. 22.

'Billion Dollar Men', *The Bulletin*, 1 March 1994, p. 67.

'Companies Urged to Talk to Shareholders', *Australian Financial Review*, 23 March 1994, p. 27.

'Survey: Pension Fund Investment: "Beauty Parade" Blues', *Financial Times*, 27 April 1994, p. V.

'City sets Sights on a Less Exciting Future', *Financial Times*, 28 April 1994, p. 30.

'Rowntree Shuffles Pension Fund Team', *Financial Times*, 3 May 1994, p. 22.

'Growing Concern Over Investor Lawsuits', *Financial Times*, 18 May 1994, p. 30.

'W H Smith to Change Share Structure', *Financial Times*, 20 May 1994, p. 20.

'Legal Briefs: Rolls-Royce Defeated by Shareholders', *Financial Times*, 31 May 1994, p. 12.

'Survey: German Banking and Finance: A Tightening of the Rules', *Financial Times*, 31 May 1994, p. II.

'Currency Details "Lacking" ', *Financial Times*, 6 June 1994, p. 9.

'Institutions Back ASX Reform Plans', *Financial Times*, 6 June 1994, p. 27.

'DTI Enlists the Great and the Good for its Governance Committee', *Financial Times*, 21 June 1994, p. 15.

'Times Drops to 20p in Price War with Telegraph', *Financial Times*, 24 June 1994, p. 1.

'PosTel Draws Line on Contracts', *Financial Times*, 25 June 1994, p. 24.

'When Price Cuts Prove Price Sensitive', *Financial Times*, 25 June 1994, p. 10.

'Own Goals Keep the Underdog in the Game', *Financial Times*, 5 July 1994, p. 26.

'Daimler Considers Anglo–US Policy on Dividends', *Financial Times*, 8 July 1994, p. 19.

'Pension Members Win Costs Ruling', *Financial Times*, 30 July 1994, p. 7.

'DOL Issues New Guidelines on Proxy Voting, Active Investing', *IRRC Corporate Governance Bulletin*, July/August 1994, p. 1.

'Chanticleer: Boards Must Learn to Shape Up or Starve', *Australian Financial Review*, 9 August 1994, p. 48.

'Money to Burn', *Pensions Management*, August 1994, p. 23.

'MAM Cuts Business with Parent Warburg Over Lasmo', *Financial Times*, 13 August 1994, p. 24.

'Chairman of Goodman Fielder to Stand Down', *Financial Times*, 17 August 1994, p. 19.

'Cut the Strings on the Parachute', *Financial Times*, 17 August 1994, p. 13.

'Goodman Fielder EGM Call', *Financial Times*, 18 August 1994, p. 20.

'Goodman Fielder Board Studies Call for Overhaul', *Financial Times*, 20 August 1994, p. 11.

'Insurers Join Outcry Against Large Pay-Offs', *Financial Times*, 20 August 1994, p. 7.

'Goodman Sets Date to Face Music', *Financial Times*, 23 August 1994, p. 22.

'BHP Acts on Beswick Shareholding', *Financial Times*, 25 August 1994, p. 22.

'The MSS Effect', *Pensions Management*, September 1994, p. 35.

'Institutions Agree to Share Information on Governance', *Financial Times*, 7 September 1994, p. 28.

'Goodman Fielder Bows to Rebel Investors to Head Off Proxy Battle', *Financial Times*, 8 September 1994, p. 31.

'Pension Funds in UK "Set to Cut Equities Holdings" ', *Financial Times*, 20 September 1994, p. 31.

'Government Backs Down on Pension Trustees', *Financial Times*, 23 September 1994, p. 8.

'A Click of the Mouse is all it Takes to Track the Share Raiders', *Financial Times*, 3 October 1994, p. 11.

'The Research Feature: The Price of Clean Living', *Pensions Management*, November 1994, p. 61.

'Prudential Set to Reduce Directors' Service Contracts', *Financial Times*, 11 November 1994, p. 19.

'US Investors Use Foreign Voting Rights', *Financial Times*, 29 November 1994, p. 30.

'Cabinet Will Seek City Advice on Defusing Executive Pay Row', *Financial Times*, 17 December 1994, p. 1.

'DOL Launches New Investigation of Proxy Voting by Pension Funds', *IRRC Corporate Governance Bulletin*, January/March 1995, p. 1.

'Labour Steps Up Campaign Over Utility Chiefs' Pay', *The Times*, 7 January 1995, p. 00.

'Saatchi Doesn't Work', *Financial Times*, 14 January 1995, p. 6.

'Labour Pushes Pension Funds to Fight Gravy Train', *The Guardian*, 16 January 1995, p. 13.

'Top UK Companies "Fail to Meet Code of Practice" ', *Financial Times*, 23 January 1995, p. 18.

'In House Management Hits the Buffers', *Pensions Management*, February 1995, p. 96.

'The Great Utility Scandal', *The Times*, 8 February 1995, p. 16.

'Cracks Around the Edges', *Financial Times*, 27 February 1995, p. 11.

'Major Set to Tackle Executive Pay Deals', *Daily Telegraph*, 1 March 1995, p. 1.

'Agreed Standard Needed to Judge Returns on Funds', *Australian Financial Review*, 13 March 1995, p. 28.

'Back to the Drawing Board', *Pensions Management*, April 1995, p. 100.

'Who Turned the Screws to Put PacDun in a Spin?', *The Age*, 21 April 1995, p. 21.

'Deveson Courts Institutions', *Australian Financial Review*, 28 April 1995, p. 32.

'Big Guns Back Stokes, But Not as Chair Apparent', *Australian Financial Review*, 2 May 1995, p. 1.

'Donations Come Under Scrutiny', *Sunday Telegraph*, 7 May 1995, City & Business sec., p. 6.

'Showdown Near as Stokes Lifts Seven Stake', *Australian Financial Review*, 17 May 1995, p. 22.

'British Gas Board Bruised on Pay But Wins the Day', *Financial Times*, 1 June 1995, p. 1.

'Companies Challenged on Political Gifts', *Financial Times*, 5 June 1995, p. 6.

'Labour Attacks Investor "Secrecy" ', *Financial Times*, 5 June 1995, p. 16.

'Calpers to Track Foreign Groups', *Financial Times*, 8 June 1995, p. 27.

'SIB Recognises Tradepoint: Stock Exchange', *Financial Times*, 8 June 1995, p. 13.

'Non-Executive Directors Come Under Fire', *Financial Times*, 12 June 1995, p. 11.

' "Five-year £35m" Package for WPP Chief is Attacked', *Financial Times*, 17 June 1995, p. 1.

'Shareholders Force WPP to Modify Chief's Pay Package', *Financial Times*, 22 June 1995, p. 1.

'Sorrell Backdown Appeases Rebels', *Financial Times*, 23 June 1995, p. 19.

'Spar Showdown is No Surrender', *The Guardian*, 24 June 1995, p. 38.

'Big Investors Threaten to Revolt on Pay', *The Guardian*, 26 June 1995, p. 14.

'Sorrell Wins £28m Deal But 26pc Vote Against', *The Guardian*, 27 June 1995, p. 17.

'M&S Ends Chief's Insulation from Re-Election', *Financial Times*, 29 June 1995, p. 18.

'Lew Appointment Under Fire', *The Age*, 24 July 1995, p. 35.

'Watchdogs Propose New Rules for Custody of Investors' Assets', *Financial Times*, 1 August 1995, p. 16.

'Resentment Over PacDun Grows', *Australian Financial Review*, 7 August 1995, p. 17.

'Funds Reject Blame in PacDun Sell-Off', *Australian Financial Review*, 8 August 1995, p. 20.

'Scandal Rocks Coles Myer', *Australian Financial Review*, 5 September 1995, p. 1.

'Qantas Superannuation Fund Sues Legal & General', *Australian Financial Review*, 6 September 1995, p. 21.

'Corporate Coup Begins', *Australian Financial Review*, 15 September 1995, p. 1.

'Lew Offers to Stand Down', *Australian Financial Review*, 19 September 1995, p. 1.

'ASA Joins Clamour for Lew's Scalp', *The Australian*, 20 September 1995, p. 41.

'New Trading System Set for Launch', *Australian Financial Review*, 21 September 1995, p. 22.

'Board Law Links Pay $20m', *Australian Financial Review*, 4 October 1995, p. 3.

'Coles Activist Plans Move to Force Lew Off Board at AGM', *The Australian*, 4 October 1995, p. 48.

'Super Funds Beef Up Scrutiny', *The Australian*, 6 October 1995, p. 21.

'AMP Declares War on Coles', *The Australian*, 12 October 1995, p. 1.

'Myer Family Dumps Lew', *Australian Financial Review*, 13 October 1995, p. 1.

'Chanticleer: Even PM Can't Save Lew Now', *Australian Financial Review*, 17 October 1995, p. 52.

'Institutions Unite Against Lew', *Australian Financial Review*, 18 October 1995, p. 1.

'Questions Raised on Coles, Kelty and AMP', *The Australian*, 18 October 1995, p. 1.

'Lew Succumbs in Coles Purge', *The Australian*, 20 October 1995, p. 23.

Index